Assessing
Science
Understanding

This is a volume in the Academic Press
EDUCATIONAL PSYCHOLOGY SERIES

Critical comprehensive reviews of research knowledge, theories, principles, and practices

Under the editorship of Gary D. Phye

Assessing Science Understanding

A Human Constructivist View

EDITED BY

Joel J. Mintzes

Department of Biological Sciences
University of North Carolina at Wilmington
and Department of Math, Science,
and Technical Education
North Carolina State University

James H. Wandersee
Graduate Studies in Curriculum
and Instruction
Louisiana State University
Baton Rouge, Louisiana

Joseph D. Novak
Department of Education
Cornell University
Ithaca, New York

ACADEMIC PRESS

San Diego   London   Boston   New York   Sydney   Tokyo   Toronto

Academic Press
A Harcourt Science and Technology Company
525 B Street, Suite 1900, San Diego, California 92101-4495, USA
http://www.apnet.com

Academic Press
24-28 Oval Road, London NW1 7DX, UK
http://www.hbuk.co.uk/ap/

Library of Congress Catalog Card Number: 99-64618

International Standard Book Number: 0-12-498365-0

PRINTED IN THE UNITED STATES OF AMERICA
99 00 01 02 03 04 MM 9 8 7 6 5 4 3 2 1

Deah, Binah, Vehascael

On Knowledge, Understanding, and Wisdom

Unless a man clearly understands and inwardly digests
What he studies, let him read ever so much; he can
Only be compared to a box well filled with books.
Like that box, he carries books within him, and
Like the box he is none the wiser for it.

Talmudic Saying

Contents

4. "WHAT DO YOU MEAN BY THAT?": USING STRUCTURED INTERVIEWS TO ASSESS SCIENCE UNDERSTANDING

Sherry A. Southerland, Mike U. Smith, and Catherine L. Cummins

5. DIALOGUE AS DATA: ASSESSING STUDENTS' SCIENTIFIC REASONING WITH INTERACTIVE PROTOCOLS

Kathleen Hogan and JoEllen Fisherkeller

6. DESIGNING AN IMAGE-BASED BIOLOGY TEST

James H. Wandersee

7. OBSERVATION RUBRICS IN SCIENCE ASSESSMENT

John E. Trowbridge and James H. Wandersee

8. PORTFOLIOS IN SCIENCE ASSESSMENT: A KNOWLEDGE-BASED MODEL FOR CLASSROOM PRACTICE

Michael R. Vitale and Nancy R. Romance

9. SemNet SOFTWARE AS AN ASSESSMENT TOOL

Kathleen M. Fisher

10. WRITING TO INQUIRE: WRITTEN PRODUCTS AS PERFORMANCE MEASURES

Audrey B. Champagne and Vicky L. Kouba

11. THE RELEVANCE OF MULTIPLE-CHOICE TESTING IN ASSESSING SCIENCE UNDERSTANDING

Philip M. Sadler

12. NATIONAL AND INTERNATIONAL ASSESSMENT

Pinchas Tamir

13. ON THE PSYCHOMETRICS OF ASSESSING SCIENCE UNDERSTANDING

Richard J. Shavelson and Maria Araceli Ruiz-Primo

14. CAUTIONARY NOTES ON ASSESSMENT OF UNDERSTANDING SCIENCE CONCEPTS AND NATURE OF SCIENCE

Ronald G. Good

15. EPILOGUE: ON WAYS OF ASSESSING SCIENCE UNDERSTANDING

Joseph D. Novak, Joel J. Mintzes, and James H. Wandersee

Contributors

Numbers in parentheses indicate the pages on which the authors' contributions begin.

Audrey B. Champagne (223), School of Education, State University of New York at Albany, Albany, New York 12222

Catherine L. Cummins (71), Graduate Studies in Curriculum and Instruction, Louisiana State University, Baton Rouge, Louisiana 70803

Katherine M. Edmondson (15), School of Veterinary Medicine, Cornell University, Ithaca, New York 14853

Kathleen M. Fisher (197), Center for Research in Mathematics and Science Education, San Diego State University, San Diego, California 92120

JoEllen Fisherkeller (95), Department of Culture and Communication, New York University, New York, New York 10003

Ronald G. Good (343), Curriculum and Instruction, Louisiana State University, Baton Rouge, Louisiana 70803

Kathleen Hogan (95), Institute of Ecosystem Studies, Millbrook, New York 12545

Vicky L. Kouba (223), School of Education, State University of New York at Albany, Albany, New York 12222

Joel J. Mintzes (1, 41, 355), Department of Biological Sciences, University of North Carolina at Wilmington, Wilmington, North Carolina 28403; and Department of Mathematics, Science and Technology Education, North Carolina State University, Raleigh, North Carolina 27607

Joseph D. Novak (1, 41, 355), Department of Education, Cornell University, Ithaca, New York 14853

Nancy R. Romance (167), School of Education, Florida Atlantic University, Boca Raton, Florida 33428

Maria Araceli Ruiz-Primo (303), School of Education, Stanford University, Stanford, California 94305

Philip M. Sadler (249), Science Education Department, Harvard–Smithsonian Center for Astrophysics, Cambridge, Massachusetts 02138

Richard J. Shavelson (303), School of Education, Stanford University, Stanford, California 94305

Mike U. Smith (71), Department of Internal Medicine, Mercer University School of Medicine, Macon, Georgia 31201

Sherry A. Southerland (71), Educational Studies Department, The University of Utah, Salt Lake City, Utah 84112

Pinchas Tamir (279), Israel Science Teaching Center, The Hebrew University, Jerusalem, Israel 91904

John E. Trowbridge (145), Department of Teacher Education, Southeastern Louisiana University, Hammond, Louisiana 70401

Michael R. Vitale (167), Department of Science Education, East Carolina University, Greenville, North Carolina 27838

James H. Wandersee (1, 129, 145, 355), Graduate Studies in Curriculum and Instruction, Louisiana State University, Baton Rouge, Louisiana 70803

Preface

Meaning making is the fundamental adaptation of the human species and the driving force underlying all forms of conceptual change, whether that change occurs in the mind of the experienced professional scientist or a young child confronting the wonders of nature for the first time.

This book, together with its companion volume *Teaching Science for Understanding: A Human Constructivist View* (Mintzes, Wandersee, & Novak, Eds., 1998, San Diego: Academic Press), offers a useful theoretical, empirical, and practical guide for reflective science teachers who are committed to preparing scientifically literate and technologically responsible citizens in the twenty-first century. In writing and editing these books we have been motivated by an abiding conviction that success in the new century will demand substantially new ways of teaching, learning, and assessing student progress in science education. Our views have been informed largely by the history and philosophy of science and education; by significant social, political, and economic changes of the past 25 years; and by a strong commitment to a cognitive model of meaningful learning, knowledge restructuring, and conceptual change.

In *Teaching Science for Understanding*, we focused on a series of promising new intervention strategies that offer powerful alternatives to traditional classroom instruction. These strategies represent a significant departure from previous practice and reflect our newfound role in preparing students to become meaning makers and knowledge builders.

In this follow-up volume, we turn our attention to the fundamental problem of assessment. Our concern for assessment is founded on the central role of evaluation in promoting (or discouraging) conceptual *understanding* in the natural sciences. Novak (Chapter 1) views assessment as the fifth essential *commonplace* in education, along with the teacher, the learner, the curriculum, and the social environment. As we view it, poor assessment practices in the elementary and secondary schools (and in colleges and universities) are clearly among the most significant impediments to *understanding* and *conceptual change*.

The view that "assessment drives learning" is perhaps the oldest adage in education; yet, until recently, science educators have invested precious little time in developing and testing new assessment strategies that complement and reinforce meaningful learning. As a result, we have witnessed a kind of progressive decoupling (i.e., a "misalignment") of instruction and assessment in science education. In the course of our work, we have seen many talented and conscientious science teachers take substantial risks by implementing powerful new instructional practices, only to inadvertently discourage meaningful learning through inappropriate assessment strategies. This book is our attempt to begin addressing that problem.

HUMAN CONSTRUCTIVISM

This book presents a set of heuristically powerful new tools for *Assessing Science Understanding* that have found widespread use in elementary and secondary schools and in colleges and universities around the world. The development of these tools has been guided in large part by a view of learning, creating, and using knowledge that we call *human constructivism*.

Human constructivists believe that the unique quality of the human mind is a reflection of its profound capacity for *making meanings*. This propensity of human beings to seek *meaning* in their interactions with objects, events, and other people serves as the driving force of conceptual change. To us, science is best understood as a formalized and highly adaptive way of harnessing the *meaning-making* capacity of the human mind—a capacity that develops during early childhood to facilitate learning and is the product of millions of years of evolution. Putting it somewhat differently, science is an intense, intellectually demanding struggle to construct heuristically powerful explanations through extended periods of interaction with the natural world, including other meaning makers.

As we see it, the function of formal schooling is to encourage *shared meaning* and teachers serve as *middlemen*, *facilitators*, and *negotiators* of meaning. Ultimately, we seek to develop in our students powerful shared meanings that are *coherent*, *parsimonious*, and useful in *analyzing* and *critically evaluating* knowledge and value claims. When we are successful in this effort, we help students construct progressively more powerful explanations of the world; we encourage them to wrestle with and resolve inconsistencies and unnecessary complexities in their thinking; and we empower them to evaluate and challenge the knowledge and value claims of others, including those whose authoritative views are currently accepted by the scientific establishment.

ASSESSING SCIENCE UNDERSTANDING

Within this *human constructivist* view, we recognize assessment as a potentially powerful mechanism for encouraging and rewarding meaning making.

We also recognize the limitations of many widely used assessment practices, and the destructive effects of a "sorting and selecting" mentality that these practices have sometimes engendered. One of the repeating themes of this book is the view that success in creating, learning, and using knowledge is not well captured by commonly used assessment practices that rely heavily on single, quantitative measures of subject matter attainment. Accordingly, we offer a wide range of new assessment techniques that are grounded in two principal assumptions: (1) that *understanding is not meaningfully revealed by "normalized" comparisons among students*, and (2) that *conceptual change is not adequately represented by a single, "standardized" alphanumeric score*.

Each of the chapters in this book has been written by one or more authoritative and highly regarded individuals within the field of science education assessment. Our goal, however, has been not to compile yet another treatise for experts alone, but instead to provide a readable and readily accessible volume on alternative assessment strategies within the reach of every science teacher. The suggestions we offer are supported by a strong framework of theory and research extending over a period of more than twenty-five years.

In Chapter 1 we introduce the theory and research on which our views are founded. Framed within Schwab's four *commonplaces* of education (i.e., the learner, the teacher, the curriculum, and the social context), we suggest that *assessment* belongs as the fifth element among the most important determinants of high-quality education. Chapters 2 (Edmondson) and 3 (Mintzes and Novak) offer two widely used assessment tools that are direct products of our work in representing and evaluating knowledge and knowledge creation: *concept maps* and V *diagrams*. During the past twenty-five years, these tools have been adopted by thousands of teachers in elementary and secondary schools and in colleges and universities around the world.

Interviewing has been rightly called "the workhorse" of assessment because of its central role in exploring and documenting students' understanding. Chapters 4 (Southerland, Smith, and Cummins) and 5 (Hogan and Fisherkeller) introduce several types of interviewing strategies that are immediately applicable to classroom use. Among other contributions, the authors of these chapters provide useful, step-by-step instructions on ways of interviewing students and evaluating their responses.

Wandersee and Trowbridge (Chapters 6 and 7) introduce several new visual and observational assessment strategies that tap into the "nonverbal" component of science learning. They rightly suggest that much about the nature of science depends on observation and that expertise in these critical skills may be encouraged through the use of observational rubrics and image-based assessment strategies.

In an effort to broaden the range of assessment strategies in current use, the authors of Chapters 8 (Vitale and Romance), 9 (Fisher), and 10 (Champagne and Kouba) focus on the value of portfolios, SemNet software, and written products as measures of understanding in natural science.

One of the potentially valuable spin-offs of the extensive research program on students' alternative conceptions is a growing body of "conceptual diagnostic tests." These widely used assessment tools (e.g., Hestenes' *Force Concept Inventory*) typically employ a traditional multiple-choice format, but depend critically on the well-documented knowledge base of students' understandings in science. In Chapter 11, Sadler describes the use of item response theory to analyze the psychometric characteristics of one such instrument developed to assess astronomy concepts at Harvard's Project STAR.

The remaining chapters in the book address critical issues in science education assessment, including national and international testing programs (Chapter 12 by Tamir), the psychometics of performance measures (Chapter 13 by Shavelson and Ruiz-Primo), and the limitations of paper and pencil examinations in science assessment (Chapter 14 by Good). In the Epilogue (Chapter 15), we summarize the main points of these chapters and offer a cautionary note on assessment based on our human constructivist view.

OUR AUDIENCE

This book and its companion volume, *Teaching Science for Understanding*, are intended primarily for science teachers, graduate students, teacher educators, researchers, and curriculum developers. However, we have found that the companion volume has served a useful function in the hands of administrators, parents, supervisors, school board members, and indeed anyone concerned about the current state of science education and what might be done to improve it. We trust that this volume on assessment will fill a complementary niche.

Joel J. Mintzes
James H. Wandersee
Joseph D. Novak

Dedication

We dedicate this book to our life-long companions, Susan Mintzes, Carol Wandersee, and Joan Novak. Without their constant support and encouragement this book (and everything else) would have been impossible.

Joel J. Mintzes
James H. Wandersee
Joseph D. Novak

Acknowledgment

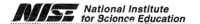

The research reported in this paper was supported by a cooperative agreement between the National Science Foundation and the University of Wisconsin-Madison (Cooperative Agreement No. RED-9452971). At UW-Madison, the National Institute for Science Education is housed in the Wisconsin Center for Education Research and is a collaborative effort of the College of Agricultural and Life Sciences, the School of Education, the College of Engineering, and the College of Letters and Science. The collaborative effort is also joined by the National Center for Improving Science Education, Washington, DC. Any opinions, findings, or conclusions are those of the author and do not necessarily reflect the view of the supporting agencies.

CHAPTER

1

Learning, Teaching, and Assessment: A Human Constructivist Perspective

JOSEPH D. NOVAK
Cornell University

JOEL J. MINTZES
University of North Carolina and North Carolina State University

JAMES H. WANDERSEE
Louisiana State University

THE ROLE OF ASSESSMENT

In 1973, Joseph Schwab argued that every educative episode involves four *commonplaces*: (1) the learner, (2) the teacher, (3) the subject matter or knowledge, and (4) the social milieu. We see value in these basic elements suggested by Schwab, but would add a fifth element: (5) assessment (Novak, 1998). Whether in school, work, or recreation, so much of what we achieve as learners is controlled in good measure by how our performance is appraised, evaluated, or rewarded. While we believe the primary motivation for learning should be the satisfaction that comes with achieving competence, we need assessment to gauge the degree to which we approach or attain high competence. High-quality assessment can facilitate high-quality learning, but unfortunately, poor assessment can deter or prevent high-quality learning and may reward performance that is deleterious to the learner in the long run. Much has been written to show that too much

Assessing Science Understanding

school testing can play this deleterious role, and some of the authors in this book will address this problem. Our objective, however, is less to castigate poor school evaluation practices than to provide promising alternatives.

We agree with Schwab (1973) that each of the commonplaces or elements of education interacts with all of the other elements, and therefore no element can be considered in isolation from the others, as is too often the practice in books on testing or evaluation. Therefore, we begin by considering each of the first four elements before proceeding to our focus on assessment.

THE LEARNER

In the last quarter century, much progress has been made in our under-standing of how humans learn and of the factors that influence their learn-ing. There is general agreement on the idea that, except for the neonate, all learners come to a learning task with some relevant knowledge, feelings, and skills. By school age, children have already attained several thousand concepts and language labels for these concepts. We see *concepts* as playing a primary role in our theory of learning and our theory of knowledge and hence we wish to define concepts very explicitly: *Concepts are perceived regularities in events or objects, or records of events or objects, designated by a label.*

Our evolutionary history has conferred on every normal child the capac-ity to recognize regularities in events or objects and to use language to label these regularities. Thus children learn to recognize and correctly label moms, dads, raining, running, and other such regularities. The language they use to label these regularities depends on the social milieu in which they are raised, but the capacity is universal. Of course, there are genetic variations in the capacities to perceive specific kinds of regularities, and some children see color, sounds, personal characteristics, and myriads of other events or objects with greater acumen than others. This has led peo-ple to propose many "faces of intellect" (Guilford, 1959) or, more recently, "multiple intelligences" (Gardner, 1983); but such classifications may do more to obfuscate the fundamental capacity of humans to perceive regular-ities of various kinds and to label and use concepts than to illuminate the process by which this basic form of learning occurs.

Learners do not store concepts as isolated bits; instead, they form rela-tionships or connections between concepts to form *propositions*. Propositions are statements about how some aspect of the universe is perceived or func-tions. Thus "sky is blue," "doggies have four legs," and "cells are units that make up living things" are propositions about how some things are per-ceived, whereas "parties are fun," "ice cools drinks," and "electrons move in conductors" are propositions about how some things function. Propositions are *units of meaning*, whereas concepts are the "atoms" that make up these units. The idea that all knowledge is constructed from concepts and relationships between concepts represents our fundamental epistemological beliefs, which are discussed further in the next section.

Learning may proceed in two different ways. *Rote learning* occurs when the learner makes no effort to relate new concepts and propositions to prior relevant knowledge he/she possesses. *Meaningful learning* occurs when the learner seeks to relate new concepts and propositions to relevant existing concepts and propositions in his/her cognitive structure. There is a continuum from rote learning to highly meaningful learning in that the degree of the latter depends on the quantity of relevant knowledge the learner possesses, the quality of organization of relevant knowledge, and the degree of effort made by the learner to integrate new with existing concepts and propositions. These ideas can be illustrated using *concept maps.* Two concept maps are shown in Figure 1. Map (A) illustrates some of the missing concepts and misconceptions that are charactistic of rote learners, whereas map (B) shows the organized knowledge of an "expert" meaningful learner.

Another distinction in learning is the contrast between *surface* and *deep* learning (Marton & Saljo, 1976). Surface learning can be related to near rote or very low levels of meaningful learning, whereas deep learning would be characterized by relatively highly levels of meaningful learning.

Perhaps the best-known classification scheme is Bloom's (1956) *Taxonomy.* Bloom described 6 taxonomic levels for evaluation of learning ranging from level 1.0, "recall of specifics," to level 5, "synthesis," and level 6, "evaluation." Studies of classroom testing have shown that most test items do not require more than level 1 performance. The consequence is that learning by rote can in some ways best achieve high performance on such test items. When the curriculum presents almost innumerable "factoids" or bits of information to be recalled, it is almost impossible for most students to consider how each of these "factoids" relates to what they already know or to integrate the changed meanings that result as this information is assimilated. The "overstuffed" curriculum in many science courses is one of the reasons students resort to rote learning.

Another reason students resort to rote learning is that they often possess many invalid notions or misconceptions in virtually every domain of knowledge. Unless students have the time, encouragement, and the inclination to reconstruct their faulty conceptual frameworks, they can do better on tests in most content domains if they simply memorize the "correct" information, procedure, or algorithm. Furthermore, teachers and textbooks can have idiosyncratic descriptions for specific concepts and propositions, and rote learning may be the most efficient strategy when verbatim recall of this information is required. Other pitfalls of typical classroom testing will be discussed in this book.

In the course of meaningful learning, the learner's knowledge structure, or cognitive structure, becomes more complex and better organized. According to Ausubel (1963, 1968, 1978) this occurs as a result of four

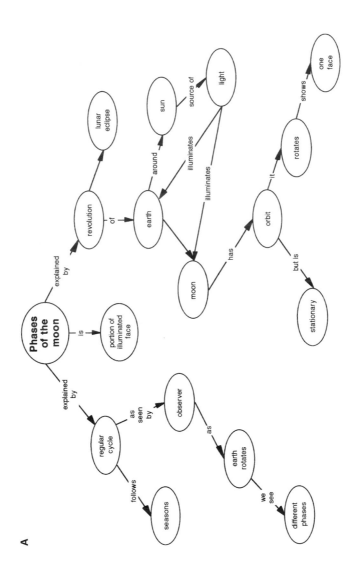

4

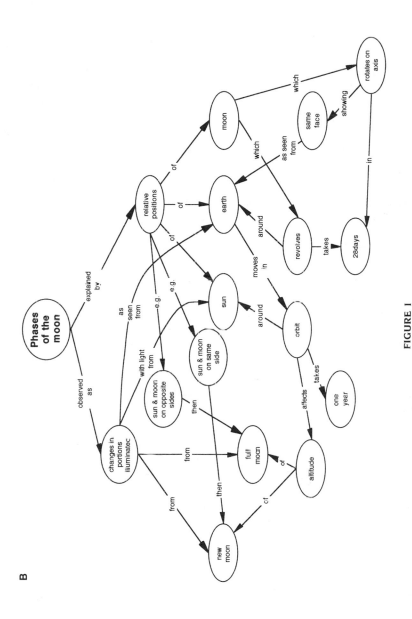

FIGURE 1

Two concept maps for the phases of the moon showing (A) the misconceptions and missing concepts that are characteristic of students learning primarily by rote and (B) the highly organized knowledge structure of an "expert" teacher, which is characteristic of meaningful learners.

5

processes: *subsumption, progressive differentiation, integrative reconciliation,* and *superordinate learning.* First and most common is the process of *subsumption,* wherein new concepts and/or propositions are subsumed under and related to more inclusive concepts and propositions. For example, a young child perceives a variety of dogs and acquires the concept of *dog.* Subsequently the child learns that some dogs are called terriers, some are collies, and so on. These latter concepts are subsumed under the child's concept of dog and give greater clarity, complexity, and meaning to his/her *dog* concept. For the domain of knowledge *dogs,* the child has achieved what Ausubel calls *progressive differentiation.* His/her *dog* concept may now include the ideas that terriers have short hair and collies have long hair. A young child may see a cow or horse at a distance and call these doggies also, but the child soon learns that these animals have features that are designated by different concept labels. Thus the child's cognitive structure undergoes further progressive differentiation and also *integrative reconciliations;* that is, things that were first confused as dogs are now recognized as similar but also as different in significant ways—and designated by different concept labels. This sorting out and refining of meanings that at first appear confusing or contradictory is achieved through integrative reconciliation, which in turn leads to further progressive differentiation of cognitive structure.

Cognitive structure development usually proceeds in an "up and down" manner. First, a learner may acquire a concept of average generality and inclusiveness. He/she then proceeds from this to distinguish concepts with greater and greater detail or specificity and to gain some concepts of greater generality and inclusiveness. Thus, in our example, dog or doggies may be the initial concept developed, followed by concepts of terrier or collie, and perhaps concepts of canine or mammal. In due course, a more complex, well-integrated knowledge structure emerges. The challenge we face in evaluation is to assess the degree to which learners are developing their conceptual framework by which they can achieve both greater precision and specificity of conceptual understanding, as well as mastery of more powerful, more general, more inclusive relevant concepts.

Recognizing that distant things *appear* to be smaller (cows look like dogs) is also part of cognitive development, whereby concepts of scale and context are being developed and refined. The importance of the context in which events and objects are embedded is one aspect of constructing valid meanings that all learners come to recognize with lesser or greater sophistication. Some researchers have also found this to be important in what they describe as "situated cognition" (Brown, Collins, & Duquid, 1989).

One threat to assessment validity is that information learned in one context may not be transferred and utilized in a different context. Test items that require use of knowledge only in the same context in which it was learned do not assess higher levels of meaningful learning. When learners achieve a high degree of differentiation and integration of knowledge in a particular subject matter domain, they are capable of transferring or applying that knowledge in a wide variety of new contexts. We return to this issue in later chapters.

The fourth process of meaningful learning described by Ausubel is *superordinate learning*. Early in a child's cognitive development, the most general, most inclusive concepts the child acquires are relatively limited in the scope of events and/or objects they refer to. Mommies, daddies, and doggies serve as some of these fundamental concepts that subsume other more specific concepts. However, as cognitive development proceeds, the child acquires more general, more inclusive *superordinate* concepts. For the preschool youngster, these may include concepts such as people, mammals, energy, and time. In later years superordinate concepts such as religion, the Dark Ages, evolution, and entropy may be acquired. Meaningful learning of superordinate concepts confers new meaning to relevant subordinate concepts and propositions and may also facilitate integrative reconciliation of concepts. Thus the acquisition of powerful superordinate concepts should be a primary goal of effective science teaching (Novak, 1977; Mintzes, Wandersee, & Novak, 1998). Unfortunately, for much science teaching, students and teachers are preoccupied with the acquisition (usually by rote learning) of numerous facts, problem-solving algorithms, and information classification schemes with little underlying conceptual coherence. The result is that students fail to acquire well-organized conceptual frameworks including powerful superordinate concepts.

One of the challenges we address in this book is how to design assessment strategies that encourage high levels of meaningful learning, including the development of well-integrated superordinate concepts. We focus on this commitment in each of the following chapters, albeit within a variety of perspectives.

THE TEACHER

Given what we have said about learning and the learner, it is evident that teachers have a very challenging role to play in the educative process. First, they must seek to understand the major superordinate and subordinate concepts of their field and to integrate these into a complex, integrated, hierarchical structure. This is no small task. So many preservice science courses in colleges and universities are little more than a deluge of information or problem-solving algorithms to be memorized and reproduced on tests. Both the pedagogy and the assessment practices in these courses often do little to foster development of the kind of knowledge frameworks that are needed for effective science teaching. So prospective science teachers must seek on their own initiative to build this kind of understanding of their field.

Second, the context in which teachers learn most of their science is divorced from the real world. To create an appropriate context for their own teaching, teachers must seek other experiences, such as field courses and laboratory research opportunities, and they must work to integrate the "book learning" with the knowledge, skills, and attitudes acquired through these experiences.

Third, teachers must learn ways to plan their own curriculum, they must be able to sequence topics in such a way that new knowledge is more easily built on previous learning, and they must master a set of strategies that aim at helping learners restructure their scientific understandings. In the past 25 years we have come to recognize that helping learners change the way they think about natural objects and events is far more difficult than we used to believe and that often this process extends well beyond the time constraints of the typical school year. Finding appropriate contexts for meaningful learning within the constraints of school structures is a major challenge that we have not even begun to seriously address.

Finally, teachers must plan and implement assessment strategies that support meaningful learning and help to achieve the kind of conceptual understandings, feelings, and actions that empower students to be more effective in whatever future work they pursue.

We have offered many ideas on how to achieve these goals in *Teaching Science for Understanding*, and we shall not repeat them here. Nevertheless, we shall attempt to be consistent with the suggestions in that book as we focus on new ideas for assessment in this book.

KNOWLEDGE AND KNOWLEDGE CREATION

There is the age-old question, What is knowledge? Humans have pondered the question for millennia. There have been significant advances in the past 3 decades in our understanding of the nature of knowledge, and also in our understanding of the process of knowledge creation. Perhaps the most important idea is that knowledge is not "discovered" as are diamonds or archeological artifacts, but rather it is "created" by human beings. *Knowledge is a human construction that is a natural outgrowth of the capacity of human beings for high levels of meaningful learning* (Novak, 1977; 1993; 1998; Mintzes, Wandersee, & Novak, 1998). Just as the building blocks for learning and acquisition of knowledge by an individual are concepts and propositions, these are also the building blocks of knowledge. Understanding the process of meaningful learning is fundamental to understanding the process of knowledge creation.

With the explosive growth of information on the Internet, anyone who "surfs the net" soon recognizes the overwhelming amount of information available. But is information knowledge? From our perspective, knowledge has *organization* and potential for *application* in problem solving. The difficulty with all of the information on the Internet is that much of it is not available in a form that allows easy organization and application. There are search engines and "crawlers" that seek out and organize some of the information available, but these are usually for special-purpose searches. Unless we design special-purpose search engines or crawlers for our own needs, information taken from the Internet can be overwhelming chaos. There is a bright future on the horizon, with new special-purpose search tools appearing, but at this writing, gaining information that can be easily structured to our specific needs can be a daunting challenge.

Another characteristic of knowledge stored in the human brain is that every piece of knowledge is associated to some degree with feelings or affect. Thus the successful application of knowledge depends not only on how much knowledge we have and how we organize it, but also on the feelings we associate with our knowledge. This is discussed in Keller's biography (1983), A *Feeling for the Organism: The Life and Work of Barbara McClintock*. In a more prosaic manner, Herrigel (1973) presented some of the same ideas in his *Zen in the Art of Archery*. Biographies of geniuses almost always emphasize not the amount of these information that people possess but rather their dogged perseverance and their feelings regarding the best questions or approaches to pursue. This is as true in the arts and humanities as it is in the sciences, or perhaps even more so.

In so much of school assessment, emotion plays little or no role; strong feelings may even prove a liability. While we tend to see more emphasis on expressing emotions in the arts and humanities, too often an individual's freedom to express emotions is suppressed in these disciplines as well. Emotions or feelings motivate. We seek to do those things that make us feel good, and we avoid those things that make us feel bad. If one of our goals is to make students more creative, more motivated to do something positive with their lives, then we face the challenge of using evaluation strategies that reward high levels of meaningful learning.

Poor testing practices can reward the wrong kind of learning. One way to increase the distribution or "spread" of scores on a test is to require recall of relatively minute details or bits of insignificant information. Such practices tend to discourage learners from looking for the "big ideas" in a domain of study and seeking to organize knowledge hierarchically, with the "big ideas" playing a dominant role. The development of strong positive feelings toward "elegant" organizations of knowledge and the wide span of relevant applications of powerful ideas is also discouraged. These are some of the issues we shall address in this book.

The process of knowledge creation involves the interplay of at least 12 elements. We have found it helpful to represent the process using the vee heuristic developed by Gowin (1981; Novak & Gowin, 1984). Figure 2 shows how these epistemological elements can be defined and related. Elements

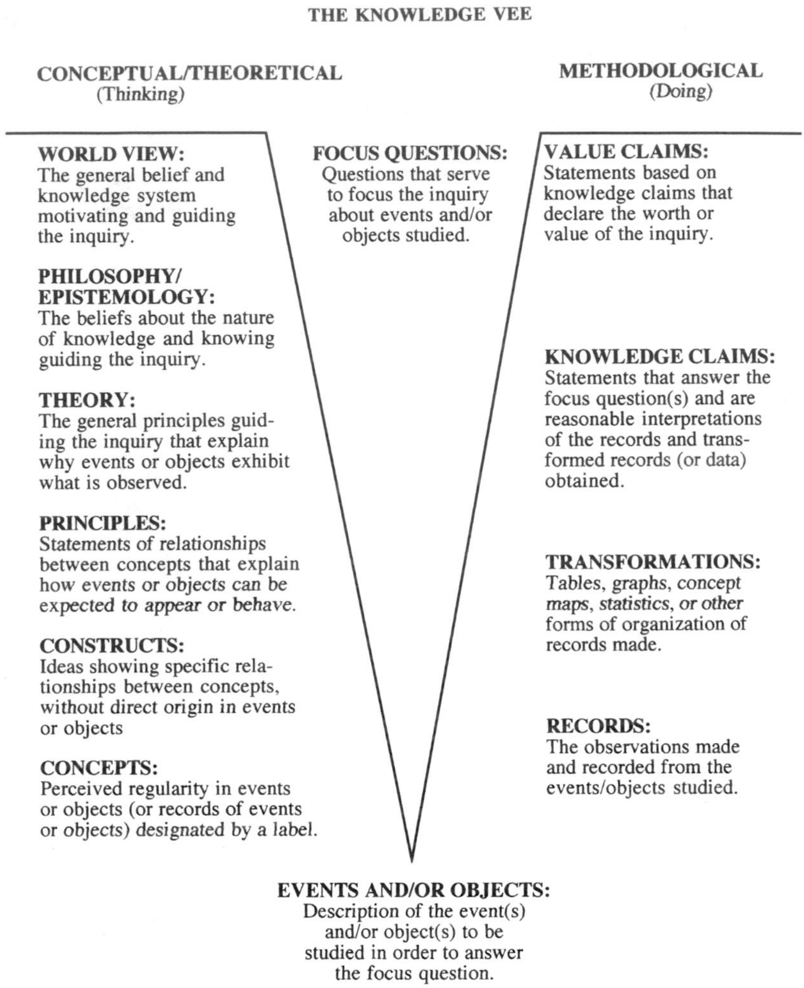

THE KNOWLEDGE VEE

| CONCEPTUAL/THEORETICAL | | METHODOLOGICAL |
| (Thinking) | | (Doing) |

WORLD VIEW:
The general belief and knowledge system motivating and guiding the inquiry.

FOCUS QUESTIONS:
Questions that serve to focus the inquiry about events and/or objects studied.

VALUE CLAIMS:
Statements based on knowledge claims that declare the worth or value of the inquiry.

PHILOSOPHY/ EPISTEMOLOGY:
The beliefs about the nature of knowledge and knowing guiding the inquiry.

KNOWLEDGE CLAIMS:
Statements that answer the focus question(s) and are reasonable interpretations of the records and transformed records (or data) obtained.

THEORY:
The general principles guiding the inquiry that explain why events or objects exhibit what is observed.

PRINCIPLES:
Statements of relationships between concepts that explain how events or objects can be expected to appear or behave.

TRANSFORMATIONS:
Tables, graphs, concept maps, statistics, or other forms of organization of records made.

CONSTRUCTS:
Ideas showing specific relationships between concepts, without direct origin in events or objects

CONCEPTS:
Perceived regularity in events or objects (or records of events or objects) designated by a label.

RECORDS:
The observations made and recorded from the events/objects studied.

EVENTS AND/OR OBJECTS:
Description of the event(s) and/or object(s) to be studied in order to answer the focus question.

FIGURE 2

The knowledge vee for the 12 elements that are involved in creating or understanding knowledge in any domain. The elements on the left side of the vee are used by the learner to select events and focus questions and to perform the actions on the right side of the vee that lead to learning and the creation of knowledge. All elements interact with each other.

on the left side represent the conceptual/theoretical elements. These are the knowledge structure and values that guide the inquiry. On the right side of the vee are the methodological or procedural elements that are involved in the creation of new knowledge and value claims. Selecting the "right" focus question and the "right" events and/or objects to observe depends on the knowledge, feelings, and values the creator brings to the process. It is evident from the elements shown in the vee that the process of knowledge creation is in some ways simple—only 12 elements are involved—and in other ways enormously complex. There are almost an infinite number of questions that may be asked and almost an infinite number of events or objects to be observed in any domain of knowledge. How do students learn to ask the right questions, observe the appropriate objects and events, make the important records, perform the best transformations, and construct the most powerful knowledge and value claims? There are no simple answers to these questions. The best we can hope to do is to help the learner develop the most powerful knowledge structures possible and help to impart a deep respect for and drive to create new knowledge. We shall attempt to show how improved assessment practices can help to achieve these goals. The use of the vee heuristic as an assessment tool is discussed in Chapter 4.

THE SOCIAL MILIEU

Education takes place in a social context. As societies change, new demands are placed on schools. After the USSR launched *Sputnik* in 1957, there was a public outcry for improving science and mathematics education in our schools. One response was to increase funding for science education at the National Science Foundation (NSF). The primary goal of these programs was to devise new textbooks and support for teacher education programs. Despite the expenditure of several billion dollars by federal agencies and school districts to improve science and mathematics education, there is little evidence that we have made significant progress, as indicated by international comparisons of student achievement in the United States and other developed democracies (see Chapter 12). There are, of course, many reasons for this, but at least one important factor is that little was done to improve assessment practices in past "reform" movements. As long as the predominant mode of assessment stressed recall of facts and problem-solving algorithms, students continued to engage in rote learning practices. While there were attempts to produce laboratory study guides with more emphasis on enquiry approaches to learning, these were often taught in a way that reduced the labs to little more than "cookbook" verification exercises. Additionally, most schools did not adopt the new NSF-sponsored curricula, for a variety of social, political, and economic reasons.

Currently the dominant factor influencing change in science and mathematics education comes from the recent effort to establish "standards." The two most prominent efforts in this have been the work of the American Association for Advancement of Science (AAAS), *Benchmarks for Science Literacy—Project 2061* (1993), and the National Academy of Sciences (NAS), National Research Council, *National Science Education Standards* (1996). Both of these publications were developed with counsel from scientists, outstanding teachers, and science educators. The participants in the process of creating the standards were obviously well-recognized experts, but as is so often the case, there were other experts whose ideas were not solicited or not included. For example, the views of those experts who do not feel that inquiry approaches are the best method of instruction for all science content were not included in the NAS committees. This, in fact, is a principal problem in the way science curricula are currently organized, taught, and evaluated.

Although the AAAS *Benchmarks* give more recognition to the variety of views on teaching approaches and grade level appropriateness of certain science topics, they are nevertheless very conservative in what they suggest can be taught in the lower grades. This, in our view, is a serious limitation. Some concepts, such as the particulate nature of matter, are so fundamental to understanding most of science that postponing instruction on these concepts postpones the chance for developing understanding of most basic science phenomena. As Novak and Musonda (1991) showed in their 12-year longitudinal study of children's science concept development, instruction in the particulate nature of matter in grades 1 and 2 can influence children's science learning throughout their schooling.

Another area that is largely ignored by the *Standards* and *Benchmarks* is the important role that metacognitive instruction can play when it is an integral part of the curriculum for grades K–12. To ignore this is to ignore research that suggests enormous gains in learning when metacognitive tools and ideas are properly taught and utilized (Mintzes et al., 1998; Novak, 1998).

The net result of most current curriculum efforts is that there is still an emphasis on what is essentially a "laundry list" of topics to be taught. Although most curriculum groups expound the idea that "more is less," the lists of topics to be taught in the *Standards, Benchmarks,* and other curriculum proposals remain overwhelming. All are a far cry from the guidelines proposed in 1964 by the National Science Teachers Association Curriculum Committee suggesting seven major conceptual schemes and five characteristics of the process of science (Novak, 1964, 1966) as the basis for the design of K–12 science curricula.

With growing public and political pressure on accountability in schools, we are witnessing today a renewed emphasis on testing in science and other areas of the curriculum. While we support the need for accountability, much of the testing done in school, state, and national programs falls far short of evaluation that assesses *understanding* of science concepts and methodologies. The net result may be inadvertently to encourage classroom activities that support rote rather than meaningful learning. We recognize the central role of traditional assessment practices as one of the most significant deterents to meaningful learning, and this recognition has led us to develop and evaluate several powerful new alternative assessment strategies that are described in this book.

A FOREWORD

In the chapters that follow, we expand on the nature of science learning and constuctivist views that underlie the alternative assessment practices we recommend. Each of the well-known contributors to this volume has had experience in applying the ideas presented, and each draws on this experience to suggest ways of improving teaching and assessment in science. With this brief introduction to four of the five *commonplaces* of education, we invite you now to consider the fifth: new approaches to *assessing science understanding.*

References

American Association for the Advancement of Science (1993). *Benchmarks for science literacy: Project 2061.* New York: Oxford University Press.

Ausubel, D. (1963). *The psychology of meaningful verbal learning.* New York: Grune & Stratton.

Ausubel, D. (1968). *Educational psychology: A cognitive view.* New York: Holt, Rinehart & Winston.

Ausubel, D., Novak, J., & Hanesian, H. (1978). *Educational psychology: A cognitive view* (2nd ed.). New York: Holt, Rinehart & Winston.

Bloom, B. (1956). *Taxonomy of educational objectives: The classification of educational goals. Handbook 1: Cognitive domain.* New York: David McKay.

Brown, J., Collins, A., & Duquid, P. (1989). Situated cognition and the culture of learning. *Educational Researcher,* 18, 32–42.

Gardner, H. (1983). *Frames of mind: The theory of multiple intelligences.* New York: Basic Books.

Gowin, D. B. (1981). *Educating.* Ithaca, NY: Cornell University Press.

Guilford, J. (1959). Three faces of intellect. *American Psychologist,* 14, 469–479.

Herrigel, E. (1973). *Zen in the art of archery* (R.F.C. Hull, trans.). New York: Vintage Books.

Keller, E. F. (1983). *A feeling for the organism. The life and works of Barbara McClintock.* New York: Freeman.

Marton, F., & Saljo, R. (1976): "On Qualitative Differences in Learning: 1. Outcome and Process." *British Journal of Educational Psychology,* 464–471.

Mintzes, J., Wandersee, J., & Novak, J. (Eds.) (1998). *Teaching science for understanding: A human constructivist view.* San Diego: Academic Press.

National Research Council. (1996). *National science education standards.* Washington, DC: National Academy Press.

Novak, J. (1964). Importance of conceptual schemes for science teaching. *The Science Teacher,* 31, 10.

Novak, J. (1966). The role of concepts in science teaching. In H. J. Klausmeier & C. W. Harris (eds.), *Analysis of Concept Learning* (pp. 239–254). New York: Academic Press.

Novak, J. (1977). *A theory of education.* Ithaca, NY: Cornell University Press.

Novak, J. (1993). Human constructivism: A unification of psychological and epistemological phenomena in meaning making. *International Journal of Personal Construct Psychology,* 6, 167–193.

Novak, J. (1998). *Learning, creating and using knowledge: Concept maps™ as facilitative tools in schools and corporations* Mahwah, NJ: Lawrence Erlbaum.

Novak, J., & Gowin, D. B. (1984). *Learning how to learn.* Cambridge, UK: Cambridge University Press.

Novak, J., & Musonda, D. (1991). A twelve year longitudinal study of science concept learning. *American Educational Research Journal,* 28, 117–153.

Schwab, J. (1973). The practical 3: Translation into curriculum. *School Review,* 81, 501–522.

CHAPTER

2

Assessing Science Understanding through Concept Maps

KATHERINE M. EDMONDSON

Cornell University

The fundamental goal of educating is to facilitate learning through shared meaning between teacher and student. As Gowin states:

> A back-and-forthness between teacher and student can be brief or it can last a long time, but the aim is to achieve shared meaning. In this interaction both teacher and student have definite responsibilities. The teacher is responsible for seeing to it that the meanings of the materials the student grasps are the meanings the teacher intended for the student to take away. The student is responsible for seeing to it that the grasped meanings are the ones the teacher intended. (Gowin, 1981, p. 63)

Regardless of the subject matter, the nature of the setting, or teaching methods, shared meaning lies at the heart of the interaction between teachers and students. How might this best be accomplished? How do teachers know when their understandings are congruent with those of their students? Implicit in the goal of shared meaning is the assumption that teaching and learning is a shared enterprise, that teachers and students must work together to construct knowledge and negotiate meaning. For this to be realized, students must be regarded as active participants in the process of knowledge construction (not as passive recipients of knowledge that is "transferred" by the teacher), and as being capable of generating meaning which may then be shared.

Teachers routinely ask whether their students understand the material or, perhaps more explicitly, how well their students understand. How complete or comprehensive is a student's understanding? Does a student who seems to grasp some concepts also grasp others? If a student understands, will he or she build upon that understanding as new information is introduced, or will learning progress in discrete units that seem independent from one another? To what extent does one student's understanding compare to another's? Inextricably linked to these questions are others that relate to teaching: What strategies for presenting the material are most effective? What qualities characterize the concepts students find more difficult to grasp? How might teachers structure a curriculum to make complex information more accessible to students? Only by maintaining a focus on the quality of student learning can teachers get meaningful answers to questions such as these. And meaningful answers to thoughtful questions about the factors that influence shared meaning and meaningful learning are essential to improving education.

Shared meaning leads to meaningful learning, in which students build upon prior knowledge and make conscious attempts to integrate new information with what they already know (Ausubel, Novak, & Hanesian, 1978; Novak, 1977, 1998). The important role prior knowledge plays in new learning has been well documented (Ausubel et al., 1978; Entwistle & Ramsden, 1983; Hegarty-Hazel & Prosser, 1991; Kulhavy & Schwartz, 1986). Prior knowledge may facilitate (Novak, 1993; Pankratius, 1990; Willerman & MacHarg, 1991) or impede subsequent learning (Novak & Musonda, 1991; West, 1988), and it is important for teachers to engage students actively with the material so that they employ meaningful learning strategies. Implicit in this assertion are the assumptions that students' approaches to learning influence their cognitive structure (Biggs, 1989; Edmondson & Novak, 1993; Entwistle, 1988) and that cognitive structure reflects qualitative differences in understanding (Bezzi, 1996; Novak & Musonda, 1991; Prosser, 1987; West & Pines, 1985). As Pearsall, Skipper, and Mintzes (1997) noted, "It appears that students who report employing 'active,' 'deep' information processing strategies tend to construct more elaborate, well-differentiated frameworks of knowledge" (p. 213). And the way in which knowledge is structured by an individual determines how it is used (Baxter & Elder, 1996; Chi, Feltovich, & Glaser, 1981; Zajchowski & Martin, 1993).

Students who learn meaningfully relate information from different sources in an attempt to integrate what they learn with the intention of imposing meaning. They form connections between new information and material that has been previously studied, and they think about the underlying structure of what is learned (Entwistle & Ramsden, 1983). Material that has been learned meaningfully is retained longer and serves as an anchor for subsequent learning (Novak & Gowin, 1984; Novak & Musonda, 1991; Prosser, 1987). It also more closely resembles the knowledge structure of experts:

> Research in the cognitive aspects of science learning has provided strong evidence that successful science learners as well as professional scientists develop elaborate, strongly hierarchical, well-differentiated, and highly integrated frameworks of related concepts as they construct meanings. Furthermore, it is apparent from studies by cognitive scientists that the ability to reason well in the natural sciences is constrained largely by the structure of domain-specific knowledge in the discipline, which accounts for differences seen in the performance of novices and experts in many science-related fields. (Pearsall et al., 1997, pp. 194–195)

The developing structure of student understanding has been compared to the knowledge structures of novices and experts in domains such as engineering, physics, and medicine. Johnson and Satchwell (1993) noted that "a key to expert performance lies in the organization of the expert's domain knowledge. Experts appear to possess a large knowledge-base that is organized into elaborate, integrated structures, while novices tend to possess less domain knowledge that is not as coherently organized" (p. 74). Zajchowski and Martin (1993) also reported differences in the structure of experts' and novices' domain-specific knowledge: "Experts in physics appear to organize subject-matter knowledge ... hierarchically under fundamental concepts... . The knowledge structure of novices in physics tends to be amorphous and based on surface features rather than underlying conceptual frameworks" (p.459). The parallels between the process of knowledge transformation as an individual develops expertise in a given area and the process of meaningful learning are clear and are consistent with the research previously cited. Helping students organize their learning according to key concepts in a hierarchical, integrated manner (i.e., helping them to learn meaningfully) facilitates understanding and the development of expertise.

The construction metaphor for learning (building upon prior knowledge, structuring understanding,) is not accidental. In several chapters of this book, authors emphasize the student's role in constructing understanding. This is based on the epistemological view of constructivism, which holds that truth, or any claim about the nature of knowledge, does not exist separate from human experience (Prawat, 1996; von Glasersfeld, 1995). Rather, interactions with the world result in the construction of knowledge claims, which may then be tested according to criteria such as validity, coherence, and correspondence. This philosophical view is compatible with psychological theories of human learning (Ausubel et al., 1978; Novak, 1998) described in Chapter 1, and has served as the theoretical underpinning for much of the recent research and calls for reform in science education (Fensham, Gunstone, & White, 1994; Mintzes, Wandersee, & Novak, 1997; Tobin, 1993; White & Gunstone, 1992). It is useful to educators because it emphasizes the necessity of actively engaging students in learning so that they may construct knowledge, test ideas, integrate what they learn, and refine their understanding. Together, constructivism and assimilation theory provide a framework for educational research and teaching practice that promotes shared meaning and has demonstrated increases in the use of meaningful learning strategies (Cliburn, 1990; Heinze-Fry & Novak, 1990) and gains in student achievement (Okebukola, 1990; Willerman & MacHarg, 1991; Wilson, 1994).

The relationship between teacher and student is dynamic; it is a continual process of "back-and-forthness." How might the essence of this dynamic process be captured for purposes of assessing whether educational goals have been achieved? How might student understanding best be portrayed? Understanding, as a process and product, involves more than simply "getting the right answer." As Hetlund, Hammerness, Unger, and Wilson state:

> ...understanding is often difficult to recognize. It reveals itself in fragments, looking more like a case built from evidence than a conclusive fact. It looks like a dynamic system in the process of change, not a static judgment stamped upon a student as an identity. Most important, it looks multifaceted—more a profile of strengths and weaknesses than the simple numerical composites of traditional evaluations. (Hetlund, Hammerness, Unger, & Wilson, 1998, p.230).

This description of understanding presents a challenge for anyone interested in assessing learning outcomes. To effectively assess understanding, educators must consider the purposes of assessment and the best methods for achieving those goals. What should be assessed? Clearly, an answer to this question depends on a teacher's educational goals, available resources, and constraints of the educational setting. In addition, the purposes of the assessment influence the type of assessment vehicles used. If the results of the assessment are used for summative purposes (to make judgments about learning outcomes), teachers may choose formats that allow comparisons between students to be made easily. If the results are to be used for formative purposes (to improve the process of learning and teaching), other assessment vehicles may be selected.

In most cases, the focus of student evaluation is propositional knowledge. It is aimed at determining the level of content and factual knowledge they have mastered, not the degree to which they have developed a well-integrated understanding. Yet, if meaningful learning is a worthwhile educational goal, and educators recognize what has been learned from cognitive research, we need to look beyond traditional assessment vehicles to assess understanding and the assimilation of new knowledge in the form of integrated frameworks. If teachers strive to capture the essence of shared meaning, which lies at the fulcrum between teaching and learning, alternative evaluation methods are necessary. Science educators have called for the need to pay attention to a "wider range of educational outcomes" and to adopt "a broader view of the purposes of testing," and they have been encouraged to develop "new techniques to probe student understanding" (Welch, 1995, pp. 102–103). As Pendley, Bretz, and Novak noted:

> ...regardless of how conceptually complete the material presented to the student is, the instruction alone does not convey understanding. ... answering numerical prob-

lems correctly does not necessarily indicate or reflect a student's conceptual understanding of the material. (Pendley, Bretz, & Novak, 1994, p. 15)

Recent literature focusing on assessment in science education has promoted the use of "authentic" examination formats (Baxter & Elder, 1996;
Welch, 1995), which often include a measure of performance. The goals of
performance assessments (chaps. 10 & 13) are consistent with the theoretical principles articulated above; their main purpose is to more closely align
teaching with the assessment of learning in a manner consistent with contemporary theories of student learning, as part of the iterative cycle of learning and instruction. Their formats involve various activities that make "the
thinking of the learner overt," and provide "opportunities for it to be examined, questioned" (Baxter & Elder, 1996, p. 134). In this way, assessment
itself becomes a more integral part of the processes of teaching and learning. Activities are "seamlesslessly" incorporated into instructional plans,
providing important information to teachers (and students) about what has
been learned.

Maintaining a focus on student learning requires educators to consider
whether the available methods of assessment are appropriate or satisfactory. Any effort to more accurately portray and assess student understanding should examine the merits of additional approaches, many of which are
described in this book. The remaining sections of this chapter focus on concept mapping as a strategy for assessing understanding in science. As vehicles for assessing understanding, concept maps provide teachers with an
avenue for developing insight into student understanding, as evidenced by
well-organized and richly elaborated knowledge structures, valid propositional relationships, and interrelationships. They also help to identify
errors, omissions, or misunderstanding, and they depict the important organizational function certain concepts play in shaping understanding as well
as the resistance of some conceptions to change.

CONCEPT MAPPING TO PORTRAY SHARED
MEANING AND MEANINGFUL LEARNING

For more than two decades, cognitive psychology has been the dominant
paradigm for research on human learning (Chi et al., 1981; Ericsson &
Smith, 1991; Glaser, 1987; Novak, 1977). Emphasizing cognitive structure, or
the way in which students structure what they learn, this large body of
research has yielded important contributions for improving educational
practice. As greater attention has been paid to applying cognitive theory to
classroom instruction (Ausubel et al., 1978; Entwistle & Ramsden, 1983;
Novak, 1998; Schmidt, Norman, & Boshuizen, 1990), these theories have
also served as a framework for research in science education, much of which
has focused on improving the quality of students' conceptions of science

(Novak, 1987; Posner, Strike, Hewson, & Gertzog, 1982; Wandersee, Mintzes, & Novak, 1994; West & Pines, 1985).

Educational researchers have taken numerous approaches to representing learners' cognitive frameworks. Many of these methods have included some form of graphical depiction (Johnson, Goldsmith, & Teague, 1995; McKeachie, Pintrich, Lin, & Sharma, 1990; Novak & Gowin, 1984; Olson & Biolsi, 1991; Trowbridge & Wandersee, 1998). These different approaches share a common purpose: to understand the ways in which students structure what they learn so that teachers will be better able to tailor their teaching approaches to achieve educational goals. Depicting student understanding in graphic or pictorial terms makes it accessible; when the structure of knowledge is made explicit, teachers (and students) can more easily correct common errors or misconceptions. They can also focus explicitly on interrelationships, promoting integration, and tie examples or particulars to important key ideas, facilitating assimilation of the concrete with the abstract. Traditional paper and pencil tests are often inadequate for assessing these properties of the developing structure of students' knowledge.

Concept maps have been used successfully in many disciplines, particularly in science (Heinze-Fry & Novak, 1990; Novak, 1990; Novak, Gowin, & Johansen, 1983; Starr & Krajcik, 1990; Willerman & MacHarg, 1991) to promote meaningful learning and effective teaching. Concept maps have been particularly helpful in representing qualitative aspects of students' learning. They may also be used by students as a study tool, or by teachers to evaluate learning, to enhance teaching, or to facilitate curriculum planning. Applicable to any discipline at any level, they are metacognitive tools that can help both teachers and students to better understand *the content and process* of effective, meaningful learning. Concept maps have also been used as "road maps" for learning, to communicate to students how new learning will build upon their previous knowledge. As heuristic devices, concept maps make the structure of knowledge explicit to students, and they reveal to teachers the idiosyncrasies in students' cognitive structures due to prior knowledge and experiences. They also reveal students' errors, omissions, and alternative frameworks.

Concept mapping is a tool for representing the interrelationships between concepts in an integrated, hierarchical manner. Concept maps depict the structure of knowledge in propositional statements that dictate the relationships among the concepts in a map. Connected by labeled lines, the concepts depicted in concept maps have superordinate–subordinate relationships as well as interrelationships (Figure 1). Based on assimilation theory (Ausubel et al., 1978; Novak & Gowin, 1984), concept maps facilitate meaningful learning by making conceptual relationships explicit and by serving as advance organizers to subsequent learning. The knowledge portrayed in concept maps is context-dependent. Different maps containing the

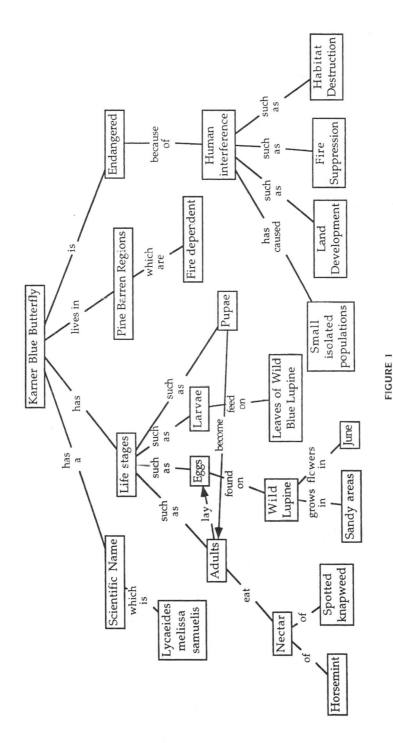

FIGURE 1

Sample concept map illustrating hierarchy and integration of concepts related to the Karner Blue butterfly.

same concepts convey different meanings depending on the relative emphasis of superordinate concepts, linking descriptors, and arrangement of individual concepts. Concept maps are idiosyncratic: they depict key concepts of a domain as portrayed through valid propositions, but necessarily reflect the knowledge and experience of the mapmaker. This feature makes concept mapping particularly helpful for illustrating the ways in which context influences the structure and application of knowledge. It allows knowledge to be portrayed as dynamic and subject to change while preserving a network of interconnected ideas, illustrating the integrated nature of meaning and understanding.

The notion of the student as *meaning-maker* (Pearsall et al., 1997; Mintzes et al., 1997) is fundamental to the effective use of concept maps, as they portray the characteristics and richness of the knowledge students construct. Concept maps provide a useful approach for promoting and assessing meaningful learning by providing a tangible record of conceptual understanding. Not only are concept maps useful for determining whether or to what extent shared meaning has occurred, they also portray the areas where it has not been achieved. Concept maps, as a technique for representing understanding "provide a unique window into the way learners structure their knowledge, offering an opportunity to assess both the propositional validity and the structural complexity of that knowledge base" (Pearsall et al., 1993 p. 198). Concept maps allow educators to gain insight into these aspects of student learning, and constitute a valuable addition to every teacher's repertoire of assessment techniques.

CONCEPT MAPS AS ASSESSMENT TOOLS

Consistent with an emphasis on the quality of student learning, concept maps may be used effectively to depict an array of qualitative aspects of student understanding. For example, concept maps allow teachers to evaluate attributes of propositional knowledge (such as structure, elaboration, validity, complexity) and portray knowledge as an integrated network, rather than a collection of discrete facts. As assessment tools, concept maps may be used summatively, as tests, but they may also be used to document changes in knowledge and understanding over time and as a vehicle for determining degrees of correspondence between students' maps and experts' maps. They may be used in classroom activities that provide students with immediate feedback about the depth of their understanding, or to assess learning from specific instructional units (i.e., lectures or laboratory exercises) (Markow & Lonning, 1998) that might not otherwise be reflected on a paper and pencil test. Hoz, Tomer, and Tamir (1990) stated that "the knowledge structure dimensions yielded by ... concept mapping are unique in comparison to traditional achievement tests, whose limitations render them inadequate for tapping certain characteristics of knowledge structures" (p. 984). Concept maps may be used for formative or summative purposes; the range of classroom settings in which they have been used to assess student learning includes elementary and secondary schools and undergraduate and professional programs.

Concept maps have been used successfully to improve student performance on traditional measures of achievement. Wilson (1993) found that concept maps predicted achievement test scores, if the test was aimed at transfer and application of knowledge. When concept maps were used as advance organizers in classes of eighth-grade physical science, Willerman and MacHarg (1991) found significant differences and improved performance on achievement tests. They attributed this outcome to the visual nature of concept maps in helping students organize their conceptual frameworks and to the fact that "model" maps were constructed by teachers and therefore served as a more complete and accurate framework upon which to build new knowledge. Esiobu and Soyibo (1995) also documented significantly better achievement scores among students in ecology and genetics courses who constructed concept maps to facilitate learning. They explained these improvements by noting the capacity of concept maps to help students see the interrelationships among concepts and to link new concepts effectively to prior knowledge. Pankratius (1990) also reported improved student performance on achievement tests in physics; maps constructed at different times "demonstrated the development of a student's understanding as the unit progressed" (p. 323).

The use of concept maps as evidence of progressive change over time is perhaps one of the most promising applications of concept maps in assessing student learning. Trowbridge and Wandersee (1996) used concept maps to analyze differences in students' comprehension of material in a lecture-based course on evolution. They found concept mapping to be a "highly sensitive tool for measuring changes in knowledge structure" (p. 54), particularly for depicting changes in students' selection of superordinate concepts, which have a great impact on students' conceptions of a discipline. Wallace and Mintzes (1990) used concept maps to document conceptual change in biology. Students' concept maps revealed significant and substantial changes in the complexity and propositional structure of their knowledge base. These results have been borne out in other fields such as chemistry (Nakhleh & Krajcik, 1994; Wilson, 1994) and engineering (Johnson & Satchwell, 1993). Johnson and Satchwell (1993) claimed that the use of "functional flow diagrams during technical instruction enhances the student's ability to develop more accurate knowledge structures" (p. 85), greatly influencing the student's understanding of relevant content.

Pearsall et al. (1997) noted "successive and progressive changes in the structural complexity of knowledge" (p. 193) as depicted by the concept maps constructed at 4-week intervals in university-level biology courses.

They reported a substantial amount of knowledge restructuring on the part of their students in general, but perhaps a more exciting finding was their ability to document the kinds of structural changes that occurred and whether those changes occurred incrementally or at particular times during the semester:

> ...clear and incremental growth in every scoring category over the course of the semester and the analyses of variance confirm that the observed differences are significant ($p < .01$). A review of these "structural complexity profiles" reveals substantial differences between the first and fourth maps; for example, the mean number of concepts and relationships increased by a factor of eight, while the mean number of crosslinks grew five times. In contrast, the number of levels of hierarchy tended to stabilize after an initial period of rapid growth, suggesting that concept differentiation and integration continue over the span of the semester while subsumption seems to peak at about week 9 or soon thereafter. (Pearsall et al., 1997, p. 204)

When teachers are able to gain access to the structure of students' knowledge as depicted by concept maps, they may notice organizational patterns in the form of common errors or misconceptions or in the form of "essential critical nodes" (Nakhleh, 1994), which are concept clusters around which expert knowledge appears to be organized. Markham, Mintzes, and Jones (1994) noted that the "appearance of these [essential critical nodes] in cognitive structure marks the strong restructuring ... [which is] characteristic of expertise in a discipline" (p. 97). Similar to the notion of "critical concepts" used by Wallace and Mintzes (1990), Nakhleh and Krajcik (1994) speculated that "students who increased their use of essential critical nodes from initial to final maps had begun to structure their understanding around a more acceptable framework than those students who did not exhibit this shift to essential critical nodes" (p. 1091). They suggest that essential critical nodes serve an important role in helping students to develop a framework for organizing understanding, which facilitates subsequent learning. Interestingly, propositional relationships in students' maps that were considered valid and appropriate were not clustered according to any particular pattern. However, inappropriate understandings were clustered around a few main ideas, suggesting both the potential for restructuring based on explicit instruction targeted to a small set of key concepts, and the challenge of modifying superordinate, organizing concepts that may be resistant to change.

Concept maps have been used to document the learning that takes place in cooperative groups of students, leading teachers to a deeper understanding of the ways in which learning progresses through the give and take of conversation (Botton, 1995; Roth & Roychoudhury, 1993; Roth, 1995). This application of concept mapping offers important insights into the process of knowledge construction. As Roth observed:

> Rather than being logical consequents, the outcomes of students' collaborative work was always a contingent achievement impossible to predict from our previous knowledge about individual students. ... The talk took place over and through an

> emerging concept map. As the session progressed, the design of the concept map took shape as the result of joint talk. At the same time, the unfolding design shaped the discussion and influenced future talk. In this way, the unfolding design and the talk stood in a reflexive relationship, each taking part in constituting the other. … we must understand the emerging map as a result of the interaction which did not have an existence independent of the context. (Roth, 1995, p. 81)

Concept maps may also prove to be useful for portraying learning that traditional methods of assessment have not captured effectively, such as experiential settings (e.g., field study, clinical education), and for assessing the types of knowledge that learners (or teachers) bring to bear on specific problems.

A variety of schemes for scoring concept maps have been suggested. Most are variations of a scheme outlined by Novak and Gowin (1984), who defined the criteria for evaluating concept maps as levels of hierarchy, the validity of the propositions and cross-links, and use of examples. These may be evaluated as general criteria, or differentially weighted point values may be assigned to the various map characteristics. In the scoring scheme Novak and Gowin devised, 1 point was assigned for each valid relationship, 4 points for hierarchy, 10 points for each cross-link, and 1 point for each example. Novak and Gowin also suggested that teachers construct a "criterion map" of the subject matter against which students' maps could be compared; the degree of similarity between the maps could then be given a percentage score.

Markham et al. (1994) scored concept maps using a modified version of Novak and Gowin's (1984) scheme. They scored six observed aspects of students maps: (1) the number of concepts, as evidence of extent of domain knowledge; (2) concept relationships, which provide additional evidence of the extent of domain knowledge; (3) branchings, which they viewed as evidence of progressive differentiation; (4) hierarchies, providing evidence of knowledge subsumption; (5) cross-links, which represent evidence of knowledge integration; and (6) examples, which indicate the specificity of domain knowledge. As in Novak and Gowin's scheme, these attributes were scored according to differential point values: 1 point was assigned to the number of concepts and concept relationships (1 point for each concept, 1 point for each valid relationship); the scores for branching varied according the amount of elaboration (1 point for each branching, 3 points for each successive branching); 5 points were assigned for each level of hierarchy; each cross-link received 10 points; and each example received 1 point.

Assigning scores to students' concept maps allows them to be used for summative purposes, while providing students with detailed feedback about the quality of their understanding. Scores on particular attributes of concept maps can also be used as a basis for comparing the extent to which different dimensions of understanding have been achieved between groups of students. In research comparing differences in the concept maps of biology majors with those of nonmajors, Markham et al. noted:

Scores on the branchings and hierarchies suggest substantial differences in the degree of concept differentiation and subsumption, which together reflect a more significantly more robust knowledge structure among the more advanced students. The biology majors depicted almost four times as many instances of branching and a 50% differential in hierarchical levels. (Markham et al., 1994, p. 97)

Austin and Shore (1995) attempted to assess the degree to which concept maps measured meaningful learning in a high school level physics class, when applied to the knowledge required to solve multistep problems. They scored concept maps according to linkage, score, "good links," error, and number of components. Links were scored on a three-point scale, taking into account the quality of the links. Each link was assigned a weighted point value, and these were added together to produce the score. The number of links scored 3, or best, produced the value of "good links." Error was determined by noting the number of any unlinked concepts, and "number of components" represented integration or connectivity, which they defined as "the minimum number of components whose removal results in a concept map in which no concepts are related" (p. 43). They observed, "While is it quite clear that a numerical score from a concept map does not pinpoint areas of misunderstanding any more than does a score on a conventional examination, close scrutiny of the concept map may more quickly serve this purpose" (p. 44).

Others have sought to develop methods for making comparisons among maps constructed by students enrolled in the same course, but that account for varying degrees of difficulty represented. Trowbridge and Wandersee (1994) suggested a concept map "performance index," which they describe as "a compound measure one could calculate that includes the student's concept map scores, the difficulty level of each map produced, and the total number of maps submitted" (p. 463). They posited that such an index would allow comparisons to be made over time, or it could serve as a basis for making comparisons among students in different educational settings. However, they were unable to show strong correlation between a student's map index and his or her course grade. Perhaps not surprisingly, there was a stronger correlation between a student's final grade and his or her average map score (Trowbridge & Wandersee, 1994).

The use of concept maps for summative assessment is not without its problems, however, and a number of issues should be addressed before applying them on a large scale. Any assessment tool must be valid (the test should measure what it purports to measure) and reliable (scores should be consistent from instance to instance). Establishing the validity and reliability of concept maps has proven to be challenging, due to the great variation in their implementation. Although Liu and Hinchey (1993) determined that concept maps had high construct validity, content validity, predictive validity, and high reliability, and Pearsall et al. (1997) reported "strong evidence of internal consistency and both construct and concurrent validity" (p. 201), these claims should be more strongly substantiated by additional research before concept maps may be used with confidence for large-scale assessment purposes.

Rice, Ryan, and Samson (1998) developed a method of scoring concept maps based on the correctness of propositions outlined in a table of specifications of instructional and curriculum goals. These criteria (whether specific information was present or missing, present and correct, or present and incorrect) were closely tied to the instructional objectives of the seventh-grade life science classes, which served as the basis for their study. They found high correlations between students' concept map scores and their scores on multiple choice tests aimed at assessing the same instructional objectives. The scoring scheme they devised "represents a distinct departure from those [methods] that focus on criteria such as hierarchy and branching. ... and it provides strong evidence for the content validity of the concept map scores" (p. 1122). They suggest that methods for scoring concept maps are directly related to the intended use of the assigned scores, and that "different methods of scoring maps measure different constructs or different aspects of the construct domain" (p. 1124).

Ruiz-Primo and Shavelson (1996) (see also Chapter 13), summarized their concerns about the use of concept maps as assessment tools based on variation in three important areas: the nature of the concept mapping task, the format of student responses, and the scoring scheme applied. Tasks requiring students to construct concept maps have varied in the conventions applied to the maps themselves (hierarchical vs weblike, flow charts, etc.). The format of students' responses have included filling in blanks, creating maps based on lists of concepts provided by the teacher, or completely open-ended tasks in which students determine which concepts are included in the map. They may be done as individual exercises, within the context of a cooperative group, or in one-on-one conferences with teachers. Scoring schemes vary widely and include those described above. Ruiz-Primo and Shavelson (1996) cite many examples of theses variations and suggest that limitations, based on relevant educational theory, should constrain the application of the technique. They state:

> Criteria such as differences in the cognitive demands required by the task, appropriateness of a structural representation in a content domain, appropriateness of the scoring system for evaluating accuracy of the representation, and practicality of the technique deserve to be explored. ... we favor scoring criteria that focus more on the adequacy of the propositions over those that focus simply on counting the number of map components (i.e., nodes and links). Finally, if concept maps are to be used in large-scale assessment, mapping techniques that require one on one interaction between student and tester should be discarded on practical grounds. (Ruiz-Primo & Shavelson, 1996, p. 595)

These concerns are shared by Rice et al. (1998). However, they caution against perpetuating the dichotomy that exists between traditional and alternative forms of assessment:

> With recent concerns about science achievement and the growing interest in authentic or alternative assessment, there seems to be an increasing tendency to consider traditional and alternative assessment as competing strategies for collecting information about what students know and can do, and that the latter is somehow superior to the former. … [This] perpetuates the perception that concept maps must necessarily measure or reflect more complex levels of thinking in much the same way that portfolios, performance or other hands-on assessment methods are designed to do. Identifying concept maps with alternative assessment methods reflects the assumption that concept maps cannot be used to assess knowledge and understanding of facts, terms, and concepts or that using concept maps for such assessments would be inappropriate. (Rice et al., 1998, p. 1104)

Given the problems associated with establishing validity and reliability, should concept maps be used for summative purposes? Are the benefits of assigning scores to students' concept maps worth the complications and problems inherent in applying any of the various scoring schemes? Clearly, an answer to this question depends on a number of factors, including the role concept maps play in a given instructional context. But for some, the benefits of using concept maps seem to lie more in improving the process of learning and in providing formative feedback than in providing additional quantitative information that may be translated into a grade:

> At the beginning, we tried to use them as assessment devices: scores were assigned to post-instruction maps for the number and correctness of the relationships portrayed, for the levels of hierarchy, and for cross-linking. We also tried to assign scores for the convergence of the students' maps to teacher-constructed maps. But soon we had to recognize that students' concept maps are highly idiosyncratic representations of a domain-specific knowledge, and the interindividual differences displayed among them were far more striking than their similarities. Taking into account the critical opinions on the scoring of concept maps, this observation led us to shift emphasis and focus on changes in content and organization of concept maps over time, and on helping the students to become aware of and criticize their own learning frames and those of the others. (Regis, Albertazzi, & Roletto, 1996, pp. 1087–1088)

White and Gunstone (1992) found that concept maps promoted science learning by stimulating discussion and debate over maps produced by cooperative groups. By engaging students in meaningful discussions of the material, they noted that concept maps portrayed a great deal of information about the quality of student learning as well as the effectiveness of the teaching. In comparison to other assessment methods they noted that concept maps "are quicker (both for students to do and the teacher to consider), more direct and considerably less verbal than essays" (p. 15). However, they found the process of concept map construction to be more valuable for pedagogical purposes than the utility of any score assigned:

> …no single map is ever demonstrably better than all the rest. The contrast with traditional forms of tests of detail is marked. It is rare for students to perceive competitive threat in concept mapping, although the intellectual demands of the task cannot be denied. This friendly aspect of this form of probing student understanding is

why we prefer to use concept mapping in teaching rather than in summative assessment. (White & Gunstone, 1992, p. 35)

Good assessment techniques reveal information about student learning
that may then be translated into teaching practice. As evidence of the reflex-
ive relationship between teaching and learning, Willerman and MacHarg
(1991) noted that the process of concept map construction reveals as much
about the teacher's conceptions of the subject matter as it does about a
student's. Concept maps may be used effectively on a small scale as an
informal mechanism for providing feedback to a teacher about a specific
unit of instruction, but they may also be used as the basis for more formal
faculty development activities such as in-service workshops or continuing
education (Edmondson, Wandersee, Novak, & Coppola, 1995; Shymansky,
Woodworth, Norman, Dunkhase, Matthews, & Liu, 1993). Teachers' concept
maps inform and reflect their conceptualizations of the subject matter, as
well as embedded assumptions "about the links between main ideas within
and across subject matters. Nodes in such maps that are linked to many
other ideas are often worth singling out as the focus of understanding goals"
(Wiske, 1998, p. 69). Concept maps are also effective for identifying and
illustrating the interrelationships that exist between teachers' disciplinary
knowledge and pedagogical content knowledge (Hoz et al., 1990; Jones, Rua,
& Carter, 1998) and any changes that may occur over time.

It is important to bear in mind that the assessment of student learning is
an integral part of a larger process of teaching and learning; it is not an end
in itself. For educators who strive to build a new culture in their classrooms
(Coppola, Ege, & Lawton, 1997) in which students learn meaningfully and
assessments are closely aligned with instruction, concept mapping provides
an approach for gaining insight into students' and teachers' cognitive structures that may be tailored to different purposes. Rice et al (1998) refer to
the dichotomy that exists between traditional and alternative forms of
assessment, yet their work holds great promise for moving beyond it, while
increasing efficiency and facilitating meaningful learning:

> The bulk of the research on concept mapping supports their value in assessing more
> complex learning outcomes, while the research … demonstrates clearly that concept
> maps can be scored for declarative knowledge of the sort commonly assessed with
> multiple choice tests. While more research needs to be conducted to further develop
> practical and efficient scoring rubrics to assess both types, … concept maps may
> become very useful as a single-format assessment technique with multiple scoring
> approaches. (Rice et al., 1998, p. 1125)

The potential for using multiple scoring approaches for one assessment
vehicle remains to be seen. However, it is exciting to consider the savings of
effort that could be realized with an approach that promotes meaningful
learning and the development of students' integrated understanding. Until
such economies of scale are realized, educators who adopt the philosophical and theoretical principles described earlier will need to combine an

array of complementary approaches in assessing their students' learning, and channel those outcomes into subsequent teaching practice.

CASES IN POINT: ASSESSING SHARED MEANING IN SPECIFIC DISCIPLINES OR CONTENT DOMAINS WITH A VIEW TO THE LARGER WORLD

Encouraging students to develop an integrated understanding of a discipline has larger implications for learning that extends beyond the scope of immediate instructional objectives. The quality of students' propositional knowledge relates directly to their ability to apply that knowledge to problems presented in a classroom and beyond. In many fields there are alternative routes to a solution; students must learn to accept that more than one solution may be correct and that "real world" problems often present with a number of constraints. Despite the fact that students perform well within the context of a specific course, they may not elaborate their understanding to include related concepts in other disciplines. Coles (1990) states:

> Students need to be encouraged to recognize that merely understanding what they are learning (deep-processing) is not in itself sufficient. They need to elaborate their knowledge; to build up more and more complex networks; to "structure" their knowledge. ... It is also important that students make connections between courses. ... Students need to see that all their courses are related in some way ... and to see that their task is largely one of seeking out and establishing those links. (pp. 305–306)

The Structure and Reactivity course at the University of Michigan provides an excellent example of an approach to promoting shared meaning through teaching and assessment in the chemistry classroom. Coppola and his colleagues (1997) have taken an innovative approach to course design that combines a variety of classroom activities and assessment vehicles. These activities have been selected to help achieve educational objectives that emphasize general concepts and patterns of mechanistic similarities that underlie the structure of the discipline, rather than only stressing long lists of reactions and syntheses. Begun in 1989, the Structure and Reactivity course sequence enrolls 1250 students each fall, about 65% of whom are in their first term of college. The course uses organic chemistry as a vehicle for students to develop new learning skills in the context of the subject matter, and deliberately aims to illustrate the connections between chemistry and the larger world. Throughout the course, students are encouraged to actively engage in the material, and to view chemistry as "one model of inquiry among many."

Assessment vehicles (which include concept maps) are chosen specifically to address different aspects of clearly articulated instructional goals. They are part of an array of assessment methods that also includes case-study format examinations, performance of an expert task, survey work and demographic analysis, and observation by outside experts. Experts' concept maps are used as a template for evaluating students' maps. Coppola and his colleagues observed that concept maps are a powerful tool for evaluating performance-based assessment of laboratory skills, and they reported that attributes of the concept maps in this course were similar in structure to experts' maps:

> Although true expertise is an amalgam of skills, appropriate and highly integrated knowledge and experience, and knowledge of what skills and information are needed in a given situation, students in the new first-year course appear to hold a more "expert" conception of the assigned task than students from the traditional course. (Coppola et al., 1997, p. 89)

Similar to the Structure and Reactivity course at the University of Michigan, the veterinary curriculum at Cornell University shares the goals of encouraging students to engage actively with the material and to apply knowledge to real problems. It incorporates an array of approaches to assessing student learning that complement the teaching goals. As described above, concept maps may be used for formative and summative purposes to assess learning and promote understanding. Concept maps have been used effectively to facilitate and assess learning with veterinary students at Cornell. As part of a series of faculty development activities, concept maps were first introduced in 1991 to faculty in the College of Veterinary Medicine responsible for teaching Small Animal Gross Anatomy, a course that at the time was required of all first-year veterinary students. Those responsible for teaching the course had noted that students commonly had great difficulty understanding the organization of the peripheral nervous system. They commented that students came to the course with a wide range of backgrounds, and that for many students, prior knowledge and misconceptions interfered with their ability to learn effectively. Concept maps were introduced as a way to assess students' prior knowledge so that learning might progress more easily.

After receiving an introduction to concept mapping and practicing the technique, all 80 first-year students were asked to construct concept maps representing their understanding of the peripheral nervous system. They were given a list of concepts that appeared in bold type in their laboratory dissection guide that related to the peripheral nerves and told to use a subset of that list when creating their maps (Figure 2). The students' concept maps then served as a basis for discussion in small groups with course faculty. The maps drawn by the students were effective at identifying areas of understanding, but, more importantly, patterns of misunderstanding became apparent. The faculty were much better able to target subsequent instruction so that these concepts could be more effectively addressed. Students found the concept mapping exercise very helpful in clarifying their thinking about a complex subject; they requested that concept maps be incorporated in examination questions in place of other forms of diagrams.

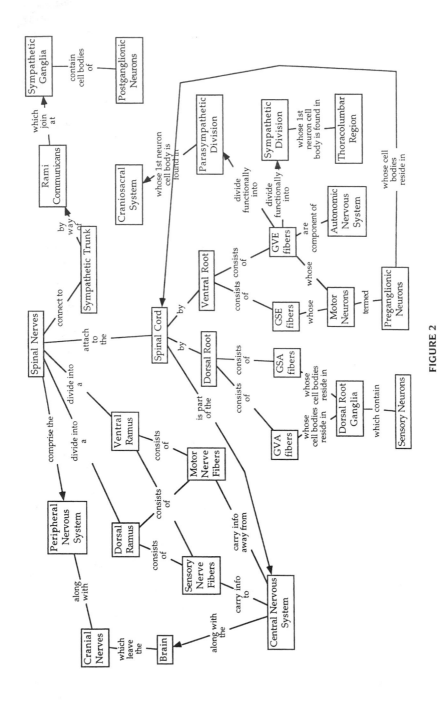

FIGURE 2

Concept map representing key concepts related to spinal nerves.

From this humble beginning, concept mapping gradually became a more integral part of the process of teaching and learning at the College. Concept maps were subsequently used as the basis for developing an innovative, problem-based curriculum (Edmondson, 1995), a range of course materials (Edmondson, 1994), and as an integral means for teaching and assessment within individual courses (Edmondson & Smith, 1998). As a mechanism for providing ongoing formative assessment, students working in tutorial groups are encouraged to construct concept maps at the conclusion of case exercises in courses taught using a problem-based approach. This offers opportunities for self-assessment as group members reflect on their learning, and additional opportunities for the faculty tutor to probe dimensions of understanding that are difficult to assess in cooperative group settings. Figure 3 shows a concept map constructed by a group of six first-year veterinary students as their attempt to synthesize the group's learning following a week-long case that focused on the mechanisms of wound healing.

Concept maps provide a flexible framework for curriculum planning that allow the veterinary faculty a vehicle for promoting and assessing knowledge transformation and for retention of the material. For example, in a course on fluid and electrolyte disorders, concept maps were incorporated into teaching, learning, and assessment activities. Most class sessions featured concept maps prominently as the basis for lecture or discussion; both the midcourse assessment and final examination have required students to construct concept maps. Students reacted positively to the task of concept mapping as being helpful for synthesizing knowledge. As a follow-up to this approach to teaching, students were asked to construct concept maps a year after the course had been completed. These maps required students to apply course concepts to new disease states or specific clinical problems, and showed high levels of retention, good integration, and the ability to apply knowledge that was learned meaningfully to novel problems. Figure 4 illustrates a student's concept map describing the pathophysiologic changes associated with large colon volvulus in a horse, building upon a list of course concepts (provided) and additional concepts of the student's own choosing (provided concepts are in bold type).

According to Baxter, Elder, and Glaser (1996), "assessments aligned with instruction and theories of knowledge development can help teachers and students attend to the relevant cognitive activities underlying knowledge-based performance" (p. 133). These examples portray assessment as an integral part of meaningful learning and effective teaching, and demonstrate an approach for determining whether shared meaning has been achieved. Concept maps allow educators to gain insight into these aspects of student learning, and should be part of every teacher's repertoire of assessment techniques.

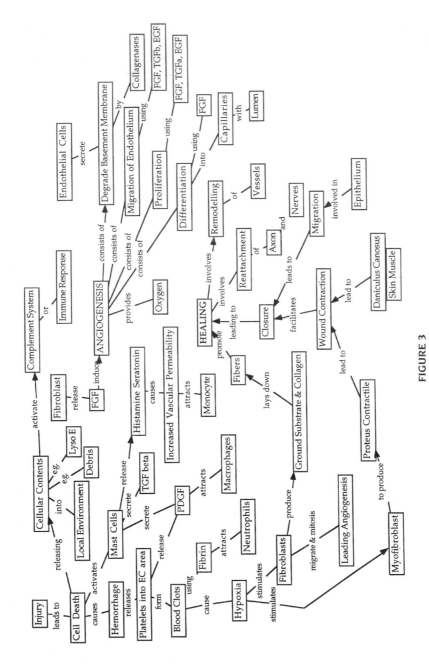

FIGURE 3

Concept map summarizing mechanisms of wound healing.

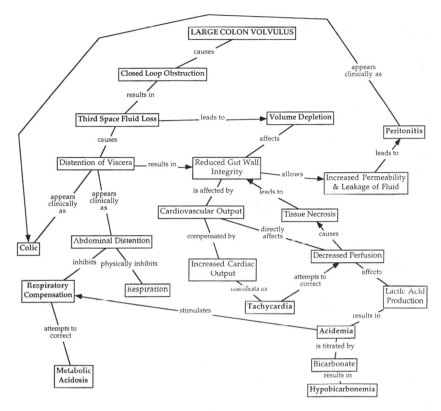

FIGURE 4

Concept map created one year following a course in fluid and electrolyte disorders depicting pathophysiologic changes associated with large colon volvulus.

SUMMARY AND CONCLUSIONS

This chapter has focused on the use of concept mapping to assess shared meaning in science classrooms. As a dimension of meaningful learning and effective teaching, assessment informs future practice as well as confirming whether instructional goals have been achieved. Concept maps may be used in a variety of settings and they portray the scaffolding of ideas that reflect the richness of students' developing conceptions of the subject matter. Concept maps are meant to represent the qualitative nature of understanding, since knowledge is constructed from experience. Personal and idiosyncratic, concept maps capture the "work in progress" that students' thinking represents.

Any assessment tool reflects the values of the individual who implements it, or the purposes and priorities of the larger context in which results are reported. Consistent with constructivist epistemology and cognitive psychology, the theoretical framework that supports the use of concept mapping hinges on the notion of meaning. Because meaning is both constructed and shared, the expectation of the student as an active agent in participating in the development of understanding is implicit. This carries a number of assumptions about the nature of the classrooms in which concept maps are employed: Students may be encouraged to challenge each other, to work together in cooperative groups, or to "mess about" with materials as they learn to think like scientists. While science educators attend to the business of conveying the defining attributes of their disciplines, other, broader, views of teaching and learning are also communicated to students. As students adopt meaningful learning strategies and develop well-organized, coherent frames of understanding, they also learn to accept greater responsibility for their learning and an awareness of their role in generating knowledge:

> *Interviewer*: What do you think the responsibilities of your professors are?
>
> *Student*: To try to get the material across in a comprehensible way. So that I can understand it—what they understand—and get my own meanings from it. They're there to teach me what they know, so I can grasp what they know and add my own information and experiences, too. (Edmondson, 1985, p. 104)

Concept maps may not be the panacea for assessing students' understanding of science, but they do represent an approach that more effectively taps the dimensions of student thinking that many traditional assessment formats miss. Future research focusing on validity and reliability issues may resolve some of the problems associated with using concept maps for large-scale or summative assessment, and it may open new avenues for assessing understanding if multiple scoring methods can be developed to measure different aspects of a content domain. As a relatively simple approach to formative assessment, concept maps are instructive to the mapmaker as well as to the map reader. Because of their capacity for portraying the changes that occur in students' thinking over time, concept maps can reflect the process of knowledge transformation that occurs as students progress from the knowledge of a relative novice to that of an expert. The examples described above illustrate the potential that concept mapping holds for improving the quality of science learning and teaching, and support the use of concept mapping for assessing understanding.

References

Austin, L. B., & Shore, B. M. (1995). Using concept mapping for assessment in physics. *Physics Education* 30 (1), 41–45.

Ausubel, D., Novak, J. D., & Hanesian, H. (1978). *Educational psychology: A cognitive view* (2nd ed.). New York: Holt, Rinehart, & Winston.

Baxter, G. P., Elder, A. D., & Glaser, R. (1996). Knowledge-based cognition and performance assessment in the science classroom. *Educational Psychologist*, 31(2), 133–140.

Bezzi, A. (1996). Use of repertory grids in facilitating knowledge construction and reconstruction in geology. *Journal of Research in Science Teaching*, 33(2), 179–204.

Biggs, J. B. (1989). Institutional learning and the integration of knowledge. In J. I. Balla, M. Gibson, & A. M. Chang (Eds.), *Learning in medical school* (pp. 21–38). Hong Kong: Hong Kong University Press.

Botton, C. (1995). Collaborative concept mapping and formative assessment key stage 3: Understandings of acids and bases. *School Science Review*, 77(279), 124–130.

Chi, M. T. H., Feltovich, P. J., & Glaser, R. (1981). Categorization and representation of physics problems by experts and novices. *Cognitive Science*, 5(2), 121–152.

Cliburn, J. W. (1990). Concept maps to promote meaningful learning. *Journal of College Science Teaching*, 19(4), 212–217.

Coles, C. R. (1990). Helping students with learning difficulties in medical and health-care education. *Medical Education*, 24, 300–312.

Coppola, B. P., Ege, S. N., & Lawton, R. G. (1997). The University of Michigan undergraduate chemistry curriculum: 2. Instructional strategies and assessment. *Journal of Chemical Education*, 74(1), 84–94.

Edmondson, K. M. (1985). *College students' conceptions of their responsibilities for learning*. Master's thesis, Cornell University, Ithaca, NY.

Edmondson, K. M. (1995). Concept mapping for the development of medical curricula. *Journal of Research in Science Teaching*, 32(7), 777–793.

Edmondson, K. M., & Novak, J. D. (1993). The interplay between epistemological views, learning strategies, and attitudes of college students. *Journal of Research in Science Teaching, 32(6)*, 547–559.

Edmondson, K. M., & Smith, D. F. (1998). Concept mapping to facilitate veterinary students' understanding of fluid and electrolyte disorders. *Teaching and Learning in Medicine*, 10(1), 21–33.

Edmondson, K. M., Wandersee, J. H., Novak, J. D., & Coppola, B. C. (1995). Using metacognitive tools to facilitate faculty development. Paper presented at the annual meeting of the National Association for Research in Science Teaching. 22–25 April 1995, San Francisco, CA.

Entwistle, N., & Ramsden, P. (1983). *Understanding student learning*. London: Croom Helm.

Entwistle, N. J. (1988). *Styles of learning and teaching*. London: David Fulton.

Ericsson, K. A., & Smith, J. (Eds.). (1991). *Toward a general theory of expertise*. Cambridge, UK: Cambridge University Press.

Esiobu, G. O., & Soyibo, K. (1995). Effects of concept and Vee mappings under three learning modes on students' cognitive achievement in ecology and genetics. *Journal of Research in Science Teaching*, 32 (9), 971–995.

Fensham, P., Gunstone, R., & White, R. (Eds.). (1994). *The content of science*. London: The Falmer Press.

Glaser, R. (1987). Learning theory and theories of knowledge. In E. DeCorte, H. Lodewijks, R. Parmentier, & P. Span (Eds.), *Learning & instruction* (pp. 397–414). Oxford, UK: Pergamon Press.

Gowin, D. B. (1981). *Educating*. Ithaca, NY: Cornell University Press.

Hegarty-Hazel, E., & Prosser, M. (1991). Relationship between students' conceptual knowledge and study strategies, Part 2: Student learning in biology. *International Journal of Science Education*, 13(4), 421–429.

Heinze-Fry, J. A., & Novak, J. D. (1990). Concept mapping brings long-term movement toward meaningful learning. *Science Education*, 74, 461–472.

Hetlund, L., Hammerness, K., Unger, C., & Wilson, D. G. (1998). How do students demonstrate understanding? In M. S. Wiske (Ed.), *Teaching for understanding* (pp. 197–232). San Francisco: Jossey-Bass.

Hoz, R., Tomer, Y., & Tamir, P. (1990). The relations between disciplinary and pedagogical knowledge and the length of teaching experience of biology and geography teachers. *Journal of Research in Science Teaching*, 27(10), 973–985.

Johnson, P. J., Goldsmith, T. E., & Teague, K. W. (1995). Similarity, structure, and knowledge: A representational approach to assessment. In P. D. Nichols, S. F. Chapman, & R. L. Brennan (Eds.), *Cognitively diagnostic assessment* (pp. 221–249). Hillsdale, NJ: Lawrence Erlbaum Assoc.

Johnson, S. D., & Satchwell, R. E. (1993). The effect of functional flow diagrams on apprentice aircraft mechanics' technical system understanding. *Performance Improvement Quarterly*, 6(4), 73–91.

Jones, M. H., Rua, M. J., & Carter, G. (1998). Science teachers' conceptual growth within Vygotsky's zone of proximal development. *Journal of Research in Science Teaching*, 35(9), 967–985.

Kulhavy, R. W., & Schwartz, N. H. (1986). Working memory: The encoding process. In G. D. Phye & T. Andre (Eds.), *Cognitive classroom learning*. San Diego: Academic Press.

Liu, X., & Hinchey, M. (1993). Validity and reliability of concept mapping as an alternative science assessment. Published in the *Proceedings of the Third International Seminar on Misconceptions and Educational Strategies in Science and Mathematics*. Department of Education, Ithaca, NY: Cornell University.

Markham, K. M., Mintzes, J. J., & Jones, M. G. (1994). The concept map as a research and evaluation tool: Further evidence of validity. *Journal of Research in Science Teaching*, 31(1), 91–101.

Markow, P. G., & Lonning, R. A. (1998). Usefulness of concept maps in college chemistry laboratories: Students' perceptions and effects on achievement. *Journal of Research in Science Teaching*, 35(9), 1015–1029.

McKeachie, W. J., Pintrich, P. R., Lin, Y.-G., & Sharma, R. (1990). *Teaching and learning in the college classroom* (No. 90-B-003.1). National Center for Research to Improve Postsecondary Teaching and Learning, The University of Michigan, Ann Arbor.

Mintzes, J. J., Wandersee, J. H., & Novak, J. D. (Eds.). (1997). *Teaching science for understanding*. San Diego: Academic Press.

Nakhleh, M. B. (1994). Chemical education research in the laboratory environment. *Journal of Chemical Education*, 71(3), 201–205.

Nakhleh, M. B., & Krajcik, J. S. (1994). Influence of levels of information as presented by different technologies on students' understanding of acid, base and pH concepts. *Journal of Research in Science Teaching*, 31(10), 1077–1096.

Novak, J. D. (1977). *A theory of education*. Ithaca, NY: Cornell University Press.

Novak, J. D. (ed.). (1987). *Proceedings of the second international seminar on misconceptions and educational strategies in science and mathematics*. Ithaca, NY: Department of Education, Cornell University.

Novak, J. D. (1990). Concept mapping: A useful tool for science education. *Journal of Research in Science Teaching*, 27(10), 937–949.

Novak, J. D. (1993). How do we learn our lesson? Taking students through the process. *The Science Teacher*, 60(3), 50–55.

Novak, J. D. (1998). *Learning, creating, and using knowledge*. Mahwah, NJ: Lawrence Erlbaum Associates.

Novak, J. D., & Gowin, D. B. (1984). *Learning how to learn*. Cambridge, UK: Cambridge University Press.

Novak, J. D., & Musonda, D. (1991). A twelve-year longitudinal study of science concept learning. *American Educational Research Journal*, 28(1), 117–153.

Novak, J. D., Gowin, D. B., & Johansen, G. T. (1983). The use of concept mapping and knowledge vee mapping with junior high school science students. *Science Education*, 67, 625–645.

Okebukola, P. A. (1990). Attaining meaningful learning of concepts in genetics and ecology: An examination of the potency of the concept-mapping technique. *Journal of Research in Science Teaching*, 27(5), 493–504.

Olson, J. R., & Biolsi, K. J. (1991). Techniques for representing expert knowledge. In K. A. Ericsson & J. Smith (Eds.), *Toward a general theory of expertise* (pp. 240–285). Cambridge, UK: Cambridge University Press.

Pankratius, W. J. (1990). Building an organized knowledge base: Concept mapping and achievement in secondary school physics. *Journal of Research in Science Teaching*, 27(4), 315–333.

Pearsall, N. R., Skipper, J. E. J., & Mintzes, J. J. (1997). Knowledge restructuring in the life sciences: A longitudinal study of conceptual change in biology. *Science Education*, 81(2), 193–215.

Pendley, B. D., Bretz, R. L., & Novak, J. D. (1994). Concept maps as a tool to assess learning in chemistry. *Journal of Chemical Education*, 71(1), 9–15.

Posner, G., Strike, K., Hewson, P., & Gertzog, W. (1982). Accommodation of a scientific conception: Toward a theory of conceptual change. *Science Education*, 66, 211–227.

Prawat, R. S. (1996). Constructivisms, modern and postmodern. *Educational Psychologist*, 31(3/4), 215–225.

Prosser, M. (1987). The effects of cognitive structure and learning strategy on student achievement. In J. T. E. Richardson, M. W. Eysenck, & D. W. piper (Eds.), *Student learning* (pp. 29–38). Milton Keynes, UK: Open University Press.

Regis, A., Albertazzi, P. G., & Roletto, E. (1996). Concept maps in chemistry education. *Journal of Chemical Education*, 73(11), 1084–1088.

Rice, D. C., Ryan, J. M., & Samson, S. M. (1998). Using concept maps to assess student learning in the science classroom: Must different methods compete? *Journal of Research in Science Teaching*, 35(10), 1103–1127.

Roth, W.-M. (1995). *Authentic school science.* Dordrecht: Kluwer Academic.

Roth, W.-M., & Roychoudhury, A. (1993). The concept map as a tool for the collaborative construction of knowledge: A microanalysis of high school physics students. *Journal of Research in Science Teaching*, 30(5), 503–534.

Ruiz-Primo, M. A., & Shavelson, R. J. (1996). Problems and issues in the use of concept maps in science assessment. *Journal of Research in Science Teaching*, 33(6), 569–600.

Schmidt, H. G., Norman, G. R., & Boshuizen, H. P. A. (1990). A cognitive perspective on medical expertise: Theory and implications. *Academic Medicine*, 65(10), 611–621.

Shymansky, J. A., Woodworth, G., Norman, O., Dunkhase, J., Matthews, C., & Liu, C.-T. (1993). A study of changes in middle school teachers' understanding of selected ideas in science as a function of an in-service program focusing on student preconceptions. *Journal of Research in Science Teaching*, 30(7), 737–755.

Starr, M. L., & Krajcik, J. S. (1990). Concept maps as a heuristic for science curriculum development: Toward improvement in process and product. *Journal of Research in Science Teaching*, 27(10), 987–1000.

Tobin, K. (Ed.). (1993). *The practice of constructivism in science education.* Hillsdale, NJ: Lawrence Erlbaum Associates.

Trowbridge, J. E., & Wandersee, J. H. (1996). How do graphics presented during college biology lessons affect students' learning? *Journal of College Science Teaching*, 26 (1), 54–57.

Trowbridge, J. E., & Wandersee, J. H. (1994). Identifying critical junctures in learning in a college course on evolution. *Journal of Research in Science Teaching*, 31(5), 459–473.

Trowbridge, J. E., & Wandersee, J. H. (1998). Theory-driven graphic organizers. In J. J. Mintzes, J. H. Wandersee, & J. D. Novak (Eds.), *Teaching science for understanding* (pp. 95–131). San Diego: Academic Press.

von Glasersfeld, E. (1995). *Radical constructivism: A way of knowing and learning.* London: The Falmer Press.

Wallace, J. D., & Mintzes, J. J. (1990). The concept map as a research tool: Exploring conceptual change in biology. *Journal of Research in Science Teaching*, 27(10), 1033–1052.

Wandersee, J. H., Mintzes, J. J., & Novak, J. D. (1994). Research on alternative conceptions in science. In D. L. Gabel (Ed.), *Handbook of research on science teaching and learning* (pp. 177–210). New York: MacMillan.

Welch, W. W. (1995). Student assessment and curriculum evaluation. In B. Fraser, J. & H. J. Walberg (Eds.), *Improving science education* (pp. 90–116). Chicago: University of Chicago Press.

West, L. (1988). Implications of recent research for improving secondary school science learning. In P. Ramsden (Ed.), *Improving learning: New perspectives* (pp. 51–68). London: Kogan Page.

West, L. H. T., & Pines, A. L. (Eds.). (1985). *Cognitive structure and conceptual change.* Orlando, FL: Academic Press.

White, R., & Gunstone, R. (1992). *Probing understanding.* London: The Falmer Press.

Willerman, M., & MacHarg, R. A. (1991). The concept map as an advance organizer. *Journal of Research in Science Teaching*, 28(8), 705–711.

Wilson, J. (1993). The predictive validity of concept mapping: Relationships to measures of achievement. Published in the *Proceedings of the Third International Seminar on Misconceptions and Educational Strategies in Science and Mathematics*. Department of Education, Ithaca, NY: Cornell University.

Wilson, J. M. (1994). Network representations of knowledge about chemical equilibrium: Variations with achievement. *Journal of Research in Science Teaching, 31*(10), 1133–1147.

Wiske, M. S. (Ed.). (1998). *Teaching for understanding*. San Francisco: Jossey-Bass.

Zajchowski, R., & Martin, J. (1993). Differences in the problem solving of stronger and weaker novices in physics: Knowledge, strategies, or knowledge structure? *Journal of Research in Science Teaching, 30*(5), 459–470.

CHAPTER

3

Assessing Science Understanding: The Epistemological Vee Diagram

JOEL J. MINTZES

University of North Carolina and North Carolina State University

JOSEPH D. NOVAK

Cornell University

> During his scientific enculturation, the apprentice physicist or biologist learns not
> only how to explain phenomena within the scope of his science by applying its exist-
> ing concepts; he learns also what is involved in criticizing those concepts and so
> improving its current content. Indeed, learning one without the other—learning how
> to apply an existing repertory of concepts, without learning what would compel us to
> qualify or change them—does nothing to make a man a "scientist" at all. (Toulmin,
> 1972, p. 165)

The ability to unravel and evaluate complex assertions made by scientists and other knowledge-makers, and to trace their conceptual and
methodological origins is an essential outcome of high-quality science
teaching and learning. In many ways, this ability is the essence of critical
thinking and constitutes one of the major goals of science education (AAAS,
1993; NRC, 1996). In this chapter we describe a powerful tool that can be
used to assess the extent to which students are capable of "unpacking"
knowledge and value claims in the natural sciences. The tool, known as the
epistemological vee (or V diagram), was developed in the 1970s and 1980s
by D. Bob Gowin (1981) and, along with the concept map, has proven to
be one of the singular contributions of Human Constructivists to the

assessment of science understanding (Novak & Gowin, 1984; Trowbridge & Wandersee, 1998). Applying this powerful tool wisely, however, requires that potential users first understand what it means to *understand*.

UNDERSTANDING UNDERSTANDING

> The intellectual transmit of a scientific discipline—the common inheritance that all practitioners of the science collectively learn, share, apply and criticize—thus comprises a particular **constellation of explanatory procedures** and in showing that he (sic) recognizes how and when to apply these procedures a man gives all the proof needed for professional purposes that he has acquired a "conceptual grasp" of the discipline. (Toulmin, 1972, p. 160)

This book offers several useful strategies for helping teachers assess science understanding. Before we continue, it might be helpful to ask ourselves two fundamental questions; first, What does it mean to *understand* within the domain of the natural sciences?, and second, How will I know when my students have developed this ability?

> If we learn only the words and equations of a science, we may remain trapped in its linguistic superstructure; we come to understand the scientific significance of those words and equations, only when we learn their application. (Toulmin, 1972, p. 161)

Webster (1958) defines understanding as "the power to render experience intelligible by bringing perceived particulars under appropriate concepts." In other words, understanding is a product of conceptual restructuring that is driven by a need to make meaning out of objects and events in the real world. We say we *understand* or *have an understanding* (1) when the meanings we construct are resonant with or shared by other people; (2) when internal contradictions in our views have been reconciled; (3) when our explanations lack extraneous or unnecessary propositions, and (4) when our views can be justified by the conceptual and methodological standards of the prevailing scientific paradigm. Unlike many others, we scientists and science teachers are scrupulous in our application of these criteria.

To make matters more concrete, let us consider understanding of a specific set of theoretical assertions; the case of the cell theory. Cell theory is one of only a handful of major generalizations in the biological sciences, which, along with Darwin's theory of natural selection and Mendel's particulate theory of inheritance, provides a coherent conceptual framework that enables scientists to "make sense" of myriads of discrete, seemingly unrelated observations about the structure, function, and origin of living organisms. In its simplest form, the theory is composed of two overarching principles: *All living organisms are composed of cells* (Schlieden & Schwann, 1839; quoted in Brock, 1961) and *all cells come from the division of other cells*, i.e., "*omnis cellula e cellula*" (Virchow, 1863). At this point in the development of biological thought, neither of these claims is controversial and few serious scientists would question their validity. And yet, as a consequence of cell theory biologists have had to disown some strongly held views about the origins of living things. Foremost among these views is the notion of "spontaneous generation."

In *Hamlet*, Shakespeare spoke of "the sun breeding maggots in dead dogs." The idea that living organisms might arise from the decaying flesh of other organisms was widely accepted in the sixteenth century. Frogs, toads, and salamanders were thought to originate in the scum of ponds and lagoons, and bats were a product of the muddy waters of the Nile delta (Baumel & Berger, 1973). In 1668 Francesco Redi demonstrated quite conclusively, however, that maggots are derived directly from the droppings of flies, and not from the decay of meat. More than a century passed before Lazzaro Spallanzani (1799) showed that boiled and hermetically sealed infusions of hempseed, lentils, peas, and rice did not serve as a breeding ground for microorganisms. However, the notion of spontaneous generation wasn't put to rest until Pasteur's (1861) well-known experiments employing specially prepared glass flasks with drawn-out necks.

This episode in the history of biology speaks volumes about the intransigence of well-entrenched ideas and the difficulty of dislodging a view that has achieved widespread acceptance, even in the face of strong counterevidence. It is significant in this instance that a change in our *understanding* of biological origins required centuries of rethinking and ultimately came about only as a result of a felt need by knowledgeable individuals to explain or make sense of a commonly observed phenomenon (i.e., rotting meat). What does this episode tell us about the nature of *understanding*, and how understanding understanding can help us in our work with young science students?

Sharing Meanings (Intersubjectivity)

To begin with, this episode suggests that *understanding rests on shared meanings*, a trait that philosophers sometimes call *intersubjectivity*. Elizabethans could claim to understand biological origins in part because the views they held were widely shared by knowledgeable people of the sixteenth century. In this context, it is important to note a characteristic and commonly misunderstood trait of the natural sciences: The warrant on understanding (and the authority for adjudicating among competing explanations) does not emerge from "democratic processes"; it rests instead on agreement among those who make up the recognized "reference group" within a discipline.

> A new concept, theory, or strategy, for example, becomes an effective "possibility" in a scientific discipline, only when it is taken seriously by influential members of the profession, and it becomes fully "established," only when it wins their positive endorsement. (Toulmin, 1972, p. 266)

Accordingly then, the first (and possibly most important) criterion of *understanding* is shared meaning. We say a student (or a scientist) *understands* when the meanings (s)he constructs are resonant with the prevailing scientific paradigm. Concept maps (Chapter 2) are an exceedingly useful way to explore the meanings students construct as a product of formal instruction in a scientific discipline (Novak & Gowin, 1984; Novak, 1998). The value of such a map is to "externalize" the student's knowledge structure in such a way as to reveal its fundamental concepts and propositions and to display the complexity of the relationships among them.

In our last book (Mintzes, Wandersee, & Novak, 1998) we stressed that human beings are "meaning-makers" and the goal of the educational enterprise is to construct shared meanings. Since that time, many teachers have asked us in essence, "Shared by whom?" For example, around the world there are apparently many groups of people who share the belief that alien beings regularly visit Earth and that UFOs are visible evidence of their existence. Does this shared meaning constitute understanding? Hmm. ... If an authoritative and highly esteemed sixteenth-century scientist were suddenly and mysteriously to materialize at a meeting of the AAAS, would those in attendance put much stock in his explanation of the origin of life?

There are two points here: First, science is an authoritative, intellectual enterprise, and while its doors are open to any and all, it doesn't follow that all viewpoints are given equal weight. Some views count more than others. The other point is that scientific explanations change over time and that the authority vested in individual scientists also evolves as new evidence accumulates. As competent science teachers, our ultimate job is to challenge students' understanding by encouraging them to interact with objects, events, and other people. Through these interactions and the meanings students share, we hope to accomplish three things: (1) to encourage them to construct progressively more powerful explanations; (2) to wrestle with and resolve inconsistencies and unnecessary complexities in their thinking; and (3) to evaluate and challenge the knowledge claims of others, including those whose authoritative views are currently accepted by the scientific establishment.

Resolving Inconsistencies (Coherence)

So far we have argued that understanding rests in part on shared meanings. But as we have seen, not all meanings are given equal weight in science, and meanings change over time as a result of our interactions with objects, events, and other people. Science does not claim to offer final answers; science provides only heuristically powerful explanations that are logical, internally consistent, and parsimonious. And that brings us to the second of our criteria for understanding—*internal consistency* or, as philosophers sometimes say, "coherence."

The claim of sixteenth-century scientists that maggots originate in the decaying flesh of dead animals provided an explanation that was consistent with much that was known about living organisms. (Interestingly, fly eggs are visible with the naked eye and can be easily discerned by the knowledgeable observer, but the spontaneous generation view was well entrenched and the concept of insect metamorphosis was not well recognized until the work of Jan Swammerdam, a contemporary of Redi and the early microscopists, Malpighi, van Leeuwenhoek, and Hooke.) It took the development of the microscope and some 200 years before another group of contemporary scientists (Pasteur, Lister, and Koch) firmly established the significance of microorganisms. Clearly, by the time of Pasteur's work, the notion that living things might arise spontaneously from nonliving matter was inconsistent with scientific knowledge of the day. Scientists interpret inconsistencies of this sort as evidence of lack of understanding.

This illustrates another important aspect of the scientific enterprise and the nature of *understanding* in scientific domains: the way inconsistencies or anomalies are resolved. Often scientists and philosophers talk about the resolution of inconsistencies as *conceptual change*. What is clear from the episode just described is that scientists are capable of living with inconsistencies for long periods of time and that uncertainty and ambiguity may reign for decades or even centuries until an adequate explanatory framework becomes available. As Kuhn (1962) suggests, during these periods of "normal science" anomalous findings (inconsistencies) accumulate and occasionally scientists patch up the prevailing paradigm to accommodate these departures. But at some point the departures from the orthodox view become so significant as to require a major restructuring of the established explanation; it is these periods in the history of scientific disciplines that Kuhn calls "revolutions." They have been likened to the punctuated shifts in biological speciation and the abrupt tectonic movements that accompany a major earthquake.

From the Human Constructivist perspective, analogous changes in the way students understand natural phenomena are a normal part of learning and typically result from attempts to reconcile inconsistencies in our explanatory frameworks. Our basic assertion (Mintzes et al., 1998)—that *meaning-making is the fundamental adaptation of the human species and the driving force underlying all forms of conceptual change*—applies equally to Nobel laureates and kindergarten children; it is a characteristic feature of the complex structure of the human nervous system and a product of millions of years of evolution.

Inconsistencies are a normal part of everyday sense-making by human minds and the incremental, cumulative, and often compartmentalized way we create knowledge. Typically these inconsistencies build up over a period of time and, like a mental earthquake, are often resolved by wholesale, abrupt, and extensive restructuring of our knowledge. Viewed through the lens of the cognitive sciences, the everyday cumulative events are products of a form of "weak restructuring" and the radical, abrupt changes result from a kind of "strong restructuring." The psychological mechanism (Ausubel, Novak, & Hanesian, 1978) responsible for much weak restructuring of our knowledge frameworks is known as *subsumption*, while that responsible for much strong restructuring we call *superordination*.

Seeking Simplicity (Parsimony)

As scientists (and science students) resolve inconsistencies in their thinking, the resulting explanatory frameworks they construct tend to be simpler than their original ideas. This is not to say that scientifically useful explanations lack complexity, but, rather, that they are *parsimonious*.

The fourteenth-century philosopher William of Ockham is perhaps most widely known for his principle of parsimony. Born around 1285, William studied at Oxford and completed his theological studies in 1318 when he was licensed to hear confessions. Ockham never became a regent master (*magister actu regens*) or "professor" but several of his writings (including the *Tractatus de praedestinatione*, *Tractatus de successivis*, and the *Summulae in libros Physicorum*) are considered masterpieces of medieval philosophy. Embedded within his work are several criticisms of contemporary "modernist" epistemologies that were grounded in part on his principle of parsimony, a principle that has come to be known as Ockham's razor (quoted in Adams, 1987):

> It is futile to do with more what can be done with fewer.
>
> When a proposition comes out true for things, if two things suffice for its truth, it is superfluous to assume a third.
>
> Plurality should not be assumed without necessity.
>
> No plurality should be assumed unless it can be proved (a) by reason, or (b) by experience, or (c) by some infallible authority.
>
> ...there are many things that God does with more that He could do with fewer. Nor should any other explanation be sought. And it follows from the fact that He wills it that it is fitting and not futile for it to be done. The matter is otherwise where natural and created voluntary causes are concerned. For these voluntary causes should conform themselves especially to right reason ... and they do nothing justly or rightly otherwise.

To most scientists, the principle of parsimony is among the most important criteria of understanding; so much so that some our our most illustrious Nobel laureates have spent a lifetime seeking simplicity in the explanations they offer. This is especially true in the physical sciences where, for example, Einstein and many of his successors have sought "general" or "grand unifying" theories to explain natural objects and events by invoking the fewest number of descriptive propositions. Currently there are those in the fields of astrophysics and particle physics who hope to explain the most complex physical phenomena through an elaboration of "string theory." String theory is yet another example of the way scientists aim for simplicity in their attempts to understand and explain the natural world.

Thinking Critically (Transparency)

The fourth criterion we apply to *understanding*, and the one that will consume the remainder of this chapter, is the ability to "unpack," analyze, and critically evaluate knowledge (and value) claims (Gowin, 1981). In literary criticism people speak about the "deconstruction" of text, and philosophers sometimes speculate on the "transparency" of knowing. The commonality among these notions is that those who have a deep understanding of a knowledge domain can trace its major claims to their conceptual and methodological roots and see through the fuzzy or cloudy thinking that typifies the novice's view. As Toulmin (1972) suggests in the excerpt we quote at the beginning of this chapter, novice scientists learn not only to apply current concepts, but also to subject them to critical analysis and, when appropriate, to modify or change them "Indeed, learning one without the other ... does nothing to make a man a 'scientist' at all."

In this sense, *understanding* requires us to master a set of epistemological ideas and metacognitive techniques. For many if not most scientists, these ideas and techniques are never taught or learned in any explicit, overt, or intentional way; rather they are acquired informally as part of an "unconscious" socialization into the profession. Nonetheless, the ability to critically analyze and evaluate the often subtle conceptual and methodological strengths and weaknesses embedded within a set of scientific knowledge claims is one of the most prized outcomes of a scientific education. The V diagram provides a formal mechanism for teaching and learning these critical skills.

INTRODUCING GOWIN'S V DIAGRAM

The epistemological vee (or V diagram) is the product of Bob Gowin's 20-year search to find a useful strategy for helping students understand the way knowledge is constructed, and to help them unpack, analyze, and critically evaluate complex knowledge and value claims in the natural sciences. In this section we describe the elements of the V diagram and suggest ways it may be profitably integrated into traditional laboratory instruction. In doing so we have chosen to "lay the V" on Pasteur's (1861) seminal paper on spontaneous generation in order to introduce a study on V diagramming in our introductory cell biology course.

The introductory biology program for science majors at the University of North Carolina at Wilmington comprises three one-semester courses focusing on the structure and function of cells, and the adaptive characteristics and environmental relationships among plants and animals. Each of these courses typically enrolls 200–300+ students and instruction is traditional in almost every respect. Students attend three 50-minute lectures and one 3-hour laboratory each week. The lectures are given by a senior professor with 25 years of college teaching experience, and the laboratories are led by graduate teaching assistants who are enrolled in the M.S. or cooperative Ph.D. programs in biology or marine biology. In most respects, this arrangement parallels that found at hundreds of research institutions and comprehensive state universities and colleges around the country. The mean combined SAT score of our first-year students is approximately 1070, which places them very near the national average.

Pasteur's (1861) paper on spontaneous generation is certainly one of the milestones in the history of biology. It is read today for its clarity of thought and simplicity of expression, even among biologists who lack any serious interest in the history of the discipline. The original paper, "Memoire sur les corpuscles organises qui existent dans l'atmosphere; Examen de la doctrine des generationes spontanees," consumes some 93 pages of the *Annals of Natural Science* and is available in redacted English. In our course we provide students with an abridged, 5-page translation (Brock, 1961) that includes all the critical passages of the original paper and an *incomplete* V diagram that identifies the epistemological elements and their definitions (Figure 1). Students enrolled in the course have had several weeks of experience with concept mapping (Chapter 2) prior to this laboratory exercise and are familiar with the terms *objects*, *events*, *concepts*, *principles*, and *theories*. Nonetheless, these epistemological terms are reviewed and the remaining elements are discussed.

At this point we introduce the view that creating new knowledge in the natural sciences involves a critical interplay between *conceptual* and *methodological* issues; we sometimes refer to the "thinking" and "doing" sides of the V. We also stress the role of theory as a guiding force in knowledge building and suggest that good research grows out of and ultimately contributes to a strong theoretical framework. In the following paragraphs we attempt to capture the flavor of this laboratory exercise.

Since our objective is to have our students analyze Pasteur's paper, we introduce the elements of the V using an overhead transparency that focuses on an unrelated knowledge domain—in this case, an explanation of seasonal variations in light intensity, day length, temperature, and precipitation. The lab begins with a viewing of the 18-minute videotape A *Private Universe* (Schneps, 1987), which reveals some of the conceptual difficulties that even our brightest students experience in this area. The video is followed by a class discussion in which the instructor elicits each of the elements of the V and records these elements on the transparency. Students are encouraged to consult, argue, and debate with each other and to complete their own V diagrams as we proceed.

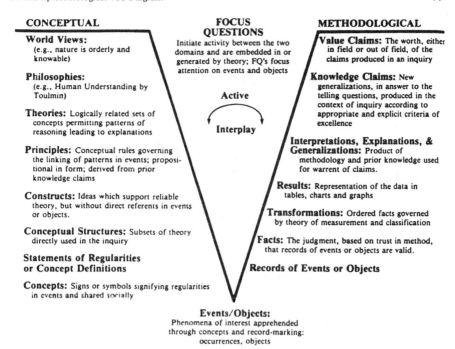

FIGURE 1
Gowin's epistemological V.

Focus Question

The *focus question* is the beginning point of any scientific investigation and typically addresses issues of what, when, how, or why. Choosing this question is almost certainly the most important decision a scientist makes, and reveals much about his or her *values* and *philosophy* or *worldviews*. Ultimately the decision to focus on one question rather than another depends on the scientist's interests and prior knowledge as well as a host of other social, political, and economic factors (e.g., availability of funding sources, opportunities for collaboration, cost of equipment and supplies, likelihood of success). In this laboratory exercise, we encourage students to suggest focus questions that are worthy of intense investigation over an extended period of time and to differentiate them from otherwise good questions that are less amenable to scientific investigation. Our focus is on precision and specificity. In a recent lab the following focus question was suggested: *How do seasonal, climatic differences in local light intensity, temperature, day length, and precipitation vary as a function of geographic distance from the equator?*

Objects and Events

Using this focus question as a point of departure, we then ask students to think about the *objects and events* that must be investigated to develop a tentative answer or hypothesis. An *object* is a material substance that can be perceived and/or manipulated through one or more of our sense organs; that is, it is something we can see, smell, hear, touch, or taste. Often scientists use instrumentation to extend their senses. For example, microscopes, telescopes, oscilloscopes, audiometric devices, and pressure gauges are all designed to make records of objects that are inaccessible to our "naked" sense organs. It is important for students to understand that science is limited in its reach to those things that humans can sense either directly or indirectly; however, this does not preclude the possibility of the extrasensory or supernatural; it merely means that scientists are not equipped to investigate those things. It also suggests that science is a powerful, but not exclusive, way of knowing and that other realms of human endeavor (such as religion) can help us construct meaning in our lives.

Events are things that happen (or can be made to happen) to *objects*. In other words, an event is an occurrence or potential occurrence that can be recorded. Events and objects are related in that the former always requires the latter. One of the fundamental epistemological assumptions of natural science is the principle of *cause and effect*, which implies that things don't happen by themselves; nature consists of matter and energy and all *events* are products of the interaction between them.

Based on the *focus question* we developed, students in our lab section were asked to reflect on the objects and events we would need in order to address the issue of seasonal differences in light intensity, temperature, day length, and precipitation as a function of geographic latitude. Grouped at tables of four students each, the research teams were given 10 minutes to discuss, argue, debate, and resolve this matter among themselves.

Ultimately the class agreed on the following objects and events: (With observation and recording stations set at intervals of 5 degrees north and south of the equator and 5 degrees east and west of the prime meridian), observe times of sunrise and sunset each day, measure light intensity (photometer) and temperature (thermometer) every hour, and determine precipitation accumulated (rain gauge) at 24-hour intervals over the span of one year.

Conceptual (Thinking) Side

Once we have agreed on a focus question and the objects and events needed to answer it, we then ask students to reflect on the *ideas* they must understand before they can begin the study. The purpose here is to encourage students to think deeply about their prior knowledge and how prior knowledge drives the questions we ask, the objects and events we choose to study, the records and transformations we make, and ultimately the knowledge and value claims we assert. The fundamental issue posed by the left side of the V is *What do I need to know* before I can answer the focus question?

Concepts are perceived regularities in objects or events that are designated by a sign or symbol. The signs and symbols that make up a language enable us to communicate these regularities rapidly and succinctly. For example, in the English language the five-letter word *chair* designates an object used for sitting that has a seat, a back, and (usually) four legs. Most children learn to recognize concrete concepts of this sort at an early age and continue to elaborate or expand on and delimit or constrain their understandings over many years. *Concepts* are important because they constitute the basic units of meaning and thereby the fundamental building blocks of knowledge.

When linked together in precise ways, two or more concepts form a **proposition** (e.g., My *chair* is made of *oak*). In the natural sciences, the important propositions are those that are generalizable, that is, they apply to more than a single instance (e.g., *Chairs* are important *pieces of furniture*). Such widely applicable propositions we call **principles.**

A **theory** is a set of interrelated principles that enables us to explain or predict the interactions among objects and events. Put somewhat differently, theories are powerful conceptual frameworks that enable us to make useful claims about the natural world (e.g., Chairs and other pieces of furniture provide comfortable living and working environments for people).

In our lab sections we discuss the nature of *concepts, principles,* and *theories* and elicit examples of each in a class discussion. We then break down again into our 4-member teams, and students are asked to consider what concepts, principles, and theories they *need to know* to address the focus question on seasonal climatic variations. In a recent lab the following concepts were identified: seasons (summer vs winter), climate, solar system, planet, Earth, sun, 23.5-degree tilt, rotation, revolution, equator, prime meridian, northern hemisphere, southern hemisphere, solar radiation (direct vs indirect), global atmospheric circulation, global oceanic circulation, latitude, longitude, light intensity, temperature, precipitation.

Among the most important principles are these: The Earth revolves around the sun; the sun radiates solar energy; the Earth is tilted on its axis; because of the tilt, one hemisphere receives direct and the other receives indirect solar radiation; during the winter the northern hemisphere receives indirect radiation; during the summer it receives direct radiation; the angle of sunlight reaching Earth's surface determines the total amount of heat absorbed/unit of surface area; major climatic differences are a function of total heat absorbed; total heat absorbed is further mediated by atmospheric and oceanic currents.

Several underlying theories were thought to be essential to understanding seasonal climatic variations. The two theories that encompass most of the principles previously identified are *modern heliocentric model of the solar system* and *molecular-kinetic theory of heat.*

In addition to the concepts, principles, and theories that drive scientific investigations, scientists are guided in their choice of a focus question, selection of objects and events, decisions about records and transformations, and ultimately about how to interpret their findings, by a set of strongly but often unconsciously held views about the nature of knowledge and the structure of the universe. These epistemological and ontological commitments are rarely stated in the text of scientific papers but commonly underly the entire intellectual enterprise. In our introductory lab on the use of the V diagram, students identified two issues of **philosophy** that undergird a study on variation in seasonal climate: *the "law" of cause* and *effect* (all natural events have a proximate cause) and *the principle of parsimony or Ockham's razor* (simpler explanations are preferred over more complex ones).

Methodological (Doing) Side

The fundamental issue posed by the right side of the V is W*hat do I need to* <u>*do*</u> to answer the focus question? Our experience has been that most students have an easier time reflecting on the methodological elements of a scientific investigation than on the conceptual ones. Nevertheless, most of our students have never been asked to think deeply about the differences between objects and events or (hu)man-made *records* of those objects and events and *transformations* of those records that enable people to make *knowledge* and *value claims*.

A **record** is simply a tangible artifact that encodes information about an object or an event. Because objects and events are not always accessible and sometimes have a fleeting existence, a scientist needs to construct a way of storing and retrieving information that preserves those attributes (s)he deems important. Records enable scientists to review the attributes of objects and events at times and places that are removed from the actual phenomenon and thus they provide a measure of convenience and permanence; they also permit other scientists to experience phenomena vicariously and thereby to evaluate knowledge and value claims based on tangible evidence. The most common forms of scientific records are written documents, photographs, and audio, visual, and electronic recordings.

It is important for students to understand that the records a scientist chooses to make are a reflection of his or her observations, and that all observations are filtered through a set of "conceptual goggles." Simply put, what we see depends on what we know; the attributes of any object or event we attend to and elect to record are products of the vast store of prior knowledge and values we accumulate over a lifetime. In this way the "doing" side of the V is strongly influenced by the "thinking" side; and, ultimately, the products of doing science (i.e., knowledge and value claims) become a part of our thinking.

Records of objects and events are simply artifacts that scientists choose to construct. The *meaning* of those artifacts, however, depends critically on the scientist's store of prior knowledge and values and is reflected in the **transformations** (s)he chooses to perform. In transforming records, scientists seek to establish connections or relationships between those records, and this typically requires some manipulation or rearrangement of the recorded objects and events. Ultimately, the purpose of a transformation is to seek answers to the focus question.

Transformations may take many forms and sometimes involve several steps. Among the most common transformations are calculations of differences or similarities, graphs, tables, figures, statistics, and flow charts. Usually such a transformation enables the scientist to represent his or her records in a form that leads directly to a set of inferences, conclusions, or knowledge and value claims. The distinction between records and transformations is often a subtle one, and students usually need help in understanding it. The important point is that a transformation is not dictated by the object or event itself or even by the records scientists make; it is a manipulation conducted by the scientist who is guided in his or her actions by a store of prior knowledge and values.

In our laboratory exercise on climatic variation, students suggested the following records: latitude and longitude of recording station, date, time of day, time of sunrise, time of sunset, light intensity (photometer), temperature (thermometer), and precipitation level (rain gauge). The transformations included statistical analyses (ANOVA), tables, and graphs depicting differences in light intensity, day-length, temperature and precipitation as a function of latitude and longitude.

Knowledge claims are statements that provide (tentative) answers to the focus questions and pose issues that invite new investigation. To be taken seriously, the knowledge claims (i.e., inferences; conclusions) that scientists make must be consistent with the concepts, principles, theories, and philosophies driving the investigation, and they must be logically and rationally related to the records and transformations the investigator has made. Additionally, knowledge claims state the limitations or constraints of the investigation and may offer guidance to subsequent investigators.

Value claims are statements of worth or quality and may have a prescriptive or ethical dimension. To be taken seriously, the value claims a scientist makes must be consistent with his or her knowledge claims. However, as with all other elements of the V, we recognize that these statements are filtered through the scientist's prior knowledge and values and the concepts, principles, theories, and philosophies that underly the study.

Among the knowledge and value claims our students suggested are light intensity, day length, temperature and precipitation are inversely related to distance from the equator, and people who live in equatorial countries suffer needless deprivation and require assistance of "first-world" nations.

V DIAGRAMS IN COLLEGE BIOLOGY

In this section we present an "expert" template and three V diagrams constructed by students enrolled in our introductory biology course, along with the scoring rubric we currently use for assessment. Our purpose is to offer some tangible referents to those who might consider using this powerful tool as an adjunct or even a substitute for more traditional assessment techniques. The V diagrams we offer represent a substantial range of ability and interest levels. It is important to keep in mind that each diagram is a unique and idiosyncratic representation of the learner's understanding of the knowledge-making process. We caution readers to take care in generalizing these findings to other populations and suggest that quantitative scoring rubrics, such as the one we offer, may need modification as local conditions dictate.

Template and Rubric

Normally, in assessing the quality of student-constructed V diagrams, we develop a template or "expert" diagram that depicts our own view of the knowledge-making process as revealed in the journal articles we read or the experiments we conduct in the laboratory. It is important to stress that this template is *not* a key in the traditional sense; that is, it does not provide "right" and "wrong" answers. Instead, the template serves as a useful vehicle for orienting us to the significant epistemological elements in a piece of research and, at the same time, it reminds us that there may be a diverse set of conceptually acceptable ways of depicting these elements.

The scoring rubric we currently use (Figure 2) is an adaptation of that suggested by Novak and Gowin (1984). We assign value to the quality, accuracy, and completeness of the focus question(s), objects, and events, conceptual elements, records, and transformations, and the knowledge and value claims our students make. The reliability and validity of similar scoring rubrics for evaluating V diagrams have been addressed in several studies (Ault, Novak, & Gowin, 1984; Brody, 1985; Gurley-Dilger, 1982; Novak, Gowin, & Johansen, 1983; Peled, Barenholz, & Tamir, 1993). In general, these studies reveal that teacher-scored V diagrams possess relatively strong psychometric qualities, comparable in most respects to commonly used measures of classroom learning.

In the template V diagram we developed for Pasteur's paper on spontaneous generation (Figure 3), the *focus question* asks whether "germs" are present in the air, and if so, whether they are present in sufficient numbers to account for the appearance of "organized bodies" in previously heated infusions. The *objects and events* are observations of odor, flavor, and organized bodies in previously heated, "extremely alterable" liquids incubated in glass flasks with drawn-out necks. The *records* are verbal descriptions and drawings

Focus Question (FoQ)
0: No focus question identified
1: Question identified, but does not focus on objects OR events OR conceptual side of vee
2: Question identified; includes concepts, but does not focus on BOTH objects AND events; OR focuses on inappropriate objects or events
3: Question identified; includes concepts; focuses on appropriate objects AND events

Objects and Events (O/E)
0: No objects or events identified
1: Objects OR events identified AND consistent with focus question; OR objects AND events identified, but inconsistent with focus question
2: Objects AND events identified AND consistent with focus question, but records not identified
3: Objects AND events identified AND consistent with focus question AND indication of records taken or needed

Conceptual Side (Con)
0: No conceptual side identified
1: Concepts OR principles identified, but not consistent with objects/events
2: Concepts AND principles identified, but not consistent with objects/events; OR concepts or principles identified AND consistent with objects/events
3: Concepts AND principles identified AND consistent with objects/events, but relevant theory OR philosophy omitted
4: Concepts AND principles identified; consistent with objects/events, AND relevant theory AND philosophy identified

Records/Transformations (R/T)
0: No records or transformations identified
1: Either records OR transformations identified, but records inconsistent with objects/events OR transformations inconsistent with focus question
2: Records identified AND consistent with objects/events, but transformation not identified or inconsistent with focus question
3: Records identified; consistent with objects/events, AND transformation identified; consistent with focus question

Knowledge and Value Claims (KVC)
0: No knowledge or value claims identified
1: Knowledge claim identified, but inconsistent with conceptual side of vee OR inconsistent with the records and transformations; OR value claim identified but inconsistent with knowledge claim
2: Knowledge claim identified AND consistent with conceptual side of vee or records/transformations, but value claim not identified OR inconsistent with knowledge claim
3: Knowledge claim identified AND consistent with conceptual side of vee and records and transformations; value claim identified AND consistent with knowledge claim

FIGURE 2

Scoring rubric for V diagrams.

depicting the liquids and the *transformations* reveal changes in the liquids over a period of 18 months. Our *knowledge claims* suggest Pasteur's principal conclusion that changes arising in the infusions are a result of solid particles carried in the air; the *value claims* suggest that boiling is a good way to prevent food spoilage.

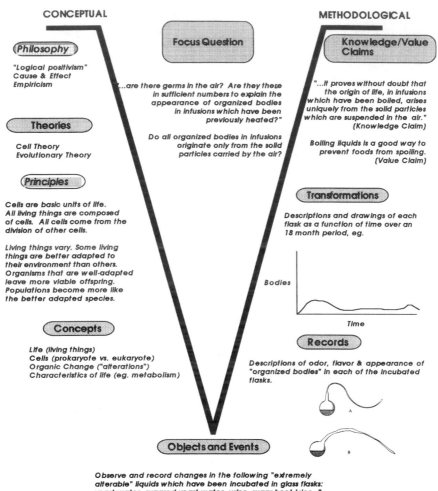

CONCEPTUAL

METHODOLOGICAL

Focus Question

Philosophy

"Logical positivism"
Cause & Effect
Empiricism

"...are there germs in the air? Are they there
in sufficient numbers to explain the
appearance of organized bodies
in infusions which have been
previously heated?"

Do all organized bodies in infusions
originate only from the solid
particles carried by the air?

Theories

Cell Theory
Evolutionary Theory

Principles

Cells are basic units of life.
All living things are composed
of cells. All cells come from the
division of other cells.

Living things vary. Some living
things are better adapted to
their environment than others.
Organisms that are well-adapted
leave more viable offspring.
Populations become more like
the better adapted species.

Concepts

Life (living things)
Cells (prokaryote vs. eukaryote)
Organic Change ("alterations")
Characteristics of life (eg. metabolism)

**Knowledge/Value
Claims**

"...it proves without doubt that
the origin of life, in infusions
which have been boiled, arises
uniquely from the solid particles
which are suspended in the air."
(Knowledge Claim)

Boiling liquids is a good way to
prevent foods from spoiling.
(Value Claim)

Transformations

Descriptions and drawings of each
flask as a function of time over an
18 month period, eg.

Bodies

Time

Records

Descriptions of odor, flavor & appearance of
"organized bodies" in each of the incubated
flasks.

A

B

Objects and Events

Observe and record changes in the following "extremely
alterable" liquids which have been incubated in glass flasks:
yeast water, sugared yeast water, urine, sugar beet juice, &
peppered water. The neck of each flask was drawn over a
flame to produce curves; the liquid was boiled for several
minutes "until steam issued freely through the extremity of the
neck"; flasks were cooled. Liquids were examined for
changes in odor, flavor and occurence of "organized bodies."

FIGURE 3
Template V diagram on Pasteur's paper.

The methodological side of our template rests on a series of underlying conceptual elements. The most important *concepts* we identify are life or living things, cells as the basic units of life, organic change in living things, and metabolic processes and other "characteristics of life." The *principles* and *theories* that subsume these concepts are the mid-nineteenth-century version of cell theory and Darwin's (1859) views on natural selection. The epistemological perspective (i.e., *philosophy*) revealed in Pasteur's paper is that of an empirical realist—in modern parlance, a "logical postivist."

Blaine

Blaine is a first-year student and an active member of Chi Phi fraternity. He lives off campus in an apartment that he shares with several fraternity brothers. He attended a public high school in a rural community in western North Carolina and intends to major in environmental studies. Currently Blaine has achieved a 2.5–2.8 grade-point average and prefers to spend his spare time playing lacrosse, riding horses, camping, hiking, and participating in student government activities. His career goal is to work for the U.S. Fish and Wildlife Commission or to serve as an environmental consultant to industry. His midterm course grade average is 56%. Blaine has remained relatively anonymous in class (he sits in the back row of a lecture hall that seats 100 students) and his attendance record has been less than perfect.

The *focus question* Blaine identifies (Figure 4) is somewhat vague ("Can spontaneous generation take place in liquids that are highly variable?"). However, he does address appropriate objects and events and includes several important concepts (3 points). The *objects and events* are identified; they are consistent with the focus question, and he does offer a vague suggestion ("Check daily") about the records that need to be taken (3 points). Unfortunately the *records and transformations* fail to explicitly identify the important objects and events or to suggest an answer to the focus question (1 point). Although a scientifically acceptable *knowledge claim* is offered ("it is due to the air particles that the liquids change."), the records and transformations are too vague for us to conclude that the claim can be justified (1 point). On the *conceptual side*, Blaine identifies a significant number of important concepts. He omits "cells," "germs" or "organisms," however, and the principles and theories he depicts fail to address the objects and events (2 points). Blaine's combined total score on the V diagram is 10 (out of 16).

Melodie

Melodie is an attractive and friendly African-American student who sits in the second row. Except for an instance of illness, she has missed no class sessions this semester and consistently maintains an alert, involved demeanor. She attended a public high school in a moderate-sized community not far from the Virginia state line and worries that her current grade-point average (3.251) may not be high enough to admit her to medical school. In addition to her strong professional goals, she says she wants to "become spiritually strong, married with one or two kids, and cruise the Bahamas." In addition to a full course load, Melodie is heavily involved in the biology club, student government, the "Technology College," and the Mormon church. Her midterm course grade average is 86%.

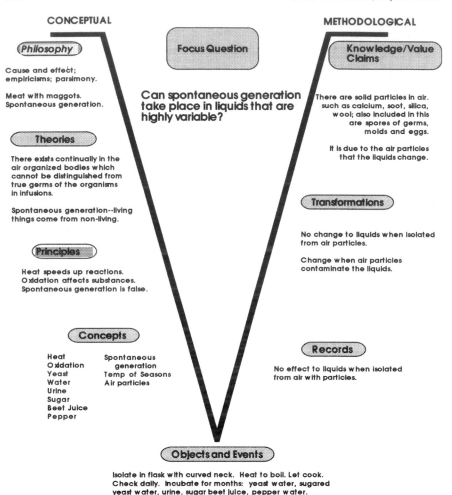

CONCEPTUAL

Philosophy

Cause and effect;
empiricisms; parsimony.

Meat with maggots.
Spontaneous generation.

Theories

There exists continually in the
air organized bodies which
cannot be distinguished from
true germs of the organisms
in infusions.

Spontaneous generation--living
things come from non-living.

Principles

Heat speeds up reactions.
Oxidation affects substances.
Spontaneous generation is false.

Concepts

Heat   Spontaneous
Oxidation   generation
Yeast   Temp of Seasons
Water   Air particles
Urine
Sugar
Beet Juice
Pepper

Focus Question

Can spontaneous generation
take place in liquids that are
highly variable?

METHODOLOGICAL

*Knowledge/Value
Claims*

There are solid particles in air.
such as calcium, soot, silica,
wool; also included in this
are spores of germs,
molds and eggs.

It is due to the air particles
that the liquids change.

Transformations

No change to liquids when isolated
from air particles.

Change when air particles
contaminate the liquids.

Records

No effect to liquids when isolated
from air with particles.

Objects and Events

Isolate in flask with curved neck. Heat to boil. Let cook.
Check daily. Incubate for months: yeast water, sugared
yeast water, urine, sugar beet juice, pepper water.

FIGURE 4
Blaine's V diagram.

The *focus question* Melodie depicts (Figure 5) is vague and fails to address the objects and events of the study, although it does identify "spontaneous generation" as the conceptual issue of concern (2 points). The *objects and events* are identified and are consistent with the focus question, but no indication of records are suggested (2 points). On the *conceptual side*, Melodie includes "germs" and "cell division" among the important concepts, and an indication of cell theory and evolution are suggested; however, the principles she depicts are not derived from relevant theory and

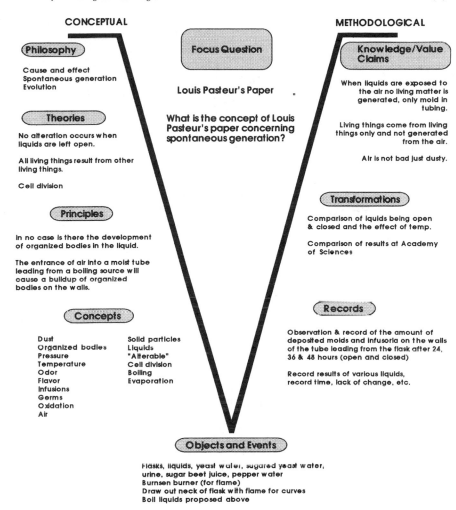

CONCEPTUAL

METHODOLOGICAL

Philosophy

Cause and effect
Spontaneous generation
Evolution

Theories

No alteration occurs when
liquids are left open.

All living things result from other
living things.

Cell division

Principles

In no case is there the development
of organized bodies in the liquid.

The entrance of air into a moist tube
leading from a boiling source will
cause a buildup of organized
bodies on the walls.

Concepts

Dust   Solid particles
Organized bodies Liquids
Pressure   "Alterable"
Temperature   Cell division
Odor   Boiling
Flavor   Evaporation
Infusions
Germs
Oxidation
Air

Focus Question

Louis Pasteur's Paper

What is the concept of Louis
Pasteur's paper concerning
spontaneous generation?

Knowledge/Value Claims

When liquids are exposed to
the air no living matter is
generated, only mold in
tubing.

Living things come from living
things only and not generated
from the air.

Air is not bad just dusty.

Transformations

Comparison of iquids being open
& closed and the effect of temp.

Comparison of results at Academy
of Sciences

Records

Observation & record of the amount of
deposited molds and infusoria on the walls
of the tube leading from the flask after 24,
36 & 48 hours (open and closed)

Record results of various liquids,
record time, lack of change, etc.

Objects and Events

Flasks, liquids, yeast water, sugared yeast water,
urine, sugar beet juice, pepper water
Burnsen burner (for flame)
Draw out neck of flask with flame for curves
Boil liquids proposed above

FIGURE 5
Melodie's V diagram.

this confusion is compounded by the inclusion of "spontaneous generation" as a guiding philosophy (3 points). The *transformations and records*
Melodie identifies are not as specific as we would like to see, but they are
consistent with the objects, events, and focus question (3 points). Finally,
Melodie includes a *knowledge claim*, but her knowledge claim is inconsistent
with the records and transformations and therefore her claim ("Air is not
bad just dusty.") is invalid (2 points). Melodie's combined total score is 12
(out of 16).

Corrie

Corrie is a mature, "nontraditional," first-year student who has returned to the University after several years to qualify for a teaching certificate in elementary education. She volunteered that her favorite pasttime is reading but, "I don't have much time for that right now because I'm 8 months pregnant." She is a graduate of a small private academy in rural South Carolina and currently maintains an overall grade point average of 2.8 (out of 4.0). Corrie, like Blaine, sits in the back row of the lecture hall where she is quiet and unobtrusive. She says her goals are to "get a masters in school administration. ... [and] to be very successful in my career as well as in my family life." Her midterm grades in biology suggest that she is performing somewhat above average among students enrolled in the course. This is the second time she has taken the course; the first time, she had Dr. R and made a grade of D. In that context she says, "it seems I'm in a totally different course. I find it difficult but interesting."

Corrie's V diagram (Figure 6) is sparse but relatively complete and, in most respects, scientifically accurate. Her *focus question asks*, "How do organized bodies. ... originate...?" which might be rephrased as, "Do organized bodies ... originate...?" Nonetheless, the question focuses on appropriate objects and events and includes several important concepts (i.e., organized bodies; infusions; heat; atmosphere) (3 points). The important *objects and events* are identified and they are consistent with the focus question, but there is no indication of the records that are needed (2 points). On the *conceptual side* of the V, Corrie identifies several important concepts but the principle she offers is confused and she identifies the theory of "spontaneous generation" as one of two underlying frameworks in Pasteur's paper (2 points). On the methodological side, her *records and transformations* are somewhat incomplete, but they are consistent with the objects and events and the focus question (3 points). Finally, Corrie does identify a knowledge claim that is consistent with the records and transformations but fails to suggest a value claim {2 points}. Her combined total score on the V diagram is 12 (out of 16).

COMMENTS AND REFLECTIONS

In this concluding section we limit our comments to two general issues: (1) the specific findings and implications of our experience with V diagrams, and (2) several broader issues concerning the value of V diagrams as assessment tools in science education.

V Diagrams in College Biology

Our own experience with V diagrams in introductory college biology suggests several conclusions: (1) The strategy can be introduced to average col-

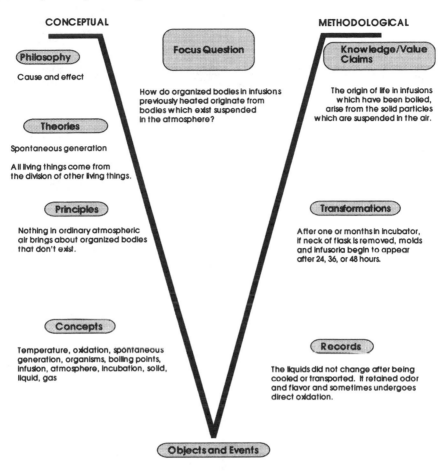

CONCEPTUAL

METHODOLOGICAL

Focus Question

How do organized bodies in infusions previously heated originate from bodies which exist suspended in the atmosphere?

Philosophy

Cause and effect

Knowledge/Value Claims

The origin of life in infusions which have been boiled, arise from the solid particles which are suspended in the air.

Theories

Spontaneous generation

All living things come from the division of other living things.

Principles

Nothing in ordinary atmospheric air brings about organized bodies that don't exist.

Transformations

After one or months in incubator, if neck of flask is removed, molds and infusoria begin to appear after 24, 36, or 48 hours.

Concepts

Temperature, oxidation, spontaneous generation, organisms, boiling points, infusion, atmosphere, incubation, solid, liquid, gas

Records

The liquids did not change after being cooled or transported. It retained odor and flavor and sometimes undergoes direct oxidation.

Objects and Events

Glass flask to place yeast water, sugared yeast water, urine, sugar beet juice, or peppered water or milk in. Burner to boil these liquids. Incubator and file to remove neck of flask.

FIGURE 6
Corrie's V diagram.

lege students in a single 3-hour laboratory with reasonable success; (2) the quality of the V diagrams students construct improves with practice and seems to be related only loosely to conventional measures of academic success, such as scores on locally constructed, multiple-choice tests; and (3) the epistemological issues addressed by the V diagram are substantially new to most students, and many could benefit from diagramming experiences at the secondary or even elementary school levels.

The V diagrams our students constructed are products of a single 3-hour introductory experience in a first-year college biology course. Only 1 of the

92 students enrolled in the course had previous experience with the technique {having taken an advanced course at an affluent public high school in upstate New York}. Despite this lack of previous experience, over 50% of these students achieved a score of 10 (out of 16) or higher. This suggests that average students with minimal prior experience can apply the technique successfully within a relatively brief period of time.

Nonetheless, it is also clear that these students might improve markedly with continued practice, and possibly with some ancillary reading and discussion in the history and philosophy of science and epistemology. Among the three students we highlighted in this chapter, the range of *total* scores appears to be relatively narrow {10 to 12}, but these total scores mask substantial differences in the students' relative abilities to "unpack" each of the nine epistemological elements depicted in the V diagram; these differences are revealed in the subscores (Figure 7).

For example, it appears that Blaine excels in the more concrete tasks of identifying the focus question of the study and in suggesting objects and events that are consistent with it, but he apparently has considerable trouble picking out the records and transformations, and offering appropriate knowledge and value claims. In contrast, it seems that Melodie excels on the conceptual side of the V but encounters some difficulty ferreting out the precise focus of the study and the objects and events. Corrie seems to share some of the strengths and several of the weaknesses of both Blaine and Melodie.

Among the three students, Blaine's scores on the midterm examinations place him within the bottom quartile of students enrolled in the course; Melodie is clearly in the top quartile, as is Corrie. Concept maps {on the topic of "cells"} constructed by these students at four intervals during the semester reinforce the view that Blaine's understanding of this domain is considerably less sophisticated than that of Melodie and Corrie.

Improvement of Laboratory Study Guides

Students often find science laboratory studies boring, confusing, and/or of little value. Some of these negative results derive from the poor design of laboratory study guides. The vee heuristic can be of value in evaluating and redesigning science laboratory guides. For example, Chen (1980) found that the vee analysis of one troublesome introductory college physics laboratory activity dealing with kinematics did not help students draw on their previous related knowledge and did not guide them well to understanding the application of physics concepts to the lab work. When the study guide was rewritten, based on this vee analysis, student performance was enhanced. The course was taught in a mastery learning format where students were required to pass exams to a criterion level of 70% or more. Chen found that students using the traditional study guide required on average twice as many trial exams to reach the passing criterion than the students using the

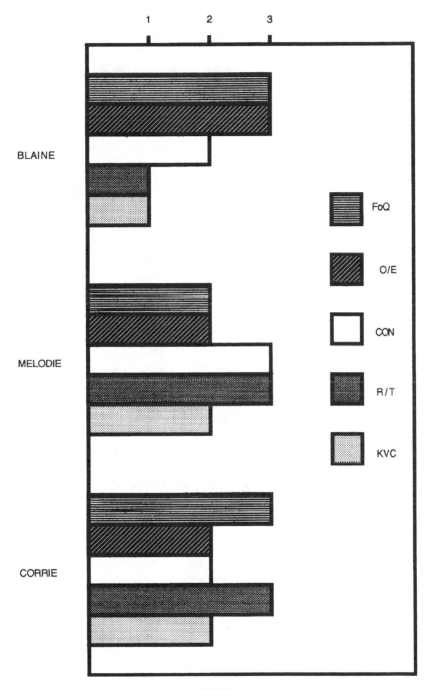

FIGURE 7
Profile of V diagram scores.

revised study guide. Moreover, questionnaire responses from students to the statement "I enjoyed doing this lab" showed highly significant differences favoring the students using the modified study guide.

In another study, in an advanced college physics laboratory class, Buchweitz (1981) found that vee analysis and concept map analysis of the laboratories showed a variety of defects, including repetition of concepts already well understood, key concepts and ideas missing from the study guide, and improper sequencing of laboratories to build on previous knowledge and to lay foundations for subsequent laboratories. Empirical analysis of performance on physics tests and questionnaire assessment of the students' perceived difficulty and value of the experiments done indicated that most learning occurred when experiments built upon and expanded students existing conceptual knowledge. Experiments that focused on developing methodological skills led to little conceptual development.

These studies showed that the vee heuristic can be of value in analyzing laboratory work and finding ways to modify this work to improve student's conceptual understanding. Further studies of this kind would be useful to improve science teaching at all levels and in all subjects.

V Diagrams in Junior High School

To provide some indication of how well our relatively inexperienced college students might perform on the V diagram task with some additional practice, we close this paper with a brief synopsis of a study that focused on the use of V diagrams among junior high school students.

Shortly after the vee was invented by Gowin in 1977, we sought to evaluate its use with junior high school students. With funding from the National Science Foundation, and cooperation from schools near Ithaca, we trained teachers and students in several seventh- and eighth-grade classrooms in the use of the vee heuristic. We also trained these groups in concept mapping and soon learned it was easier to begin the training with concept maps than with the vee. Over the years, with groups of all ages, including corporate employees, we have continued to observe that individuals generally come to accept and understand the vee more readily when they are first given some training and practice in concept mapping. Logically, one might expect that an epistemological understanding of the nature of concepts and principles would aid in understanding concept mapping, and we began our work by applying the vee to student laboratory studies and teacher demonstrations. What soon became evident is that students (and also most teachers) are so imbued with positivistic epistemological ideas that the vee nomenclature and constructive underpinnings presented a major hurdle. Psychologically, it was more appropriate and therefore easier to begin with concept mapping, and this in turn laid *some* of the groundwork needed to help move students and their teachers to more constructivist views.

TABLE 1

**Comparison of Vee Map Mean Scores for Grade 7 (School A) and Grade 8 (School B)
Students on Three Scoring Criteria**

		N	Mean	S.D.	*t*-value	df	*p*<
Identifying parts	School A (7th)	75	17.87	1.15	7.82	133	.0001
of vee	School B (8th)	80	14.39	3.87			
Defining terms	School A (7th)	75	14.23	2.93	3.85	133	.0001
of vee	School B (8th)	80	11.92	4.42			
Picking out examples	School A (7th)	75	13.35	3.18	0.703	133	.472
of vee terms	School B (8th)	80	12.89	4.85			

Working with both seventh- and eighth-grade classes (Table 1), we found that the age differential was not the significant factor. In fact, seventh grade students performed somewhat better than the 8th-grade students, partly as a result of the more extensive use of concept maps and vees in seventh-grade classrooms (Novak et al., 1983). Although we used a simplified version of the vee that did not include world view philosophy, and constructs as elements, the key epistemological idea that what we hold in our heads controls how we ask questions, seek answers to these questions, and interpret the data from our studies, remained important features in the use of the vee. As the work progressed, both teachers and students reported the value of the vee in illustrating their understanding of a lab, demonstration, or textbook section. Figure 8 shows an example of a vee constructed by one of the students.

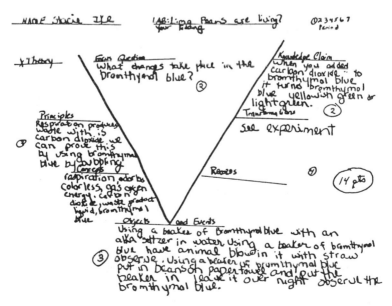

FIGURE 8

V diagram of a seventh-grade student.

Scoring of vees was done using a set of criteria shown in Table 2. Note that not all elements of the vee were involved in our work with junior high school students. Using these criteria, vees prepared by students were scored by our research staff. Since the seventh-grade classes did more work with vees than the eighth-grade class, their performance was used to illustrate student success with the vee. Table 3 shows the mean score values on various parts of the vee for 9 different laboratory activities. Note that there was improvement as the year progressed, but even later performance was less than perfect. Nevertheless, the data show clearly that most of the students had acquired reasonable proficiency with the use of the vee. We also collected qualitative data from students and teachers, and some of this is reported elsewhere (Novak et al., 1983). In general, both students and teachers found the vee to be valuable to facilitate student understanding of their lab work and as an indicator of what students were learning.

Over the years we have come to appreciate increasingly the need for teachers and students to engage in discourse on the nature of world views and philosophical/epistemological issues. If we were repeating our work with junior high schools students, we would include these elements of the vee in our program.

Vee diagrams have been used successfully with students from grade one through adults. However we do not have at this time systematic data on use of the vee in earlier grades. This kind of research would make good MS and PhD studies for graduate students.

THE NEED FOR GREATER EPISTEMOLOGICAL UNDERSTANDING

Although we were able to report only a limited number of studies in this chapter, a fact that these and other studies demonstrate clearly is that both teachers and students lack strong understanding of the nature of knowledge and knowledge creation in the sciences. This problem has been recognized by others, including most of the reports on the need for improved standards for science education. The reality is that it is very difficult to encourage the building of these competencies if we do not have adequate means to evaluate learning progress in this area. We have found that the vee can be a powerful evaluation tool that can and should be used more widely to improve science curriculums and to facilitate student learning in the area of epistemology.

In many of our more recent research studies we have observed a close relationship between commitment to meaningful learning and commitment to constructivist epistemological ideas. There is evidence that a kind of symbiosis exists and that advancing students' understanding and commitment to constructivist ideas will also advance commitment to high levels of meaningful learning. We have seen that use of the vee heuristic with

TABLE 2
Comprehensive Form for Assessing Student-Constructed V's

Focus Question

0—no focus question is identified.

1—a question is identified, but does not focus upon the objects and the major event OR the conceptual side of the V.

2—a focus question is identified; includes concepts, but does not suggest objects or the major event OR the wrong objects and event are identified in relation to the rest of the laboratory exercise.

3—a clear focus question is identified; includes concept to be used and suggests the major event and accompanying objects.

Object/Event

0—no object or event is identified.

1—the major event OR the objects are identified and is consistent with the focus question, OR an event and objects are identified, but are inconsistent with the focus question.

2—the major event with accompanying objects is identified, and is consistent with the focus question.

3—same as above, but also suggests what records will be taken.

Theory, Principles, and Concepts

0—no conceptual side is identified.

1—a few concepts are identified, but without principles and theory, or a principle written is the knowledge claim sought in the laboratory exercise.

2—concepts and at least one type of principle (conceptual or methodological) OR concepts and a relevant theory is identified.

3—concepts and two types of principles are identified, OR concepts, one type of principle, and a relevant theory are identified.

4—concepts, two types of principles, and a relevant theory are identified.

Records/Transformations

0—no records or transformations are identified.

1—records are identified, but are inconsistent with the major focus question or the major event.

2—records OR transformations are identified, but not both.

3—records are identified for the major event; transformations are inconsistent with the intent of the focus question.

4—records are identified for the major event; transformations are consistent with the focus question and the grade level and ability of the student.

Knowledge Claim

0—no knowledge claim is identified.

1—a claim that is unrelated to the left-hand side of the V.

2—a knowledge claim that includes a concept that is used in an improper context OR any generalization that is inconsistent with the records and transformations.

3—a knowledge claim that includes the concepts from the focus question and is derived from the records and transformations.

4—same as above, but the knowledge claim leads to a new focus question.

students both for science instruction and for evaluation can significantly advance their understanding of and commitment to constructivist ideas. In many respects, we see this need as the fundamental problem facing education. We encourage much more research to be done to explore ways the vee heuristic can be employed to enhance science education.

TABLE 3
Mean Scores and Standard Deviations (Below) for Nine Student-Constructed Vees

Criteria category	Maximum value	#1 (78)	#2 (55)	#3 (76)	#4 (58)	#5 (63)	#6 (29)	#7 (79)	#8 (60)	#9 (43)
Focus question	3	1.77	1.92	2.42	2.74	2.27	2.34	2.91	2.12	2.33
		0.60	0.47	0.59	0.54	0.45	0.48	0.29	0.32	0.60
Objects/events	3	1.69	2.24	1.51	2.12	2.19	2.41	2.35	2.88	2.72
		0.93	0.74	0.68	0.72	0.39	0.56	0.56	0.32	0.67
Theory/principles/ concepts	4	1.54	1.71	2.60	3.09	2.89	2.72	2.69	2.38	3.18
		0.83	1.04	0.73	0.96	0.76	0.64	0.65	0.98	0.63
Records/transforma- tions	4	3.28	2.33	3.28	3.55	3.32	3.27	3.90	3.45	3.14
		1.16	0.79	1.27	0.78	0.69	0.70	0.50	0.81	0.64
Knowledge claims	4	1.92	1.51	2.04	2.57	2.82	2.37	2.33	2.43	2.58
		1.13	1.03	0.97	0.80	0.78	0.82	0.65	2.22	0.75
Total score	18	10.20	9.71	11.86	14.07	13.19	13.14	14.19	13.27	13.95
		2.90	2.27	2.30	2.10	1.57	1.66	1.26	2.22	1.75

Note: Data are for School A, Grade 7, Number in parentheses indicates sample size, and content of each lab is indicated in the key.

Key to laboratory content: #1, lima bean variation; #2, protective coloration; #3, cell structure; #4, earthworm dissection; #5, peach dissection; #6, pulse rate exercise; #7, blood pressure; #8, saliva digestion; #9, seed growth.

References

Adams, M. M. (1987). *William Ockham*. South Bend, IN: University of Notre Dame Press.

American Association for the Advancement of Science (1993). *Benchmarks for science literacy—Project* 2061. New York: Oxford University Press.

Ault, C. R., Novak, J. D., & Gowin, D. B. (1984). Constructing vee maps for clinical interviews on molecule concepts. *Science Education*, 68, 441–462.

Ausubel, D. P., Novak, J. D., & Hanesian H. (1978). Educational psychology: A cognitive view. New York: Holt, Rinehart and Winston.

Baumel, H. B., & Berger, J. J. (1973). *Biology—its people and its papers*. Washington, DC: National Science Teachers Association.

Brock, T. D. (Ed.), (1961). *Milestones in microbiology*. Englewood Cliffs, NJ: Prentice-Hall.

Brody, M. (1985). *Concept mapping, vee diagrams and individual interviews applied to the design of marine trades extension curricula and organizational feedback system*. Unpublished PhD dissertation, Cornell University.

Buchweitz, B. (1981). *An epistemological analysis of curriculum and an assessment of Concept learning in physics laboratory*. Unpublished PhD dissertation Cornell University.

Chen, Hai Hsia (1980). *Relevance of Gowin's structure of knowledge and Ausubel's learning theory for a method of improving physics laboratory instructions*. Unpublished MS thesis, Cornell University.

Darwin, C. (1859). *On the origin of species by means of natural selection*. London: John Murray

Gowin, D. B. (1981). *Educating*. Ithaca, NY: Cornell University Press.

Gurley-Dilger, L. (1982). *Use of Gowin's vee and concept mapping strategies to teach responsibility for learning in high school biological sciences*. Unpublished PhD dissertation, Cornell University.

Kuhn, T. (1962). *The structure of scientific revolutions*. Chicago: University of Chicago Press.

Mintzes, J. J., Wandersee, J. H., & Novak, J. D. (Eds.), (1998). *Teaching science for understanding: A human constructivist view*. San Diego, CA: Academic Press.

National Research Council (1996). *National science education standards.* Washington, DC: National Academy Press.

Novak, J. D. (1998). *Learning, creating and using knowledge: concept maps as facilitative tools in schools and Corporations.* Mahwah, NJ: Erlbaum.

Novak, J. D., & Gowin, D. B. (1984). *Learning how to learn.* Cambridge, UK: Cambridge University Press.

Novak, J. D., Gowin, D. B., & Johansen, G. T. (1983). The use of concept mapping and knowledge vee mapping with junior high school science students. *Science Education, 67, 625–645.*

Pasteur, L. (1861). Memoire sur les corpuscles organises qui existent dans l'atmosphere: Examen de la doctrine des generations spontanees. *Annales des Sciences Naturelles, 16, 5–98.*

Peled, L., Barenholz, H., & Tamir, P. (1993). Concept mapping and Gowin's categories as heuristic devices in scientific reading of high school students. In J.D. Novak (Ed.), *Proceedings of the third international seminar on misconceptions and educational strategies in science and mathematics* (distributed electronically). Ithaca, NY: Department of Education, Cornell University.

Schneps, M. H. (1987). *A private universe.* Santa Monica, CA: Pyramid Films.

Spallanzani, L. (1799). *Tracts on the nature of animals and vegetables.* Translated by J.G. Dalyell, Edinburgh.

Toulmin, S. (1972). *Human understanding,* Vol. 1: *The collective use and evolution of concepts.* Princeton, NJ: Princeton University Press.

Trowbridge, J. E., & Wandersee, J. H. (1998) Theory-driven graphic organizers. In Mintzes, J.J., Wandersee, J.H., & Novak, J.D. (Eds). *Teaching science for understanding: A human constructivist view.* San Diego, CA: Academic Press.

Virchow, R. (1971). *Cellular pathology.* New York: Dover (from 1863 edition).

Webster's (1958). *New collegiate dictionary.* Cambridge, MA: Riverside Press.

CHAPTER

4

"What Do You Mean By That?" Using Structured Interviews to Assess Science Understanding

SHERRY A. SOUTHERLAND
University of Utah

MIKE U. SMITH
Mercer University School of Medicine

CATHERINE L. CUMMINS
Louisiana State University

As she reviewed the results of yesterday's biology test, Ms. Benson found it difficult to determine just where things had gone wrong. Her 10th-grade students had seemed to understand the unit on evolutionary change, they had done well on the weekly quizzes, and appeared to be engaged in the material. But the findings from these, somewhat informal, assessment techniques differed drastically from the results of the unit tests. This difference was particularly marked when she focused on the essay portion of the test. Her students clearly did not understand even the basics of evolution. Ms. Benson sat, mulling over the papers, trying to figure out where to go from there. Should she just enter the poor grades, chalking them up to lack of understanding and dismal student effort, or should she review the unit trying to target the areas of difficulty? As is true for all teachers, Ms. Benson felt the need to move ahead, and she didn't have a great deal of time to devote to repeating this single topic, but she knew that understanding what this year's students missed would help her plan more effectively for this unit next year.

This chapter offers a means for Ms. Benson to determine the source of students' conceptual difficulties. The structured interview techniques we describe can provide an avenue into understanding students' meanings,

Assessing Science Understanding
71

providing information that can be used to shape further instruction. In this particular case, by using two or three structured interview prompts with a sample of five students of varying abilities, Ms. Benson could generate a description of the alternative views students hold on fundamental issues related to evolution, such as sources of variation in a population and processes of natural selection. While these interviews may take an entire class period or afternoon to complete, their findings may allow Ms. Benson to explicitly address students' conceptions during later class sessions in order to help shape students' present ideas toward more scientific explanations. Such interviews and the information they provide are not cure-alls, but becoming familiar with students' conceptions certainly allows for more focused instruction and may prevent nights spent puzzling over unexpected exam responses.

THE NEED FOR QUALITATIVE ASSESSMENT TOOLS

As science educators, we all want to know what our students have learned in our classrooms—How good a job have they done? How good a job have we done? What do they know, and what do they understand? Have they learned only to parrot definitions and recognize axioms, or can they use their newfound knowledge in meaningful ways? Assuming that meaningful learning involves active restructuring of a learner's preexisting conceptions, an accurate understanding of those conceptions is of paramount importance, but how can we assess this learning in ways that are valuable to both the learner and the teacher/researcher? There is a growing consensus that traditional quantitative assessment tools are largely inadequate for producing an adequately fine-grained description of both what learners know and how they build and revise that knowledge. In recent years teachers, researchers, and curriculum planners have found that a rich understanding of the common alternative conceptions can be a useful guide for planning effective instruction. To build these thick descriptions of student conceptual frameworks, researchers have turned to more descriptive tools, such as the structured interview, in which we ask students to explain their understandings in their own words and/or apply that knowledge in selected tasks. Interest in personal meanings and individual conceptual frameworks, as opposed to assigning scores that can be used to measure the proportion of students who have learned to recognize certain scientific conceptions, marks a significant shift in recent science education (Driver & Easley, 1978). Such interpretive research provides much more detailed snapshots not only of what students know, but also what they understand (Gallagher, 1991; Smith, Blakeslee, & Anderson, 1993).

WHAT IS A STRUCTURED INTERVIEW?

The structured interview provides an excellent opportunity to gain a well-grounded understanding of the meanings learners assign to a concept. Carefully structured and implemented interviews serve as deep probes of a student's understanding of a single concept or small groups of concepts. During a structured interview, the teacher/researcher uses a set of questions called "probes" (and sometimes selected photographs or other props) designed in advance of the interview to elicit a portrait of the learner's understanding about a specific concept. In this one-on-one setting the student may be asked to use her own words to explain a concept (e.g., "What is natural selection?"). The student is required to go beyond simple recognition of a concept to construct a detailed personal explanation. Typically the student is also asked to use that concept explicitly to solve a problem or other application task (e.g., "Explain why cave fish have no color"). The teacher/researcher watches and listens closely to everything the student says and does, asking questions only as necessary to better understand the learner's dialogue and actions (Opper, 1977; Smith, 1983). For instance, if a student is sorting a set of terms, the important data include not only the learner's final sort of cards, but also her verbal and nonverbal expressions during the sorting task.

The structured interview differs from other research tools in the wealth of data regarding a learner's understanding of a concept it can provide. This potential diversity of data allows for a richer and more useful portrait of what a learner knows. However, there are drawbacks to this approach. Structured interviews are best completed with an individual student, thus time becomes a factor as the teacher/research attempts to schedule interviews. In a typical classroom, selective sampling must be employed for this technique to be practical. More importantly, however, significant amounts of time are required to make sense of the data collected from these interviews. Despite these constraints, structured interviews can be useful tools in assessing learners' conceptions.

STRUCTURED INTERVIEW TASKS

The selection of the task to be used in a structured interview, including any graphics or other props, is the most critical decision in planning an interview. The interview task should be tightly focused on the concept of interest and at a level of difficulty appropriate to the learner. It should be carefully structured to focus on likely conceptual difficulties based on prior experience with similar students. Depending on the purposes of the study, the degree to which the student is likely to be familiar with the type of application should be carefully considered (for instance, will the stu-

TABLE 1
Degree of Understanding Required by Interview Probes

Degree of Understanding	Interview Probe
Concept recognition/definition	Interview about instances
Concept application	Interview about instances
	Prediction interview
	Problem solving
	Process interview
	Sorting task
Construction of causal explanations	Sorting task

dent recognize the plant or animal species involved in the interview prompt?).

Different kinds of interview tasks also require different levels of understanding. Can the student recognize the concept? generate an example? apply the concept? use the concept to predict phenomena or solve problems? Table 1 compares the various interview probes described in this chapter with the degree of understanding they are likely to require.

The greatest insights are typically obtained when the interview requires the student to apply her understanding in a specific task. In this chapter we describe structured interviews that require applications in four different settings: *interviews about instances, prediction interviews, sorting interviews,* and *problem-solving interviews.*

Interviews about Instances

In interviews about instances a student is typically presented with a specific set of examples and counterexamples of the concept of interest and is asked to identify which cases are examples of the concept, and then to explain that decision. For practical reasons the examples are usually graphics such as line pictures, drawings, or diagrams. An example of a series of graphics used to probe student understanding of the concept *species* is provided in Figure 1. The graphics should be carefully chosen to require application of the concept. The design of graphics should illustrate a wide range of variations in response and highlight typical student difficulties (e.g., for a sophisticated audience one might include examples of members of races or subspecies). Interviews about instances may involve a number of instances. In Demastes-Southerland (1994), as many as 15 cards were used to characterize students' notions of biological adaptation. However, it is important to remember that even one well-chosen graphic can provide great insight into a student's understanding of a concept.

In the interview about instances of the species concept in Figure 1, a student is shown the graphics one at a time and asked the initial focusing question, "How many species do you see?" The teacher/researcher then

FIGURE 1
Line drawings for interviews about instances of species concept. *Top*: one card, holding three different flowers; *middle*: one card, holding three different dogs; *bottom*: one card, holding three different primates.

follows the student's response with planned questions designed to make sense of what the student is saying: "Why did you say that?" "Why did you say there was one species shown?" "What makes all these one species, but *these* three members of *different* species?" "What makes something a species?" Then the teacher/researcher *gently* probes into the student's reasoning for each decision, gaining insight into the student's understanding of the species concept. Questions should be designed to gain an understanding of how the student understands, explains, and applies a concept and what the student means by her explanations.

The following rules of thumb for structuring the questions employed in an interview about instances may be helpful:

1. Focus questions should require the application of the concept, without forcing an explicit definition. A more traditional assessment might ask the student to choose the correct definition of the concept from among four choices or to write down a definition of the concept. The more indirect approach of the interview about instances is usually the more productive because it allows the student to evince her understanding without first committing to an explicit definition that may be memorized by rote with little or no understanding. This also allows the teacher/researcher to gain an idea of how the student applies the *implicit* concept.

2. Do not force the student into a specific response to each graphic. If the student needs to "waffle" in her answer, she should be allowed to do so. If the student does not have an understanding of the concept that allows her to make a decision about a specific instance, do not force her to choose. This lack of understanding is, in fact, an important piece of the description of her conceptual framework as it is being built. The next step for the interviewer is to understand what part of the graphic cannot be interpreted by the student, what part of her understanding is missing or fuzzy. And the interview interpretation should reflect this murkiness.

3. Specific definitions of the concept, if needed, should be asked for only after understanding the student's response to the focusing questions. Again, this prevents students from early closure on a rote definition. Thus, in our example it would be inappropriate to ask, "Well, what is a species?"

4. As with all the interview formats we describe, it is important for the interviewer to wait at least 3 to 5 seconds after each prompt before trying to interpret the question or ask another. Classroom research has shown that when this wait time is observed, both the length of the student responses and the cognitive level of the responses increases (Rowe, 1974). Observing adequate wait time is often difficult for novice interviewers and often requires considerable practice. Audio taping practice interviews and reviewing the tape with a stopwatch is a useful tool for interviewer training.

Prediction Interviews

Prediction interviews require students to anticipate an outcome of a situation and explain or justify that prediction. The strength of this kind of inter-

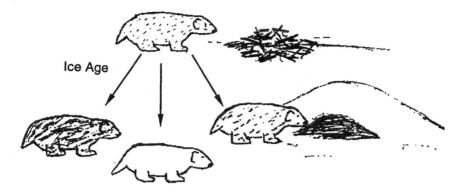

FIGURE 2

Line drawings for use in a prediction interview about origin of variation in a population.

view is that it focuses on the ways students apply their personal meanings of the concept. Unlike interviews about instances, which require students to explain a concept, prediction interviews emphasize the application of that knowledge. And because they require application, prediction interviews are very useful in teasing out what has been learned by rote with minimal understanding from what is meaningful knowledge. Questioning for prediction interviews should follow the same rules of thumb as interviews about instances described above. Figure 2 exemplifies a graphic used in a prediction interview on students' understandings of the origin of biological variation.

A Prediction Interview: "Origin of Variation"

R: This is my ancestral mammal. It's kind of fat. It has kind of short hair. And it makes a nest on the ground in sticks; that's how it nests. Then the ice age comes and it gets really cold.

Student: Okay.

R: So then there is a mutation. Something happens to produce new variation. Would one of these mutations be more likely? This one [bear] gets long hair. This one [loses its hair] and this one learns to kind of burrow in the ground.

S: Which one do I think would happen?

R: Is one of these more likely? Which one?

S: Ahm, most likely let's see. Number three.

R: Most likely, number three [the graphic of the burrowing bear]. Why did you say that?

continued

S: Just because it's easy to ah. Did you say he [the original bear] just likes warms up right there and the ground and stuff?

R: Yeah.

S: Like in his nest or something like that?

R: Yeah, individuals of this species nest on the ground.

S: Right.

R: But an individual of the initial species undergoes a mutation. Which variation, if one, would you most expect to see?

S: Well. Either one [bear with the longer hair] or three [burrowing bear]. (Small laugh)...

R: And why do you say that?

S: Well with three that's just natural. I mean when you get cold you bundle up ... Or if you could, you could get longer hair ... to be able to live in the cold.

R: Okay. (Pause) So what causes mutations, do you know?

S: When something changes outside that affects the animal ... and they have to change to adapt to that.

The goal of this interview task is for the student to make a prediction and then to explain the basis of her prediction. In this case, the student explained that a mutation for burrowing or long hair may have occurred in response to a period of severe cold. The student's explanation shows that she does not understand that genetic variability in the population occurs independently of external events and thus predates those changes. While the mutation is not caused by the cold, this idea is common among students (Demastes-Southerland, Good, & Peebles, 1996). This interview excerpt demonstrates that the most valuable information from a structured interview often comes not from how a student completes the task, but from how the student explains, justifies, or rationalizes her thinking.

White and Gunstone (1992) describe a more extensive approach to prediction interviews. These interviews require four tasks of students: (1) to predict an outcome of an event, (2) to explain or justify this prediction, (3) to describe a graphic of the actual outcome of the event, and (4) to reconcile conflicts between their personal predictions and the actual outcome. In addition to the strengths of simple prediction interviews, such *Prediction–Observation–Explanation* (POE) interviews allow the teacher/researcher to see the effects of prior knowledge on a student's evidence evaluation because the student must also interpret the actual outcome of the event in light of her previous prediction.

In our experience, however, this additional requirement is sometimes also an assessment liability. We have found that the process of reconciliation required in POEs encourages students to reevaluate their understanding. When confronted by the discrepancy between what they predicted on the basis of their current understanding and the actual outcome observed, many students will revise their understanding on the spot. Describing the student's *current* understanding becomes a moving target. Thus, we view the POE interview as an excellent teaching tool but less acceptable as a pure form of assessment.

This version of the Heisenberg uncertainty principle, of course, applies to all assessment practices, including the various forms of structured interview described in this chapter. Participation in an assessment procedure of this sort may act as a catalyst for learning by the student. Although an assessment is intended to explore the student's knowledge framework, the very act of assessment may stimulate change in that knowledge (Demastes-Southerland, 1994). Accordingly, as we use structured interviews, we must recognize that assessment tools can inadvertently serve as teaching tools. This fact must be recognized as the we try to make sense of what students know.

Sorting Interviews

In a sorting interview the student is presented with a group of objects to be sorted according to specific instructions that can be structured in many different ways to match the purpose of the assessment. For example, the interviewer may present a series of graphics depicting some natural phenomenon. The student may then be asked to select any number of the cards to be used in any order to explain the phenomenon. Alternatively, a student may be presented with a set of genetics problem cards and asked to sort them according to similarity (e.g., Smith, 1992). As with other kinds of interviews described in this chapter, students are encouraged to talk about their reasoning as they attempt to construct an explanation for their sorting.

In one example (Figure 3), a student is asked to construct an explanation of how the pelage color of a population of rabbits changes over time. One advantage of this particular sorting task is that it allows for investigation of anthropomorphic and teleological reasoning patterns. It also provides insight into those factors the student viewed as necessary for evolution driven by natural selection (Demastes-Southerland, 1994).

A Sorting Interview: "Natural Selection"

R: What I want you to do is sort through these cards to explain something. But as you sort through 'em, if ahm, you would talk aloud while you're thinking about why you [used this card]. Okay. It's about evolution. (...) Here's the initial population of rabbits. And they're all white. And, they live on brown background.

S: Okay.

continued

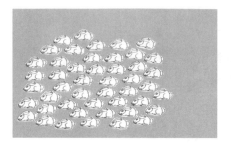

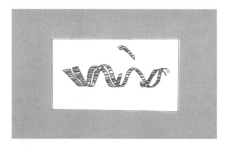

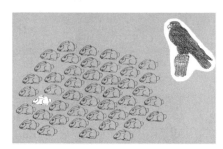

FIGURE 3

Line drawings for use in a sorting interview about the evolution of biological populations. (Pelage color change in a population of rabbits.)

R: That's our initial population. Now, after the bout of evolution, we'll call it, that's what the population looks like. [Indicating the card with a hawk, brown rabbits, and one white rabbit.]

S: Um hum. (Yes.)

R: And they [the rabbits] are still on the brown background. I have some other cards here that you could use to explain this. You don't have to use all of them. I don't care if you use all of them. And, but if you need them to explain how this happened, you can use them.

S: Okay, what is that? [pointing to a card]

continued

R: That ah, genetic material that's kind of broken.

S: Okay. Well, let me sort them first. Let me put them here and I'll explain. [Long pause] Ahm, wait, I'm confused.

R: Okay. So what are you confused about? Can you talk at all?

S: Okay. Well, I'm kinda confused about the hawk and why the rabbits here are the same.

R: Right.

S: But ahm, you've got the hawk … And, so, ahm, obviously something about the hawk is, you know, destroying the rabbit population. I guess you could say?

R: So the two cards you're looking at really hard is the card that has a lot of white rabbits with two brown ones. And you've got the one in your hand, the hawk with a lot of white rabbits and two brown ones.

S: Okay. Well, I think that, ahm, all the hawk ones, are supposed to, will be together. I mean, if you could put one of these before the other, this one should come before this one.

R: Why is that?

S: Because ahm, you, you start, you have ahm, this same number of rabbits and on this thing and at this point, I guess, the hawk is ahm … You introduce the hawk into eating the population and then in here you have nothing. And so you've got to have nothing here and then the hawk. Then the brown bunnies are born. (Long pause)

R: Okay. So how did those rabbits (become brown)?

S: Ahm, I, some kind of genetic, I mean I guess it's this. (Indicating DNA graphic.)

R: If you don't want to use that card, you don't have to.

S: Oh, yeah, I don't want to use it.

R: Okay. So, we'll put this card away.

S: Ah, it's a, it's a some kind of, it's evolution. Some kind of change in, the change occurring to the different color.

R: Okay. Do you think, you've got the two brown rabbits appearing before the hawk appears. Ah, do you think that the brown is some-how dependent upon the hawk?

S: No. Just because you have brown rabbits doesn't mean that you're gonna all of the sudden have a hawk.

R: Um hum. (Yes.) Let's turn that around. Just because you have a hawk, do you think that the rabbits would be more prone to turn brown?

S: That, yeah, that's kinda like ahm, I don't know if that would neces-sarily be their, be the reason why they're brown, but that sorta like, you know, ah, animals evolving ahm, the white fur for winter time and, and just because that's, you know, the survival of the fittest kind of thing. … They're evolving browns in order to be less noticeable to the hawk … 'Cause the hawk here is predator. It's to their advantage to be brown rather than white.

As the above interview excerpt demonstrates, a common difficulty with card sorting interviews is the complexity of the resulting transcript. On the other hand, that complexity is also a strength of this approach due to the additional insight it provides into the factors students consider as they form an explanation.

At the outset of a sorting interview it is essential that the teacher/researcher introduce the task instructions and remind the student to give voice to her thoughts as she constructs explanations. Subsequent interview questions come in response to the explanations the student is constructing. As is the case in all structured interviews, the goal of the interviewer's questions is to understand not only what the student does, but also gain insight into the basis of the student's thinking, reasoning, and understanding.

One of the strengths of sorting tasks is the variety of sources of data they provide. Depending on the exact nature of the task, these may include the student's verbal explanations and nonverbal cues, the specific graphics used by the student during the task, the groupings of cards produced, and the order in which they are arranged. On the other hand, the information obtained in a sorting task is particularly sensitive to exactly what objects are initially selected for inclusion. In addition, some researchers have voiced concern over the reliability of card sorts based on the observation that a re-sorting of the objects after a brief period sometimes produces a very different pattern (Smith, 1992). Once again, we must recognize the need to include sorting tasks as one of several possible interview probes in order to generate a rich but reliable portrait of what a learner knows.

Problem-Solving and Process Interviews

Teachers in disciplines such as mathematics, physics, chemistry, and genetics have long included problem solving in formal assessments. Such assessments are useful for distinguishing between successful and unsuccessful problem solvers, but they provide only limited insight into how the student solves a problem and even less information about the student's understanding of the concepts involved. The problem-solving interview is designed to fill those needs. In the interview setting, a student is asked to attempt to solve a problem while "thinking aloud," explaining as much as possible about what she is doing, why she is doing it, and what her symbols and actions mean.

Selection of the problems to be solved during the interview is perhaps the most crucial planning task, and pilot testing is strongly recommended. Otherwise, the procedures are similar to those in other assessment interviews. This technique has been very useful to science educators and has led to numerous new understandings about student difficulties, typical performance patterns, and conceptual understandings in a wide range of disciplines from physics to genetics. The following interview excerpt is an example of a typical problem-solving interview first reported by Smith and Good (1984).

A Problem-Solving Interview: "Monohybrid Cross"

After receiving the basic instructions from the interviewer, a student receives a card on which is printed a simple monohybrid cross problem whose solution requires computing the proportion of offspring from a given cross that would be expected to have a specified genetic makeup (genotype). After reading the problem, the student begins:

S: Well, all I remember is, is that we had a chart that said when you have, ahm, heterozygous offspring like it was Ss. ... I don't even remember what was here. If I ... I guess it was a ss that bred with a ..., oh, ssh. I don't remember. But anyway, I remember that the recessive was over there in the corner (writes "ss" in the bottom right corner of a 2 × 2 Punnett square), and that is was $1/16$ of all the stocks.
R: Yeah.
S: And it was, it was when we matched two heterozygotes.

This excerpt suggests that for this student and many students like her, solving a problem is a task of reproducing from memory something that has been seen before in texts and/or in lectures. This conclusion is further supported by students' nonverbal behavior in the same study. For example, during these interviews some students closed their eyes and pointed in the air, apparently attempting to remember some visual pattern.

Another technique commonly used in various interview assessment protocols, but especially in problem-solving interviews, is to include individuals of varying skill levels in the group of interviewees—novice students, expert practitioners, graduate students, faculty members within (or sometimes outside) the discipline. Comparison of the performances of individuals of such different experience levels who can be expected to have very different conceptual understandings has been a tool fruitfully employed by many researchers in a wide variety of fields in recent years. When very different levels of performance are juxtaposed, important characteristics of each that may not have been so obvious when considered alone often become readily apparent. In the study of genetics problem solving just described, for example, the tendency of unsuccessful subjects to view the task as one of memorization and reproduction was most obvious when their problem solving was compared to that of successful subjects who clearly approached each problem as a task requiring analysis and reasoning based on their understanding of genetic concepts. Clearly, a broad approach to sampling would also be information in classroom interviews, in that it allows the teacher to gain an understanding of the diverse students in her classroom.

The process interview resembles the problem-solving interview except that the interviewee is asked to explain how a process occurs. For example, an individual might be asked to explain why metal objects may feel cooler than nonmetal objects (Lewis & Linn, 1994), how a battery works to light a bulb (Fredette & Clement, 1981), or the events that occur during mitosis and meiosis (e.g., Smith, 1991; Kindfield, 1994). Process interviews are clearly most useful when assessing a student's understanding of a multistep process, a series of interrelated events, or perhaps a constraint-based interaction (Chi, Slotta, & de Leeuw, 1994).

Problem-solving and process interviews are unique among the methods discussed here because they focus more on performance as a means to assess knowledge, although understanding the student's conceptual framework remains the overarching goal. Like some sorting interviews, the strength of such tasks is that they require application of the individual's understandings more than direct description of that knowledge.

CONDUCTING STRUCTURED INTERVIEWS

The key to conducting a successful structured interview is remembering the goal of this assessment tool, which is *generating a trustworthy description of a student's understanding of a science topic.* Planning a successful interview requires that a teacher/researcher attends not only to careful selection of the tasks and props but also to the practicalities of preparation, assuring student comfort, choosing an appropriate timeframe, planning appropriate prompts and follow-up questions, and completing necessary pilot studies.

Practicalities of Preparation

It is possible to walk into an interview situation with wonderfully designed prompts, a battery of thoughtful questions, and keen insight into students, and still fail to walk away with usable findings. Some of the most common-sense interviewing needs are the easiest to forget. Be sure to prepare a checklist of needed materials to review before beginning the interview. This checklist should include *a relatively quiet location* (students and interviewers are easily distracted, and audiotapes are notorious for picking up background noise), *functioning recording equipment, prelabeled fresh tapes, backup batteries or access to a power source,* and, of course, *copies of interview questions and all necessary props.*

Student Comfort

Because a central goal of the structured interview is for the student to describe as much as possible what she is thinking as she completes a task, it is essential that she feels as comfortable as possible about the interview process and the interviewer. Thus, it is not advisable for a researcher to simply "pop-in" to interview a student; a nervous or frightened student tends to talk very little. Interviews are usually much more fruitful after the student has developed some degree of comfort with the teacher/researcher, comfort that can be fostered by spending time with the student informally or observing or teaching in the student's classroom.

Interview assessments are typically used to provide the teacher/researcher with insight about student understanding, rather than to evaluate individual students. When interviews are conducted to provide insight about understanding, it is important that the teacher/researcher make the intent of the interview clear to the interviewee, emphasizing that the goal of interview is to describe what the student understands and that this requires the student to explain as much as possible of what she is thinking (White and Gunstone, 1992). It is crucial for the teacher/researcher to emphasize that the interview is not a test to be scored and that her performance will in no way affect her course grade. The teacher usually has an advantage over the researcher because the teacher is familiar with the student, but it may be more difficult for the teacher to convince the student that the interview is not to be graded. Once the student is convinced that she is not being graded, she will become comfortable enough to reveal both what she knows and what she does not.

Timeframe

Establishing a high degree of student comfort also can be fostered through providing an adequate timeframe for the interview. Scheduling is often a particular challenge for the classroom teacher whose time is very limited, but interviews that are conducted on the fly during the last five minutes before the bell rings may produce little of value. It is difficult for a student to mull over her answers and express herself as clearly as possible if she feels that the interview time is tightly constrained. It is therefore advisable to allow a generous amount of time when scheduling interviews. Remember that although the task itself may not seem time intensive, the follow-up questions and answers may require substantial thought on the part of the student. Such thought requires time. Probably the best way for a teacher/researcher to ensure adequate time is to conduct a pilot study using the planned tasks with a few students in the age group of interest. Ideally, the pilot study should include individuals with a variety of personality types and ability levels to give some understanding of the range of times that may be required. When scheduling the study interviews, it is also advisable to schedule some time between interviews to allow for the occasional interview that may run overtime.

Prompts, Follow-up Questions, and Interviewer Comments

Ideally, the prompts should allow for in-depth examination of the student's understanding of a carefully defined concept or limited set of concepts.

Therefore, the prompts should be focused, direct, and planned verbatim as much as possible before the interviews begin. Care must be exercised to ensure that the interviewer is always nonevaluative and that the interview does not become either an evaluation or a teaching session. Be careful to avoid leading the student in any way, either verbally or nonverbally. In general, no feedback about acceptability of the performance should be given during the interview. (Interviewers often find it difficult, for example, to avoid saying, "Good," "That's right," "Are you sure about that?")

Impromptu responses should be limited and as neutral as possible. Piaget's first concrete suggestion for the interview—his golden rule—is "to avoid suggestion, that is to say, to avoid dictating a particular answer among all the possible answers" (1929/1976, p. 13). This is particularly important for ensuring that the student's responses are what Piaget calls "liberated convictions" and not "suggested convictions." In the former, the child replies after reflection, drawing the answer from the stores of his own mind, without suggestion, although the question is new to him. ... It is an original product of the child's thought. ... The liberated conviction is, thus, strictly speaking neither spontaneous or suggested: It is the result of reasoning. (Piaget, 1929/1976, p. 11).

Avoiding suggestion is one of the most difficult aspects of interviewing. Piaget (1929/1976) points to two types of suggestions that are particularly dangerous, *verbal suggestion* and *suggestion by perseveration*. "[The former] is very difficult to describe in detail. The only means of avoiding it is to learn children's talk and to frame questions in this language. ... Suggestion due to preseveration is still harder to avoid, for the simple fact of continuing the conversation after the child's first answer tends to make him perserverate along the line he has already adopted" (p.15). Even asking for simple clarification (e.g., "How did you get that?") can be recognized as negative feedback if the interviewer asks such questions only when the student has made an error.

Indeed, Piaget maintains that it is so difficult not to be suggestive that his second cardinal rule is simply "not to talk too much" (Piaget, 1929/1976, p. 9). Complicating this process further, however, is a recognition of differing patterns of communication as described by Belenky, Clinchy, Goldberger, and Tarule (1986). This work suggests that it can also be important to take an active role in promoting communication with some students, magnifying the need to acknowledge that the interviewer is actually attending to what the student is saying. Comments such as "yes," "I hear you," or the more conversational "right" are often helpful for keeping the discussion flowing as long as the interviewer is clearly not also implying evaluation of the student's performance. Supporting this approach, both Piaget (1967) and Seidman (1991) imply that it is possible to be too silent as well, making the student unlikely to talk and eliminating the possibility of meaning checks. As described by Flynn (1978, p. 267), the interviewer must "'maintain a talk–time ratio' that facilitates information gathering."

Easley (1977) suggests that the teacher/researcher "must watch and try to understand what the pupil is doing and saying, and take the pupil's words and actions seriously, not just as mischievous or sloppy, though occasionally they may be that" (p. 26). Whenever necessary, the interviewer should probe the student as gently as possible as much as possible to insure that the teacher/researcher understands the student's meaning. (Use comments such as "What do you mean?" and "I don't think I understand what you're saying.") The art of interviewing seems to lie not only in knowing what to say and when to say it, but also in recognizing the relevant cues from the student's words, actions, and attitudes and the general context of the moment.

Above all, the interviewer must be cognitively engaged with the thought processes of the interviewee at all times, must be able to follow the mental logic the student uses to move from one step to another. While following the structured prompts, the interviewer must also be flexible enough to ask for clarification when she does not follow the student's logic. As soon as the interviewer recognizes that that she no longer understands a student's reasoning, the interview protocol should be put aside and clarifying questions asked, such as "What did you mean by that?" or "Help me understand why you sorted those two terms together." Such simple questions conducted sparingly during the interview allow the student an opportunity to further clarify her meaning and allow the teacher/researcher an opportunity to verify the emerging portrait of the student's understanding. The use of such participant verification adds face validity to the resulting description.

Pilot Studies

Perhaps the most important piece of advice we can offer about conducting successful structured interviews is to *conduct a pilot study* (or "dry run") during which the teacher/researcher finalizes all the task, props, prompts, and procedures to be used. The pilot study should include a small number of students similar in age, ethnicity, gender to the group eventually to be studied, and representing the range of differences among the target group.

In our work, we have found that students can see things in our prompts that we did not see, leading to interpretations and reasoning patterns in the students that we did not expect. Such events may not be learning events for the students, but they have definitely been so for us, emphasizing the need for a small pilot study before a large-scale assessment or research project. If these initially unexpected interpretations can be anticipated, they may allow the teacher/researcher to modify the graphics, problems, or other props so as to avoid the possibility of certain interpretations or to modify the protocol to address those interpretations more directly.

The pilot study provides answers to many important questions that will make the study interviews more productive. Are the problems too easy or too difficult for these subjects? How well do the prompts work? Do they need to be modified? Are other prompts needed? How much time should be scheduled for the interview? How should the recording device(s) be set up to maximize their value? Do I use enough wait time? Do I talk too much? Are my prompts brief and neutral? Do students feel comfortable in this setting?

Recognizing that structured interviews are usually somewhat loosely structured, some interviewers tend to omit a pilot study. In contrast, we have found pilots to be essential in predicting and correcting areas of potential difficulties, ensuring that the interview will go smoothly and generate worthwhile findings.

Potential for Formal Evaluation

Because structured interviews can provide for a wealth of information regarding a student's understanding, interviews would seem to be likely candidates for use in formal evaluation. However, there are several features of interviews that would make such uses problematic. The first of these are logistical in nature. Interviews are time-intensive processes, requiring a teacher/researcher to sample the population to be studied. We argue that careful sampling allows for a small number of interviews to provide an overall portrait of the various understandings that the students in a class might hold. But formal evaluation would require interviews with each student, which logistically the time constraints of normal classroom teaching would not allow.

The second argument against the use of structured interviews for formal evaluation centers on the strength of this technique. Structured interviews are useful, despite amount of time and labor they require, because they allow students to express what they know and how they can apply that knowledge in their own words in a relatively open format. Such interviews allow teacher/researchers to build thick descriptions of students' conceptual frameworks. We argue and other studies have demonstrated that such thick descriptions can be very useful in planning and refining instruction (Bishop & Anderson, 1990; Lewis & Linn, 1994). However, the use of structured interviews for formal evaluation would require that the teacher/researcher forgo the analysis of unexpected alternative conceptions and unanticipated applications in order to focus on assessing the degree to which the student understands/can apply a concept in scientific terms. This approach negates the very strength of structured interviews. Additionally, the novelty of such tasks would allow more articulate and less tentative students to outshine their peers, not because of more scientific understandings, but simply by virtue of particular personality traits. Thus, the validity of such a measure for formal evaluation must be questioned. We suggest that formal evaluations of individual students' conceptual frameworks could be better achieved through less complex and more focused measures, leaving structured interviews to be used as a means of assessment to inform instruction.

HOW TO MAKE SENSE OF INTERVIEW RESPONSES

Note-taking during an interview can be beneficial, but it generally provides only a superficial picture of a student's meaning. Because of the potential depth of information generated in an interview, it is usually better to record them, allowing for more intensive data analysis. Ideally, recording should include both audio and video tapes. The use of two taping methods provides a back up if one tape fouls; it also permits cross checking for unintelligible responses. Each form of recording has its own strengths. Transcription is much easier from an audio tape, because videotapes often have reduced audio quality. However, video recordings provide a wealth of nonverbal information, such as facial expressions and hand gestures. A procedure that we have found to be useful is to make the initial transcriptions from the audiotape and add important nonverbal information obtained from the video to the initial transcript. Transcriptions, although labor intensive, allow for detailed analysis of the interview that can provide invaluable insight into a student's understanding.

As with most classroom research activities, analysis of interview data may be accomplished in a variety of ways, some capturing a richer and more multilayered perspective than others. (For a more detailed discussion of data analysis refer to Miles & Huberman [1994].) We favor approaches wherein the teacher/researcher attempts to put her expectations aside to the extent possible, and instead reads the transcript with a fresh "eye," looking for important trends from the learner's responses to emerge. This approach is often referred to as *grounded theory*, in that hypotheses regarding the data are generated *as* (and not before) the data are reviewed (Glaser & Strauss, 1967). The grounded theory approach builds on a strength of the structured interview in that it allows a learner's unique perspective of the interview situation to inform data analysis. As trends are identified, the teacher/research reviews the data to indicate areas in which important trends are noted (a process known as *coding* the data). As transcripts are coded, more trends are accumulated. Ideally, a sample of interview transcripts should be reviewed several times, so that ideas emerging from one transcript can inform subsequent readings. As strong trends are noted throughout several interviews, the teacher/researcher should take care to look for *negative examples*, that is, occasions for which the tentative trend fails to hold true. This inductive approach to data analysis—looking for similarities and differences in sets of data—allows for a more informative and reliable portrait of learners to emerge.

ISSUES TO CONSIDER IN THE USE OF STRUCTURED INTERVIEWS

Mode Validity

Patton (1989) argues that the use of multiple sources of data is one of the intrinsic characteristics of trustworthy descriptive/qualitative research. White and Gunstone (1992) argue that reliance on only one research probe results in a very limited interpretation of the student's understanding: "Just as your house cannot be described completely by a single measure, nor can understanding. The more measures you take, the more complete the assessment" (p. 177). A research finding with a high *mode validity* is understood to be one that is achieved through the use of multiple modes of investigation and thus represents a richer and more faithful description of a learner's conceptions.

Different methods of data collection often provide different insights into a student's understandings. These insights should be complementary, but sometimes appear to be contradictory. For example, Demastes-Southerland (1994) found that students responded in contradictory manners when the results of concept maps, interviews about instances, and prediction interviews were compared. Thus, the context of the question changed the nature of the students' responses. Just as written responses have been found to be incomplete sources for capturing a teacher's conception of the nature of science (Lederman & O'Malley, 1990), structured interviews provide only an incomplete portrait of what a student knows. Often it is the accumulation of multiple observations obtained through different interview probes and the attempt to make sense of those data in a single, coherent description that results in the greatest insights.

There are signs that mode validity is becoming a common concern of individuals interested in science learning. Many of the current studies of learners' conceptions have employed two interview techniques, such as questioning along with concept maps (Beyerback & Smith, 1990); written explanations along with discussion of these explanations (Bishop & Anderson, 1990); or prediction interviews along with discussion of these explanations (Kargbo, Hobbs, & Erickson, 1980). The work by Songer and Mintzes (1994) is an excellent example of increasing the mode validity of research, with their inclusion of concept maps, structured interviews, as well as more traditional, quantitative testing instruments. Unfortunately, because of the intensive labor associated with descriptive/qualitative data collection and analysis, few studies within science education have been accomplished using multiple means of data collection. However, the use of both quantitative and qualitative data, or even the use of multiple interview probes allows for the generation of a much richer and more informative portrait of what a student knows.

Content Specificity

Researchers are also beginning to note the *extreme content specificity* of students' thinking. For instance, when dealing with biological knowledge, the type of organism included in an interview prompt has been shown to radically change the nature of a student's response. Through the use of individual interviews with 15- to 17-year-old students, Tamir and Zohar (1992) found that while 30% of the students described plants in anthropomorphic terms, fully 62% of the students understood animals in a similar manner. In this example, the type of organism seems to change the nature of a student's explanation of a biological phenomenon.

Another example of content specificity is seen most dramatically in research on the structure of biological knowledge: a knowledge framework that exhibits *multiple levels of causality*. One of the most important differences between the physical and life sciences is the distinction between proximate and ultimate causation. The need for distinguishing ultimate from proximate causes in biology emerges from the historical information encoded in genes (Mayr, 1988). Evolution, the unifying theory of biology, is what Mayr calls the ultimate cause of all biological phenomena (such as snowshoe hares changing color in winter). Proximate causes include the physiological or mechanistic basis of evolutionary change (such as differences in enzymatic reactions that allow for color changes in the hare). In our research we have found that students often do not recognize the influence of ultimate causation; sometimes they see ultimate and proximate causes as competing explanations (Cummins & Remsen, 1992). Most experiments and demonstrations in science classrooms expose students only to proximate causation. Consequently, students lack exposure to reasoning based on ultimate causation.

USING STRUCTURED INTERVIEWS TO INFORM TEACHING

Conducting structured interviews with a small sample of students in a class can be a useful way of gathering information about what students know about a topic as well as the degree to which they can apply that knowledge. As discussed in this chapter, such interviews require careful planning to select the appropriate probes and follow-up questions, a reasonable amount of time to schedule a discussion with individual students, as well as time to review the data. Despite these constraints of effort and time, structured interviews can provide invaluable insights into a learner's meaning. Because the teacher/researcher's interpretations are grounded in the learner's voice, we may more fully understand what a learner knows and how she can apply that knowledge. Such thick descriptions of several students' conceptual frameworks in a classroom are invaluable tools in planning classroom instruction.

There is ample evidence that much of the of the assessment used in the classroom has failed in helping many students achieve the level of understanding required for successful application of their knowledge. In the past, testing has focused on memorization rather than application and other forms of higher order thinking skills. Unfortunately, in teaching "what you test is what you get." In our view, the highest goal of science teaching should be for students to learn to apply their knowledge effectively in personal and professional settings. To accomplish this goal we must increasingly turn to assessments such as structured interviews that require the *use* of scientific knowledge.

References

Belenky, M., Clinchy, B., Goldberger, N., & Tarule, J. (1986). Women's ways of knowing: The development of self, voice, and mind. New York: Basic Books.

Beyerback, B. A., & Smith, J. M. (1990). Using a computerized concept mapping program to assess preservice teachers' thinking about effective teaching. Journal of Research in Science Teaching, 27, 961–971.

Bishop, B. A., & Anderson, C. W. (1990). Student conceptions of natural selection and its role in evolution. Journal of Research in Science Teaching, 27, 415–427.

Chi, M. T. H., Slotta, J. D., & de Leeuw, N. (1994). From things to processes: A theory of conceptual change for learning science concepts. Learning and Instruction, 4, 27–43.

Cummins, C. L., & Remsen, J. V. 1992. The importance of distinguishing ultimate from proximate causation in the teaching and learning of biology. In Skip Hills (Ed.), History and philosophy of science in science education: Proceedings of the second international conference for history and philosophy of science in science teaching, Vol. 1 (pp. 201–210). Kingston, Ontario, Canada: Mathematics, Science, Technology and Teacher Education Group and Faculty of Education, Queen's University.

Demastes-Southerland, S. (1994). Factors influencing conceptual change in evolution: A longitudinal, multicase study. Doctoral dissertation, Louisiana State University.

Demastes-Southerland, S., Good, R., & Peebles, P. (1996). Patterns of conceptual change in evolution. Journal of Research in Science Teaching, 33, 407–431.

Driver, R., & Easley, J. (1978). Pupils and paradigms: A review of literature related to concept development in adolescent students. Studies in Science Education, 5, 61–84.

Easley, J. (1977). On clinical studies in mathematics education. Eric Center for Science, Mathematics, and Environmental Education. (ERIC Document Reproduction Service No. ED 146 015).

Flynn, P. T. (1978). Effective clinical interviewing. Language, Speech, and Hearing Services in Schools, 9, 265–271.

Fredette, N., & Clement, J. (1981). Student misconcepts of an electric current: What do they mean? Journal of College Science Teaching, 10, 280–285.

Gallagher, J. J. (Ed.) (1991). Interpretive research in science education. NARST monograph, 4.

Glaser, B. G., & Strauss, A. L. (1967). The discovery of grounded theory: Strategies for qualitative research. Chicago: Aldine.

Kargbo, D. B., Hobbs, E. D., & Erickson, G. L. (1980). Children's beliefs about inherited characteristics. Journal of Biological Education, 14, 137–146.

Kindfield, A. C. H. (1994). Assessing understanding of biological processes: Elucidating students' models of meiosis. The American Biology Teacher, 56, 367–371.

Lederman, N. G., & O'Malley, M. (1990). Students' perceptions of tentativeness in science: Development, use, and sources of change. *Science Education, 74*, 224–239.

Lewis, E. L., & Linn, M. C. (1994). Heat energy and temperature concepts of adolescents, adults, and experts: Implications for curricular improvements. *Journal of Research in Science Teaching, 31*, 657–677.

Mayr, E. (1988). *Toward a new philosophy of biology: Observations of an evolutionist.* Cambridge, MA: Belknap Press of Harvard University Press.

Miles, M. B., & Huberman, A. M. (1994). *Qualitative data analysis.* Thousand Oaks, CA: Sage Publications.

Opper, S. (1977). Piaget's clinical method. *Journal of Children's Mathematical Behavior, 1*, 90–107.

Patton, M. Q. (1989). *Qualitative evaluation methods.* Beverly Hills, CA: Sage Publications.

Piaget, J. (1929/1976). *The child's conception of the world.* (J. Tomlinson, and A. Tomlison, Eds. and trans.) Totowa, NJ: Littlefield, Adams.

Piaget, J. (1967). Cognitions and conservations: Two views. *Contemporary Psychology, 12*, 530–533.

Rowe, M. B. (1974). Wait-time and rewards as instructional variables. *Journal of Research in Science Teaching, 11*, 81–94.

Seidman, I. E. (1991). *Interviewing as qualitative research.* New York: Teachers College Press.

Smith, E. L., Blakeslee, T. D., & Anderson, C. W. (1993). Teaching strategies associated with conceptual change learning in science. *Journal of Research in Science Teaching, 30*, 111–126.

Smith, M. U. (1983). A comparative analysis of the performance of experts and novices while solving selected classical genetics problems (Doctoral dissertation. The Florida State University) *Dissertation Abstracts International, 44*, 451A. (University Microfilms No. 8314200).

Smith, M. U. (1991). Teaching cell division: Student difficulties and teaching recommendations. *Journal of College Science Teaching, 21*, 28–33.

Smith, M. U. (1992). Expertise and the organization of knowledge: Unexpected differences among genetic counselors, faculty, and students on problem categorization tasks. *Journal of Research in Science Teaching, 29*, 179–205.

Smith, M. U., & Good, R. (1984). Problem solving and classical genetics: Successful versus unsuccessful performance. *Journal of Research in Science Teaching, 21*, 895–912.

Songer, C., & Mintzes, J. (1994). Understanding cellular respiration: An analysis of conceptual change in college biology. *Journal of Research in Science Teaching, 31*, 621–637.

Tamir, P., & Zohar, A. (1992). Anthropomorphism and teleology in reasoning about biological phenomena. *Journal of Biological Education, 25*, 57–67.

White, R., & Gunstone, R. (1992). *Probing understanding.* New York: The Falmer Press.

CHAPTER

5

Dialogue as Data: Assessing Students' Scientific Reasoning with Interactive Protocols

KATHLEEN HOGAN
Institute of Ecosystem Studies

JOELLEN FISHERKELLER
New York University

A major goal of education is to help students think effectively with the knowledge they have. In science classrooms, this goal becomes manifest by engaging students in scientific reasoning—the practice of thinking with and about scientific knowledge. We have achieved some consensus as a nation about the reasoning processes that science education should foster (American Association for the Advancement of Science, 1993; National Research Council, 1996), including the ability to modify prior ideas through deliberative reflection, integrate theory and data to build explanations, buttress conclusions with evidence, and confirm claims with logical arguments that distinguish warranted statements from conjectures.

Yet despite consensus on the importance of learning to reason, science classroom assessments typically fall short in this area. This is understandable. Although it is not hard to recognize good reasoning when we see it, it can be much more challenging to formally assess the processes than the products of thinking. This is the challenge that we tackle in the pages that follow.

Devising feasible ways to assess students' reasoning is important because what we assess sends messages to students about what we value.

If we want to promote good thinking and reasoning practices among students, then reasoning itself should be examined, shaped, and evaluated as an object of learning (Glaser, 1994). By emphasizing thinking and reasoning processes in assessments in science classrooms we also communicate messages about the nature of science. Science largely is a way of reasoning about phenomena, alone and within a larger community of peers. Yet students tend to think of science more as a set of facts than as a dynamic process of knowledge building (Lederman, 1992). Broadening our focus of assessment can in turn help to broaden students' conceptualizations of the practices of science.

The techniques for assessing students' scientific reasoning described in this chapter complement the information on assessing students' cognitive structures presented within other chapters of this book (e.g., Southerland, Smith, & Cummins). We look especially at what can be learned about students' scientific reasoning by analyzing their verbal interactions. But before delving into specific assessment techniques, we provide some background on scientific reasoning and on the use of interactive protocols as data.

THE KNOWLEDGE AND REASONING CONNECTION

Knowledge and thinking are inextricably linked. A well-structured knowledge base can sustain higher levels of reasoning than poorly structured knowledge (Novak & Gowin, 1984). Likewise, engaging in reasoning processes, such as seeking information to support claims, can multiply and strengthen connections within a person's cognitive framework of ideas. Thus, we use knowledge to reason, and we reason to construct knowledge.

Some researchers emphasize that it is knowledge itself, not reasoning abilities, that distinguishes expert and novice scientific thinkers (Brewer & Samarapungavan, 1991). Although there certainly are important knowledge-based differences that distinguish these two groups, this does not help to explain the differences in thinking and learning among novice science students who have equally underdeveloped knowledge about a topic. For instance, some learners are better able than others to overcome their naive beliefs to integrate new information and build more comprehensive understandings of phenomena. Those learners may in fact have stronger reasoning skills, metacognitive abilities, and dispositions to engage in effortful cognition, rather than possessing more prior knowledge or higher basic cognitive capacities (Klaczynski, Gordon, & Fauth 1997; Kuhn & Pearsall, 1998; Stanovich & West, 1997).

Imagine, for instance, two eighth-grade science students, Michele and Micah. They have a similar level of understanding about the potential impacts of exotic species on ecosystem processes following an ecology unit in which they did field work and modeled ecosystem perturbations using software tools. But when completing an assessment task that asked them to evaluate the validity of different conclusions that 10 hypothetical students might draw from a set of observations of a marsh where the exotic plant purple loosestrife had begun to dominate, Michele and Micah performed quite differently. Michele failed to recognize when conclusions went beyond the data, so long as the conclusions were consistent with her own beliefs about the impact of exotics on native plant communities. Micah, however, was able to identify why such conclusions were weak, and articulate why other conclusions were stronger, such as those that took seemingly contradictory evidence into account.

Because reasoning such as that which Micah demonstrated requires examining one's own thinking and comparing it to standards of rationality, it is inherently metacognitive (Moshman, 1998). So although we cannot ignore the role of a well-integrated knowledge structure in enabling thinking, we also must attend to the habits and skills that enable students to use their knowledge mindfully. We should become aware of when students' thinking is strong even when their ideas are not fully developed, as well as when their ideas are correct, yet their inferencing processes weak. Assessing reasoning skills in these ways can provide the basis for instruction that helps students become better learners and thinkers.

Although we can shift the focus of an assessment lens to place cognitive structure or reasoning processes in the foreground, both must be in the final picture if we are to understand how students learn and perform in science. This chapter contributes to a complete picture for science assessment in part by suggesting how judging the soundness of students' ideas can be integral to judging the quality of their reasoning.

BROADENING CONCEPTUALIZATIONS OF SCIENTIFIC REASONING

Students use reasoning processes whenever they work to make sense of things while learning. Reasoning can occur in science classes while students listen to a lecture, read a text, do labs, run computer simulations, search library or Internet sources, participate in debates, do applied projects, prepare and give public exhibitions of their work, and so on. In its broadest sense, reasoning is the process of figuring things out (Paul, 1995).

Although science classrooms present many opportunities for developing and assessing students' reasoning skills, scientific reasoning most often is equated with the thinking processes that occur during scientific inquiry. Typically scientists pursue inquiry and employ associated reasoning processes to explain and predict natural phenomena. There are diverse traditions of inquiry within different scientific disciplines (Loving, 1997), but the inquiry process generally includes the following phases of activity:

Form questions and hypotheses—make observations and use prior research and theories to generate productive questions; develop hypotheses

Design investigations and generate data—operationally define and control variables; choose appropriate methods; run experiments or investigations and collect data

Interpret data and integrate information—manage and analyze data; discern patterns and draw inferences; relate results back to a hypothesis or theoretical framework to build explanations, make new predictions, and form generalizations

Build and communicate arguments—persuade a community of peers of the validity and significance of scientific findings; use critical response skills to judge, evaluate, and defend knowledge claims

Most research on the development of reasoning skills has focused on logical hypothetico-deductive and inductive causal reasoning skills that are used when forming hypotheses, designing experiments, controlling variables, making inferences, and integrating theory and data (e.g., Dunbar, 1993; Klahr & Dunbar, 1988; Koslowski, 1996; Kuhn, Amsel, & O'Loughlin, 1988; Kuhn, Garcia-Mila, Zohar, & Andersen, 1995; Lawson, 1993; Schauble, 1996). Many of these studies have roots either in classic information-processing models (for a review see Mayer [1996]), or Piagetian theory (Inhelder & Piaget, 1958), which attributes skilled reasoning to the development of content-independent logical operations that allow people to mentally manipulate abstract representations of the concrete world. However, most of the researchers cited above have expanded these theoretical frameworks in a Human Constructivist (Mintzes, Wandersee, & Novak, 1998) direction by considering the interplay of students' conceptual structures and reasoning operations.

In addition to expanding studies on scientific reasoning by recognizing the interplay of knowledge and reasoning, another possible expansion could come from recognizing that not all of the thinking practices by which scientists make progress conform to rules of logic. For instance, scientists may employ confirmatory biases (i.e., seeking information that supports a hypothesis or premise while ignoring contradictory evidence) when their hypotheses are new and fragile, delaying disconfirmation until they have established some corroboration for fledgling hypotheses (Tweney & Chitwood, 1995). Also, the types of manipulative experiments used in the vast majority of studies of children's scientific reasoning do not represent the range of practices used in scientific disciplines in which techniques such as modeling, long-term monitoring, and historical analysis are more useful approaches to answering the discipline's central questions.

It seems wise then, to broaden our conceptualization of scientific reasoning beyond logical, rule-based procedures such as isolating variables. Although such thinking processes certainly are an important part of scientists' reasoning repertoire, there are limits to what can be learned about how students reason while doing science when reasoning is studied only in narrow task contexts.

One way in which researchers have broadened the investigation of students' scientific reasoning practices is to focus on how students build explanations, arguments, and models from their own data within classroom contexts (e.g., Kelly, Druker, & Chen, 1998; Palincsar, Anderson, & David, 1993; Reddy, Jacobs, McCrohon, & Herrenkohl, 1998). Tracking students' knowledge-building interactions over time within a community of inquiry yields insights into how students reason within a setting that is more similar to scientists' real-world social intellectual contexts than logic problems.

Many researchers who situate studies of students' scientific reasoning within the social context of classrooms employ an interpretive framework that integrates sociocultural and constructivist theory (Driver, Asoko, Leach, Mortimer, & Scott, 1994; Hatano, 1993; O'Loughlin, 1992). Whereas Piagetians have viewed social interaction primarily as a stimulus for internal constructive activity (Mugny & Doise, 1978), social constructivists view scientific thinking and reasoning much as scholars of the history and philosophy of science do (e.g., Kuhn, 1962)—as a practice that is intricately enmeshed in social, cultural, and historical contexts. Recent models of cognition (e.g., Mayer, 1996; Pintrich, Marx, & Boyle, 1993) portray the influence of these external contexts on thinking and reasoning, and also expand representations of internal cognitive contexts to include elements such as epistemological and motivational beliefs.

All of this empirical and theoretical activity presents compelling reasons to expand existing notions of scientific reasoning, and thereby its assessment. Even when assessing students' reasoning only while they are engaged in the phases of scientific inquiry, there is much to analyze in addition to their logical thinking processes. The following list defines six modes of reasoning that can be examined as elements of students' scientific thinking practices, when they are reasoning alone and with others (adapted from Halpern, 1996; Marzano et al., 1988; Moshman, 1998; Paul, 1995; Stiggins, 1997):

Analytical reasoning—To examine the parts of a whole and how they function together, including analysis of the components of one's own reasoning such as one's assumptions, claims, and interpretations.

Analogical reasoning—To discern similarities between two or more things (and by default recognize their differences), often to understand or illuminate significant features of a novel situation, idea, or problem by comparison with a more familiar case.

Dialogical reasoning—To consider different points of view or think within multiple frames of reference. A subset of dialogical reasoning is dialectical reasoning in which the strengths and weaknesses of opposing points of view are tested.

Inferential reasoning—To link two conditions to conclude that something is so because of something else. There are two types of inferential thinking: Inductive thinking is drawing conclusions and generalizations from specific instances or evidence. Deductive thinking is applying a general principle or premises to form conclusions or interpret instances.

Evaluative reasoning—To judge the worth or quality of something, such as an idea, proposition or knowledge claim, according to some external criteria.

Integrative reasoning—To bring together different pieces of information or sources of knowledge into a unified whole.

Table 1 presents a matrix of these six types of reasoning and the four general stages of scientific inquiry described earlier. Although some types of reasoning may be more central during some stages of inquiry than others (e.g., inferential reasoning during data interpretation; dialogical reasoning during argumentation), the questions in each cell illustrate how each of the types of reasoning can come into play during all stages of scientific inquiry.

USING VERBAL INTERACTIONS TO ASSESS SCIENTIFIC REASONING

A traditional method of assessing covert cognitive processes such as those used during problem solving and reasoning employs "think-aloud protocols." These protocols typically are derived from clinical situations in which the researcher minimizes interaction with the research participant (Ericsson & Simon, 1984). The researcher acts as a monitor whose only actions are to remind the subjects to keep verbalizing their thoughts as they solve the problem, rather than to prompt responses to substantive questions. The research subjects are not asked to describe, explain, justify, rationalize, or elaborate on what they are doing, but are expected simply to verbalize the information they are attending to while generating a solution. Analyzing the resulting protocol is a deductive process of comparing the sequence of problem-solving steps the person used to a previously determined analysis of the ideal solution path (Chi, 1997).

In contrast, we use the term "interactive protocols" to describe data derived from situations in which an interviewer actively probes or participates in thinking with an interviewee, or in which there is a natural dialogue between two or more people whose thinking is being assessed. Whereas think-aloud protocols capture verbalizations of thinking processes that normally would not be expressed aloud, interactive protocols are the result of intentional and purposeful communication. Therefore, interactive protocols are records of communicative events, rather than reports of private sense-making.

Verbal data gathered in interactive settings can provide a useful but undertapped source of information about students' reasoning as they do science. Scientific reasoning fundamentally is a dialogic process, whether undertaken independently or with others. Reasoning aloud with others simply brings the dialogic out into the open.

TABLE I

Questions Illustrating How a Scientist Could Use Six Types of Reasoning in Each Stage of Scientific Inquiry

Stages of inquiry	Types of reasoning					
	Analytical	Analogical	Dialogical	Inferential	Evaluative	Integrative
Form questions and hypotheses	• How can I break down this topic or phenomenon of interest into several discrete or inter-related questions?	• What questions have been asked about similar phenomena, and what ideas do they provide for questions that I might ask?	• What are all of the alternative hypotheses that I should consider?	• Given what already is known about this topic, can I infer that others will consider my questions to be important?	• Is the question significant, researchable, and interesting?	• What questions emerge when I combine my own observations with what is written about this topic in the literature?
Design investigations and generate data	• What steps should I take to address my question fully?	• Since the problems I face in my research are a lot like the problems that scholars in another discipline face, could I adapt their methods to my own situation?	• What are the strengths and weaknesses of the research methods I'm considering using?	• Since most researchers use this method to tackle questions similar to mine, can I infer that the methodology must be appropriate and effective?	• Are these methods appropriate and rigorous enough for generating the kinds of data that I'll need to answer my question?	• Could I combine a variety of data gathering techniques to strengthen my research?
Interpret data and integrate information	• Does this finding make sense in relation to that finding?	• What techniques have other researchers used to analyze data sets similar to mine?	• Is there more than one way to interpret these data?	• What can I conclude about the workings of the phenomenon I studied given my set of results?	• Are the results conclusive or ambiguous?	• How do the findings fit within or expand my theoretical framework?
Build and communicate arguments	• What are all of the points I want to make in my argument?	• What similar case could I compare to my work to make my points more clear or to highlight important attributes for my audience?	• What counter-arguments are others likely to make, and how can I take them into consideration?	• Can I infer from the principles of argumentation that I should use more evidence than assumptions to build a strong case for my conclusions?	• Do my conclusions follow logically from my premises?	• Are there findings from other studies that I can use to corroborate my findings?

Although reasoning spontaneously in verbal interchange certainly is an important dimension of scientists' work, ultimately it is through painstakingly deliberative reasoning communicated in writing that scientists make contributions to their discipline. So does it make sense to focus on assessing the interactive form of reasoning in science classrooms? We think that it does, for several reasons. One is that verbal data can reveal the dynamic nature of reasoning in ways that the end products of reasoning cannot. Would we not come to understand scientific reasoning better, for instance, by witnessing the reasoning processes that scientists engage in while producing a written argument for their findings? Another reason that gathering verbal data is valuable for assessment purposes is that many students are unable to translate their reasoning into written form. Their thinking may be more sophisticated than their writing abilities, which would be the case with the first and second graders who have been shown to engage in amazingly complex verbal argumentation about their science studies (Gallas, 1995; Reddy, 1995). Additionally, thinking is optimized in richly contextualized, motivating events (Bronfenbrenner & Ceci, 1994), which social/intellectual exchange can create. Students can more completely display their abilities when engaging with the thoughts and reactions of reasoning partners. So although verbal exchange should not be the only source of evidence for making judgments about students' scientific reasoning, it can yield information that other means of assessment cannot.

STEPS FOR ASSESSING REASONING THROUGH VERBAL INTERACTIONS IN CLASSROOM AND INTERVIEW CONTEXTS

Talk abounds in science classrooms, but teachers cannot directly siphon it into a grade book, nor can researchers simply recount the dialogues they record. Both practitioners and researchers need to use disciplined procedures to formally assess students' scientific reasoning. The following seven steps provide guidelines for a procedure for assessing the reasoning that students exhibit through verbal interactions in science classroom and interview contexts.

Step 1. Determine a Purpose and Approach

We describe three approaches to studying scientific reasoning: microgenetic, diagnostic (formative and summative), and transactive. Each reflects different research and evaluation purposes.

Microgenetic Approach

The main purpose of microgenetic research is to gain insight into the mechanisms that cause cognitive growth and development. Researchers begin by presenting people with a challenge, such as by asking fourth graders to determine what variables affect the speed of a model boat (Kuhn et al., 1995). They then observe how a person's strategies change from the time they first tackle a problem, through repeated trials, until they reach a stable state in their problem-solving approach. Microgenetic researchers make numerous observations over multiple sessions that occur over several weeks or months, and then infer the processes that led to changes in how each person approached the task (Siegler & Crowley, 1991). The microgenetic approach allows researchers to get beyond the limited information available from pre- and post-testing of learning to understand exactly how growth in cognition occurs.

Since cognitive competencies, including reasoning abilities, are dynamic attributes, a "movie" rather than a "snapshot" of reasoning provides a more accurate portrayal of students' capabilities. Also, developing a fine-grained understanding of how a range of students reason can yield essential information for helping students who do not reason well, and for tailoring learning experiences to other types of individual differences. However, microgenetic research requires labor-intensive methods that are more feasible for researchers than for practitioners to carry out.

Diagnostic Approach

The diagnostic approach is taken when the goal is to determine the level of reasoning that a student is capable of demonstrating at a given point in time. Diagnostic assessment can be either formative or summative. Formative diagnoses occur, for instance, during a classroom activity when teachers take note of the gaps in students' understanding, reasoning, or other skills, and then plan subsequent instruction to address the gaps. Teachers constantly use such informal diagnostic processes as they teach. Summative diagnoses are made when classroom teachers want to know how students' thinking has or has not changed after a period of instruction. A researcher who conducts interviews to determine patterns in the reasoning of students in different age groups as they work on a given task also is carrying out a form of summative diagnosis.

Transactive Approach

The purpose of transactive assessment is to determine a student's potential level of performance. Unlike in microgenetic or diagnostic approaches, a teacher or researcher intentionally tries to move a student's thinking along. Once assessors interact with a student to gather information about how he or she is thinking, they provide hints, suggestions, and other types of supports to see if the child can perform at a higher level than he or she achieved alone. Central to this technique is the notion of the zone of proximal development (Vygotsky, 1978), which is the range of performance between what a child is capable of achieving alone, and what he or she can do with support from a more skilled or knowledgeable partner. This type of assessment is embedded within an instructional technique known as scaffolding (Forman, Minick, & Stone, 1993; Hogan & Pressley, 1997a; Palincsar, 1986; Wood, Bruner, & Ross, 1976) in which a teacher or parent provides just enough assistance to enable learners to continue to make progress on their own.

An evaluation technique called dynamic assessment embodies the transactive approach (e.g., Day, Engelhardt, Maxwell, & Bolig, 1997; Feuerstein, Rand, Jensen, Kaniel, & Tzuriel, 1987; Lidz; 1987; Magnusson, Templin, & Boyle, 1997). Dynamic assessment provides information about a child's potential for learning, rather than solely about the knowledge and skills he or she already has acquired, by providing support for the child to form new conceptual connections or develop skills while doing an assessment task. Researchers are recognizing that even when unintended, most interview interactions are as much learning events as they are assessment events (Ackerman, 1995; Ginsburg, 1997; Mishler, 1986; Smagorinsky, 1995; Welzel & Roth, 1998).

Using dynamic assessment to make direct measurements of a child's ability to benefit from instruction is important given that two learners might achieve the same outcome on an assessment, yet differ in the strategic strength, speed, or efficiency with which they learn (Day et al., 1997). In the realm of reasoning, dynamic assessment can reveal, for instance, if students are able to strengthen their arguments when a researcher or teacher hints at potential weaknesses or suggests new information for the student to consider.

Step 2. Establish and Communicate Standards
for Reasoning

Generating proficiency standards for reasoning is particularly crucial in classroom settings because it makes students aware of the teacher's criteria and expectations for reasoning. Students often are unaware of exactly what teachers value, so standards help to make learning goals explicit. For instance, it can be a new notion to students that thinking and reasoning well with others in science class are important skills to develop. Standards also can become metacognitive tools for students to use to evaluate their own performance, perhaps at first while they reflect on a reasoning event, and then eventually in a self-regulatory manner while reasoning. Ideally, students should help to determine the assessment criteria for reasoning so that they can develop a personal understanding of and investment in the standards.

It is equally important for researchers to have a framework for reasoning in mind before designing tasks, choosing classroom events to observe, or developing analysis tools. General standards for reasoning differ from task-specific rubrics (see step 6), even though a rubric also communicates standards. Standards are applicable across tasks as a general framework that distinguishes effective from ineffective reasoning.

Fictional portraits of good and poor reasoners, such as the vignettes of Michele and Micah presented earlier, potentially are an effective means of communicating reasoning standards to younger students. For older students, a list that contrasts elements of good and poor reasoning is an effective way to present standards. Using a list of intellectual standards such as is provided in Table 2, students could generate specific examples for each dimension of high- and low-quality reasoning in science.

In addition to assessing the products and processes of reasoning, teachers, researchers, and students can assess reasoning dispositions (Ennis, 1987; Perkins, Jay, & Tishman, 1993). General standards for three important dispositions that underpin scientific reasoning—respect for evidence, open-mindedness, and reflection—are presented in Table 3 (from Hogan, 1994).

Once standards for reasoning are established, students need to gain experience using them before their reasoning practices are formally assessed. Although describing educational opportunities and instructional techniques that help students develop scientific reasoning skills is beyond the scope of this chapter, some assessment activities also can serve as learning events, as noted earlier.

Step 3. Choose Interactive Settings for Assessment

Both classrooms and interviews are social settings in which the fluid nature of students' reasoning becomes manifest in dialogue. The following sections describe a variety of interactive configurations within classroom and interview settings that can be used to assess students' reasoning.

TABLE 2
Intellectual Standards for Reasoning

High-quality Reasoning Is	Low-quality Reasoning Is
Clear	Unclear
Precise	Imprecise
Specific	Vague
Accurate	Inaccurate
Relevant	Irrelevant
Plausible	Implausible
Consistent	Inconsistent
Logical	Illogical
Deep	Superficial
Broad	Narrow
Complete	Incomplete
Significant	Trivial
Adequate (for purpose)	Inadequate
Fair	Biased or one-sided

Source. Adapted with permission from Paul, R. (1995). *Critical thinking: How to prepare students for a rapidly changing world* (p. 63). Santa Rosa, CA: Center for Critical Thinking.

TABLE 3
Standards for Assessing Three Reasoning Dispositions

Respect for evidence
- Generates accurate and reliable evidence by watching patiently, measuring carefully, and revising or repeating procedures
- Presents evidence in an honest, unbiased, objective fashion, even when it contradicts expectations
- Recognizes how prior ideas and perspectives can influence interpretation of evidence
- Uses evidence to make appropriate claims and build arguments
- Suspends judgments and conclusions until sufficient and convincing evidence is acquired
- Carefully evaluates the evidence behind claims and the credibility of sources
- Shows appropriate and productive skepticism for claims that don't make sense

Open-mindedness
- Considers multiple possibilities and approaches
- Seeks out different points of view
- Can reason from alternative perspectives
- Reconsiders own ideas in light of input from others
- Uses input to improve work
- Shifts gears when a strategy isn't working

Reflection
- Monitors own thinking and progress toward goals
- Uses personal standards for evaluating success and effectiveness of own actions
- Identifies own strengths, limitations, and ways to improve
- Can provide and explain evidence of growth
- Evaluates the ideas of others to give useful feedback

1. Verbal Interactions in Classroom Settings

The regular course of events in inquiry-based science classrooms provide abundant opportunities for assessing students' reasoning. Researchers and teachers can choose from among the following options depending on the nature of their research or assessment question.

A. Whole class discussions moderated by a teacher

Teachers orchestrate class discussions during all stages of inquiry, from developing questions to building arguments, in order to induct students into modes of scientific discourse, assess their level of understanding, and help them learn from one another. A number of researchers (e.g., Duschl & Gitomer, 1997; Hogan & Pressley, 1997b; Reddy, 1995; van Zee & Minstrel, 1997; Varelas, 1996) and classroom teachers (e.g., Gallas, 1995; Simpson, 1997) have described how class discussions yield information about the thinking and reasoning of students from kindergarten through high school levels.

B. Teacher dialogue with small groups

Samples of student/teacher dialogue can be gathered as teachers check in with student groups who are working on a task. Since teachers often challenge or assist students when they visit groups, this setting provides opportunities to see how students' reasoning changes as a result of teacher input.

C. Peer dialogue

Working with peers on tasks during science class automatically presents a social demand and necessity for students to reason aloud. As long as students are working on a task that requires them to reason, small groups can be a productive setting for gathering verbal data for assessment purposes.

D. On-line computer network discussions

Students can interact through written as well as spoken dialogue. Their written interchange is especially dynamic when done via

---

A Sample Class Discussion That Probes Students' Reasoning

In the following excerpt from a class discussion in a middle school physical science classroom, the class was reflecting on the results of a lab activity. As part of a unit on matter and molecules, the students participated in a demonstration that gas has mass. They arranged plastic bags into which straws were inserted around the edges of a lab table. They then placed another lab table face down on top of the bags. Several students blew into the straws, and the expanding plastic bags lifted the top table. This excerpt begins after students had recounted their observations of what happened as they blew into the bags.

Eliza: If someone sat on top of it (the table) and it was really really heavy and like there wasn't enough room, then how could the air get in? If it was like really heavy?

Teacher: That's a good question. Just a minute. Eliza, will you repeat your question again?

Eliza: If like it was really heavy, how would the air get into the bag?

Teacher: So you're saying you think if this is really heavy then you would probably not be able to inflate the bag, is that right?

Eliza: Yeah, because the air couldn't get in.

Teacher: Do you think there's a point at which that would occur? Now obviously here it didn't. Here we were able to lift up, but do you think there's a point at which you would not be able to lift it up?

Eliza: I don't know (she giggles as other students' hands go up). Umm, probably.

Teacher: Let's look into it; in fact, let's move right into the next question I was going to have which is to explain, to get into the explanations. Eliza is saying that she thinks if there's too much weight you would not be able to lift it. But what does cause it to rise, 'cause that's what I asked you to do, to explain why you think whatever happened happened. So Eliza is saying that she thinks after a while it wouldn't be able to rise. But

continued

what causes it to rise? Why did that table lift up, when we were up here and all of you blew into the bags, what caused the table to rise, this table isn't all that light. What caused the table to rise? (She pauses, and more hands gradually go up.) Anthony?

Anthony: Because when we blew into the bags the air had to have someplace to go, so the bags pushed up on the table, but I think if it was a lot heavier you wouldn't be strong enough to blow into the bag because the bags would be too crushed.

Teacher: Okay, so you're saying that the air, the exhaled air that's blowing into it is pushing up, but air, it's like this stuff right here (she waves her hand around), but how can this stuff be able to cause this to lift that table? What's happening?

Anthony: The air pressure inside, it has to have someplace to go.

Teacher: When you say air pressure, what do you mean by that, air pressure? What does the term air pressure mean? I just need to know what you mean.

Anthony: Like the pressure of the air, like when you have air inside a basketball it's trying to get out because if you put too much air in it will pop because of the air pressure—it's too much air in one little space and it can't all fit in there.

Teacher: So you're saying…

Anthony: …like if you put too much water in a water balloon it will pop, it's the same thing with air.

Teacher: So the air is in the bags? But could you see the air in here?

Anthony: Well, you could see the bag fill up, but I guess, can you see the air all around you, is that what you mean?

Teacher: I guess I'm having a hard time thinking about the air, like with water I can see that, but with air here, this is just filled up with air. (The bell rings.) Wait one second before you go, don't leave yet. What I've done with Anthony is what I'm going to do with all of you for the rest of this unit is question, question, question. After I get done questioning I'll question some more.

In this discussion, the teacher prompted students to think by continually asking them to clarify, explain, and elaborate on their ideas. She did not close off their thinking by evaluating their contributions. During exploratory dialogue such as this, students display not only what they think, but also how they reason. For instance, Anthony offered a reason for his assertion that it would not be possible to lift a heavier table by blowing into bags "because the bags would be too crushed." He also reasoned analogically by relating the inflated plastic bags to a basketball and a water balloon. He also sought clarity by asking the teacher in his final turn if she was talking about the air inside the bag or "the air all around you." A teacher or a researcher, then, could use this dialogue that occurred in a whole class setting as one indicator of a student's reasoning practices.

computer. Several educational research/development projects (e.g., Scardamalia, Bereiter, & Lamon, 1994; Vye et al., 1998) link students within and across classrooms to create knowledge-building communities. When students provide a rationale for their claims or critique another student's conclusions on-line, they leave tangible evidence of their interactive reasoning in a computer data base, which then is readily available for analysis for assessment or research purposes.

2. Verbal Interactions in Interview Settings

We suggest that interview transcripts be regarded as interactive protocols in which a student's responses are interpreted in light of the verbalizations of the interviewer.

A. Solo interviews

One-to-one interactions are the most typical clinical interview setting for assessing students' understanding, thinking, and reasoning. Two advantages of solo interviews are that they allow a researcher to be responsive to one child, and they narrow down the variables that need to be considered when interpreting the child's responses. Although some teachers find time for 5- to 10-minute interviews with individual children while others in the class work on self-guided tasks, it is time-consuming to interview all of the children in a class in this way, so it is not something that teachers can do very often. Another potential disadvantage of solo interviews is that not all children are comfortable or forthcoming in a one-to-one interview situation with an adult.

B. Group interviews

Holding small-group interviews with two or more students is a more practical way for teachers to interview all students in a class. Another advantage is that some students might be more talkative and spontaneous when responding to peers than when talking just with an adult. But the disadvantage of a group interview is that adding peers requires taking more contextual variables into consideration when analyzing the results. The unit of analysis becomes the individual-in-a-group, or simply the group itself. If a teacher wants to use an interview as a summative assessment, then it becomes more difficult to assign individual students a grade when they are interviewed within a group than when they are interviewed alone.

Given that different classroom and interview settings provide different kinds of opportunities for students to display their reasoning, a well-rounded assessment or research approach would be to gather samples from several settings within a given time period. This is perhaps more feasible for teachers than for researchers to do since they see their students every day. But collecting data in multiple settings also is worth the effort for researchers because it provides triangulation (Lincoln & Guba, 1985) to strengthen research claims.

Step 4. Choose Tasks for Eliciting
and Assessing Reasoning

Some of the most valuable assessment activities are those that provide students with opportunities to exercise important competencies while doing them (Wiggins, 1993). Good assessment tasks are distinguishable from good learning tasks only because students' performance on them is measured in some explicit way. Such tasks provide ideal contexts for assessing students' reasoning through verbal interactions since they are likely to engage students and motivate them to perform to capacity.

The five examples provided below illustrate a variety of learning activities that could serve as authentic assessments of students' reasoning if data were gathered and analyzed while students participated in them. The examples are drawn from an ecology unit called "Who Eats What?" within a curriculum for the upper elementary and middle grades called *Eco-Inquiry* (Hogan, 1994). Over the course of 4–6 weeks, students investigate the feeding interactions on their schoolyard or a nearby piece of property, do supplementary investigations, construct and work with food webs, and do a variety of applied activities, such as creating interpretive signs to teach others about animals' food resources. The following examples describe some of the unit's activities that occur at various stages of inquiry, suggest an interactive setting that teachers or researchers could use to gather data, and outline some types of reasoning that could be assessed.

Example 1: "A Landowner's Request"

Phase of Inquiry: Forming Questions and Hypotheses
Task: Generate and Refine Focus Questions
Students receive a request from a landowner to investigate the animals and their food resources on a piece of property. They decide together on the questions they will try to answer.
Setting: Class Discussion
The teacher prompts the students to consider what exactly they will study with questions such as What do we already know about the study site? What could we find out by doing observations? What might be difficult to figure out on our own? What would be important to try to figure out? Why?
Reasoning to Assess:
Dialogical—Do students consider their own interests along with what information might be useful for a variety of audiences, such as naturalists, landowners, and resource managers?
Evaluative—Can students determine which questions are more feasible to address or more important than other questions?

Example 2: "Learning More about Animal Feeding Habits"

Phase of Inquiry: Designing Investigations and Generating Data

Task: Planning Feeding Investigations

Once students do an initial survey of the property to look for animals, animal signs, evidence of feeding interactions, and potential food resources, they plan indoor and outdoor investigations to learn more about animals' feeding habits and relationships.

Setting: Teacher Interacting with Peer Groups

The teacher circulates around the classroom to interact with each group of students as they plan their investigations. For instance, one group might be planning to test which species of leaf earthworms prefer to eat. The teacher asks questions such as How will you know which leaf they prefer? How can you make sure your test is fair?

Reasoning to Assess:

Analytical—Can students break down a problem into logical steps for generating valid data?

Analogical—Can students draw analogies between situations they know a lot about and those that are less familiar to help them devise investigations, such as between how they would determine what a human family eats and what wildlife eats (e.g., look at what is in cupboards/stashes of food; find leftovers/partially eaten plant material; observe grocery shopping/foraging activities)?

Example 3: "Who Eats What?"

Phase of Inquiry: Interpreting Data and Integrating Information

Task: Making Food Webs

Students use their field observations, investigation results, and other sources of information to make food web diagrams that show who eats what on their study site.

Setting: Peer Groups

As students work together to construct food webs, their communications with one another reveal their reasoning processes, such as how they interpret physical evidence and how they apply prior knowledge to their analysis task.

Reasoning to Assess:

Inferential/Inductive Reasoning—Can students induce which animal might eat what based on the type and location of certain signs (e.g., a pile of pine cone bracts; holes in leaves on a treetop branch)?

Integrative Reasoning—Can students combine evidence based on observations with evidence from other sources, such as field guides?

Example 4: "Reverberations in a Food Web"

Phase of Inquiry: Building and Communicating Arguments
Task: Figuring out how single changes can affect an entire food web
Students are presented with a scenario in which their study site is altered in some way, such as by a landscaping crew taking away all of the leaf litter and dead branches. They then trace how the changes could reverberate through their entire food web.
Setting: Group Interview
Three or four students from different groups are brought together for an interview. They are asked to present their groups' food web analyses to one another, and resolve any discrepancies between the analyses.
Reasoning to Assess:
Analytical Reasoning—Can students identify the assumptions behind their peers' conclusions?
Dialogical/Dialectical Reasoning—Can students point out the strength and weaknesses of their own and their peers' inferences?

Example 5: "Thinking about What We Learned"

Phase of Inquiry: Reflecting on Reasoning
Task: Stimulated Recall
During a stimulated recall task, students look at a record of a learning event, which they then interpret or evaluate. For instance, students could watch a videotape of a small group interview or peer discussion in which they participated. This is a good method for assessing students' metacognitive knowledge about reasoning. Researchers also can use stimulated recall for member checking (Lincoln & Guba, 1985) to note the similarities and discrepancies between how the participant and the researcher interpret a learning event.
Setting: Solo Interview
Showing individual students a videotape of their group as the basis for an interview probably is more feasible for a researcher than for a teacher to do, since it should be done in a private setting where playing the tape will not disturb others students, and where the interviewee will feel free to share his or her thoughts.
Reasoning to Assess:
Analytical Reasoning—Can students identify the components of their own reasoning?
Evaluative—Can students judge how well their own and others' reasoning meet a set of standards?

Step 5. Collect Data

There are two main approaches to gathering data on the reasoning students demonstrate through verbal exchange. The first is to make judgments immediately on a checklist or rating scale while students are talking, and the second is to record their verbalizations for later analysis.

1. Checklists and Observational Rating Scales

   Checklists and observational ratings scales for assessing students' reasoning are prewritten lists of the types of reasoning or sets of reasoning skills that students are expected to demonstrate during an assessment task. They are filled out while students are being assessed, or shortly thereafter, based simply on the researcher's or teacher's observations of students' performance. Whereas a checklist provides an opportunity just to note the presence or absence of a reasoning skill, a rating scale delineates various levels of performance of the skill. Since judgments are made on the spot, these methods are the least time-consuming way to assess students' reasoning, and so are especially practical for teachers to use. Students also can complete checklists to give feedback to peers by taking turns participating in and observing a group reasoning task.

   One disadvantage of using checklists and observational rating scales is that they leave no record of the students' actual performance. This makes it difficult for teachers and researchers to go back to reconsider a judgment, and for researchers to get interrater reliability for their data. It also makes it difficult for teachers to give useful feedback to students, unless she or he also jotted down notes paraphrasing what the students said or describing the exact behavior and context that led to a certain judgment. Also, since the assessment criteria are predetermined, checklists and rating scales provide no opportunity for inducing new categories or criteria of performance based on what emerges during the assessment task. Although checklists and rating scales have these drawbacks, they still add practical and efficient tools to a repertoire of data-collection techniques.

A Sample Checklist for Rating Students' Reasoning

The checklist below was constructed for assessing the reasoning of students in a high school environmental studies course. The students have spent several weeks constructing environmental impact statements for two areas that the school is considering as possible sites to pave for a parking lot. They have examined biological, ecological, and hydrological characteristics of the two plots of land, and now are preparing their rec-

continued

ommendations. This is an ideal type of task for rating students' reasoning because the quality of answers depends on the reasoning used—there is not one right answer, nor can valid responses simply be matters of opinion (Paul, 1995).

Small groups of students are deliberating about which site would be better suited for a parking lot from an environmental perspective before pooling their ideas to come up with a single recommendation as a whole class. The teacher circulates around to each group, and asks the students to show their best thinking as they talk through the question "Which site do we recommend be chosen for the parking lot, and why." She explains to the students that they will be in a "fish bowl," meaning that she will position herself outside of their circle to watch and listen to them interact. Since the teacher acts as an observer in this situation, this is an example of a *diagnostic* rather than a *transactive* assessment of students' reasoning. Alternatively, the teacher could interact with the students by actively probing their reasoning, still using the same checklist to note students' responses, but taking her role into account when she interprets the results.

This checklist provides space for the teacher to note the reasoning of each student in the group (in this case a group of three, S1–S3). However, depending on the timing of the assessment, one student may act as a spokesperson by articulating reasoning that already had emerged from their group discussion. The teacher will use her judgment to determine whether to rate the reasoning of the group as a whole or to note reasoning skills demonstrated by individual students.

A Reasoning Checklist

Names: S1 _____ S2 _____ S3 _____

Reasoning Target	Demonstrated (checks)	Notes
Provides solid evidence to support a claim or idea	S1 S2 S3	
Synthesizes different points of view or strands of evidence	S1 S2 S3	
Builds on and strengthens an idea	S1 S2 S3	
Weighs strengths and weaknesses of alternative choices/interpretations	S1 S2 S3	
Seeks clarity after recognizing points of confusion or muddled thinking	S1 S2 S3	

2. Record and Transcribe Verbal Interchange for Textual Analysis

Audio or video recordings of students as they reason aloud provide a rich data base for analysis. The disadvantage, especially for teachers, is that simply replaying the recording doubles the time that would be required just to make judgments during the assessment activity itself, and transcribing increases the time commitment at least tenfold, depending on the level of detail and accuracy desired for the transcription. Also, dealing with recording equipment and keeping track of all of the resulting tapes present managerial challenges that can be especially daunting for teachers who must focus their primary attention on teaching while with their students.

A good compromise for both teachers and researchers, depending on the nature of a research question or the purpose and stakes of an assessment, is to use recordings as a backup to written notes and checklists. Tapes then do not necessarily have to be transcribed, but rather can be consulted if necessary to make sure that the written records capture the most genuine interpretation of the students' task performance.

Step 6. Analyze Data

One of the first analysis decisions is to determine the unit of analysis, meaning the data that will be considered as a whole for analysis purposes. In research on reasoning in interactive settings, the unit of analysis can range from a whole class, to small groups, to dyads, to individuals-in-interaction. Then coding schemes (typically used by researchers) or rubrics (typically used by teachers) are inductively or deductively devised and applied to the data.

Analyses should consider both the elements and the quality of students' reasoning. Including benchmarks or exemplars of each type or level of reasoning within a coding scheme or rubric makes them easier to apply. The following sections present criteria that can form the basis for developing task-specific rubrics or research-specific coding schemes to judge various reasoning skills (e.g., making inferences) and reasoning practices (e.g., building arguments). When developing or choosing an analysis scheme, teachers and researchers should bear in mind their goals and purpose.

1. Judging the Structure and Quality of Arguments

Halpern (1996) outlines the five core elements of arguments as follows:

- Conclusion—a final judgment, claim, decision, or belief that a reasoner purports to be true or reasonable
- Premise—a statement that supports a conclusion

- Assumption—an implied or explicit statement for which no proof or evidence is offered
- Qualifier—a constraint or restriction on the conclusion
- Counterargument—a statement that refutes or weakens a conclusion

Students' arguments can be analyzed to see if they contain each of these core elements. The quality of the argument then can be assessed along a continuum from being unsound to being completely sound. Halpern suggests basing judgments of the quality of

---

Analyzing an Argument

For a high school biology class assignment, students did background research and then identified what they considered to be our nation's top three most urgent environmental problems. One pair of students included the problem of invasive exotic species in its list. The teacher asked the two students to explain to the rest of the class their choice of this issue as an environmental threat. The following transcript of the girls' interchange demonstrates one approach to analyzing students' argumentation by embedding the following symbols into the text to identify the core elements of their argument:

(C) = Conclusion
(P) = Premise
(A) = Assumption
(Q) = Qualifier
(CA) = Counterargument

Shana: Exotic species are bad for our environment because they make it hard for the plants and animals that already live here to keep on growing and living **(C)**. It is like they outcompete them for food, water, space, and everything **(P)**.

Nicole: But we said not all exotics are bad, only those that are invasive **(Q)**. That means that they spread almost uncontrollably once they get here. But you never know if an exotic will be invasive or not, so it is best just to try to keep new species out of our country **(C)**.

Shana: Yeah, they are really good at taking over because they reproduce a lot and can live just about anywhere **(P)**.

Teacher: So why is this issue more pressing than some of the other issues you considered for your list of the top three worst environmental threats?

Nicole: What really made it sink in for us was when we read that many exotic plants grow best on soil that has been disturbed **(P)**. The article had this graph of how much land gets plowed

continued

> up for development and stuff every year to show that more and more land gets disturbed by people, and so we just create conditions for non-native plants to thrive **(P)**.
>
> Shana: Also people travel around all over the world a lot more, and merchandise gets shipped all over the place **(P)**. So plants and animals get transported our of their own region all the time, every day, and it is just going to keep happening more and more unless we try to control it better **(C)**.
>
> Nicole: Once exotic species get established in a new area they are almost impossible to get rid of **(P)**, So we have to pay attention to this issue before it's too late **(C)**. You could just say that this one doesn't belong in the top three because exotic species don't directly affect our health **(CA)**, but if our whole ecosystems change, that can't be good for anybody in the long run. [An unstated assumption **(A)** is that environmental issues of most concern are those that have a direct impact on human health.]
>
> (For examples of research studies that have analyzed students' scientific arguments see Eichinger, Anderson, Palincsar, & David [1991] and Kelly et al. [1998].)

an argument in part on whether (a) the premises are acceptable and consistent; (b) the premises are relevant to the conclusion and provide sufficient support for it; and (c) no essential premises are missing. Note that although an argument's conclusion may be judged to be acceptable or true, the argument itself is not strong unless the premises also are sound and supportive.

2. Judging the Adequacy of a Theory

Students' reasoning might yield a theory or model, rather than an argument. Or students could be asked to judge rather than to generate theories as an assessment task. Four criteria (Samarapungavan, 1992) for judging both students' theories and their judgments of theories are:

- Range of explanation—A theory that can account for more observations is more desirable than one that accounts for fewer observations.
- Ad-hocness—A theory that does not include ad hoc, auxiliary assumptions that explain away empirical anomalies, but that are not independently testable, is preferable to a theory that does contain ad hoc explanations.

- Empirical adequacy—An adequate theory must be consistent with the empirical evidence.
- Logical consistency—An adequate theory cannot have logical inconsistences or mutually contradictory propositions.

3. Judging Inferences

   Several researchers (Kuhn et al., 1988, 1995; Schauble, 1996) have developed coding schemes to judge the type and validity of students' inferences. These have been used to judge students' performance in multivariable experiment tasks, such as determining which variables causally affect the speed with which a race car travels down a track.

   A. Types of inferences

      The first distinction these coding schemes make is between theory-based and evidence-based inferences. When people make theory-based inferences, they justify a causal connection between a variable and an outcome with their own prior beliefs rather than by referring to empirical evidence. In contrast, evidence-based inferences use empirical evidence to justify a claim of a causal connection. There are three main types of evidence-based inferences.

      - Inclusion inferences are judgments that a variable is causally related to an experimental result.
      - Exclusion inferences are judgments that a variable is not causally related to a result.
      - Indeterminant inferences judge that insufficient information or confounded evidence make it impossible to judge whether a variable is causally related to an outcome.

   B. Validity of inferences

      Each type of evidence-based inference can be valid or invalid, depending on whether or not the data justify the inference. For instance, three types of invalid inclusion inferences are

      - Co-occurrence inferences—assuming that one variable caused another based on only one instance in which the variable was an antecedent of an outcome.
      - Co-variation inferences—assuming that one variable caused another based on multiple instances in which the variable was an antecedent of an outcome, but without considering the occurrence of additional covariates
      - Generalized inferences—summarizing in an undisciplined manner across a number of uncontrolled instances

      A coding scheme or rubric for judging these types of inferences is most suitable for traditional, variables-manipulation tasks, such as testing how the length of string and the weight of a bob affect the period of a pendulum. Although computer simulations make it possible for students to manipulate variables and get results that would be impossible to get in real time, in the life sciences as compared to in the physical sciences it is much harder to devise tasks using real phenomena (as opposed to records of data or computer simulations) that are suitable for efficiently assessing these types of reasoning skills.

4. Judging Reasoning Complexity

For a study of eighth-grade students who worked together over a number of weeks building mental models of the nature of matter, Hogan (1997) developed a scheme for coding and judging the key elements of the reasoning the students expressed aloud. Procedural definitions of the six elements within her Reasoning Complexity Rubric are as follows:

- Generativity—Judging the number and type (i.e., lower level reiteration of observations or confirmed generalizations, and students' own ideas, conjectures, or propositions) of subtopics brought forth within a discussion
- Elaboration—Gauging the amount of detail that is added to subtopics that are articulated
- Justifications—Noting two types of justifications of ideas and assertions: evidence-based and inference-based
- Explanations—Marking the presentation of mechanisms that account for a phenomenon
- Logical coherence—Scoring the soundness of a justification or explanation
- Synthesis—Determining if opposite views are accounted for

Table 4 presents the entire rubric, which delineates different levels of performance for each reasoning criterion. By including criteria for judging the logical coherence of ideas, this rubric links assessments of the substance and processes of students' reasoning.

Another tool for judging students' reasoning complexity that blends analysis of the substance of students' ideas with their reason-

---

Applying the Reasoning Complexity Rubric

Here is a sample of interactive reasoning of two eighth graders who were trying to explain, on a molecular level, how sugar cubes dissolve in water.

Elana: Sugar cubes. In the water, the crystalline solids they un-organize themselves, and so then they just floated in with all the other molecules.

continued

Jamus: What do you mean by unorganize themselves?

Elana: Well, you know how they showed the molecules being like a row, you know. (She draws a diagram of circles packed tightly together in a row.)

Jamus: Ya.

Elana: (Refers to drawing.) And this is like the water, so they un-organize themselves and they were like this.

Jamus: Well maybe the liquid came in between those molecules and like separated them.

Elana: Ya, exactly.

Jamus: So we supposedly have that one.

This interchange was scored using the Reasoning Complexity Rubric as follows:

Generativity = 1

Only one observation of the dissolving sugar cube was discussed.

Elaboration = 1

There was one elaboration on one idea when Elana responded to Jamus's request to explain what she meant by "unorganize them-selves."

Justifications = 0

There were no justifications present in this discussion.

Explanations = 3

Two mechanisms were proposed to explain the single phenomenon of sugar dissolving in water. One was that molecules of water come in between molecules of the sugar, and another was that as the sugar molecules "unorganize" they "float in with all the other molecules."

Logical Coherence = 3

Although the connections made between the phenomenon of dis-solving and the molecular-level mechanisms were sound, they did not include supporting details.

Synthesis = 0

No contrasting views emerged, so there was no opportunity to syn-thesize ideas.

Thus, this interchange received a total score of 8 out of 24 points for rea-soning complexity.

ing processes is the Bidimensional Coding Scheme (Hogan & Fish-erkeller, 1996). This scheme (Table 5) can be used to assess how com-patible students' ideas are with expert propositions, as well as how elaborately the students can reason about the ideas. The coding scheme is thus a tool for analyzing students' conceptual understand-ing and their reasoning proficiency. The bidimensional coding scheme can be applied across different topic areas, but requires generating a

TABLE 4

Reasoning Complexity Rubric

Criteria	Rating Scale				
	0	1	2	3	4
Generativity	No observations or ideas	1–2 observations or confirmed generalizations	3 or more observations or confirmed generalizations	1–2 own conjectures/ideas/assertions	3 or more own conjectures/ideas/assertions
Elaboration	No elaboration	1–2 elaborations of 1 idea	1–2 elaborations of more than 1 idea	3 or more elaborations of 1 idea	3 or more elaborations of more than 1 idea
Justifications	No justifications	Single justification of 1 idea	Single justifications of more than 1 idea	Multiple justifications of 1 idea	Multiple justifications of more than 1 idea
Explanations	No explanations	Single mechanism of 1 phenomenon	Single mechanism of more than 1 phenomenon	Multiple or chained mechanisms of 1 phenomenon	Multiple or chained mechanisms of more than 1 phenomenon
Logical coherence	No logical connections invoked	Nonsensical connections made	Vague, underspecified connections making superficial sense	Clear and reasonable connections, but lack support	Solid, principled, and coherent connections
Synthesis	No contrasting views emerged	2 counterideas coexist separately and unresolved	2 counterideas explicitly combined without deeper conceptual resolution	1 counter idea prevails through support given for it	2 or more counterideas synthesized into a more complex, coherent idea

TABLE 5
Bidimensional Coding Scheme for Comparing Students' Statements
to Expert Propositions

Code	Definition
Compatible elaborate	Statements concur with the expert proposition and have sufficient detail to show the thinking behind them and/or recur throughout the transcript in the same form.
Compatible sketchy	Statements concur with expert proposition, but essential details are missing. Often represent a correct guess among choices provided, but no ability to explain why choice was made.
Compatible/incompatible	Makes sketchy statements that concur with proposition, but that are not elaborated, and makes sketchy statements that disagree. Contradictory statements are often found in two parts of the transcript in response to different questions or tasks on the same topic.
Incompatible sketchy	Statements disagree with proposition, but very few details or logic is given, and do not recur throughout transcript. Often seem to be responses given just to say something, a guess.
Incompatible elaborate	Statements disagree with proposition and students provide details or coherent, personal logic backing them up. Same or similar statements/explanations recur throughout transcript.
Nonexistent	Use when students respond "I don't know" or do not mention the topic when asked a question calling for its use.
No evidence	Use when a topic was not directly addressed by a question and students did not mention it within the context of response to any question.

set of expert propositions about a given topic that can be used as a basis of comparison with students' ideas.

Step 7. Give Feedback or Make Claims

Giving feedback to students about the elements and quality of their reasoning is crucial for classroom assessment, although it is seldom a component of academic research. Not only can feedback help students become more aware of how they can strengthen their reasoning skills, it also can help them understand how effortful reasoning helps them achieve larger goals, such as producing and communicating real-world research results in a way that an audience beyond the classroom would find compelling.

Whereas teachers share assessment results primarily with students and parents, researchers must convince their peers of the worth and validity of their findings. When building claims from verbal reasoning data it is particularly important to acknowledge how all of the aspects of an interactive setting could affect students' reasoning, a point that we take up again in the next section.

CHALLENGES, CAVEATS, AND CONCLUSIONS

Using interactive protocols to assess students' reasoning can be quite time-consuming, and so it can be especially challenging for teachers who must fit assessment activities into days filled with many other responsibilities. One practical suggestion is to hand over responsibility for interactive reasoning assessments largely to students. Having students use checklists and rating scales to evaluate their peers' reasoning already has been mentioned. Another suggestion is to stock a classroom with inexpensive cassette recorders and tapes, so that students can create audio portfolios of their reasoning conversations throughout a semester. The tapes can document conversations with the teacher as well as with peers. Then by rating their own reasoning with a rubric that ideally they have helped to develop, or simply by writing reflective comments about their performance, students can learn a tremendous amount about reasoning. The ultimate goal of assessment—to promote students' learning—will then have been achieved.

Involving students in collecting samples of their reasoning over time is a way to address an additional challenge, which is that students' reasoning is affected by the nature of task and social contexts. A given assessment situation does not reveal students' absolute reasoning abilities, but rather reveals what they can or choose to do in a particular setting with particular people. For instance, some students might reason better within a task that provides latitude to use an empathetic, co-constructive orientation rather than traditional refutational argumentation (Belenky, Clinchy, Goldberger, & Tarule, 1986). Another example of contextual variation is that high-ability students working in homogeneous high-ability groups perform differently from high-ability students working in heterogeneous ability groups (Webb, Nemer, Chizhik, & Suqrve, 1998). Also, students tend to work better, and thus probably reason better, with their friends (Zajac & Hartup, 1997). Therefore, students' reasoning abilities should be judged by considering their performance across different social configurations and types of classroom activities. Students are in the best position to comment on how different settings affect their motivation and ability to reason well, so their reflective commentaries can provide crucial information for interpreting their performance.

One caveat is that just as some students have trouble expressing their thoughts in writing, others may have weak oral discourse skills or lack basic conversational competencies (Cherry Wilkinson & Calculator, 1982), such as knowing how and when to listen and take turns and how to speak so that others will listen. Students who are more aggressive, competitive, self-assured, or talkative in social settings are not necessarily the best reasoners, so it is important to try to separate such factors out from the quality of the reasoning itself. One way to minimize the influence of these factors, which can play a large role in face-to-face interactions, is to provide opportunities for exchange via computer networks. On-line dialogues were described earlier as a method that provides teachers and researchers with an automatic record of interactive reasoning to assess. Yet the caveat in this case is that contextual factors pertaining to students' competencies and comfort levels in communicating via the computer will have some bearing on students' display of reasoning.

Assessing students' reasoning via interactive protocols is only one approach that can expand our system of science assessments, just as the assessment of reasoning itself is only one objective within a system of valued science learning outcomes. Perhaps the most important feature of this mode and focus of assessment is its potential to positively affect the intellectual culture of classrooms. Teachers who openly value and assess students' reasoning expect students to take on substantive parts of the conversation in science class (Duschl & Gitomer, 1997; Hogan & Pressley, 1997b; van Zee & Minstrel, 1997), such by proposing interpretations, building on each other's ideas, discussing their views and assumptions, and resolving their differences interactively. In these ways students, with their peers and teacher, actively construct both the reasoning practices and the substance of science.

References

Ackerman, E. (1995). Construction and transference of meaning through form. In L. P. Steffe, & J. Gale (Eds.), *Constructivism in education* (pp. 341–354). Hillsdale, NJ: Erlbaum.

American Association for the Advancement of Science. (1993). *Benchmarks for science literacy*. New York: Oxford University Press.

Belenky, M. F., Clinchy, B. M., Goldberger, N. R., & Tarule, J. M. (1986). *Women's ways of knowing: The development of self, voice, and mind*. New York: Basic Books.

Brewer, W. F., & Samarapungavan, A. (1991). Children's theories vs. scientific theories: Differences in reasoning or differences in knowledge? In R. R. Hoffman & D. S. Palermo (Eds.), *Cognition and the symbolic processes* (pp. 209–232). Hillsdale, NJ: Lawrence Erlbaum.

Bronfenbrenner, U., & Ceci, S. J. (1994). Nature–nurture reconceptualized in developmental perspective: A bioecological model. *Psychological Review, 101*, 568–586.

Cherry Wilkinson, L., & Calculator, S. (1982). Effective speakers: Students' use of language to request and obtain information and action in the classroom. In L. Cherry Wilkinson (Ed.), *Communicating in the classroom* (pp. 85–100). New York: Academic Press.

Chi, M. T. H. (1997). Quantifying qualitative analyses of verbal data: A practical guide. *The Journal of the Learning Sciences, 6*, 271–315.

Day, J. D., Engelhardt, J. L., Maxwell, S. E., & Bolig, E. E. (1997). Comparison of static and dynamic assessment procedures and their relation to independent performance. *Journal of Educational Psychology, 89*, 358–368.

Driver, R., Asoko, H., Leach, J., Mortimer, E., & Scott, P. (1994). Constructing scientific knowledge in the classroom. *Educational Researcher*, 23, 5–12.

Dunbar, K. (1993). Concept discovery in a scientific domain. *Cognitive Science*, 17, 397–434.

Duschl, R. A., & Gitomer, D. H. (1997). Strategies and challenges to changing the focus of assessment and instruction in science classrooms. *Educational Assessment*, 4, 37–73.

Eichinger, D. C., Anderson, C. W., Palincsar, A. S., & David, Y. M. (1991, April). *An illustration of the roles of content knowledge, scientific argument, and social norms in collaborative problem solving*. Paper presented at the annual meeting of the American Educational Research Association, Chicago.

Ennis, R. H. (1987). A taxonomy of critical thinking dispositions and abilities. In J. B. Baron, & R. J. Sternberg (Eds.), *Teaching thinking skills: Theory and practice* (pp. 9–26). New York: W. H. Freeman.

Ericsson, K. A., & Simon, H. A. (1984). *Protocol analysis*. Cambridge, MA: MIT/Bradford.

Feuerstein, R., Rand, Y., Jensen, M. R., Kaniel, S., & Tzuriel, D. (1987). Prerequisites for assessment of learning potential: The LPAD model. In C. S. Lidz (Ed.), *Dynamic assessment: An interactional approach to evaluating learning potential* (pp. 35–51). New York: Guilford.

Forman, E. A., Minick, N., & Stone, C. A., (Eds.) (1993). *Contexts for learning: Sociocultural dynamics in children's development*. New York: Oxford University Press.

Gallas, K. (1995). *Talking their way into science: Hearing children's questions and theories, responding with curricula*. New York: Teachers College Press.

Ginsburg, H. P. (1997). *Entering the child's mind*. New York: Cambridge University Press.

Glaser, R. (1994, July). *Application and theory: Learning theory and the design of learning environments*. Keynote Address presented at the 23rd international Congress of Applied Psychology, Madrid, Spain.

Halpern, D. F. (1996). *Thought & knowledge* (3rd ed.). Mahwah, NJ: Lawrence Erlbaum.

Hatano, G. (1993). Time to merge Vygotskian and constructivist conceptions of knowledge acquisition. In E. Forman, N. Minick, & C. A. Stone. (Eds.) *Contexts for Learning: Sociocultural dynamics in children's development* (pp. 153–166). New York: Oxford University Press.

Hogan, K. (1994). *Eco-Inquiry: A guide to ecological learning experiences in the upper elementary/middle grades*. Dubuque, IA: Kendall/Hunt.

Hogan, K. (1997, March). *Comparative cognitive models of teacher student and student/student knowledge-building discourse*. Paper presented at the annual meeting of the National Association for Research in Science Teaching, Chicago.

Hogan, K., & Fisherkeller, J. (1996). Representing students' thinking about nutrient cycling in ecosystems: Bidimensional coding of a complex topic. *Journal of Research in Science Teaching*, 33, 941–970.

Hogan, K., & Pressley, M. (Eds.) (1997a). *Scaffolding student learning: Instructional approaches and issues*. Cambridge, MA: Brookline Books.

Hogan, K., & Pressley, M. (1997b). Scaffolding scientific competencies within classroom communities of inquiry. In K. Hogan & M. Pressley (Eds.), *Scaffolding student learning: Instructional approaches and Issues* (pp. 74–107). Cambridge, MA: Brookline Books.

Inhelder, B., & Piaget, J. (1958). *The growth of logical thinking from childhood to adolescence*. New York: Basic Books.

Kelly, G. J., Druker, S., & Chen, C. (1998). Students' reasoning about electricity: Combining performance assessments with argumentation analysis. *International Journal of Science Education*, 20, 849–872.

Klaczynski, P. A., Gordon, D. H., & Fauth, J. (1997). Goal-oriented critical reasoning and individual differences in critical reasoning biases. *Journal of Educational Psychology*, 89, 470–485.

Klahr, D., & Dunbar, K. (1988). Dual space search during scientific reasoning. *Cognitive Science*, 12, 1–48.

Koslowski, B. (1996). *Theory and evidence: The development of scientific reasoning*. Cambridge, MA: MIT Press.

Kuhn, D., & Pearsall, S. (1998). Relations between metastrategic knowledge and strategic performance. *Cognitive Development*, 13, 227–247.

Kuhn, D., Amsel, E., & O'Loughlin, M. (1988). *The development of scientific thinking skills.* New York: Academic Press.

Kuhn, D., Garcia-Mila, M., Zohar, A., & Andersen, C. (1995). Strategies of knowledge acquisition, *Monographs of the Society for Research in Child Development*, Serial No. 245, 60(4).

Kuhn, T. S. (1962). *The structure of scientific revolutions.* Chicago: University of Chicago Press.

Lawson, A. E. (1993). Deductive reasoning, brain maturation, and science concept acquisition: Are they linked? *Journal of Research in Science Teaching.* 30, 1029–1051.

Lederman, N. G. (1992). Students' and teachers' conceptions of the nature of science: A review of the research. *Journal of Research in Science Teaching.* 19, 331–359.

Lidz, C. S. (Ed.) (1987). *Dynamic assessment: An interactional approach to evaluating learning potential.* New York: Guilford.

Lincoln, Y. S., & Guba, E. G. (1985). *Naturalistic inquiry.* Thousand Oaks, CA: Sage Publications.

Loving, C. C. (1997). From the summit of truth to its slippery slopes: Science education's journey through positivist-postmodern territory. *American Educational Research Journal.* 34, 421–452.

Magnusson, S. J., Templin, M., & Boyle, R. A. (1997). Dynamic science assessment: A new approach for investigating conceptual change. *The Journal of the Learning Sciences.* 6, 91–142.

Marzano, R. J., Brandt, R. S., Hughes, C. S., Jones, B. F., Presseisen, B. Z., Rankin, S. C., & Suhor, C. (1988). *Dimensions of thinking: A framework for curriculum and instruction.* Alexandria, VA: Association for Supervision and Curriculum Development.

Mayer, R. E. (1996). Learners as information processors: Legacies and limitations of educational psychology's second metaphor. *Educational Psychologist.* 31, 151–161.

Mintzes, J. J., Wandersee, J. H., & Novak, J. D. (Eds.) (1998). *Teaching science for understanding: A human constructivist view.* San Diego, CA: Academic Press.

Mishler, E. G. (1986). *Research interviewing: Context and narrative.* Cambridge, MA: Harvard University Press.

Moshman, D. (1998). Cognitive development beyond childhood. In W. Damon (Ed.), *Handbook of child psychology*, Vol. 2: *Cognition, language and perception* (5th ed., pp. 947–978). New York: Wiley.

Mugny, G., & Doise, W. (1978). Socio-cognitive conflict and structure of individual and collective performances. *European Journal of Social Psychology*, 8, 181–192.

National Research Council. (1996). *National science education standards.* Washington, DC: National Academy Press.

Novak, J. D., & Gowin, D. B. (1984). *Learning how to learn.* New York: Cambridge University Press.

O'Loughlin, M. (1992). Rethinking science education: Beyond Piagetian constructivism toward a sociocultural model of teaching and learning. *Journal of Research in Science Teaching*, 29, 791–820.

Palincsar, A. S. (1986). The role of dialogue in providing scaffolded instruction. *Educational Psychologist*, 21, 73–98.

Palincsar, A. S., Anderson, C. W., & David, Y. M. (1993). Pursuing scientific literacy in the middle grades through collaborative problem solving. *The Elementary School Journal*, 93, 643–658.

Paul, R. (1995). *Critical thinking: How to prepare students for a rapidly changing world.* Santa Rosa, CA: Foundation for Critical Thinking.

Perkins, D., Jay, E., & Tishman, S. (1993). Beyond abilities: A dispositional theory of thinking. *The Merrill-Palmer Quarterly*, 39, 1–21.

Pintrich, P. R., Marx, R. W., & Boyle, R. A. (1993). Beyond cold conceptual change: The role of motivational beliefs and classroom contextual factors in the process of conceptual change. *Review of Educational Research*, 63, 167–199.

Reddy, M. (1995, April). *Becoming second grade scientists: Teaching and learning in science discussions.* Paper presented at the annual meeting of the American Educational Research Association, San Francisco.

Reddy, M., Jacobs, P., McCrohon, C, & Herrenkohl, L. R. (1998). *Creating scientific communities in the elementary classroom.* Portsmouth, NH: Heinemann.

Samarapungavan, A. (1992). Children's judgments in theory choice tasks: Scientific rationality in childhood. *Cognition, 45*, 1–32.

Scardamalia, M., Bereiter, C., & Lamon, M. (1994). The CSILE Project: Trying to bring the classroom into World 3. In K. McGilly (Ed.), *Classroom lessons: Integrating cognitive theory and classroom practice* (pp. 201–228). Cambridge, MA: MIT Press.

Schauble, L. (1996). The development of scientific reasoning in knowledge-rich contexts. *Developmental Psychology, 32*, 102–119.

Siegler, R. S., & Crowley, K. (1991). The microgenetic method: A direct means for studying cognitive development. *American Psychologist, 46*, 606–620.

Simpson, D. (1997). Collaborative conversations: Strategies for engaging students in productive dialogues. *The Science Teacher, 64*, 40–43.

Smagorinsky, P. (1995). The social construction of data: Methodological problems of investigating learning in the zone of proximal development. *Review of Educational Research, 65*, 191–212.

Southerland, S. A., Smith, M. U., & Cummins, C. L. (2000). "What do you mean by that?" Using structured interviews to assess science understanding. In J. J. Mintzes, J. H. Wandersee, & J. D. Novak (Eds.), *Assessing science understanding: A human constructivist view*. San Diego, CA: Academic Press.

Stanovich, K. E., & West, R. F. (1997). Reasoning independently of prior belief and individual differences in actively open-minded thinking. *Journal of Educational Psychology, 89*, 342–357.

Stiggins, R. J. (1997). *Student-centered classroom assessment* (2nd ed.). Upper Saddle River, NJ: Merrill.

Twency, R. D., & Chitwood, S. T. (1995). Scientific reasoning. In S. E. Newstead & J. Evans (Eds.), *Perspectives on thinking and reasoning: Essays in honor of Peter Wason* (pp. 241–260). Englewood Cliffs, NJ: Lawrence Erlbaum.

van Zee, E. H., & Minstrel, J. (1997). Reflective discourse: developing shared understandings in a physics classroom. *International Journal of Science Education, 19*, 209–228.

Varelas, M. (1996). Between theory and data in a seventh-grade science class. *Journal of Research in Science Teaching. 33*, 229–263.

Vye, N. J., Schwartz, D. L., Bransford, J. D., Barron, B. J., Zech, L., & The Cognition and Technology Group at Vanderbilt. (1998). SMART environments that support monitoring, reflection, and revision. In D. J. Hacker, J. Dunlosky, & A. C. Graesser, (1998). *Metacognition in educational theory and practice* (pp. 305–346). Mahwah, NJ: Erlbaum.

Vygotsky, L. S. (1978). *Mind in society*. Cambridge, MA: Harvard University Press.

Webb, N., Nemer, K., Chizhik, A., & Suqrve, B. (1998). Equity issues in collaborative group assessment: Group composition and performance. *American Educational Research Journal, 35*, 607–651.

Welzel, M., & Roth, W-M. (1998). Do interviews really assess students' knowledge? *International Journal of Science Education, 20*, 25–44.

Wiggins, B. (1993). *Assessing student performance*. San Francisco: Jossey-Bass.

Wood, S. S., Bruner, J. S., & Ross, G. (1976). The role of tutoring in problem solving. *Journal of Child Psychology and Psychiatry, 17*, 89–100.

Zajac, R. J., & Hartup, W. W. (1997). Friends as coworkers: research review and classroom implications. *The Elementary School Journal, 98*, 3–13.

CHAPTER

6

Designing an Image-Based Biology Test

JAMES H. WANDERSEE
Louisiana State University

Biology textbooks are replete with images. Knowledge construction and progress in the life sciences have typically been associated with definitive and explanatory images of natural objects and phenomena. Perusal of histories of biology serves to document that it is one of the most visual of the sciences. Research biologists have long realized that the well-chosen image can communicate what they have learned about the living world much better than words do. Seldom do their research journal articles consist entirely of text and numbers; in fact, it is not uncommon to see the images in an article predominate.

Words are just one way of probing students' understanding of biological knowledge. If that is so, why do biology test items, from elementary school to graduate school, seldom employ images, or frame challenging or complex questions about them? In the past, printing technologies may have made placing image-based items on biology tests economically infeasible, but in the twenty-first century, the cost factor and lack of access to the requisite printing technology are no longer convenient rationalizations for their omission.

Can it be that we have been trying to assess what biology students know in ways that do not coincide with the thought processes, practices, and values held by those who actually work within the domain of biology? Can it be that sometimes our students really understand the very concepts and principles we are probing, but our verbal probes are unable to detect this understanding or do not activate the same kind of responses as visual probes might?

Since biology assessment seeks to identify, inform, and assign current scientific value to what has been learned, it seems logical to conclude that, up to now, there have been virtually no targeted, test-based rewards for students who study and learn from the graphics in their biology textbooks and courses. Yet, our own research indicates that those students who actively transform and practice applying their knowledge from biology text to biology graphics (and, conversely, from graphics to text) attain greater understanding (Wandersee, 1988, 1990). In addition, as Hayes and Readence (1983) have carefully demonstrated, the images in a text enhance learning to the extent that the text depends on them for a full understanding and integrates them well.

For the past two decades, my research group, the 15° Laboratory (and its forerunners), has been studying the effects of various visual approaches on biology learning. Our studies, ranging from concept maps and biogeochemical cycle diagrams to electron micrographs and photographic images, have convinced us that both the activity of representing and the form of representation greatly influence biology learning (Abrams & Wandersee, 1992; Wandersee, 1994, 1996; Trowbridge & Wandersee, 1994, 1996; Wandersee & Schussler, 1999).

Years ago, Ausubel, Novak, and Hanesian (1978) pointed out that "much potentially meaningful knowledge taught by verbal exposition results in rotely learned verbalisms" (p. 28) and they warned that "excellence is not synonymous with high examination scores; one must consider the way in which such scores are achieved, the kind of knowledge they reflect, and the motivation underlying them. More important than what pupils know at the end of the sixth, eighth, and twelfth grades is the extent of their knowledge at ages 25, 40, and 60" (p. 34). Just as few investors can realistically expect their short-term investments to be high-yield ones, neither can biology instructors expect both spectacular and immediate learning outcomes. Meaningful learning takes time, adequate prior knowledge, and conscious effort. Sufficient time must also be allowed for it to bear intellectual dividends. Thus, we may have been expecting to see too many of those dividends too soon, and looking for them in the wrong places—namely, encapsulated in the biological terms we ask our students to read, write, and speak.

The term "graphics" encompasses, tables, graphs, charts, diagrams, maps, line drawings, illustrations, photographic images, and so forth. In this chapter, because of their commonality and accessibility, we shall focus specifically on the use of still *photographic images* as the basis of biology test items. What is set forth here may or may not apply to other forms of representation or other fields of science.

Without being reductionistic or apologetic, the operating assumption here is that science education research makes the most progress when it intentionally and carefully delimits its field of view. If the reform catch phrase, "less is more," applies to science teaching, then less is also more in science education research. To this author, such baseline studies seem necessary prior to conducting high-quality holistic ones. In contrast, pseudo-holistic science education research is an exercise in vagueness, vacuosity, and imprecision. Theories of Everything (TOEs) may indeed be worthwhile and attainable goals in physics, but not in science education, given its current state of development.

WHAT CAN AN IMAGE-BASED TEST REVEAL ABOUT BIOLOGY LEARNING?

The *National Science Education Standards* (National Research Council, 1996, p. 76) endorse a new view of assessment, namely that "assessment and learning are two sides of the same coin." Your author sees image-based biology testing as being in harmony with the following *Standards'* statements as well, because It expands the range of performance evaluated so that "students have adequate opportunity to demonstrate their achievements" (p. 83) and because it "elicit[s] the full extent of students' understanding ... [and is] set in a variety of contexts ... [and can be shown to have] meaning outside the classroom" (p. 87). It also aligns well with *Science for All Americans'* (AAAS, 1989) principles that "science demands evidence ... [and that, in science,] great value is placed on ... instruments and techniques of observation" (pp. 26–27). "Teaching [and testing] should be consistent with the nature of scientific inquiry" (p. 147) and "concentrate on the collection and use of evidence" (p. 148). All of these consensual recommendations seem consistent with image-based instruction and assessment

Blystone and Dettling (1990, p. 21) aptly observe, "Virtually every science course employs the use of a textbook." Typically, biology textbook reviewers and adopters alike focus on the quality of the prose and downplay the quality and range of the illustrations. Your author thinks that photographs and other graphics found in biology textbooks are a vastly underused learning resource. Teachers expect to see them there but devote little class or homework time to extracting meaning from them. Interviews with biology teachers have shown us that many consider them to be more motivational than educational.

Some self-proclaimed "rigorous" biology instructors have sneered that those are just "window dressing," pretty pictures and line art that boost the price of the book. What a Luddite-like response!

In contrast, Seymour Pappert (1993, p. 137) wisely counsels a return to "more concrete ways of knowing" and considers the overvaluing of abstract reasoning (invoking complex mazes of words and numbers) as the principal barrier to progress in education. If computer magnate software Bill

Gates (1995, p. 224) is spending significant sums of money to purchase the rights to major image collections and has founded a digital stock agency named Corbis as a source for various visual material, it seems fair to assume that images will play an important future role in our students' futures.

Cognitive scientist Donald Norman (1993) claims that "cognitive artifacts" (units of key information abstracted into a representational form) comprise the basis of human intellectual power. Since the majority of photographs taken involve human choice, judgment, and framing, under Norman's typology, photographs might be considered "experiential artifacts" (p. 52), in passive, surface representational form (pp. 80–81), that allow biology students to experience objects and events as if they were there, to see critical features, to become informed about things that are otherwise inaccessible to them, to reason about these objects and events, and, sometimes, to make new discoveries using them.

When used in common with other students in the course, life science photographs can:

1. Serve as a "shared workspace" for thinking about biological questions and issues (Norman, 1993, p. 83)
2. Provide external memory storage that maintains an accurate view of objects or events, and stores more information than human memory alone can store
3. Capture (freeze in time) the spatial arrangement of objects or events of interest
4. Provide the imagery necessary to anchor relevant concepts, principles, and theory in long-term memory
5. Serve as a primary, complementary, or redundant communication channel for biology learning.

It should be obvious that these same characteristics can inform and facilitate image-based biology test-item design and construction.

As a cautionary note, dangers of relying on images include (1) thinking that the photographic representation is exactly equivalent to the actual object or event in nature; (2) ignoring important information that the representation did not or could not capture; and (3) overgeneralizing from photographs, failing to realize the limited range of images being supplied to the learner.

WHAT ARE THE TESTING IMPLICATIONS OF PAIVIO'S DUAL CODING THEORY?

"Dual coding is the principle which proposes that texts are processed and encoded in the verbal systems [of the cerebral cortex] whereas pictures or graphics are processed both in the image and verbal systems. Dual coding was seen as a way to explain why memory for pictures may be better than that for texts" (de Jong et al., 1998).

The dual-coding idea is actually the basis of a theory advanced by psychologist A. Paivio (1971, 1975, 1983, 1991) to explain how visual experiences enhance learning. This theory proposes that people can encode information as language-like propositions or picture-like mental representations. His research has shown that pictures contain information that is not contained in text, that information shown in pictures is easier to recall because it is encoded in *both* memory systems, not just text, and that verbal concepts are, so to speak, "hung on visual pegs," providing a visual–verbal linkage that facilitates recall.

While some authors (de Jong et al., 1998) argue that other graphic effects may outweigh the influence of dual coding, not all researchers agree (Paivio, 1991). Our research group has used this well-established theory for years and found it to be quite useful in biology understanding and enhancing visual effects on biology learning.

The implications of Paivio's theory (1991) for biology testing, in the context of this chapter, would seem to be as follows:

1. Well-chosen photographic images can serve as an alternative cognitive portal for accessing what the learner understands about a given biological topic.
2. To eliminate rote learning effects, images that have *not* been analyzed previously in biology class are preferable for use in testing.
3. The most important concepts, constructs, propositions, and theories to be assessed by the biology test should be probed by both an exclusively verbal test item, and, a photograph-based, visual–verbal test item. This two-portal approach provides single and dual avenues of cognitive access into the student's long-term memory.
4. For the sake of authenticity, imaging, image-based analysis, and visual learning approaches should be part of the biology learner's weekly in-class learning experiences.

WHAT ARE SOME SALIENT PRINCIPLES OF VISUAL PERCEPTION AND COGNITION?

Research has shown that most visitors to an art museum spend less than 5 seconds considering an individual artwork on site (Barrett, 1996). Why does such minimal observation occur? Is it because the typical visitors are not trained observers? Is it because they don't expect anything more from the experience than a fleeting sensation? Do biology students spend similarly infinitesimal amounts of time when they view the photographs in their biology textbooks?

Our research group has found that biology students need transformative tasks such as the following to expand their viewing time of textbook photographs and to construct scientific meaning related to each image. Such tasks can include (1) writing detailed descriptions of the photographs; (2) exchanging these written descriptions with peers to uncover and eliminate previously "missed" features; (3) orally interpreting the photographs in terms of the biological content knowledge learned in the course to date; (4) individually evaluating and rank-ordering a biology textbook chapter's photographs using a reporting template prepared by the instructor; and (5) informally debating the resulting evaluations and ranks in class. We have found that, at least initially, observing a photograph must have an explicit purpose for the student, or it is simply treated as a pleasurable activity of little educational consequence.

Using Barrett's helpful book (1996, pp. 113–118), your author has identified four major photographic styles that may be found in contemporary biology textbook photographs:

1. *Realism* (mimesis) uses the world as the standard of truth and the intent behind the photograph is to accurately portray nature as clearly and sharply focused as possible. This is, by far, the most common type of photograph in most biology textbooks. A photograph of a fish scale or an excavated tree root system or a mosquito piercing human skin would fall into this category.
2. *Expressionism* (pictorialism) emphasizes the photographer's individuality and experiences while imaging the object or event. Props, soft-focus, staging, costuming, distortion, pseudo-coloring, and texturing may be used to make an artistic statement about the subject. Actors dressed as Pasteur, Darwin, Leeuwenhoek, Fleming, and McClintock, and holding appropriate scientific props in their hands, might appear in a chapter on scientific methods.
3. *Formalism* is a twentieth-century aesthetic theory that emphasizes the importance of the harmonious formal organization and composition of the image. Context is down-played and the photograph's meaning lies in its form, not the actual subject matter. A photograph of a fly's compound eye might be used for its geometric pattern and the strange curiosity it evokes, rather than to teach about insect vision.
4. *Instrumentalism* is a theory that embraces life for art's sake, rather than vice versa. Photographs are taken to make social, moral, or economic statements in order to help people. Victims of a tropical disease might be portrayed to evoke pity and serve as a call to action. Seeing such human suffering might inspire someone to a career in tropical medicine or provoke better sanitation practices.

It is your author's fieldwork-based opinion that learning to recognize and attending to the aforementioned four basic photographic styles is an important first step in teaching and testing with photographic images. Students can then begin to see the photographs in their textbooks and in everyday life (and, subsequently, on your tests) as serving different purposes. This provides a natural transition to the next question we consider.

HOW CAN THE STUDENT'S ATTENTION BE FOCUSED ON SELECTED ASPECTS OF THE PHOTOGRAPHIC IMAGE?

For novices, it may be best to try to choose photographs that have an obvious center of interest. When too much information is present in a single photograph, students can feel overwhelmed. As a result, they may miss or selectively filter out some of its content, oversimplify it by grouping its elements, or choose to avoid it entirely (Zakia, 1997). When students become more visually literate, as your course unfolds, you can use increasingly complex images when testing them. There's nothing inherently wrong with photographic complexity, it's just that one has to introduce it by degrees.

WHEN SHOULD A COLOR IMAGE BE USED INSTEAD OF A MONOCHROME IMAGE?

First of all, recall your human physiology. Each eye has about 125 million rods and about 7 million cones (Solso, 1994)—almost 18 times more "shades of gray" detectors (rods) than color detectors (cones). Consider, too, that if you are projecting an image for the class to see, rods work under conditions of lower light intensity, so class members, regardless of where they are seated, are more likely to see your image if it is a monochrome image ("black and white"). Such photographs should have an ample range of gray values and not be excessively high in contrast.

When color is important to the interpretation of an image of an object or event, then a color image should definitely be used. Some organisms such as birds and stained bacteria are more easily identifiable and distinguishable when presented in color: Inflamed human tissues appear visibly redder, laboratory colorimetric tests depend on color for interpretation of results, pseudocolored maps of marine algae need to be shown in color, and so forth. Admittedly, sometimes only one kind of image (monochrome or color) is available. However, when given a choice and both images are equally sharp and well exposed, weigh the visibility and interpretability issues.

Your local copying center should have a color copier that you can use to prepare a color overhead transparency, or even to prepare a monochrome overhead transparency version of a color image. If you have a computer with scanner and color printer peripherals, you can do this yourself. You can store digital images for later use in presentation software to be displayed via LED projection panels or video projectors. Use of images from the adopted biology textbook for local testing purposes usually poses no legal risks; some publishers even supply them on CD-ROM as an ancillary to the text. Image libraries are also available for purchase on CD-ROMs, or for free on some on-line image bases, so you don't always have to begin with a hard copy. You can even capture still images from your own videotapes or live TV using a frame-grabbing device such as Snappy. But make sure each image is of sufficient resolution for both testing and projection purposes. Note that color or black and white 35-mm slides currently offer much higher resolution than any other medium. Some teachers may even prefer to print out a classroom set of color or black and white copies of each image for testing purposes, so projection is completely unnecessary.

Make sure you comply with all legal requirements for image use. *Finding Images Online* (Berinstein, 1996) is a fine reference to consult whenever questions related to finding, capturing, viewing, and (legally) using images have arisen.

WHAT IS THE AUTHOR'S MODEL OF IMAGE-BASED BIOLOGY TEST-ITEM DESIGN?

Even today, too much of what passes for science instruction in our schools and colleges is predicated on helping students read and memorize a lifeless, albeit updated, "rhetoric of conclusions in which current and temporary constructions of scientific knowledge are conveyed as empirical, literal, and irrevocable truths"—a danger that Joseph Schwab (1962, p. 24) warned biology educators about long ago.

Table 1 presents the 20-Q Model of Visual Biology Test Design (Wandersee, 1997). Your author has taught biology at both the high school and college level, with a decade of science teaching experience at each level. Thus, being familiar with real-world science teaching, the model takes into account that, along with instructional concerns, there are always logistical and human factors concerns, as well as administrative constraints.

Alluding to the venerable parlor game of "20 Questions," the 20-Q Model was designed to stimulate and assist biology instructors in framing a series of image-based questions (Drummond, 1995) for visual biology testing. By intent, it also allows them to use the same image for multiple sections and yet ask different questions about it, since many readers of this book will teach multiple sections of the same biology course.

To use the model shown in Table 1, instructors, when acting as biology test designers, can draw on any image base to which they have legal access, choose a potentially challenging or evocative image, and scan the first column of the 20-Q Model (consisting of possible visual-related stems for

TABLE 1

Wandersee's 20-Q Model of Image-Based Biology Test-Item Design

Question	Code Words
1. Describe this event biologically…	describe event
2. Give the function(s) of this/these structure(s)…	give function(s)
3. Provide the next step in this process…	give next step
4. How else could this event be explained biologically…	give alternative explanation
5. Predict what will happen next…	predict results
6. What evidence do you see that suggests…	tell what evidence suggests
7. What is the limiting factor in this process…	give limiting factor(s)
8. What biological principle is operating here…	specify principle operating
9. If we didn't have or couldn't use … what could we use instead…	suggest could use—instead of
10. What is the connection between…	give connection between
11. In the past, how was this event explained by scientists…	supply past scientific explanation
12. On what basis do you suspect this organism is a…	give organism I.D. basis
13. Biologically, this organism is most closely related to…	what most closely related to
14. How would you go about measuring…	tell how you'd measure
15. Make a biological estimation how long it would take for…	make time estimate
16. What is the concept a biologist would use here to…	suggest valid concept
17. Ask an important biological question about this photograph…	ask important question
18. What would a graph of this event look like…	sketch graph of event
19. Design a device to monitor an important variable in this environment…	design monitoring device
20. Apply what you read in your last assignment to this photo…	apply reading to photo

Scoring rubric: No relevant biological understanding demonstrated = 0 points; very limited relevant biological understanding demonstrated = 1 point; partial relevant biological understanding demonstrated = 2 points; complete relevant biological understanding demonstrated = 3 points. *Note:* Item score depends on the number of aspects posted in parentheses on the test item as being necessary for a full 3-point rating.

items) to locate an appropriate question. Teachers who have used the model report that, even if the 20-Q Model doesn't always contain an appropriate stem, using the first-column scanning process usually prompts and inspires them to generate one of their own. The coding column provides model-based keywords they can use to tag the images they have used for a given test for reference when constructing future tests.

Biology instructors say that once they have used the model for a semester (incorporating timed, challenging, 3-minute, short-answer, brightly projected visual biology test items during the last 9–15 minutes of their tests), students themselves, as part of a unit review activity, enjoy choosing images and proposing unit-based questions to the instructor for possible use on the forthcoming exam. In this way, reflection and self-evaluation are encouraged, and at least two items per test are then instructor-validated, but peer-designed.

Even if the instructor uses scanable answer sheets for the other questions, scanable answer sheets are available with sufficient white space for including three to five human-scored, handwritten, short-answer items at the end. A general scoring rubric is found in the footnote to Table 1. Biology teachers have found it useful in preparing a scoring key and in explaining their item ratings to students.

Experience with the 20-Q Model has shown that students need in-class practice in answering some representative visual biology questions before they ever encounter them on a real test. For this practice, it helps to project the question, the photographic image, and four actual but anonymous, handwritten student answers to that question—each shown receiving a different score in accordance with the scoring rubric. Students need to ask questions to understand that the test performance emphasis is on demonstrating "relevant biological understanding" in each short-answer response they write.

WHAT ARE SOME EXAMPLES OF MODEL-BASED TEST ITEMS?

The following examples (see Figures 1–5) contain 20-Q-Model-based test questions and silhouetted representations of the photographs used by biology teachers who have been piloting image-based biology testing. The actual photographs could not be reproduced here because rights to use them did not extend beyond the teachers' classrooms. It is assumed that the reader will have no trouble visualizing an appropriate photograph and will begin to see the potential for application and analysis that such an image-based testing approach offers.

HOW CAN IMAGE-BASED BIOLOGY TEST RESULTS BE ANALYZED AND INTERPRETED?

David Hyerle, long a proponent of visual thinking, writes, "We are only at the beginning of integrating visual tools into learning environments in both schools and businesses." He also sees a shift in thinking that will accompany this change: "Given visual tools, learners are motivated to seek definitions that are relational, patterned, and context-driven" (1996, p. 20). In other words, the focus of learning is concomitantly switching from isolated

FIGURE 1

Biochemically, discuss the factors that limit how far this man can run.

"things" to searching for and constructing patterns that connect—so that students not only understand some important details in depth, but also keep "the big picture" in mind.

If instructors are to incorporate photographic images into their testing programs, then they have to make a conscious effort to become better observers themselves (see Chapter 7).

Many pages of contemporary biology textbooks are devoted to photographs, micrographs, and other kinds of graphics. One way to show that

FIGURE 2

Evidence suggests that this root system drawing is inaccurate. How so?

FIGURE 3
What adaptations combine to make these animals merit the title "the ships of the desert?"

FIGURE 4
What disease is likely to result if this man persists in the activity shown here, and what course does the disease typically follow?

FIGURE 5

What is the observational advantage for using artwork rather than
photographs in field guides to organisms?

you value images is to refer in class to them when you discuss the content
of a chapter, to demonstrate how you personally go about grasping their
meaning, to show you've looked at every one of them and read their cap-
tions, and to include some of them in your exams.

The other requirement for using the type of image-based testing
proposed here is that teachers need a strong and up-to-date biology background for the topic being tested. They must use their own biology knowledge base judiciously in deciding what level of understanding is being
demonstrated by the student's answer to a given image-based question.
They must grade similar answers in the same way every time. Such questions can indeed probe "depth of understanding," but instructor effort must
be made to be as objective as possible in scoring and in providing feedback
to the students.

What about preparing students for such questions? If you are going to do
this, start at the beginning of the course, and build it into your printed
course description. Let everyone know that you intend to test their learning
using the images relevant to your biology course. Explain why this is important and how it will give them additional information about their progress in
learning biology. Chances are they will not be shocked. These are the MTV
generations you are addressing! Even in 1980, Doblin estimated that 85% of
all the messages we receive daily are visual ones. No wonder school
sometimes seems archaic to today's students when tests reflect a text-only
bias.

In the past, you may have said, "These are really important for you to study"; but if you don't actually test student's understanding of the photographic images, micrographs, microscope slides, and so forth that they've viewed—along with relevant images from the real world that you'd like them to interpret—you are perceived by students as blatantly contradicting what you say. Only the most metacognitively oriented and internally motivated of learners will diligently study course content that the instructor fails to reward with grade points.

The 20-Q Model's scoring rubric provided in this chapter is intended to help biology teachers begin to probe and assess biological understanding via photographic images. It is admittedly simple and primarily qualitative, but has been classroom tested. The teachers who used it wrote little explanatory notes on their checklists. In fact, you may wish to develop a grading checklist tailored for each exam and assign points to image-based responses in this way—attaching a copy of the instructor-completed checklist to each graded exam answer sheet before you hand back a particular examination to the students. Better image-based biology assessment tools are currently being developed and field tested by our 15° Laboratory research group (http://www.15degreelab.com), as well as by others around the world.

You are cordially invited to participate in the development of new tools and techniques of visual assessment. While it may not always control teaching, testing almost always drives learning. Open your students' eyes to the images of life! Help them to "make meaning of" the still photographs they see in their textbooks and the images they encounter in their classroom biology lessons, and to interpret, biologically, their own real-time images of everyday life.

References

Abrams, E., & Wandersee, J. H. (1992). How to use a concept map to identify students' biological misconceptions. *Adaptation*, 14(1), 1, 4, 14, 16.

American Association for the Advancement of Science [AAAS]. (1989). *Science for all Americans*. Washington, DC: Author.

Ausubel, D. P., Novak, J. D., & Hanesian, H. (1978). *Educational psychology: A cognitive view* (2nd ed.). New York: Holt, Rinehart & Winston.

Berinstein, P. (1996). *Finding images online*. Wilton, CT: Pemberton Press.

Barrett, T. (1996). *Criticizing photographs: An introduction to understanding images* (2nd ed.). Mountain View, CA: Mayfield.

Blystone, R. V., & Dettling, B. C. (1990). Visual literacy in science textbooks. In M. B. Rowe (Ed.), Vol. 6, *What research says to the science teacher: The process of knowing* (pp. 19–40). Washington, DC: National Science Teachers Association.

de Jong, T., Ainsworth, S., Dobson, M., der Hulst, A., Levonen, J., Reimann, P., Sime, J.-A., van Someren, M. W., Spada, H., & Swaak, J. (1998). Acquiring knowledge in science and mathematics: The use of multiple representations in technology-based learning environments. In M. W. van Someren, P. Reimann, H. P. A. Boshuizen, & T. de Jong (Eds.), *Learning with multiple representations* (pp. 9–40). Amsterdam: Pergamon.

Doblin, J. (1980). A structure of non-textual communications. In P.A. Kolers, M. E. Wrolstad, & H. Bouma (Eds.), *Processing of visible language 2* (pp. 89–111). New York: Plenum Press.

Drummond, T. (1995). A *brief summary of the best practices in college teaching*. Seattle, WA: North Seattle Community College.

Gates, B. (1995). *The road ahead*. New York: Viking Penguin.

Hayes, D. A., & Readence, J. E. (1983). Transfer of learning from illustration-dependent text. *Journal of Educational Research*, 76(4), 245–248.

Hyerle, D. (1996). *Visual tools*. Alexandria, VA: ASCD.

National Research Council. (1996). *National Science Education Standards*. Washington, DC: National Academy Press.

Norman, D. A. (1993). *Things that make us smart*. Reading, MA: Addison-Wesley.

Paivio, A. (1971). *Imagery and verbal processes*. New York: Holt, Rinehart & Winston.

Paivio, A. (1975). Perceptual comparisons through the mind's eye. *Memory and Cognition*, 3(6), 635–647.

Paivio, A. (1983). The empirical case for dual coding. In J. C. Yuille (Ed.), *Imagery, memory, and cognition*. Hillsdale, NJ: Earlbaum.

Paivio, A. (1991). Dual coding theory: Retrospect and current status. *Canadian Journal of Psychology*, 45(3), 255–287

Pappert, S. (1993). *The children's machine: Rethinking school in the age of the computer*. New York: Basic Books.

Schwab, J. J., & Brandwein, P. F. (1962). *The teaching of science as enquiry*. Cambridge, MA: Harvard University Press.

Solso, R. L. (1994). *Cognition and the visual arts*. Cambridge, MA: MIT Press.

Trowbridge, J. E., & Wandersee, J. H. (1994). Identifying critical junctures in learning in a college course on evolution. *Journal of Research in Science Teaching*, 31(5), 459–474.

Trowbridge, J. E., & Wandersee, J. H. (1996). How do graphics presented during college biology lessons affect students' learning? A concept map analysis. *Journal of College Science Teaching*, 26(1), 54–57.

Wandersee, J. H. (1988). Ways students read texts. *Journal of Research in Science Teaching*. 25(1), 69–84.

Wandersee, J. H. (1990). Concept mapping and the cartography of cognition. *Journal of Research in Science Teaching*, 27(10), 923–936.

Wandersee, J. H. (1994). Making high-tech micrographs meaningful to the biology student. In P. Fensham, R. Gunstone, & R White (Eds.), *The content of science: A constructivist approach to its teaching and learning* (Chapter 12, pp. 161–176). London: Falmer Press.

Wandersee, J. H. (1996). The graphic representation of biological knowledge: Integrating words and images. In K. M. Fisher & M. R. Kibby (Eds.), *Knowledge acquisition, organization, and use in biology* (NATO ASI Series) (Chapter 2, pp. 25–35). Berlin: Springer-Verlag.

Wandersee, J. H. (1997, October 11). *How to design a visual biology test*. Paper presented at the 1997 National Convention of the National Association of Biology Teachers, Minneapolis, MN.

Wandersee, J. H., & Schussler, E. E. (1999). Preventing plant blindness. *The American Biology Teacher*, 61: 82, 84, 86.

Zakia, R. D. (1997). *Perception and imaging*. Newton, MA: Butterworth–Heinemann.

CHAPTER 7

Observation Rubrics in Science Assessment

JOHN E. TROWBRIDGE
Southeastern Louisiana University

JAMES H. WANDERSEE
Louisiana State University

Many people have heard the story of the Chinese bamboo tree: A farmer plants a Chinese bamboo tree seed, tends it for four years and sees nary a sprout. To the untrained eye, his extensive labors have been in vain, but the farmer knows that in the third month of the fifth year it will soon begin to grow into a tree that soon will be 90 feet tall. The moral of the story is: It takes time for important work to pay off.

There's only one small problem. Bamboo isn't a tree, it's a grass; there's no such thing as a bamboo tree. Of the 1200+ species of bamboo, not one is even treelike (Chadderon, 1998). In addition, if bamboo seeds don't germinate within a year, they probably aren't viable seeds. Normally, within a few months an aboveground shoot appears (Chadderon, 1998).

Finally, even Chinese bamboo experts have not heard of this supposedly "Chinese" tree form of bamboo. Your authors suspect what the legend calls the Chinese bamboo tree is actually *Ailanthus altissima*, the Tree of Heaven—a deciduous native to China that reaches 40–60 feet in height after about a decade of growth, and that bears orange-red to brown fruit (samara) that persists into winter. The Tree of Heaven is one of the most adaptable and pollution-tolerant trees available for planting in cities. It is the tree made famous in the novel *A Tree Grows in Brooklyn*. It's a fast-sprouting (contrary to

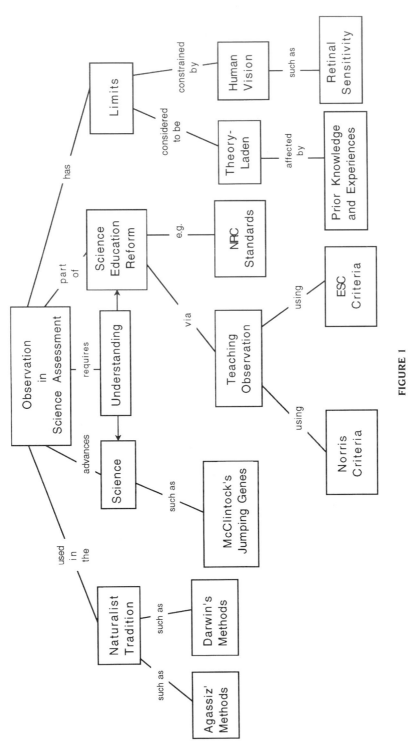

FIGURE 1

Overview of chapter.

legend), easy to grow, tenacious tree, which some consider to be a weed having no "landscape value."

What is the take-home message here? There is no substitute for direct and reliable observations. Or, "to separate the bamboo from the bamboozle," only careful observations can anchor knowledge to the real world. This chapter examines the rubrics of science assessment (Figure 1).

Elementary school science curricula and texts focus on scientific processes, often beginning with observation. Observation skills are treated as a foundation for carrying out other scientific processes such as classifying and making inferences (Abruscato, 1992). Dorothy Gabel (1984), a respected science educator and researcher, rationalizes observation to be among the most basic skills needed in the study of science. She states, "Teaching children to become discriminating observers is one of the major objectives of science education in the elementary school (p. 1)." Our own research has convinced us that not only has direct observation led to scientific discoveries, it is also a powerful approach to teaching science for understanding (Trowbridge & Wandersee, 1995).

OBSERVATION IN THE NATURALIST TRADITION

We have also explored the teaching methods of zoologist Louis Agassiz, an influential mentor of America's first generation of biologists. Though some of his scientific views may be at variance with today's science, the lasting lesson Agassiz taught his students and, thus, generations of biologists to come was the importance and power of direct observation. He contended that the laboratory ought not be a place for mere verification of generalizations. Rather, it should be a haven where each student observes, compares, and generalizes for himself or herself (Teller, 1947, p. 72). Agassiz was once asked, "What do you regard as your greatest work?" He replied, "I have taught men to observe" (Cooper, 1945, p. 1).

"Go to nature; take the facts into your own hands; look and see for yourself!"—these were the maxims Agassiz extolled wherever he went (James, 1911, p. 12). James states, "His passion for knowing living things was combined with a rapidity of observation, and a capacity to recognize them again and remember everything about them" (p. 5).

AGASSIZ' BIOLOGY TEACHING LEGACY

In a similar fashion, present-day introductory ichthyology laboratory exercises often start with a box of bones and students are asked to rearticulate a fish skeleton. The degree of help from the instructor and access to laboratory manuals does vary, because only one or two labs may be devoted to this activity. Ichthyology students then move on to morphometrics—key characteristics of body form, such as shape or fin placements. Then they learn meristics—countable characteristics such as the number of spines and rays in a particular fin or number of gill rakers. With the visible piscine body as the basic referent, the student must accomplish such observational tasks before moving inward (studying internal anatomy and physiology) or outward (studying marine ecology). In this fashion students are empowered to make critical observations that serve to anchor future learning.

Across the sciences, from marine science to cytogenetics, we think Louis Agassiz's approach rings true. Evelyn Fox Keller (1985), biographer of Nobel laureate and cytogeneticist Barbara McClintock, has written extensively about this scientist's "feelings" for her research organism, the corn plant—a feeling born of years of McClintock's method of focused observation, which she practiced first in the field and then in the laboratory. McClintock emphasized that much of today's research is done improperly, with a view of imposing answers on the organism, rather than doing the kind of sustained observation of a species in nature that allows the visual story to unfold (Griffard & Wandersee, 1997).

She admonished new students to look at your organisms every day—in the natural where they are found. She also believed firmly in focusing on *differences* that she noted in her observations, and in focusing intensively on individual organisms within the context of a population. Biographer Keller (p. 164) quotes McClintock as saying, "From days, weeks, and years of patient observations comes what looks like privileged insight: 'When I see things, I can interpret them right away.'" Thus, McClintock learned about "jumping genes" long before other geneticists did; using her sustained observation-based cytogenetics. She had to wait years for the scientific world to catch up to her discoveries. Perhaps there is a powerful message here for all of us interested in understanding how science makes significant progress through observation.

There are modern-day instances of where direct observation of nature, combined with a passion for knowing, has promoted a gain in scientific knowledge. The *Chronicle of Higher Education* (Gose, June 23, 1995), reported that a junior at Yale was publishing a book on trout. The book—the most thorough of its kind—contains watercolor paintings and short descriptions of 70 species of North American trout. The young man (20 years old at the time) has a passion for trout fishing and has noticed the lack of diversity spurred by anglers' desires for trophy-size fish. The wildlife management response to the public's trophy quest has been stocking by non-native fish that grow to a bigger size. The non-native fish may out-compete the native species, resulting in lower species diversity. The author hopes his book will stimulate wildlife biologists' attempts to preserve and restore species diversity in natural systems (Gose, 1995). Much of his information comes from an illustrated daily diary he keeps of his fishing adventures, which now fill nine notebooks. It is undisputed that much of his knowledge of trout comes from firsthand experience and self-taught observational skills.

Then there are those among us who rediscover the power of observation. Lawrence Biemiller (1995) reported on how a vacation at a lake reintroduced him to the process of observation. His rediscovery was prompted by a comment made by a member of his vacation party: "You've got to look hard at something for at least ten minutes before you start to see what you are looking at." We have chosen to name this the 10-Minute Rule and will refer to it later. Following this advice, he became more observant in a variety of contexts, such as when visiting an art museum or when looking through an old set of encyclopedias. Inquiry followed naturally. He states that, "A lesson you teach yourself, by careful observation and consideration, is still ten times as potent, and a hundred times more rewarding, as a lesson from a textbook. Observing the world around you carefully, and learning from all that it offers to teach, is about as fine a pastime as a man or woman can devise. You just have to take ten minutes to get yourself started, to begin seeing how much there is" (Biemiller, 1995, p. A39).

Nonscientists are often involved in making observations. These people may not have any scientific training beyond what is necessary for them to make and report their observations precisely and accurately. More than a century ago, the U.S. Weather Service initiated monitoring in North America, and still continues today with more than 11,000 volunteer monitoring stations. For decades, the National Audubon Society has conducted an Annual Christmas Bird Count utilizing a large number of trained volunteers (often more than 45,000 participate). Wildflower surveys are part of phenological studies, which have had a rich history in Europe during the last two centuries. Phenological studies of plants may include dates of first bud, first leaf, or first flowering of a season. These studies of plants and animals are thought to be good indicators of climate change (Mappin, 1998).

Today, nonscientist observers are used in citizen monitoring programs such as tornado spotting, whale migration charting, dolphin behavior photography, Monarch butterfly tagging, and asteroid warning. We contend that one of the best ways to teach a lasting lesson on scientific observation is in a "science for citizenship" context—where student data are seen as real contributions to a national or global scientific effort, which requires some in depth, situated understanding of a particular science topic, and where the student comes to view scientific observation, like science itself, as a transnational activity.

SCIENCE ADVANCES THROUGH OBSERVATION

Biological theories are often supported and refined through observation. Consider Schwann and Schleiden's cell theory, largely microscopy-based, and the Darwin–Wallace theory of evolution by natural selection, largely biogeography-based. In geology, plate tectonics—the modern theory of continental drift—was also confirmed by indirect observation coupled with inference. Like the cell theory and evolutionary theory in biology, plate tectonics revolutionized our understanding of the natural world.

In physics, ponder the observational skill displayed by the 19-year-old Galileo. By studying the swinging lamps in a church using only his sight and his pulse, he discovered the principle of isochronism—each swing of the pendulum takes the same time, regardless of its amplitude. Metrologists were elated. From this youthful Galilean observation came the technology for the pendulum clock, further subdividing the arrow of time.

The Russian chemist Dmitri Mendeleev noted the recurrence of the chemical and physical properties of the known elements when arranged in a table form by increasing atomic number via note cards he posted on his office wall. His work demonstrates that observations can be made indirectly, here across existing data sets—a kind of metaobservation, or the detection and observation of patterns within already-made data sets of direct observations. The periodic table and its powerful, graphic arrangement of observational data has enabled great progress to be made in understanding the current thinking about the chemical nature of matter.

Through direct and indirect observation, the current U.S. Human Genome Project in biology hopes to produce the life sciences' equivalent of the periodic table for human biology, a complete map and decoding of the human genome (human chromosomal data set).

Thus, observations can be direct, mediated by instruments, coupled with inference, pooled, collated across time and space, and distilled into principles. They can enable technological advances, unlock meaningful understanding within a knowledge domain, and drive both research and technology. From a teenager in church to a scientist on the moon, observations, both serendipitous and planned, sometimes have unforeseen but major impacts on what we know about our world.

Richard Perry (1972), in his book *The Unknown Ocean*, writes about life in the ocean:

> The bizarre variety of its [the ocean's] multitudinous life has been partially revealed by the strange harvests of fishermen, by chance encounters with mariners, and by the deep trawls of marine biologist. The latter, however, admit that much of the data they have amassed during their tens of thousands of patient dredging, and their hundreds of thousands of hours of ingenious laboratory research must be reworked, and their theories revised, in the new light of direct observation by the skin-diver's eye and the underwater camera. (pp. 13–14)

NOTABLE SCIENTISTS WHO USE OBSERVATIONS
AS A BASIS FOR THEIR WORK

The power of direct observation cannot be overestimated as a fundamental process of science. By itself, it has led to many discoveries and contributed to both scientific knowledge and scientific methods. Agassiz's instructional method, mentioned previously, also relies on direct observation. Here are several examples of the roles observation have had in science.

Stephan Jay Gould, famed Harvard University paleontologist, on a recent stroll down the beach in the Bahamas noticed a telltale change in the shells of land snails found on a mudflat. Because of his keen interest in these tropical island snails and his years of experience observing them, he hypothesized that the act of evolution was occurring there, not just hybridization. He sorted them and saw a pattern! Laboratory tests later confirmed his intuitive insight (Cromie, 1997).

Michael Goulding, a tropical ecologist, studies the relationship between fish and trees in the Amazon River basin (Wade, 1997, pp. 39–42). What relationship you may ask? Dr. Goulding studied a fish that is perfectly adapted for a fish–tree interaction. The tambaqui fish, a swift, 3-foot-long, 60-pound relative of the dreaded piranha, was observed to eat, transport, and excrete tree seeds. He found that 50% of the group of 96 tambaqui whose stomachs he dissected had crushed rubber tree seeds inside, and 20% had palm fruits, some as big as 2 inches in diameter. It was observed that the fish wait for the fruit to drop into the water or they pick the fruit off low-hanging branches that dip into the river. Who would have thought that fish and trees are directly connected ecologically? Careful observation, both anatomical and behavioral, both qualitative and quantitative, ultimately elucidated these intertwined plant and fish life cycles.

Jerome Namias, a weather expert credited for the development of the extended forecast, was able to forecast the weather for periods of weeks and seasons ahead, largely by recognizing recurrent weather patterns. He placed emphasis on the way the upper layers and surface of the ocean interact with the atmosphere. He examined statistical likelihoods and looked for analogies in the observed weather record. Here we see experience that led to an intuitive ability, founded on observation.

Naturalist and natural history approaches gave rise to ecology as a major scientific field. Ecologists immediately started creating complex mathematical models and flow diagrams and the discipline became more experimental every year. Wade Roush (1995), in the journal *Science*, reports that many ecologists are now questioning experimental techniques that do not have a natural history foundation accompanied by extended observations. We think that is how progress in science is best made—by sustained multivariate observation. He cites the example of James Brown, an ecologist at the University of New Mexico, and his 18-year study done on plots in the Chiuahuan desert. Brown and his colleagues have been manipulating one factor after another in an attempt to explain predator–prey relationships. The experiments are long-term, tedious, expensive, but very realistic. That's how progress in understanding is made.

Another mystery, this time in entomology, yields to careful observation. Where do wispy monarch butterflies get enough energy to migrate 1800 miles? Observation unraveled the mystery. Dr. David Marriott, founder of the monarch program in Encinitas, California, knows the answer. Those monarchs that develop in early fall appear to be genetically programmed to gather lots of nectar from plants, convert it into fat biologically, and store it a small area of fatty tissue (Ray, 1998, p. B12). Thus, reserve nectar-based power, plus occasional feeding enroute makes such a long migration metabolically possible.

PEDAGOGY AND THE NEW STANDARDS

Using the power of observation within a content area seems to have a good fit with meaningful learning theory. In fact, observation activities can serve as an anchor for many of the elements associated with meaningful learning. A concept map summarizing many of the principles of meaningful learning and their connections to observation is shown in Figure 2. Note how observation can serve as the linchpin of conceptual change. We think this avenue has been relatively unexploited pedagogically in the past.

The *National Science Education Standards* (NRC, 1996) provide many opportunities for observation. Several examples are given below:

Unifying Concepts and Processes
- Evidence consists of observation and data on which to base scientific explanations. Use evidence to help understand interactions and predict changes in natural observed systems (p. 117).

Science as Inquiry
- Use observations to construct reasonable explanations for questions posed (p. 121).
- In the earliest years, investigations are largely based on systematic observations (p. 122).
- As students conduct investigations and observations, they should consider questions such as "What data will answer the question?" and "What are the best observations or measurements to make?" (p. 144).
- Some investigations involve observing and describing objects, organisms, and events (p. 148).

We are already seeing changes in teaching that focus on observations. For example, Purdue physics professor Charles Holbrow was influenced by the U.S. trend to make science education a more active process. His approach is to teach science by observation, which leads to hypothesis generation and testing. For example, he will mix two flasks of different

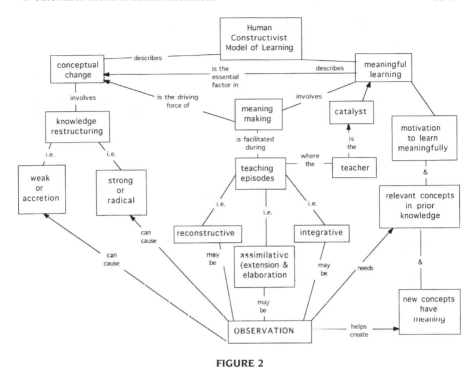

FIGURE 2

Concept map situating observation within meaningful learning.

chemicals and through a process of exhaustive questioning, students will invent the concept of molarity. The idea behind the pedagogic approaches of Holbrow and like-minded professors was to start students off on a course in which they must observe, hypothesize, and think like scientists, and thus keep more of them interested in science (Morgan, 1991).

Observation seems to be the basis for a great deal of inquiry-based teaching. Foster (1998) describes an excellent classroom example of observation leading to inquiry. Fifth-grade students were asked, What makes fruit change color and why? The students designed tests and made observations over time. It was decided that the observations needed to be inscribed with drawings and records of touch and smell. The teacher reported that "observations and questions flowed."

Other observations done by these same students included comparative molding in a carved pumpkin vs. rotten tomatoes, and fruit flies emerging from the compost pile. Misiti (1993) reports that good observations lead to good questions. Misiti makes an important point about the difference between just seeing and observation. "Seeing is a passive process whereas observing is an active process often utilizing many senses at once."

THEORY-LADENNESS OF OBSERVATION

The criteria presented next may appear to be at variance with current constructivist views in science education, and as well the idea of objective science. The criteria seem to direct the observer to seek the truth of their observations in a totally objective manner. We know that the goal of totally objective thinking has waned in the last 25 years and that, at times, even good observations cannot explain a particular phenomenon. Classical Newtonian physics was based on observation and common sense, which made the shift to classical mechanics difficult for many scientists and educators (Matthews, 1992). Observation is not theory-independent; it is very much is dependent on what Kuhn (1962) calls the observer's "conceptual goggles."

Norris (1984) qualifies the following criteria by stating they are not to be used as a necessary set or a sufficient set, but to be recognized as merely a set of conditions or frameworks. We believe that these criteria may help students to make more elaborate observations that improve the reporting of the qualities of the observed phenomena. The criteria may also compel observers to be self-reflective about their observations and explain and explore their own stances and biases. We think it is important to raise the observer's consciousness regarding the need to recognize and minimize subjectivity—not idealize objectivity.

TEACHING THE POWER OF DIRECT OBSERVATION

We have found that students can become competent observers through well-planned activities that develop observation skills. Two sets of proficiencies, skills, and criteria for observation are presented here from the seminal work of Norris (1994) and the Eisenhower Southwest Consortium for the Improvement of Mathematics and Science Teaching (1996). Teaching observational competence requires a set of proficiencies. Norris (1994) described observation competence as consisting of three broad proficiencies: (1) making observations well, (2) reporting observations well, and (3) correctly assessing the believability of reports of observation. While these are somewhat distinct activities, they are also related. Below we outline the Norris proficiencies. We have elected to call them criteria because they can serve as evaluative standards during the assessment of science understanding.

COMPLEMENTARY SETS OF CRITERIA TO ASSESS
THE QUALITY OF OBSERVATION

Making Observations Well—The Norris Criteria

To observe well an observer should:

1. Recognize emotions that may interfere with making sound judgments.

2. Be alert to the situation and give his or her observation careful consideration.
3. Have no identifiable conflict of interest.
4. Demonstrate being skilled at observing the sort of thing observed.
5. Verify having senses and sensory equipment functioning normally.
6. Attempt to use as precise a technique as appropriate.
7. Observe in well-chosen situations in which good access to the thing is available. Access is good to the extent that:
   a. There is a satisfactory medium of observation.
   b. There are sufficient several opportunities for observation.
   c. There is more than one opportunity to observe.
   d. If used, instrumentation is adequate. Instrumentation is adequate to the extent that
      i. It has reasonable precision.
      ii. It has an appropriate range of application.
      iii. It is of high quality.
      iv. It works in a way that is well understood.
      v. It is currently in good working condition.

Reporting Observations Well—The Norris Criteria

To report observations well, an observer should:

1. Report the observation no more precisely than can be justified by the observation technique that was used.
2. Prepare the report close to the time of observing.
3. Be sure to report the observation himself or herself.
4. Complete the report in the same environment in which the observation was made.
5. Report the observation in a well-designed record.

Assessing Reports of Observations—The Norris Criteria

An observation report tends to be believable to the extent that:

1. The observer has met the conditions for good observations.
2. The observer has met the conditions for reporting his or her observations properly.
3. The following conditions are satisfied:
   a. The observer has an established reputation for being honest and correct.
   b. The observer avoided exposure, after the event, to further information relevant to describing it.
   c. The observer behaved in a mature way and is unequivocally in full possession of his or her faculties.

d. The observation report commits the speaker/reader to holding a small number of things to be true.
e. The observation report is fully corroborated.
f. The observation report can affect the observer's reputation for truthfulness and the observer fully realizes this.
g. The observation report does not obviously conflict with other statements for which good reason can be given.
h. The observation is not being made about an emotionally loaded event.
i. The observation report is the first impression provided by the speaker.
j. The observation report is not made in response to a leading question.
k. The observation report does not include a recollection of something previously forgotten.
l. The observation report focuses on salient features of an event.
m. Having a record, the observation report comes from a source with a good reputation for making careful records (pp. 135–137).

Levels of Observational Competency—The ESC Criteria

The previous list could be intimidating to the average classroom science teacher. We suggest that it be used as a guideline for developing a site–classroom-specific rubric to assess observation. Included here is a useful rubric reported by the Eisenhower Southwest Consortium for the Improvement of Mathematics and Science Teaching (1996, p. 3):

"*Novice*" *is one who*
- Sees only obvious things, notices few details or changes, has poor discrimination ability.
- Doesn't use all of his or her senses.

"*Novice plus*" *is one who*
- Makes somewhat focused and active observations, but his or her quality, depth, breadth, and accuracy are inconsistent.

"*Proficient*" *is one who*
- Uses all of the senses to notice details, patterns, similarities, and differences.
- Can quantify observations using appropriate measurements.

"*Proficient plus*" *is one who*
- Follows a regular program of observations.
- Makes objective and accurate observations consistently.

"Advanced" is one who

- Judges how frequently and accurate observations need to be made for an experiment [or inquiry] and makes them accordingly.
- Uses discerned patterns and relationships to focus further observations.

HUMAN VISION

Human vision is both amazingly flexible and yet limited. For example, machine-driven robotics used to spot and eliminate out-of-specifications products on an assembly line can detect up to 256 shades of gray. In contrast the human eye sees just 64 shades of gray, at best (Ryan, 1998). Human vision is an eye–brain system capable of detecting an object's color, motion, shape, direction, and distance—each variable having distinct detection limits (Gregory, 1995).

Vision improves quickly in the first month of life, but there are subtle improvements that occur all the way up to age 6. Many visual maps have been discovered in the human brain, and in cortical development all of these maps gradually become linked. Human vision has physical limits, and, thus, human observations have visual limits.

Filtering of Human Vision

We actually "see" only a tiny band within the total electromagnetic spectrum known as visible light. We have learned how to construct devices that "see" everything from radio waves to cosmic rays—or at least our external detectors' signals can be transformed into visual representations. By harnessing the entire electromagnetic spectrum for our scientific observations, we have opened up new windows of understanding.

It is easy to think that representation is reality. But, as artist René Magritte, the surrealist, aptly demonstrated, the representation is not equivalent to the thing represented. The X-ray radiograph may contain artifacts, the radar display may portray false returns, and the sonogram cannot show air and bone. Our extrasensory "images" are altered or filtered on the basis of our detectors and processors.

Just as optical telescopes, and now radio telescopes, extend our vision of the solar system and the universe beyond, so the optical microscope and various electron microscopes extend our vision of the microworld and its molecular–atomic inhabitants. Our senses are indeed limited by their electromagnetic parameters, but these inherent limits can be circumvented via clever "prosthetic" devices sensitive to machine-detectable wave lengths, whose outputs can then be transformed into a visual representation that our eyes can decode.

Journals

Using journals to record observations is a tradition in science. Our previous examples of the trout fisher and Barbara McClintock illustrate that the value of an observation may not be revealed for quite some time. The fieldbook a biologist keeps, the written diary of an explorer, or a ship captain's log are all examples of records that capture an event when it happens. The event is not only described, but it also situated within a time frame.

Historians certainly make use of eyewitness accounts, but so do scientists. For example, it may not be convenient (or possible!) to return to the arctic regions explored by Byrd, but his diary or log will give insights into the experience within the era it occurred. Another example might be the useful information packed into the diary kept by the Lewis and Clarke expedition. Westward expansion would have been hindered were it not for their journal's vital information. Fleming's observation in 1928 that a mold interfered with the growth of bacteria in a culture dish led to the development of penicillin. Consider, too, what we learned about the human anatomy and the behavior and musculature of horses from Da Vinci's notebooks of drawings, about microorganisms from Leuenhook's description of microbes, and about the cosmos from observatory records made by astronomers like Kepler. Such carefully constructed records of observations have been vital to advancing scientific understanding.

Modern-day extensions to journals include flight-data recorders and other data loggers that can capture information without a human observer present. Within our space program, the capabilities of these automated extensions of human presence have given rise to the debate as to whether or not to continue manned space missions.

CONSTRUCTING OBSERVATION RUBRICS

We think the two sets of criteria for assessing observations should serve as a guide for developing your own observation rubrics. We do not want to give a rigid list that will apply to all contexts. Initiation of observations is very much like the classroom process of getting students to ask questions and, more importantly, appropriate questions. When do the students have enough information to ask questions or make observations? There seems to be a stage where students don't know enough to ask relevant questions or make salient observations. There is an important difference between leaving students alone to make their own discoveries and telling them enough so they can proceed on their own (Anderson, 1984). "Answering your own questions leads to the most meaningful and lasting learning" (Anderson, 1984, p.24).

A student in Anderson's (1984) study explained that she liked the type of learning that goes beyond merely just observing, what she described as just playing around. It was when the instructor came around and asked questions and raised clues that she gained the desire to know and understand.

What we propose is an observational framework. This allows for more authenticity because the assessment becomes contextualized. We also strongly advocate that observations be conducted with a specific science content. Elementary science experiences are often centered around idealized and sterile basic processes, such as observing, measuring, or classifying. Such disconnected studies can be carried out without any meaningful science learning context. A common observation or visual discrimination exercise is to distinguish inclusive and exclusive relationships among items such as those in Figure 3. This exercise is content independent, so, based on cognitive research insights, we feel it has negligible value in teaching science.

We strongly suggest that science teachers use the basic frameworks given here and supply the criteria relevant to their lessons. The Norris Framework is a very useful starting point. Its three main parts are;

1. Making observations well
2. Reporting observations well
3. Assessing observations well

A representative example may be assessing a nature walk or field trip activity. Many teachers use such activities and are often disappointed by the lack of observations made by students and the lack of richness or detail in those observations. The students may not have gleaned from the activity what the teacher expected of them.

We suggest that some sort of prefocus activity be conducted before the observation activity takes place. A student-appropriate version of the observation assessment rubric that the teacher plans to employ for the activity should be used in science-content-specific, pretrip, learning exercises. The prefocus activity may include showing slides or pictures and reviewing significant events or objects that may be the focus for the nature walk. For

FIGURE 3
Critical attribute test items—Which two are most similar?

example, the students in the classroom view a picture of a forest, and are asked to make observations about the relative abundance of the different tree species present. Thus, an important ecological consideration such as species dominance can later be determined by observation. This distribution pattern may not be apparent to the students during an unfocused nature walk. What follows is an observational skill rubric we have developed for a middle school nature walk.

Making Observations Well
1. Student made adequate and appropriate use of equipment given (binoculars, nets, etc.).
2. Student reported 10 or more on-task and focused sensory experiences.
3. Student located and spent 10 minutes at each map-designated observation station.
4. Student avoided conflicting interests (Walkman, excessive socializing, etc.).

Reporting Observations Well
1. Student made use of a journal.
2. Journal entries were neat and legible.
3. Journal entries were of sufficient length to explain each phenomenon.
4. Journal entries were made at or very close to the time of the actual observation.

Assessing Observations Well
1. Student reflects on the match between the written record and observation.
2. Conclusions are based on evidence gathered.
3. Scientific conclusions are understandable by others.
4. Any uncorroborated observations are seen as an opportunity for hypothesizing, not perceived as wrong.

This basic framework for an observation rubric focuses on the quality and quantity of objects or phenomena observed. If you have to choose between the two, aim for quality, accompanied by focus and depth of observation. We are looking for some threshold of sensory experiences and a minimum amount of time necessary to make good observations. Each of the above items could be in the form of a checklist, or rating sheet in which a range of point values is provided (for instance, 1 to 5 points).

Depending on what the teachers' goals were for the nature walk and follow-up assessment, they may want to add criteria recommended by Shepardson and Britsch (1997):

Look for observations versus deductions.
Look for level of detail in observations.
Look for observations that note differences.

Look for comparisons.
Look for careful accurate descriptions.

Furthermore, Shepardson and Britsch suggest that observation journals be assessed for conceptual understanding by looking for

- Information, facts, vocabulary
- Prior knowledge of ideas
- Use of words/language that label describe, interpret, and explain
- Changes in understanding science

What we are attempting to do here with regard to developing an observation rubric is to provide a menu of items from which the science teacher can select. Again, any rubric must be constructed with regard to the teacher's expectations and the type of content to be taught. We are very suspicious of attempts to teach process skills that are not explicitly linked to specific science concepts.

Tables 1–3 give selected proficiencies and suggested sample activities that will help develop these skills or proficiencies.

TEACHING HOW TO MAKE GOOD OBSERVATIONS

We believe that students can be taught and continuously upgraded in specific science observation skills (Table 1). We certainly advocate lots of practice before actual grades are assigned to the students' observations. A simple activity that requires focused observations is called "Oyster in the Half-Shell" (Kolb, 1986). Each student receives an oyster shell, is asked to write five descriptive observations on a card, and returns the shell and card to separate boxes. Now each student is given or selects a card (not his or her own) and must find the shell that it describes. Generally, what happens is that descriptions are too vague (such as gray on the outside and smooth

TABLE 1
Making Observations Well

Proficiency	Activity
Focus observations	Oyster shell activity
Agree on common vocabulary	Estimations of wind speed using the Beaufort Scale
Technique	Orientation competitions with compass and validation checkpoints.
Avoid conflict of interest	Written analysis of identified biases that may enter into a scientific investigation—using the recent radio-astronomy-based movie: Contact!

TABLE 2
Reporting Observations Well

Proficiency	Activity
Degree of precision	Use an array of thermometers to record the temperature of a bucket of cold water. Note the variation in readings.
Time of reporting observation	Compare in-field notes with notes written at various times after the observation was done.
The reporter	Contrast firsthand, secondhand, and film records (e.g., photographs) of an event.
Well-made record	Explore the strengths and weaknesses of a variety of record-making approaches, such as written notebooks, sketchbooks, thermal signatures, audio recordings, and video recordings.

and white on the inside) and don't zero in on the individual shell's characteristics. Visual differences that would distinguish the shells from each other are not used. However, if the instructions are given as "Write down five descriptive observations that will allow someone else to find the shell," then the results are quite different. Furthermore, if students are allowed to use rulers, scales, color scales, and other tools to quantify aspects of their shell, they can become more adept at making critical distinctions among the shells. This activity works well with peanuts, too, or any other set of objects that where individual organisms that seem similar at first can be distinguished on the basis of critical attributes.

In any case, the teacher needs to provide seasoned feedback based on observational proficiency that she/he has developed and practiced for the organism or phenomenon of interest. Note that the teacher needs to be proficient at the observational skills and content she/he is using. Without such a knowledge base, the teacher cannot adequately guide the lesson, ask the right questions, or assess student responses.

Observations may be influenced by preconceived perceptions. For, example if you were told to watch for out snakes when hiking a trail, various sticks

TABLE 3
Assessing Observations Well

Proficiency	Activity
Records unaltered	Can an embellished tale be de-embellished?
Observer is honest	Verification exercise such as a fish story—can the fisherman be trusted?
Includes salient features	Report weeding. Explore extraneous data in reports. What data are of greatest worth.
Report corroborated	Is it replicable? Or is this just "cold fusion" revisited?

you see would begin to take on the form of a snake. Scientists have demonstrated the surprising extent to which the brain's expectations can warp what it perceives (Academic Press, 1998).

Blind malacologist G. Vermeij (1997), through experience, developed a keen sense of observation of seashells. He gives a brief account of a 4th-grade science lesson with seashells.

> I wondered why the cold-water shells of the Dutch beaches were so chalky and plain, whereas tropical creations were ornate and polished. My fourth-grade teacher had not only given my hands an unforgettable esthetic treat, but she aroused in me a lasting curiosity of things unknown. Mrs. Colberg captured the essence of her task. She created an opportunity, a freedom for someone to observe, an encouragement to wonder, and in the end a permissive environment in which to ask a genuine scientific question. (p. 5)

TEACHING HOW TO REPORT OBSERVATIONS WELL

Reporting observations is a critical transference of the observed to some type of permanent record (Table 2). When using equipment to make observations, students need to know how to use the equipment and what constitutes an accurate and precise reading. For example, the range of body temperature from a healthy person to one with a fever lies within a few degrees. Therefore, a thermometer that has a scale calibrated from 32 to 212°F or 0 to 100°C, will not yield the precision needed to determine if a person has a fever. Note also that there is a marked difference in calibration points between U.S. and European fever thermometers as to what constitutes a normal body temperature.

Likewise, the neatness and accuracy of the recordings is critical. For example, when observers are writing field notes they must consider the fact that someone else may need to decipher them.

TEACHING HOW TO ASSESS OBSERVATIONS WELL

Just as observing and reporting observations may be affected by perception and expectation, so can the assessment of observations be affected by interpretation (Table 3). When telling stories there often seems to be some slight change in the story when it travels from one person to the next. How can these changes be detected and, more importantly, how can they be avoided? We recommend that a system of verification be built into the assessment of observations. This may include corroboration from different sources, such as eyewitness, photograph, or videotape. For verbal information that has been repeated, students could verify their information accounts with the person who originated the information. Just as a reporter is to supposed to verify and check her/his sources, a student making observations should have a method of verifying her/his observation records.

CONCLUSION

The power of observation cannot be overestimated in science. There is a rich history of how observation has advanced science. The message for science teaching is to develop observational skills. It is very important that these skills be developed within a context or content area. Lessons empty of content are just that, empty. By developing rubrics that assess observation, teachers and students receive helpful feedback and gain information that can enhance metalearning—a cognitive activity vital to meaningful learning. We advise teachers to aim toward developing students' observational skills within specific science contexts and within the intellectual space mapped out by the recent science standards, instead of dreaming about the Holy Grail of universal transfer and generic science process skills. Work toward refining and tracking students' observational proficiency levels throughout the science curriculum, via appropriate prefocus and situated science observation exercises and field-based activities.

Look to the histories of science to find inspiring and insightful exemplars of observation prowess in the particular science domain of interest. It is our contention that, in contrast to many other animals, humans are typically suboptimal observers—which, in turn, places unnecessary limitations on their understanding of nature. To see nature, to really see it in previously untapped ways, is to open up new avenues of scientific understanding. Yes, it is hard to assess a student's observational proficiency and we are only beginning to explore new ways of doing so. But the history of science suggests it will pay dividends for science literacy and for the advancement of science in service of the generations we hope to educate during the new millennium.

A closing example: Most people pay little attention to the green foliage they encounter in the woods. Our research shows that students say they prefer to study animals rather than plants (Wandersee, 1986). However, an irritating and uncomfortable encounter with poison ivy or poison oak can make even the most plant-uninterested hunter or backpacker a focused observer. The slogan goes, "Leaves of three, let it be." See Figure 4 and look for the similarities in foliage. After an itching experience, people who like to be outdoors usually form a strong visual search image for the leaves of these two dermatitis agents. Where once they only saw green leaves, now they see different and threatening species. This illustrates how motivation affects observation. One of the most challenging tasks in teaching science is motivating students to learn—and some topics are definitely easier to sell than others!

FIGURE 4
Leaves of three, let it be! Visually identifying poison ivy and poison oak.

References

Abruscato, J. (1992). *Teaching children science* (3rd ed.). Boston: Allyn & Bacon.
Academic Press. (1998). Fooling the mind's eye. *Daily inSight*. On-line at *http://www.academic press.com/inscight/07131998/grapha.htm*
Anderson, C. (Ed.) (1984). Observing science perspectives from research and practice. In *Observing science classrooms: 1984 AETS Yearbook*, p.24. Columbus, OH. ERIC.
Biemiller, L. (1995, August 11). On Rangeley Lake: The leisure to learn from what is around you. *The Chronicle of Higher Education* 41, A39, August 11. Washington, DC: Chronicle of Higher Education.
Chadderon, L. (1998, November). The big bamboozle. *Fast Company*, p.62.
Cooper, L. (1945). *Louis Agassiz as a teacher*. Ithaca, NY: Comstock.
Cromie, W. J. (1997, January 9). Snails caught in act of evolution. *Harvard University Gazette*, pp. 1, 6.
Eisenhower Southwest Consortium for the Improvement of Mathematics and Science Teaching. (1996). Putting numbers on performance. *Classroom Compass*, 2(2). Austin, TX: Author.
Foster, S. (1998, Spring). New perspective—new practice: A classroom example. *Principled Practice in Mathematics and Science Education* 2(1), 4–7.
Gabel, D. (1984). *Introductory science skills*. Prospect Heights, IL: Waveland Press.
Gose, B. (1995, June 23). Notes of a fly fisherman. *Chronicle of Higher Education* 42, A27–A28.
Gregory, R. (1995). Starting to see vision. In R. Gregory, J. Harris, P. H. Heard, & D. Rose (Eds.). *The artful eye* (pp. 141–156). New York: Oxford University Press.

Griffard, P. B., & Wandersee, J. H. (1997). Teaching about scientist Barbara McClintock: Bridging molecular and organismal biology. *Adaptation: The Journal of the New York Biology Teachers Association* 19(4), 8–11.

James, W. (1911). *Memories and studies.* New York: Longmans, Green.

Keller, E. F. (1985). *Reflections on gender and science.* New Haven, CT: Yale University Press.

Kolb, J. (Ed.). (1986). *Marine science activities.* Poulsbo, WA: Marine Science Project: For Sea.

Kuhn, T. (1962). *The structure of scientific revolutions.* Chicago: University of Chicago Press.

Mappin, M. J. (1998, Spring–Summer). Choosing an environmental monitoring program. *Green Teacher* (55), 12–15.

Matthews, M. (1992). History, philosophy, and science teaching: The present rapprochement. *Science & Education* 1, 11–47.

Misiti, F. (1993, January). A sense of science. *Science and Children* 30, 28–30.

Morgan, D. (1991). New methods teach science by observation, hypothesis. *Scientist* 5(4), 1–8.

National Research Council. (1996). *National science education standards.* Washington, DC: National Academy Press.

Norris, S. P. (1984). Defining observational competence. *Science Education,* 68(2), 129–142.

Perry, R. (1972). *The unknown ocean.* New York: Taplinger.

Ray, C. C. (1998, October 6). Butterflies' energy. *The New York Times,* p. B12.

Roush, W. (1995). When rigor meets reality. *Science,* 269, 313–315.

Ryan, J. (1998, December 10). Machine vision narrowing the gap between human and robot. *The New York Times,* p. D13.

Shepardson, D. P., & Britsch, J. (1997, January). The nature of student thinking in life science laboratories. *School Science and Mathematics* 97, 37–44.

Teller, J. D. (1947). *Louis Agassiz, scientist and teacher.* Columbus, OH: Ohio State University Press.

Trowbridge, J. E., & Wandersee, J. H. (1995). Agassiz's influence on marine science teaching: Promoting nature study by direct observation. In F. Finley, D. Allchin, D. Rhees, & S. Fifield (Eds.), *Proceedings,* Vol. 2, *Third International History, Philosophy, and Science Teaching Conference,* (pp. 1217–1224). Minneapolis, MN: University of Minnesota.

Vermeij, G. (1997). *Privileged hands: A scientific life.* New York: W.H. Freeman.

Wade, N. (Ed.). (1997). *The science times book of fish.* New York: The Lyons Press.

Wandersee, J. H. (1986). Plants or animals: Which do junior high school students prefer to study? *Journal of Research in Science Teaching* 23(5), 415–426.

CHAPTER

8

Portfolios in Science Assessment: A Knowledge-Based Model for Classroom Practice

MICHAEL R. VITALE
East Carolina University

NANCY R. ROMANCE
Florida Atlantic University

The goal of this chapter is to provide a research-based perspective on the use of portfolios in classroom assessment for three interrelated but diverse audiences: practicing science teachers, graduate students in science education, and science education researchers. In doing so, a primary emphasis is on developing practical recommendations and an associated rationale for the use of portfolios by science teachers as effective tools for instructional assessment in classroom settings. Concomitantly, as a foundation for supporting our perspective and recommendations, we have interwoven into the chapter representative material from a variety of sources that we feel would be of value to all three audiences.

Within the context of science instruction, portfolios may be defined as *collections of student work samples that are assumed to reflect meaningful understanding of underlying science concepts* (Archbald, 1991; Arter & Spandel, 1992; Cary, 1994; Collins, 1992; Benoit & Yang, 1996; Doran, Lawrenz, & Helgeson, 1994; Krueger & Wallace, 1996; Slater, 1994). As a form of authentic assessment, portfolios are considered by advocates to offer teachers a more valid means of evaluating student understanding than traditional forms of testing (Jorgensen, 1996; Reckase, 1995; Wiggins, 1992). Primarily, advocates have emphasized sharing portfolio assessment practices, developing implementation strategies for portfolio scoring schemes in the form of rubrics (e.g., Arter, 1995), and, in some cases, comparing the results of portfolio and traditional assessment in learning settings (Slater, Ryan, & Samson, 1997; Zeilik et al., 1997).

We agree with advocates that portfolio assessment is potentially able to contribute toward science teachers' evaluation of their students' meaningful understanding. However, we also agree with concerns (e.g., Terwilliger, 1997) that student completion of authentic assessment tasks may have little to do with whether they understand science concepts. Just as producing a cake by the rote execution of the steps in a recipe does not imply an individual is a trained chef, a student work sample in a science portfolio may not indicate meaningful conceptual understanding of science knowledge. Despite its importance, this problem has received little attention.

The focus of this chapter reflects our view that the most important practical issue concerning classroom use of portfolio assessment is the development of strategies that provide an explicit linkage between the conceptual science knowledge taught and the means used to assess student understanding of it. In addressing this issue, we first present a research-based rationale that is supportive of the use of portfolios in science classrooms to assess meaningful student understanding. Then, we offer a knowledge-based model in the form of strategies and procedures science teachers can follow to implement portfolio assessment in their classrooms.

PORTFOLIOS AND ASSESSMENT IN SCIENCE

Portfolios and Science Assessment

A variety of perspectives (e.g., Benoit & Yang, 1996) are helpful in understanding the potential role of portfolios in instructional assessment in science. Perhaps the most fundamental is what the term typically denotes in visual disciplines such as art, photography, and architecture. In each of these, a portfolio consists of a sample of products intended to represent the quality of work an individual is capable of accomplishing. In evaluating such a portfolio, the quality of work presented provides a basis for an inference that the individual, having produced such work in the past, is capable of performing work of similar quality in the future. In making an inferential conclusion, the contents of the portfolio are assumed to be the work of the individual, the evaluator of the portfolio makes a clinical judgment regarding the quality of the work, and the purpose of the evaluative judgment is usually well defined. In this context, the function of portfolios is to provide information that contributes toward inferences of future performance.

This chapter considers portfolios in science assessment in much the same fashion as the visual arts, but with an important difference regarding the kind of judgment to be made by science teachers. Specifically, within a science classroom, our view is that a portfolio considered as a work sample should inform teachers' inferences regarding the conceptual understanding of science. And, consistent with this function, the emphasis in this chapter is on a methodology for portfolio assessment that is explicitly supportive of such inferences.

Portfolios in Science Classrooms and Assessment Methodology

Within science classrooms, a wide variety of products could be included as work samples in a student portfolio. In this chapter, however, our emphasis is on student products that reflect the meaningful understanding, integration, and application of science concepts and principles (Raizen et al., 1990). Included among these products might be (1) reports of empirical research completed by students, (2) analyses of societal issues from a sound scientific view, (3) papers demonstrating in-depth understanding of fundamental science principles, (4) documentation of presentations designed to foster understanding of science concepts for others, (5) journals addressing a student's reflective observations over an instructional timespan, and (6) analytic and/or integrative visual representations of science knowledge itself in the form of concept maps. By way of contrast, some of the literature (e.g., Spandel, 1997) considers any collection of student work (e.g., tests, homework, laboratory reports) to be included in a portfolio as representative samples of student understanding. Although we do not dispute what student products teachers choose to include as a work sample, our focus is on portfolio activities and tasks that are open-ended and constructively require students to use and apply knowledge in ways that demonstrate their understanding of science concepts.

While these different forms of portfolio tasks are considered later in the chapter in some detail, the important point here is that whenever portfolios are used by teachers to make evaluative inferences regarding student understanding, the question of psychometric standards of practice must be considered. Our view (Vitale & Romance, 1995b) is that because inferential conclusions are made through an assessment process, the fundamental standards relating to the reliability and validity of student portfolios as assessment instruments are applicable. Certainly, from the standpoint of assessment reliability, no teacher would want to evaluate student performance under conditions in which the evaluative process itself evidenced a high degree of inconsistency. In a similar fashion, from the standpoint of assessment validity, no teacher would want to make conclusions regarding student understanding within a context in which the evaluative data primarily reflected characteristics of performance unrelated to student understanding.

Although a technical treatment of these concerns is beyond the scope of this chapter, our view is in agreement with Hambleton (1994) that all forms of authentic assessment (including portfolio assessment) should themselves be evaluated technically as criterion-referenced tests (Glaser, 1963). Related views by Ruiz-Primo and Shavelson (1996) also suggest that all forms of authentic assessment should be clearly defined in terms of task requirements, a response format, and a scoring (or evaluative) system. While it is certainly common to consider all forms of authentic assessment as needing new methodological standards (Delandshere & Petrosky, 1998), we do not agree. Rather, consistent with the work of Hambleton (1994), Ruiz-Primo and Shavelson (1996), and Terwilliger (1997), we caution practitioners to be sensitive to the traditional concerns relating to reliability and validity, particularly in the face of findings that successful student performance on authentic tasks, problem-solving, and laboratory activities has not always been found to indicate meaningful student understanding of course content (e.g., Baxter, Elder, & Glaser, 1996; Chi, Feltovich, & Glaser, 1981; Halloun & Hestenes, 1985; Maloney, 1994). Also, Shavelson and Ruiz (Chapter 13 in this volume) offer an in-depth exploration of these issues.

Recognizing Other Instructional Uses of Portfolios in Science Teaching

In addition to serving as products in assessment, portfolio activities and tasks also may serve as a constructivist mode of instruction. As such, the development of a portfolio work sample by a student is itself an important instructional element of the classroom learning process. For example, in considering the previous categories of work samples for portfolios, the development of a concept map by a student is well accepted as a constructive activity that is highly integrative in terms of core concepts and concept relationships (Barenholz & Tamir, 1992). Further, the use of science concepts and principles to evaluate a social issue (e.g., an environmental problem) is itself an important learning experience (Doran, Lawrenz, & Melgeson, 1994; Glaser, 1996). Additional support for this perspective, which emphasizes the constructive application of knowledge, has been established in other areas as well (e.g., Trollip & Lippert, 1987). The general point here is that the student completion of portfolio activities fits naturally within a broad constructivist process of science instruction and that the evaluation of student involvement in the activities themselves could be approached in the same fashion as assessment of any performance task.

Summary of Potential Benefits and Problems with Portfolio Assessment in Science

Portfolios clearly have the potential to demonstrate student performance that reflects the integrative understanding and application of science concepts. Their function is to provide the teacher with work samples from which inferences may be made regarding student conceptual understanding. Within this context, however, teachers must establish sufficient methodological control to insure the validity of the inferences made through portfolio assessment.

LIMITATIONS OF THE CHAPTER ON THE SCOPE OF PORTFOLIO ASSESSMENT

Although the model for knowledge-based portfolio assessment we present is a general one, the scope of its development in this chapter has been limited in order to emphasize practical classroom applications. These limitations are best understood as a set of assumptions. A primary assumption is that the model focuses on the clinical use of portfolio assessment by teachers in their classrooms rather than the use of portfolios in large-scale assessment (e.g., LeMahieu, Gitomer, & Eresh, 1995). In this sense, *clinical use* refers to teachers' informed judgments about the degree to which student portfolios indicate meaningful understanding *in conjunction with other available information*. Thus, this chapter assumes that teachers' evaluation of portfolios will be complemented by other forms of assessment.

In focusing on teachers' clinical judgment, the emphasis in this chapter is on amplifying the linkage between student portfolio work samples and the underlying science knowledge the work sample represents rather than scoring schemes or rubrics per se. Consistent with Slater et al. (1997), our view is that the articulation between course content and portfolio tasks is the key to supporting sound teacher evaluative judgments regarding student understanding. Despite their prominence in the literature, generalized numerical scoring schemes (i.e., rubrics) associated with portfolio assessment are, by themselves, not specific enough to provide evidence of meaningful student understanding.

Another simplifying assumption in the chapter is that the portfolio will be used to evaluate individual students rather than collaborative group performance. Along with the question of detailed rubric development, this constraint could be relaxed without loss of generality. However, without the complication of rubrics and with the focus on individual students, the presentation of the knowledge-based portfolio model is simplified.

Finally, other than recognizing their existence and importance, this chapter does not address emerging psychometric issues of authentic assessment having implications for portfolio assessment (e.g., Bateson, 1994; Strong &

Sexton, 1996; Ruiz-Primo & Shavelson, 1996; Terwilliger, 1997). This is because the portfolio model presented explicitly addresses the question of assessment validity by establishing a knowledge-based context within which teacher inferences are made.

A COGNITIVE SCIENCE PERSPECTIVE ON KNOWLEDGE, LEARNING, AND ASSESSMENT

Core Concepts and Concept Relationships as a Framework for Science Understanding

The question of the definition and representation of knowledge has been recognized as important in a variety of different disciplines. As used in cognitive science and related disciplines, knowledge refers to conceptual understanding rather than rote memorization of inert factual information. In computer science, Sowa (1984) developed conceptual graphs as a method for representing knowledge. In cognitive science, Anderson (1993, 1996) has studied meaningful learning as a process of first representing and then transforming declarative forms of knowledge into procedural forms of expertise. In instructional design, Engelmann and Carnine (1982) have approached the curriculum development process as one of identifying and then teaching core concepts and concept relationships that provide the basis for concept understanding and application. In educational psychology, Ausubel (Ausubel, 1963; Ausubel, Novak, & Hanesian, 1978) and Novak (Novak, 1998; Novak & Gowin, 1984) have stressed the hierarchical structure of concepts and concept relationships as a framework for meaningful learning and understanding (vs. rote performance).

Although somewhat different in emphasis, the preceding perspectives all incorporate three key elements in addressing the question of representing conceptual knowledge and understanding. The first key element is that *concepts are defined as classes or sets of instances that have one or more common characteristics.* Some examples of simple concepts in science would be *expanding* (getting larger), *contracting* (getting smaller), *hotter* (in temperature), and *colder* (in temperature). Demonstrating understanding of concepts typically requires students to identify novel instances as examples or non-examples of the class or category.

The second key element is that *science principles are represented as relationships among concepts.* Some examples of simple conceptual relationships would be that *objects expand when heated* (and contract when cooled) and that *a substance in a medium that is less dense will rise.* Demonstrating understanding of concept relationships typically requires students to apply them by making specific predictions (e.g., since the object is being heated, it will expand; since the substance is less dense, it will rise.)

The third key element is that *analysis of observed events is based on knowledge of conceptual relationships*. Some simple examples in this domain would include interpreting the fact that a substance rose in a medium as possibly (but not necessarily) being due to the fact that it was less dense or attributing the expansion of an object to the possibility that it was heated. In these cases, knowledge of relevant conceptual relationships provides the analytic basis for possible reasons as to why an event might have occurred, thus providing scientific explanations for understanding of phenomena.

A Methodological Perspective on Science Knowledge and Understanding

In considering methodological approaches for representing conceptual relationships, Anderson (1993, 1996) has used production rules to represent knowledge in an IF/THEN form. An example of a production rule would be IF *an object is heated*, THEN *it will expand*. Although a simple notion, production rules have the advantage that they have an explicit logical structure that is well understood in knowledge representation and that they are easy to transform into specified tasks for use in instructional settings. For example, demonstrating an understanding of the relationship that *objects expand when heated* follows a fundamental form of logical argument (i.e., modus ponens):

1. Given that the rule IF *an object is heated* THEN *it expands* is TRUE, and
2. Given, in a specific situation, that it is TRUE that *a designated object is heated*, then, it can be concluded that
3. It is TRUE that *the designated object will expand*.

Thus, knowledge of the conceptual relationship specified by the IF/THEN rule in combination with situation-specific factual information provides the student with the capability to demonstrate conceptual understanding by making a knowledge-based prediction.

In his work, Anderson (1993, 1996) has illustrated how simple linguistic transformations of IF/THEN production rules in declarative form can provide a guideline for representing knowledge-based applications as procedural knowledge. For example, the production rule IF *an object is heated*, THEN *it will expand* as a form of declarative knowledge can be transformed linguistically to represent procedural knowledge that is applied as follows: *To predict whether an object will expand, determine whether it is being heated* or *to make an object expand, heat it*.

In much the same way, knowledge-based production rules provide a means for representing other powerful forms of knowledge as conceptual relationships. For example, hierarchical concept definitions that involve the feature of inheritance could be approached in terms of rules such as *the young of mammals are born alive, a whale is a mammal, so the young of whales are born alive*. In such cases, by teaching knowledge relationships involving characteristics of mammals along with relationships about which animals are mammals, students are able to build a conceptual knowledge base for understanding biological classifications. Although beyond the scope of this chapter, Engelmann and Carnine (1982) have presented instructional algorithms for teaching knowledge in the form of IF/THEN production rules that are highly effective in science teaching (e.g., Muthukrishna, Carnine, Grossen, & Miller, 1993).

In addition to providing a general form for representing concept relationships, IF/THEN production rules also offer a formal way to address related processes through which knowledge is applied analytically. Such forms of argument, called abductive reasoning, ask the question of whether the observation of a rule consequence (the THEN part) provides any information regarding the occurrence of the antecedent (the IF part). For example, using the preceding rule, *heated objects expand and cooled objects contract*, the analytic question of whether the increased size of expansion joints (i.e., space between bridge segments dependent on the expansion/contraction of the segments) observed on a highway or bridge in winter could have been caused by decreased temperature may be addressed as follows:

1. Given that the rule IF *an object (i.e., bridge segment) is cooled*, THEN *it contracts* is TRUE, and
2. Given, in a specific situation, it is TRUE that *a designated object has contracted*, then, it can be concluded that
3. It is NOT NECESSARILY TRUE that *the reason is that the designated object was cooled*.

In this form of argument, the logical conclusion of *not necessarily* is due to the possibility of other causes. However, it is important and useful that knowledge of the rule in conjunction with the observed event is suggestive of a plausible explanation whose validity could be confirmed through other means. Also, considering the underlying production rule as a basis for problem solving, an expert diagnosing the problem (i.e., why the expansion joints are enlarged) would automatically reference the rule along with other relevant forms of such domain-specific knowledge to generate a list of possible reasons.

Although IF/THEN production rules have been emphasized, all of the other approaches to knowledge representation referenced earlier offer important complementary perspectives for science teaching. However, the methodological strength of production rules for the purpose of this chapter is that they illustrate clearly how scientific knowledge in the form of concept relationships can serve as the focus for teaching and assessment of student understanding. At the same time, because production rules primarily have been used as tools in computer-based systems, they have some practical limitations regarding their general use by classroom teachers.

Concept Mapping as a Practical Strategy for
Knowledge Representation in Science Classrooms

Whenever conceptual relationships can be expressed as IF/THEN rules, then production rule methodology is useful within science teaching (Vitale, Romance, Parke, & Widergren, 1994). However, production rules are not the best tool for knowledge representation by teachers and students in classroom settings. Rather, teachers and students in classroom learning need a more informal approach for representing both the hierarchical structure of core concepts and different forms of concept relationships.

A general knowledge-representation tool that has been found highly practical for classroom use is the *concept mapping* strategy developed by Novak and his associates (Ausubel et al., 1978; Novak, 1998; Novak & Gowin, 1984; Trowbridge & Wandersee, 1998). By representing conceptual relationships graphically, concept maps visually assist teachers and students as they explore knowledge. In a concept map, concepts are represented as labeled elements on a graph and concept relationships as connecting lines that are themselves labeled. Within the preceding examples, a portion of a simple concept map might include the concepts of OBJECTS, EXPAND, and CONTRACT as graphic elements. In turn, the relationship between the concepts OBJECT and EXPAND would be shown by a connecting line labeled with the word *heated*, while the relationship between the concepts OBJECT and CONTRACT would be shown by a connecting line labeled with the word *cooled* (i.e., OBJECTS *heated* EXPAND; OBJECTS *cooled* CONTRACT).

In keeping with Ausubel's (1963; Ausubel et al., 1978) theory as an instructional framework, Novak (Novak, 1998; Novak & Gowin, 1984) suggested that concept maps should be organized in hierarchical form with more general superordinate concepts at the top and subordinate concepts below. Additionally, he suggested that the labeled links that identify concept relationships should form units of meaning that express knowledge in propositional form (e.g., SKY is BLUE). As used by teachers and students, Novak's (Novak, 1998; Novak & Gowin, 1984) concept mapping strategy provides a practical means not only to explicate knowledge relationships within a knowledge domain, but also to represent the process of cumulative knowledge acquisition by continually reorganizing concept maps to include new knowledge relationships as they are learned. In evaluating Novak's (Novak, 1998; Novak & Gowin, 1984) concept mapping strategy, it is important to recognize that its emphasis on visual representation of hierarchical concepts and explicit propositional relationships provides a flexible and informal structure that, although less detailed than other approaches (e.g., Anderson, 1993, 1996; Dansereau, 1995; Sowa, 1984), is of great practical utility in teaching. As a form of knowledge representation, a large number of studies have shown that concept mapping is an effective tool in a wide variety of science classroom settings, including the use of concept maps as an instructional strategy, as an assessment tool, and as a curriculum organization guide in teaching (e.g., Novak, 1998; Trowbridge & Wandersee, 1998; Romance & Vitale, 1997).

Knowledge-Based Architectures for Science Teaching and Assessment

Knowledge-Based Approaches from Cognitive Science

The idea of a knowledge-based approach to teaching and assessment was developed in the fields of cognitive science and artificial intelligence. Primarily, it reflects a methodological effort to study and represent the knowledge (i.e., expertise) of skilled problem solvers in a fashion that may be implemented in a computer environment (see Posner, 1989). The goal of this effort is to develop intelligent machines that, by use of an explicit knowledge base of production rules, can simulate the performance of expert problem solvers. And, in developing such expert systems, the term *knowledge-based* is used to denote the fact that the system of production rules comprising the knowledge base is a distinct component of the computer system.

The original work and the general terminology of expert systems has been expanded into computer-based intelligent tutoring systems (e.g., Polson & Richardson, 1988; Sleeman & Brown, 1982) whose architecture (see Figure 1) included separate components for (1) the explicit representation of the knowledge to be taught, (2) the pedagogical strategies to be used in instruction to teach the knowledge, (3) the assessment tasks to be assigned students to determine student mastery of the knowledge, and (4) a model representing student mastery of the knowledge base. Most importantly, as Figure 1 shows, linkage to the knowledge base itself provides the overall system with the means to control the other instructional and assessment components. Thus, within the intelligent tutoring system model, both the instructional strategies and assessment tasks are based explicitly on the content knowledge base. Although not as explicitly knowledge-based, the instructional design models of both Gagne, Briggs, and Wager (1992) and Engelmann and Carnine (1982) present related approaches for linking instruction and assessment.

A Knowledge-Based Approach for Teaching In-depth Science

The potential value of adapting a knowledge-based teaching model for classroom teaching stems from the original design of intelligent tutoring systems reflecting the informal strategies of master teachers. However, what is needed for their practical use by teachers is the development of a model

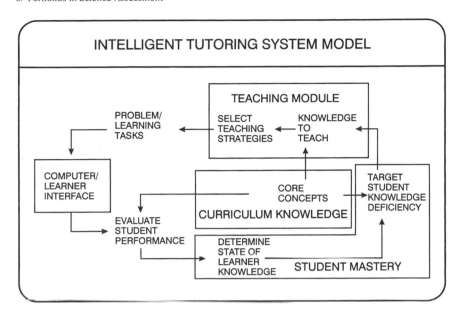

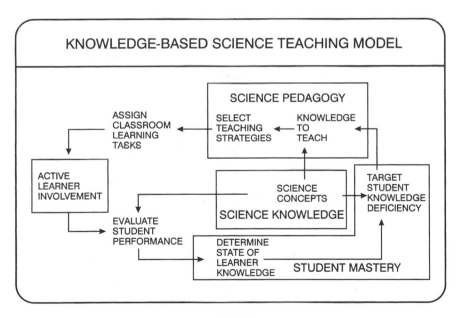

FIGURE 1

Intelligent tutoring system model as an architecture for a knowledge-based
science teaching model. Both models illustrate the role of knowledge as
the central element in teaching and assessment (Vitale et al., 1994).
Vitale and Romance © 1994.

that incorporates the underlying knowledge-based architecture in a form that is usable in classroom settings. Using Novak's (1998) and Novak and Gowin's (1984) concept mapping strategy in conjunction with Ausubel's (1963) and Carnine's (1992) emphasis on teaching core concepts (or big ideas), the authors (Romance & Vitale, 1992; Vitale & Romance, 1995a) developed and tested such a model, *Science* IDEAS, for teaching in-depth science at the upper elementary levels.

Focusing here on the implementation of a knowledge-based architecture, the *Science* IDEAS model shown in Figure 2 uses a concept mapping teaching routine as a focus for all elements of science instruction within a daily 2-hour time period. (The in-depth science instruction replaces the regular reading/language arts program.) Initially, the concept map developed in the classroom reflects students' prior knowledge in conjunction with an organizational focus on core concepts prompted by the teacher. Once initiated, the concept map is expanded on a continuing basis by adding new elements (i.e., concepts and links) and by reorganizing existing elements as student learning progresses. Thus, the concept map includes conceptual knowledge resulting from student hands-on science activities, textbooks and trade materials, teacher demonstrations, student journals, writing assignments, and individual or group concept maps. For example, if the topic is weather,

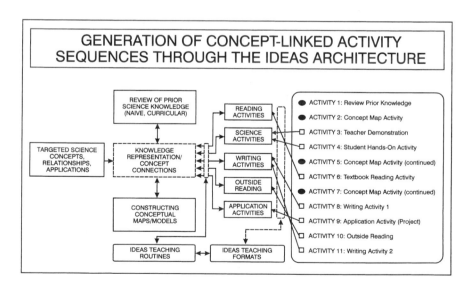

FIGURE 2

Architecture of the knowledge-based *Science* IDEAS model. As shown, core science concepts serve as focus for multiple instructional activities used to implement an in-depth learning environment (Vitale & Romance, 1995a).
Romance and Vitale © 1995.

a weather concept map is initiated and then modified over a multiweek period as students complete a variety of activities that relate to an in-depth understanding of weather.

Complementing the instructional component of the *Science* IDEAS model, a parallel knowledge-based science assessment component (shown in Figure 3) has been developed for use in the model (Vitale & Romance, 1995a). This component consists of a typology representing qualitatively different performance categories through which students demonstrate conceptual understanding of science concepts by completing various instructional activities. Because use of the performance typology with activities is contextualized within the conceptual knowledge to be taught, the assessment system is knowledge-based as well. The specific categories of the science assessment typology are as follows:

1. *Observation or recording of events in the environment.* The correspondence of science concepts with events in the world is necessary for meaningful understanding

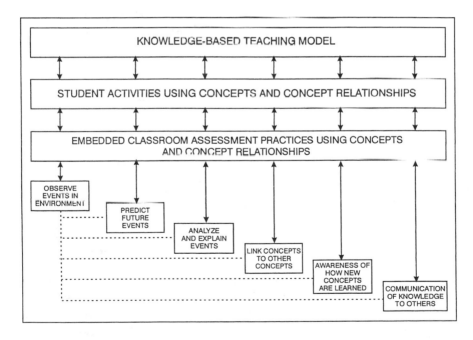

FIGURE 3

Assessment typology for knowledge-based *Science* IDEAS model. Typology represents qualitatively different student performance categories through which students demonstrate conceptual understanding in instructional activities (Vitale & Romance, 1995b). Vitale and Romance © 1998.

2. *Prediction and/or manipulative control of future events.* Applying knowledge of conceptual relationships to make accurate predictions or control events in specific situations is an important element of meaningful understanding.

3. *Analysis and/or explanation of occurring events.* Using knowledge of conceptual relationships to explain events occurring in specific situations is an important element of meaningful understanding.

4. *Construction of logical and/or visual representations of how science concepts are related to each other (such as concept maps).* The construction of concept maps to represent knowledge is recognized as an important metacognitive tool in learning.

5. *Demonstrated awareness of how science concepts and concept relationships are learned.* An important aspect of science is to understand the process through which the discipline has gained knowledge and how those processes apply to an individual gaining scientific knowledge.

6. *Demonstrations of the communication of scientific knowledge to others.* Communication of knowledge in a variety of ways is an important constituent of scientific understanding.

In general, the typology follows a hierarchical structure with an initial emphasis on concepts and concept relationships as the fundamental science knowledge to be learned and, given such fundamental knowledge, its application (2, 3), representation (4), expansion (5), and communication (6), all of which must be linked to the world (1) if meaningful understanding is to be accomplished. Considered as a hierarchy, the first three categories (1–3) reflect a production rule methodology, which, in turn, provides a knowledge-based foundation for the other three categories (4–6).

A General Knowledge-Based Teaching Model for Linking Classroom Instruction and Assessment.

The Science IDEAS model is knowledge-based since science concepts provide the organizational focus for all instructional activities. However, the assessment system is knowledge-based in an indirect fashion. That is, elements of the assessment typology are embedded in various knowledge-based instructional activities. In this sense, the assessment typology provides teachers with guidance when evaluating student performance in various activities. However, while this approach has been found to work well in upper elementary science classrooms, it clearly is not practical for secondary or college science classes, which evidence greater concept coverage and fewer student contact hours.

As a result, a more general teaching model (shown in Figure 4) in which both instructional and assessment tasks are knowledge-based has been developed as an enhancement of the original *Science* IDEAS (Vitale & Romance, 1998). As it applies to this chapter, this more general model designed for use in secondary and college, as well as elementary classrooms, is as as follows:

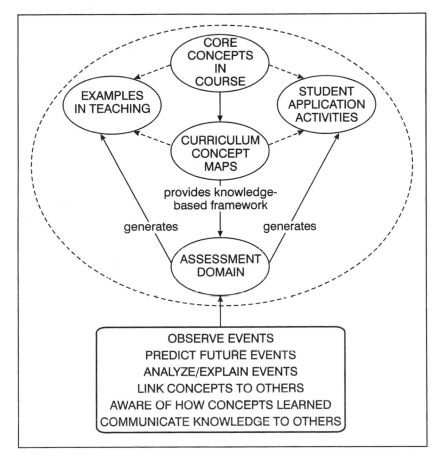

FIGURE 4

General knowledge-based teaching model linking instruction and student application activities via concept maps and core assessment categories (Vitale & Romance, 1998). In this chapter, the teaching model provides the basis for linking portfolio tasks and activities with a science knowledge base. Vitale © 1998.

1. Teachers identify the core concepts and concept relationships to be taught by topic or unit.
2. Teachers construct a concept map representing the core concepts or big ideas to use as a curriculum guide.
3. Teachers design tasks or scenarios that could be used alternatively either for instruction or assessment by combining selected elements from their concept map with appropriate categories from the assessment typology.
4. Teachers present the tasks either by modeling the application of the science concepts to the tasks, and/or by assigning the tasks as student

activities to be completed with (or without) teacher guidance, and/or by using the tasks for student assessment.

5. Teachers continually reference all instructional and assessment tasks either to the initial teacher-developed core concept map, or to a concept map developed interactively by students with teacher guidance.

The knowledge-based feature of this enhanced teaching model is the use of the core concept map in conjunction with the assessment typology to generate tasks for use with students. Thus, all tasks are explicitly knowledge-based. And, once generated, tasks may be used with equal validity for either instructional purposes by the teacher, as learning activities for students, or for student assessment.

Complementing the five components of the model, teachers use a heuristic strategy to generate the contexts (or domains) in which the conceptual knowledge is applicable (*"What settings are relevant to the concepts taught?"*) and what student performance provides evidence of conceptual understanding of course content (*"In the setting identified, what are students who understand the course content able to do that distinguishes them from students who did not understand it?"*). By applying these heuristics (see Figure 5), teachers develop informal performance specifications for student tasks, and then formalize the performance specifications by identifying, for each task, (1) a description of the activity, (2) the outcome of the activity, (3) the procedure or process to be followed by the student to complete the activity, and (4) the prior conceptual knowledge on the part of the student necessary to complete the process. Finally, the prior knowledge component of the performance specification is referenced back to the core concept map to make the tasks and associated performance specifications knowledge-based.

Although additional details are beyond the bounds of this paper, it is important to note that the linkage between student performance specifications, student tasks and activities, and the core concept map provides a framework within which teachers are able to organize and refine their course. Thus, the knowledge-based model provides a means for implementing forms of knowledge-based assessment (such as portfolios) that teachers may interpret as valid measures of conceptual understanding.

A KNOWLEDGE-BASED PORTFOLIO ASSESSMENT MODEL

Additional Perspectives Relating to Knowledge-Based Assessment

The preceding sections of this chapter provided a framework for the conceptual development of the ideas relating to knowledge-based instruction and assessment grounded in the cognitive science and related literatures.

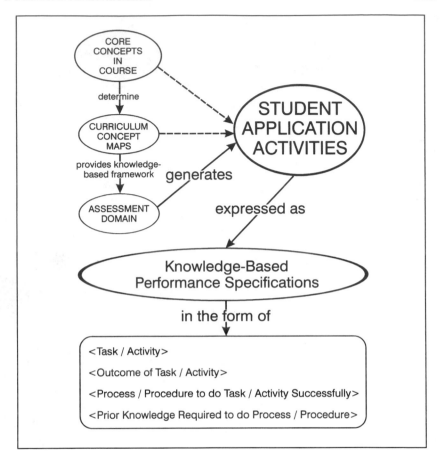

FIGURE 5

Component of general knowledge-based teaching model showing the generation of student performance specifications (Vitale & Romance, 1998). In this chapter, the format for performance specifications provides structure for representing knowledge-based portfolio tasks and activities.

Vitale © 1998.

Although not as detailed in their development, other sources from the educational literature are supportive of the importance of the relationship between knowledge and assessment. Terwillinger (1997) has noted the implications of contextually bound specific knowledge within a domain as an important consideration for evaluating any form of assessment. Glaser and Chi (1988) have shown that knowledge within a domain is nontransferable to other domains, suggesting that all forms of instructional assessment must be knowledge-based for maximum validity. In this sense, the development of mastery and understanding of course content by students is con-

sidered a form of expertise, which in the cognitive science literature is always addressed from a knowledge-based perspective (e.g., Anderson, 1993, 1996). Consistent with Glaser's (1990) call for the integration of cognitive science with learning theory, Baxter et al. (1996) have illustrated the importance of aligning assessment, instruction, and theories of knowledge in classroom settings.

Another recent source relevant to the idea of knowledge-based assessment is a framework for assessing domain-specific problem solving by Sugrue (1995). Consistent with work by Anderson (1993, 1996), Sugrue (1995) outlined elements of an assessment model whose knowledge-based typology is related to that presented here. Again, because competence in problem solving is recognized in the literature as domain-specific, Sugrue's (1995) assessment model recognizes that the transferable metacognitive and motivational elements of problem solving must be assessed conditionally within a context of domain-specific knowledge. In a related paper, addressing the question of knowledge representation in assessment, Suen, Sonak, Zimmaro, and Roberts (1997) suggested how concept maps could function as scaffolding to enhance the validity of authentic assessment tasks. Finally, in what were presented originally as demonstrations of problem-solving and reasoning skills, earlier work by Trollip and Lippert (1987) and Ennals and Briggs (1986) provide what today's literature would consider operational prototypes for a form of knowledge-based portfolio assessment. Working in computer-based environments, these studies illustrated how students could demonstrate understanding of knowledge by using it to construct dynamic computer environments. In these studies, students used software tools (expert system shells, PROLOG) to construct simple knowledge-based environments, including semantic graphs, concept classification aids, and procedural guides. In all of these examples, students demonstrated their understanding by encoding specified course knowledge into a computer environment in a form with which another person could interact. Thus, considered together, these and the references noted above are all supportive of the importance of linking portfolio and other forms assessment to the conceptual knowledge they are intended to evaluate.

A Model for Knowledge-Based Portfolio Assessment

A procedural model for knowledge-based portfolio assessment can now be presented as a variant of the general knowledge-based teaching model.

Framework for Portfolio Assessment Provided by the General Knowledge-Based Teaching Model

Step 1. Use a concept map to specify the knowledge base to be taught and assessed. The concept map should be constructed from the

course, unit, or topic content, as appropriate, to include the core concepts or big ideas to be emphasized in instruction. From the standpoint of portfolio assessment, the concept map serves as a general curriculum guide.

Step 2. *Use heuristics to identify the general settings or contexts in which the content is to be applied.* These can be limited to a classroom context or include both classroom and applied out-of-classroom settings, as appropriate. From the standpoint of portfolio assessment, the settings provide the general application context within which the portfolio tasks will fit and helps insure the relevance of instruction to assessment.

Procedure for Knowledge-Based Portfolio Assessment Within the Framework of General Knowledge-Based Teaching

Step 3. *Select the set or subset of core concepts from the concept map (step 1) that are to be the focus of the portfolio assessment task or activity.* Depending on the scope of the concept map, this could be the whole map or a portion of it. From the standpoint of portfolio assessment, this step specifies the specific conceptual knowledge that is to be linked to the portfolio assessment task.

Step 4. *Specify the application setting or context within which the portfolio assessment task or activity will be conducted.* This is particularly important if the assessment activity is framed in an out-of-classroom application setting. The setting provides the specific context for the portfolio task and, ultimately, guidelines for the performance specifications for the portfolio product. These should follow from (Step 2) above to insure the relevance of instruction to assessment.

Step 5. *Select the form of portfolio assessment task from the following list:*
   (a) Reports of empirical research completed by students
   (b) Analyses of societal issues from a sound scientific view
   (c) Papers demonstrating in-depth understanding of fundamental science principles
   (d) Documentation of presentations designed to foster understanding of science concepts for others
   (e) Journals addressing a student's reflective observations over an instructional timespan
   (f) Analytic and/or integrative visual representations of science knowledge itself in the form of concept maps
   In terms of the general knowledge-based teaching model, the above list (which is not intended to be exhaustive) is an

enhancement of the basic assessment typology presented previously. All of these portfolio activities require students to apply their understanding of science concepts to complete an open-ended task or activity that results in a portfolio product. As noted earlier, we recommend that portfolio assessment tasks or activities meet this requirement in order to distinguish between portfolio projects that require constructive application of knowledge by students from those that are completed in a rote step-by-step fashion. In designing and evaluating specific portfolio tasks, we recommend that teachers use the following guidelines to insure they are knowledge-based:

1. *In designing a portfolio task or activity*, be certain that there is no way students can complete the activity without applying the relevant conceptual knowledge.
2. *In evaluating a portfolio product*, be certain to focus on the student explanation or interpretation of the portfolio task in terms of the relevant conceptual knowledge.

Together these two guidelines insure that the portfolio activity and the student portfolio product are knowledge-based, linking the relevant conceptual knowledge to the portfolio task and product. If this is done, the portfolio product cannot be completed in a rote fashion and will provide a foundation for an inference regarding meaningful student understanding.

Step 6. *Develop knowledge-based performance specifications for the portfolio task and product as follows (using the information in steps 3, 4, and 5:)*

(a) A *description of the portfolio task or activity for the student*. This describes the general task for the student (e.g., research report) and specifies the general topic or content that is to be addressed (e.g., implications of differences in temperature associated with different insulation materials and their use in homes).

(b) *The requirements that the resulting product of the student is expected to meet*. This communicates to the student what characteristics the final product should address (e.g., the results of a research study conducted to compare insulation materials, projections comparing the effectiveness of different materials for home insulation, the specific interpretation of the results and projections in terms of fundamental concepts involving heat and temperature).

(c) *The procedure or process to be followed by the student to complete the activity (this may or may not be communicated to the student)*. The specific steps necessary to complete the project may or may not be specified. However, the linkage of the knowledge base to the task or activity should never be specified if the teacher intends to interpret the portfolio product as a measure of student understanding.

(d) *The conceptual knowledge (referencing the concept map) that is necessary for the student to complete the portfolio task or activity (this may or may not be communicated to the student).* Again, the relevant knowledge may or may not be specified in a detailed form (i.e., beyond that in (a)). However, the linkage of the knowledge base to the task or activity should never be specified if the teacher intends to interpret the portfolio product as a measure of student understanding.

Step 7. *Develop guidelines for evaluating the portfolio assessment product.* The emphasis here is that the evaluation of the portfolio by the teacher should be a clinical judgment regarding two considerations: (1) the degree to which the relevant conceptual knowledge is represented accurately in the portfolio product (step 6.d) and (2) the degree to which the portfolio product meets the specified performance outcomes (step 6.b), including the degree to which the relevant concepts are used in an explanatory or interpretative basis by students. Within this context, teachers may or may not desire to develop their own partial scoring schemes (i.e., rubrics).

Considered together, the seven-step process insures an explicit linkage of portfolio assessment activities or tasks to the meaningful understanding of science concepts. In our view, *linkage* formal or informal—is the only logical basis for making valid inferences of meaningful student understanding from a portfolio product.

Some Elaborations of the Basic Model for Knowledge-Based Portfolio Assessment

Multiple Portfolio Products Focusing on the Same Knowledge

As noted earlier, a student portfolio could consist of a variety of products that represent different forms of student performance, including a variety of student products of the form described in the basic model. However, one important qualitative elaboration of the basic model is that a student portfolio also could consist of a variety of different products, all of which are related to the same set of science concepts. Implemented informally, this was found to be an important feature of documenting student performance in the Science IDEAS model. For example, student portfolios in a classroom might include products from a variety of activities relating to basic weather concepts. Teachers using this approach reported it to be very powerful in evaluating student understanding.

Student-Constructed Concept Maps in Combination with Other Activities

One important elaboration of the basic model involves the role of concept maps in portfolio assessment. On one hand, concept maps can be portfolio assessment tasks themselves. As such, they should be evaluated by the teacher in terms of their consistency with scientific knowledge and the degree to which the elements are organized in accordance with specific performance specifications (e.g., for a textbook analysis task—hierarchical structure, concepts, and links forming propositions). However, student-constructed concept maps could also be required along with all other forms of portfolio tasks. For example, if the portfolio task is for students to develop an analysis of an environmental issue, students could also be required to construct concept maps illustrating the science concepts applied in the analysis.

Student Journaling in Combination with Other Activities

Another elaboration of the basic model is the use of student journals recording reflective perceptions of a specific portfolio activity. Used in this fashion, student journaling adds a metacognitive perspective to learning and applying science knowledge in a form that may be transferable (e.g., Sugrue, 1995).

Planning and Implementation Guidelines for Knowledge-Based Portfolio Assessment

Although the focus of this chapter is on a methodology for linking portfolio assessment to science knowledge, it is important to offer practical implementation guidelines. First, the model is presented in a form in which a teacher develops a concept map for a portion of a course and then implements the knowledge-based portfolio procedure. And, in fact, this is an approach we recommend as an informal tryout of the procedure. However, in using portfolio assessment for a course, an overall plan should be developed specifying what the portfolio (and other) assessment tasks and activities will be, when they are to be assigned, and how long students have to complete them. Within this planning context, teachers should decide whether to implement any of the elaborations of the basic model.

In some cases, particularly with concept maps, teachers may want to provide students with formal guidance if not instruction on how to complete the task. Such guidance, when necessary, is best provided in written form. Although some might object to any form of structure in an open-ended task, our belief is that the application of science knowledge to the task by the student is the open-ended portion of the activity that is important. But, we recognize that this is an individual teacher decision.

Finally, with regard to concept mapping by the teacher as a curriculum guide, we recommend that the procedures outlined in the general knowledge-based teaching model be followed. The complete model has the advantage of not only using concept maps for organizing content in a way that is meaningful to teachers and students, but also of helping teachers to focus their instructional presentations, assignments, and tests to emphasize the dynamic characteristics of scientific knowledge in the form of concept relationships. At the same time, teachers who are interested only in assessment may simply utilize the knowledge-based portfolio assessment model presented in this section. In effect, this model reduced to minimal form consists of *defining portfolio assessment tasks, specifying the scientific knowledge that is relevant, and deciding how the student product is to be evaluated.* Because knowledge-based instruction is best conducted in a coherent manner, we encourage teachers implementing it partially to work toward broadening their scope to that of a general knowledge-based approach over time.

EXAMPLES ILLUSTRATING
THE KNOWLEDGE-BASED PORTFOLIO
ASSESSMENT MODEL

Formal and Informal Processes for Developing
Knowledge-Based Portfolio Tasks

Each of the following examples was developed by applying the knowledge-based portfolio model outlined in the preceding section. However, it is also important to note some of the informal processes involved. Most teachers would consider any of the three major elements of the model (knowledge, application setting, type of task) as practical starting points for an assessment activity. Rather than applying these three steps in sequence, what is important is that all three elements are defined for the completed activity. Thus, teachers should begin with whichever element is most intuitively meaningful.

Also, in developing activities, it is important to keep the two guidelines in mind that insure the task is knowledge-based. These require (1) the task to be defined so that students cannot complete it without an understanding of the concepts involved and (2) the evaluation of the task by the teacher to focus upon student explanations and interpretations that incorporate the relevant concepts.

Finally, the emphasis in this chapter has been on open-ended knowledge-based activities that are relatively large in scope (i.e., student projects). In this regard, it is implied that each type of portfolio assessment task (e.g., a research paper project) includes aspects of the basic forms of scientific understanding in the assessment typology for the knowledge-based teaching model (e.g., predictions, applications, representation/-

communication of relationships). Within a more general assessment framework, there are categories of knowledge-based assessment following the structure of production rules that are not open-ended at all (e.g., given information about a specific situation, using knowledge of a scientific relationship to predict an outcome.) Still, our recommendation to teachers regarding portfolio assessment is to focus on the forms of knowledge-based, open-ended activities presented below.

Selected Examples of Knowledge-Based Portfolio Tasks

Each of the following examples is described in terms of the elements of knowledge-based performance specifications described earlier (task description, product requirements, procedure or process, conceptual knowledge), along with evaluative guidelines.

Portfolio Project 1: Sea Breezes

In this project, students explore understanding of sea breezes in terms of convection and related concepts. The projects activities will include (a) completing outside reading on sea breezes, (b) obtaining hourly temperatures for land and sea for a period of 24 hours, (c) obtaining hourly wind velocity for the same land–sea area for the same 24 hours, (d) summarizing the data and relationships among the land–sea temperature differential and wind velocity, and (e) explaining the findings in terms of convection and related concepts. The portfolio product will be in the form of a report including items (a)–(e). Some of the major concepts relevant to the project include *convection*, *absorption*, *radiation*, and *specific heat*. Teacher evaluation should focus on the degree to which the relevant concepts are used to explain the phenomena observed. An optional enhancement would be to have students develop a concept map showing the relationships involved.

In reviewing this example, note that without the linkage of the knowledge base to the task, this project could be completed in a rote fashion. Without meaningful understanding, students could not complete this task.

Portfolio Project 2: Effect of Oceans on Coastal Climate

In this project, students explore understanding of how oceans moderate coastal climate in terms of specific heat, convection, and related concepts. The project activities will include (a) completing outside reading on coastal climate effects, (b) studying the effects on the east coast (e.g., Charleston, South Carolina) and west coast (e.g., San Francisco, California) by obtaining average monthly temperature data (from an almanac over 1 year) for the ocean, the coastal location, and several inland locations having similar latitude and terrain, (c) summarizing the similarities and differences in temperature data in terms of distance from the coast and time of year, and (d) explaining the findings in terms of specific heat, convection, and related concepts. The portfolio product will be in the form of a video presentation including items (a)–(d). Some of the major concepts relevant to the project include *specific heat, convection, absorption,* and *radiation.* Teacher evaluation should focus on the degree to which the relevant concepts are used to explain the phenomena observed. An optional enhancement would be to have students develop a concept map showing the relationships involved.

In reviewing this example, note that without the linkage of the knowledge base to the task, this project could be completed in a rote fashion. Without meaningful understanding, students could not complete this task.

Portfolio Project 3: Insulating for Hot and Cold

In this project, students explore understanding of home insulation in terms of thermal conductivity and use of common materials. The project activities will include (a) completing outside reading on home insulation, (b) studying the thermal conductivity of selected materials (e.g., fiberglass, cotton, soil, air, wool), (c) investigating the use of the different insulation materials studied (in (b)) for heating and cooling using a standard "box" (with internal temperature probes) under varied temperature levels, (d) summarizing the results of studies (b) and (c) in terms of conductivity and insulation value, and (e) explaining the findings in terms of thermal conductivity and radiation. The portfolio product will be in the form of graphic display with relevant explanations attached. Some of the major concepts relevant to the project include *thermal conductivity, conductors, insulators, temperature gradients, and radiation.* Teacher evaluation should focus on the degree to which the relevant concepts are used to explain the phenomena observed. An optional enhancement would be to have students develop a concept map showing the relationships involved.

In reviewing this example, note that without the linkage of the knowledge base to the task, this project could be completed in a rote fashion. Without meaningful understanding, students could not complete this task.

Portfolio Project 4: Understanding the Greenhouse Effect

In this project, students explore understanding of the processes underlying the greenhouse effect in terms of radiation and transparency of materials. The project activities will include (a) completing outside reading on the greenhouse effect, (b) building a model greenhouse to study the dynamics involved under varying conditions and summarizing the findings, (c) relating the dynamics of the model greenhouse to the role of the earth's atmosphere in global warming, and (d) an explanation of (b) and (c) in terms of radiation and related concepts. Some of the major concepts relevant to the project include *radiation*, *wavelength*, *transparency*, and *opacity*. The portfolio product will be in the form of written report with graphic displays showing similarities between the model greenhouse and global warming, supported by relevant explanations attached. Teacher evaluation should focus on the degree to which the relevant concepts are used to explain the phenomena observed. An optional enhancement would be to have students develop a concept map showing the relationships involved.

In reviewing this example, note that without the linkage of the knowledge base to the task, this project could be completed in a rote fashion. Without meaningful understanding, students could not complete this task.

Some Variations on the Knowledge-Based Portfolio Examples

As knowledge-based assessment tasks, each of the preceding examples could be implemented in a variety of ways. For example, the outside reading materials in each example could serve as a context for student-developed concept maps. A wide variety of other application settings could have been selected for each example (e.g., coastal regions throughout the world vs the United States). The portfolio activities could not have included a data-collection component; rather, they could have been research papers or analyses demonstrating in-depth understanding using available sources. A number of the projects could have emphasized their relevance to societal issues. For example, the greenhouse project could have served as a context for the exploration and/or evaluation of policy issues related to consumer practices (e.g., fossil fuel consumption).

With regard to media used for portfolio products, students could have constructed multimedia presentations (e.g., *Hyperstudio*) or computer-based simulations (e.g., STELLA) as an alternative to preparing reports combining written and graphic elements. A natural use of such forms of presentation would be to foster understanding of science concepts in others. In addition, students also could have maintained journals reflecting their thoughts and growth of understanding as they completed the portfolio activity. Although beyond the scope of this chapter, it is important to note the potential value of computer-based knowledge-construction tools (e.g., Trollip & Lippert, 1987; Ennals & Briggs, 1986) through which students would encode conceptual relationships in interactive software environments to develop portfolio products.

Finally, although we have emphasized the design of portfolio tasks as individual student projects, any of the forms of knowledge-based activities could have been conducted using cooperative groups.

IMPLICATIONS OF THE KNOWLEDGE-BASED MODEL FOR SCIENCE TEACHERS AND RESEARCHERS

The knowledge-based perspective in this chapter has implications for science teachers and science education researchers. Perhaps the most important is the notion that student competence is best considered as a form of knowledge-based expertise. This suggests that the goals of science instruction are best framed in terms of the proficiency that experts in the field would display if they were to apply their knowledge. While this may not seem a radical view, it is very much at odds with popular views of science instruction and assessment whose emphasis is on the process of learning rather than knowledge itself. A fundamental view of this chapter is that instruction and assessment must be addressed interdependently because both are based on the underlying knowledge base to be taught. In fact, linking the knowledge students must apply to complete assessment tasks is the means through which teachers are able to establish the validity of the inferences they make from such tasks regarding meaningful student understanding. On the other hand, without an explicit linkage between knowledge and assessment, teacher interpretation of any form of assessment performance is tenuous.

With regard to portfolio assessment considered as one particular form of assessment, we feel the implications for practitioners are clear. To assess student understanding, work-sample portfolio tasks should require students to apply their knowledge in an open-ended fashion. In this regard, we recommend the variety of portfolio assessment tasks that meet this criterion. However, our view is that it is not sufficient to assign students open-ended tasks or simply to compile accumulations of completed work in a portfolio to realize the potential of the approach. Rather, tasks such as those we recommend, which require the constructive application of knowledge, also must be linked explicitly to the relevant conceptual knowledge to support inferences regarding meaningful student understanding. In this regard, we have suggested concept mapping as a practical methodological tool for establishing the recommended knowledge–task linkage for portfolio assessment.

Despite the research foundations that support our recommendations, we recognize that much research remains to be done. Certainly, psychometric concerns in the literature about validity of inferences made from authentic assessment approaches such as portfolios should be clarified. Of particular importance are the implications of considering student mastery as a form of knowledge-based expertise and how student knowledge is transformed into specifications for valid assessment tasks. Additional research also is needed on qualitatively different forms of portfolio assessment and the valid forms of teacher inference associated with each.

Finally, the focus of the present chapter on teachers' clinical judgments purposefully minimizes the importance of formal scoring rubrics. In our view, the linkage between knowledge and portfolio tasks provides the foundation for their validity. Given an explicit link between a knowledge and a portfolio task, the development of scoring rubrics is a minimal problem. In contrast, developing and using a rubric without such an explicit knowledge-task link to evaluate meaningful understanding makes little sense. However, in large-scale portfolio assessment (vs within-class clinical judgment), we recognize that the use of rubrics as scoring schemes is an important concern. For such applications, we encourage practitioners to consider carefully the references in this chapter that address the methodological issues of scoring schemes (including rubrics), reliability, and validity as a technical guide for their assessment systems. With this in mind, we encourage both practitioners and researchers to work toward the development of portfolio assessment systems that meet the highest levels of traditional methodological standards in educational measurement.

References

Anderson, J. R. (1993). Problem solving and learning. *American Psychologist*, 48(1), 35–44.

Anderson, J. R. (1996). ACT: A simple theory of complex cognition. *American Psychologist*, 51(4), 335–365

Archbald, D. A. (1991). Authentic assessment: Principles, practices, and issues. *School Psychology Quarterly*, 6(4), 279–293.

Arter, J. A. (1995). *Portfolios for assessment and instruction*. ERIC Digest. Greensboro, NC: ERIC Clearinghouse on Counseling and Student Services.

Arter, J. A., & Spandel, V. (1992). Using portfolios of student work in instruction and assessment. *Educational Measurement: Issues and Practice*, 11(1), 36–43.

Ausubel, D. P. (1963). *The psychology of meaningful verbal learning*. New York: Holt, Rinehart, & Winston.

Ausubel, D. P., Novak, J. D., & Hanesian, H. (1978). *Educational psychology: A cognitive view*. (2nd ed.). New York: Holt, Rinehart, & Winston.

Barenholz, H., & Tamir, P. (1992). A comprehensive use of concept mapping in design, instruction, and assessment. *Research in Science and Technological Education*, 10(1), 37–52.

Bateson, D. (1994). Psychometric and philosophic problems in "authentic" assessment: Performance tasks and portfolios. *Alberta Journal of Educational Research*, 40(2), 233–245.

Baxter, G. P., Elder, A. D., & Glaser, R. (1996). Knowledge-based cognition and performance assessment in the science classroom. *Educational Psychologist*, 31(2), 133–140.

Benoit, J., & Yang, H. (1996). A redefinition of portfolio assessment based upon purpose: Findings and implications from a large-scale program. *Journal of Research and Development in Education*, 29(3), 181–191.

Carnine, D. (1992). Introduction. In D. Carnine & E. J. Kameenui (Eds.), *Higher order thinking* (pp. 1–22). Austin, TX: Pro-Ed.

Cary, L. M. (1994) *Measuring and evaluating school learning*. (Chapter 13). Needham Heights, MA: Allyn & Bacon.

Chi, M. T. H., Feltovich, P. S., & Glaser, R. (1981). Categorization and representation of physics problems by experts and novices. *Cognitive Science*, 5, 121–152.

Collins, A. (1992). Portfolios for science education: Issues in purpose, structure, and authenticity. *Science Education*, 76, 451–463.

Dansereau, D. F. (1995). Derived structural schemas and the transfer of knowledge. In A. McKeough, J. Lupart, & A. Marini (Eds.), *Teaching for transfer: Fostering generalization in learning* (pp. 93–121) Mahwah, NJ: Lawrence Earlbaum.

Delandshere, G., & Petrosky, A. R. (1998). Assessment of complex performances: Limitations of key measurement assumptions. *Educational Researcher*, 27(2), 14–24.

Doran, R. L., Lawrenz, F., & Helgeson, S. (1994). Research on assessment in science. In D. Gabel (Ed.), *Handbook of research on science teaching and learning* (pp. 388–442). New York: Macmillan.

Engelmann, S., & Carnine, D. (1982). *Theory of instruction: Principles and applications*. New York: Irvington.

Ennals, R., & Briggs, J. (1986). Fifth-generation computing: Introducing micro-PROLOG into the classroom. *Journal of Educational Computing Research*. 1, 97–111.

Gagne, R. M., Briggs, L. J., & Wager, W. W. (1992). *Principles of instructional design* (4th ed.). Fort Worth, TX: Harcourt Brace Jovanovich.

Glaser, R. (1963). Instructional technology and the measurement of learning outcomes: Some questions. *American Psychologist*, 18, 519–521.

Glaser, R. (1990). The reemergence of learning theory within instructional research. *American Psychologist*, 45, 29–39.

Glaser, R. (1996). Changing the agency for learning. Acquiring expert performance. In K. A. Ericsson (Ed.), *The road to excellence: Acquisition of expert performance in the arts and sciences, sports and games* (pp. 303–312) Mahwah, NJ: Lawrence Earlbaum.

Glaser, R., & Chi, M. (1988). Overview. In M. Chi, R. Glaser, & M. Farr (Eds.), *The nature of expertise* (pp. 15–36). Hillsdale, NJ: Lawrence Earlbaum.

Halloun, I. A., & Hestenes, D. (1985). The initial knowledge state of physics college students. *American Journal of Physics*, 53, 1043–1055.

Hambleton, R. K. (1994). The rise and fall of criterion-referenced measurement. *Educational Measurement: Issues and Practice*, 13(4), 21–26.

Jorgenson, M. (1996). *Rethinking portfolio assessment: Documenting the intellectual work of learners in science and mathematics*. ERIC Document Reproduction Services [ED400169].

Krueger, B., & Wallace, J. (1996). Portfolio assessment: Possibilities and pointers for practice. *Australian Science Teachers Journal*, 42(1), 26–29.

LeMahieu, P. G., Gitomer, D. H., & Eresh, J. T. (1995). Portfolios in large-scale assessment: Difficult but not possible. *Educational Measurement: Issues and Practice*, 14(3), 11–28.

Maloney, D. (1994). Research on problem solving: Physics. In D. Gabel (Ed.), *Handbook of research on science teaching and learning* (pp. 327–354). New York. Macmillan.

Muthukrishna, A., Carnine, D., Grossen, B., & Miller, S. (1993). Children's alternative frameworks: Should they be directly addressed in science instruction? *Journal of Research in Science Teaching*, 30(3), 223–248.

Novak, J. D. (1998). The pursuit of a dream: Education can be improved. In J. J. Mintzes, J. H. Wandersee, & J. D. Novak (Eds.), *Teaching science for understanding: A human constructivist view* (pp. 3–29). San Diego, CA: Academic Press.

Novak, J. D., & Gowin, D. B. (1984). *Learning how to learn*. Cambridge, MA: Cambridge University Press.

Polson, M. C., & Richardson, J. J. (Eds.) (1988). *Foundations of intelligent tutoring systems*. Hillsdale, NJ: Lawrence Earlbaum.

Posner, M. I. (1989). *Foundations of Cognitive Science*. Cambridge, MA: MIT Press.

Raizen, S. A., Baron, J. B., Champagne, A. B., Haertel, E., Mullis, I. V. S., & Oakes, J. (1990). *Assessment in science education: The middle years*. Washington, DC: National Center for Improving Science Education.

Reckase, M. D. (1995). Portfolio assessment: A theoretical estimate of score reliability. *Educational Measurement: Issues and Practice*, 14(1), 12–14.

Romance, N. R., & Vitale, M. R. (1992). A curriculum strategy that expands time for in-depth elementary science instruction by using science-based reading strategies: Effects of a year-long study in grade four. *Journal of Research in Science Teaching*, 29(6), 545–554.

Romance, N. R., & Vitale, M. R. (1997). Implications of an instructional strategy emphasizing structured conceptual knowledge: Addressing causes of learning problems in undergraduate science. In R. Abrams (Ed.), *Proceedings of the Fourth International Misconceptions Seminar.* Ithaca, NY: Cornell University.

Ruiz-Primo, M. A., & Shavelson, R. J. (1996). Rhetoric and reality in science performance assessment: An update. *Journal of Research in Science Teaching*, 33(6), 569–600.

Shavelson, R. J., & Ruiz-Primo, M. A. (in press). On the psychometrics of assessing science understanding. In J. J. Mintzes, J. H. Wandersee, & J. D. Novak (Eds.), *Assessing science understanding: A human constructivist view.* San Diego, CA: Academic Press.

Slater, T. F. (1994). Portfolio assessment strategies for introductory physics. *The Physics Teacher*, 32, 415–417.

Slater, T. F., Ryan, J. M., & Samson, S. L. (1997). Impact and dynamics of portfolio assessment and traditional assessment in a college physics course. *Journal of Research in Science Teaching*, 34(3), 255–272.

Sleeman, D., & Brown, J. S. (Eds.) (1982). *Intelligent tutoring systems.* New York: Academic Press.

Sowa, J. F. (1984). *Conceptual structures.* Reading, MA: Addison–Wesley.

Spandel, V. (1997) Reflections on portfolios. (pp. 573–591). In G. D. Phye (Ed.), *Handbook of Academic Learning.* San Diego, CA: Academic Press.

Strong, S., & Sexton, L. C. (1996). Performance assessment for state accountability: Proceed with caution. *Journal of Instructional Psychology*, 23(1), 68–94.

Suen, H. K., Sonak, B., Zimmaro, D., & Roberts, D. M. (1997). Concept maps as scaffolding for authentic assessment. *Psychological Reports*, 81, 714.

Sugrue, B. (1995). A theory-based framework for assessing domain-specific problem solving ability. *Educational Measurement: Issues and Practice*, 9, 29–35.

Terwilliger, J. (1997). Semantics, psychometrics, and assessment reform: A close look at authentic assessment. *Educational Researcher*, 26(8), 24–27.

Trollip, S. R., & Lippert, R. C. (1987). Constructing knowledge bases: A promising instructional tool. *Journal of Computer-Based Instruction*, 14(2), 44–48.

Trowbridge, J. E., & Wandersee, J. H. (1998). Theory-driven graphic organizers. In J. J. Mintzes, J. H. Wandersee, & J. D. Novak (Eds.), *Teaching science for understanding: A human constructivist view* (pp. 95–131). San Diego, CA: Academic Press.

Vitale, M. R., & Romance, N. R. (1995a). *Evolution of a model for teaching in-depth science in elementary school: Longitudinal findings and research implications.* Paper presented to the National Association for Research in Science Teaching, San Francisco, CA.

Vitale, M. R., & Romance, N. R. (1995b). Technology-based assessment in science: Issues underlying teacher advocacy of testing policy. *Journal of Science Education and Technology*, 4(1), 65–74.

Vitale, M. R., & Romance, N. R. (1998). *Assessment in college teaching: A restrictive instructional systems perspective.* Region V Higher Education Consortium in Mathematics, Science, and Technology. Boca Raton, FL: Florida Atlantic University.

Vitale, M. R., Romance, N. R., Parke, H., & Widergren, P. (1994). *Teaching for student conceptual understanding in science: Research implications from an interdisciplinary perspective.* Paper presented to the National Association for Research in Science Teaching, Anaheim, CA.

Wiggins, G. (1992). Creating tests worth taking. *Educational Leadership*, 49(8), 26–33.

Zelik, M., Schau, C., Mattern, N., Hall, S., Teague, K. W., & Bisard, W. (1997). Conceptual astronomy: A novel model for teaching postsecondary science courses. *American Journal of Physics*, 65(10), 987–996.

SemNet Software as an Assessment Tool

KATHLEEN M. FISHER
San Diego State University

> [M]eaningful conceptual learning should be a central goal of good science teaching and ... such learning is possible when instruction takes into consideration recent cognitive research about student learning.

The SemNet© software is a knowledge-representation tool that can help science students shift from rote to meaningful learning as proposed by Roth above (Fisher, 1990). It supports the *minds-on* activities in hands-on/minds-on classrooms. In particular, the process of representing what they know with SemNet helps students convert their perceptual and experiential knowledge into integrated conceptual understanding.

However, it doesn't make sense to *teach* for conceptual understanding unless one also *tests* for conceptual understanding, since it is well known that the form of assessment that is used shapes students' perceptions of their learning goals. Unfortunately, multiple-choice tests, the most widely used form of assessment, generally assess only isolated fragments of knowledge (Marshall, 1989). Essays are the oldest form of generative assessment and are well-suited to measuring knowledge integration and conceptual understanding, but they are time-consuming to grade and difficult to grade consistently. As one example of this, I recently participated in a workshop in which five groups of three to five faculty each were asked to assess a set of essay questions. Three groups were in full agreement about what were the best answers, but two groups had quite a different perspective. They were applying a different set of criteria.

Asking students to self-model their knowledge about a topic with Sem-Net is a viable alternative to essays for measuring conceptual understanding and it has several advantages over essays. First, with the skeletal form of knowledge representation used in SemNet, students stick closely to what they know about the scientific topic; there is little incentive for them to pad their responses with empty phrases ("throwing the bull") as is so common in essays. Another advantage in using SemNet is that it provides a comprehensive quantitative analysis of each network (described further below). Third, the format prompts students to include many more relevant concepts and relationships than are generally elicited by essay questions.

The habit promoted by SemNet-based knowledge construction of retrieving more content in response to a question seems to have a lasting effect. For example, Gorodetsky and Fisher (1996) found that when students who used SemNet as a learning tool wrote essays at the end of the semester, they included twice as many key ideas and twice as many sentences per item as did students who did not use SemNet. The sentences of SemNet learners were also significantly shorter and easier to understand.

There are at least two significant limitations to using the current version of SemNet as a generative assessment tool. First, students should have prior experience with the software before entering the testing situation. Second, each student must have access to a Macintosh computer. Fortunately, a cross-platform successor to SemNet is currently under development, which will address the second constraint (students will still need computers but will not be limited to Macintoshes). The first constraint may actually be a benefit in disguise, since the evidence suggests that using SemNet to support knowledge construction activities promotes higher level learning and retention (see review by Fisher [in press]. Perhaps this and similar tools should be used more frequently in student learning processes.

WHAT IS THE SEMNET SOFTWARE?

SemNet is a Macintosh-based tool that has been employed with 3rd graders studying ecology, middle school children exploring difficult topics like sex and drugs, high school students studying biology, college students learning history, music, literature, and science, and students enrolled in music and physiology college courses being taught across the world wide web. It also has been used in various government organizations such as the European Common Market and businesses such as the Bank of America.

SemNet permits an individual to construct a semantic network or conceptual graph about any descriptive or declarative domain of knowledge. The SemNet software is like a word processor in that the user can enter any kind and quantity of semantic data on any topic. It differs from a word processor in that information is organized into a skeletal *semantic network* rather than into sentences or outlines.

The SemNet software provides at least 16 different views of the data that is entered (Figure 1). This is valuable in part because, according to Langer (1989, 1997), having multiple views of a topic facilitates learning. Every concept entered into the net appears as a central concept in one graphic frame (such as *evolution* in the upper left of Figure 1), and will also appear as a related concept in the frames in which it is linked to the central concept (as is the case with *natural selection* and the other four related concepts in this frame). Concepts can also be viewed in lists arranged alphabetically, in order of creation, by number of direct links, and by embeddedness (number of unique links to two nodes away). The top of the list of 119 concepts in creation order is shown in the upper left of Figure 1. *Living things* is the most embedded concept in this net with 110 unique paths to two nodes (concepts) away.

One can also examine the knowledge core, the 49 most embedded concepts in the net with the connections among them. A portion of the knowledge core is shown in the center of Figure 1, with the links emanating from *living things*. The display allows you to click on any concept to examine its links, and you can choose to look only at direct links as we are doing here, or at links going to two nodes away.

A semantic network models the way in which humans store denotative, factual information in long-term memory (Quillian, 1967, 1968, 1969; Sowa, 1984). The idea of a semantic network can be traced back to Peirce in the late nineteenth century (Roberts, 1973). Semantic network theory is robust and has been embodied in many computer-based variations (e.g., Woods, 1975). All share the same basic principle: Knowledge is represented in the form of *concepts*, typically represented by nouns or noun phrases, that are linked by *relations* or *arcs*, typically represented by verbs, verb phrases, or prepositions.

In general, constructing a semantic network or conceptual graph is a challenging task typically undertaken by cognitive scientists, computer scientists, cognitive psychologists, and their ilk. However, SemNet is a relatively simple, user-friendly semantic networking tool that was designed specifically for use by students and teachers.

Semantic network construction goes quickly. We find that beginners add about 20 linked concepts per hour to a network, and they quickly build up to 40–80 new linked concepts per hour, depending on their knowledge of the topic being represented. It is similarly easy to edit a SemNet-based semantic network.

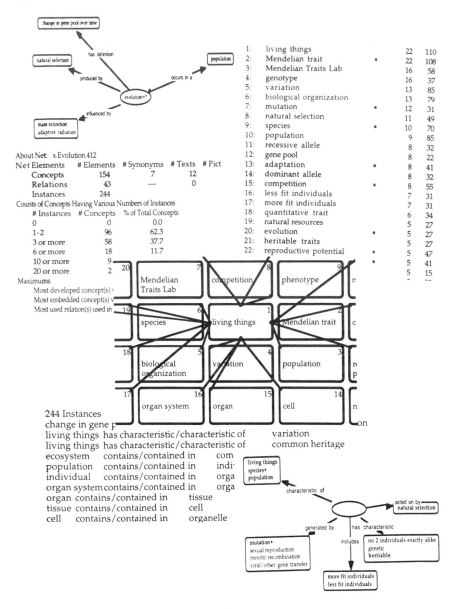

FIGURE 1

A montage of six of the 16 views provided by SemNet. From a net about evolution containing 119 concepts (nouns), 19 relations (verb phrases), and 156 instances (concept-relation-concept units). The views are: upper left–Current Concept Graphically; upper right–Concepts in Creation Order; middle left–About Net (quantitative overview of all elements); middle right–Knowledge Core (main ideas); lower left–Instances in Creation Order; lower right– Concept Graphically with central concept masked.

Many researchers have created learning and assessment programs that involve computer modeling of student knowledge by the computer system itself (e.g., Frederiksen & White, 1990; Lesgold, Lajoie, Logan, & Eggan, 1990). In contrast, students using SemNet create a model of their own knowledge using established knowledge representation techniques made accessible by this easy-to-learn software. This is known as student *self-modeling* of their knowledge.

WHAT IS MEANINGFUL CONCEPTUAL UNDERSTANDING IN SCIENCE?

Learning is not simply a process of adding in knowledge into the head; rather, learning is an active process in which the learner takes information from the environment and *constructs* personal interpretations and meanings. The learner's interpretations are influenced not only by the external environment (words in a text or by what a teacher says), they are also shaped by the learner's prior knowledge and experience.

Roth (1990), p. 143

All human thinking involves knowledge—one's accumulated information about the world—and the ability to use that knowledge to respond to events, predict outcomes, and plan ahead. Knowledge is represented by concepts, relations, and modifiers that are symbolized in language and that are used to represent meaning. Below I draw upon descriptions by several others of how these symbols are integrated to produce *meaningful conceptual understanding.*

In semantically complex task domains: "(a) complex meaningful language and other symbolic expressions, patterns, actions, and task structures occur; (b) successful performance requires complex conceptual and relational domain knowledge relevant to the task; and (c) successful performance depends on [internal] semantic representations and semantic processing operations. Semantic representation and processing are required to comprehend and produce linguistic messages and other symbolic expressions, patterns, actions, and task structures; to acquire, retrieve, and use conceptual knowledge; and to represent, plan, and control complex procedures and actions for the attainment of task-relevant goals" (Frederiksen & Breuleux, 1990, p. 353).

Stated another way, a person "makes sense of experience by organizing it into memory clusters that researchers have variously referred to as schemata..., frames..., cognitive structures..., or conceptual networks. A schema is a cluster of knowledge specifying a set of concepts and the relationships among them that [together] describe a more complex superordinate concept. According to learning theorists..., learning involves relating new experiences to what a person already knows; that is, to the person's relevant schema" (Roth, 1990).

A person with conceptual understanding has an integrated picture of the whole structure, process, event, or other topic, rather than a disconnected list of fragmented ideas about its parts. Steadily accumulating evidence suggests that a rich, coherent knowledge structure is a central aspect of competence. One set of evidence supporting this conclusion derives from studies of experts in a domain compared to novices. These studies find that experts (compared to novices):

- Have richer, more interconnected semantic networks (Derry, 1990).
- Have knowledge structures that are more internally coherent and more associated with information external to (or distant from) the topic (Tweney & Walker, 1990; Roth, 1990).
- Utilize more systematic hierarchical and temporal relations for organizing knowledge and events (Reif & Larkin, 1991; Fisher & Thornton, 1987; Fisher, 1988a–c).
- Use specific relations in consistent ways (Hoffman, 1991; Faletti & Fisher, 1996).
- Organize information into larger chunks and recognize and store more patterns (Chase & Simon, 1973; Perkins, 1981).
- Generally make finer discriminations between closely related entities (Klausmeir, 1990; Roth, 1990).

HOW CAN MEANINGFUL CONCEPTUAL UNDERSTANDING BE ASSESSED?

If we want students to develop the thinking skills, knowledge manipulation skills, and performance skills of experts, then we want to assess students in ways that will drive their learning in the desired directions. This is the primary benefit of using a cognitive-based learning and assessment tool.

In assessing for conceptual understanding, the aim is to "look into a person's mind" to see not only what that person knows, but also how that person is thinking—that is, how that person's information is constructed, organized, stored, retrieved, and manipulated. In a sense, conceptual assessments consist of special "mirrors" or "cameras" that let us capture and evaluate an image of an individual's or group's personal or collaborative knowledge and perspective at a given point in time.

Explicit construction of knowledge has powerful ramifications. For example, Baars (1988) claims that each time two concepts are brought into working memory and linked with a relation, that information is broadcast to all the modules in the brain, most of which are working subconsciously. A consequence of this broadcasting is that the linked ideas become available in many different performance situations. Cognitive-based assessment examines the extent to which such linkages exist.

Cognitive-based assessments generally serve two important purposes. Not only do they help predict how well individuals may do in some domain, much like other forms of testing, but they also contribute to the instructional process in more substantive ways by providing students and their teachers with significant insights into the cognitive and metacognitive strategies being used by the students.

USING SEMNET AS AN ASSESSMENT TOOL

SemNet-based assessment examines the declarative knowledge structures of students, or students' *knowledge about* a topic. This may at first seem like a serious limitation, but, in fact, domain-specific knowledge has been shown to be a critical component of competent performance. An especially convincing demonstration of the extent to which an individual's knowledge about a domain can be used to predict his or her problem-solving skill is provided by Gordon and Gill (1989). They interviewed students about their knowledge of one of two domains: (1) how to use mathematical vectors or (2) how to use a videotape recorder. The researchers then created a conceptual graph (semantic network) to represent each student's knowledge about the domain being studied. Gordon and Gill then used those conceptual graphs to predict each student's ability to solve problems in the domain. Their predictions of performance, based on evaluation of content knowledge, were accurate at the 85% level in one domain and the 93% level in the other!

SemNet-based assessment differs from other forms of assessment in significant ways. First, SemNet-based assessment is generative, not responsive. Second, the semantic network that a student produces allows the reviewer to see not only what concepts and relations the student chooses to include in describing a particular topic, but also reveals the student's higher order structure—that is, the way in which the student's knowledge is organized. Third, semantic network construction requires a relatively high level of precision, largely eliminating the ambiguity inherent in text and essay. Fourth, in creating knowledge representations, students must make the relations they perceive between ideas explicit (whereas those relations are often implicit in essays). Effective and consistent use of relations is difficult for many students, yet this aspect of knowledge organization is overlooked by most other assessment methods, except for the well-known Miller Analogies Test (Wandersee, in press). Fifth, an indirect but very important effect of assessment via knowledge representation is that it promotes good thinking and learning habits. And sixth, another important consideration in the use of computer-based semantic networks for assessment is that, while they do require qualitative evaluation, review is augmented by powerful automated scoring procedures. These procedures are described below.

NATURE OF RELATIONS

Since few assessments attend to relations, it may be helpful to give a brief characterization of them (Faletti & Fisher, 1996; Hoffman, 1991; Fisher, 1988a–c). First, there is a pronounced lack of standardization within biology with respect to relation names; that is, while biologists use similar relation meanings, they often use different names to refer to those meanings (see, for example, Hoffman, 1991). Second, three relations are used to construct 50% of all instances (concept–relation–concept units) in general biology. That is, three relations seem to embody our first and most basic understanding of a biology idea. These three relations are *whole/part*, *set/member*, and *characteristic*. Third, no single constrained set of relations is suitable for representing all biology knowledge. *Content drives relations.* Each different sub-domain and subtopic requires its own unique expressions. To constrain the relation set is synonymous with failing to represent the knowledge adequately and accurately at the level needed to learn biology. Fourth, mastering relations is challenging for all learners and is a particularly difficult challenge for second-language learners. This is consistent with observations made by others that children learn nouns before verbs (Gentner, 1978) and second-language learners learn nouns before verbs (Rosenthal, 1996). Concepts typically have noun names while relationships are generally expressed with verbs.

A student's failure to comprehend a relationship is rarely diagnosed without a tool like SemNet, and without diagnosis it cannot be directly remedied. Yet correction of an error in comprehending a basic relation is much more powerful than correction of any misapprehended concept. This is so because the basic relations are used over and over again. Any student who is unsure of the meaning of *"has part"* (a common condition for ESL students) is at a serious disadvantage in learning biology.

It is ironic and intriguing that while relations generally are more difficult to understand than concepts, we teach them less. Rarely will you see a relationship listed in a course syllabus as a topic to be mastered.

GENERATIVE ASSESSMENTS WITH SEMNET

In this section I'll describe some ways of using SemNet as a generative assessment tool in a course in which the software is also being used as a learning tool. Three main types of assessment occur in such a course: diagnostic assessment, embedded or formative assessment, and summative assessment. In addition, SemNet can be used to elicit students' prior knowledge about a topic. Each of these is described below. In the next section, I describe strategies for reviewing and evaluating nets.

Diagnostic Assessment

Diagnostic assessment is extremely valuable, especially early in the learning process. Identification and remediation of specific problems early in the course can help strengthen the students' cognitive and metacognitive learning skills, leading to more satisfactory and productive learning experiences.

The most challenging part of SemNet-based knowledge representation is the creation of bidirectional relations, a step that is not part of our everyday thinking. To experience the difficulty, perhaps the reader would like to generate the reverse relation ray for the four instances below. The relation is the verb phrase indicated by italics. The reverse ray would be the wording used to describe the same relation between the two underlined concepts in the opposite direction. A general rule of thumb for good relation rays is that they use the same main words in each direction:

- <u>car</u> *has part* <u>wheel</u>
- <u>glycolysis</u> *has input* <u>glucose</u>
- <u>metaphase</u> *follows* <u>prophase</u>
- <u>predation</u> *is a component of* <u>natural selection</u>

There is no one right way to word reverse relation rays, but there are acceptable and unacceptable ways. My preferred reverse relation rays for these instances are shown at the end of this chapter.

When students first begin constructing knowledge networks, I provide a set of bidirectional relations for them to use. Once they begin to construct their own nets without this help, however, these are the most common problems I see in diagnostic assessments:

- Students fail to name the reverse relation ray (and SemNet automatically names the ray "inverse of [original relation ray]").
- Students name the reverse relation ray but do so incorrectly, actually describing two different relations instead of two halves of the same relation, as in *"has input/output from."*
- Students use relations incorrectly; a common error is to use a *set/member* relation to describe a physical *whole/part* and vice versa.
- Students use relations inconsistently; second-language learners have particular problems with correct relation use, since both first and second language learners learn nouns before verbs (Gentner, 1978; Rosenthal, 1996).
- Students give sparse and inadequate descriptions of important concepts, often no more than a linear chain of concepts.
- Students fail to include important ideas in their nets.

Early diagnostic assessment and feedback typically leads to rapid improvement, greatly enhancing the quality of subsequent student nets and also, I believe, increasing the quality and precision of student thinking about biology. Providing examples of expert nets also seems to help students develop their skills more quickly.

Embedded Assessments

My students represent what they are learning in the course by creating a series of small (150- to 200-concept) semantic networks. The process of creating these nets becomes an important step in their learning of biology, and the products of their efforts allow me to "look into their minds" and "see" what they are thinking. The feedback I give on each subsequent net, as well as their own reflections and their reviews of other students' nets, lead to steady improvement in their thinking about and organization of their biology knowledge.

The students generally work in groups of four in both the wet lab and in the computer lab. In the wet lab we take the privileging approach to learning biology topics (Keys, 1997), often using experiments designed to challenge prior conceptions (Roth, 1990). In the computer lab, the students describe the ideas that were illustrated by the experiments.

So long as groups work well together, which they usually (but not always) do, they reap the benefits associated with group activities (Johnson, Johnson, & Smith, 1991). The most pronounced benefits seem to me to be tutoring or peer instruction, sharing of expertise, negotiation of meaning, mutual support in learning, and questioning of specific representations. The greatest benefit to the instructor, aside from the benefits inherent in the social learning process, is that there are only one-fourth the number of nets to review as there would be if each student worked alone! The evaluation method I use for such group work is described in the next section.

The most common error observed in embedded assessments, in addition to occasional persistence of some of the errors described above, is failure to consistently organize knowledge hierarchically and temporally. In particular, students often lack the habit of thinking "up a hierarchy," yet this step facilitates the knitting together of smaller ideas into larger ones and establishes pathways for thoughts to cascade down. Failure to link ideas to their appropriate categories can subsequently reduce a student's ability to retrieve and use that knowledge effectively (Reif & Larkin, 1991).

Likewise, when a sequence of events regularly occur together, as in the phases of cell division, it makes sense to connect them temporally as well as hierarchically. Most students do not do this spontaneously and need steady, gentle prompting to acquire these cognitive habits.

Summative Assessment

In a course of this type, midterms and final examinations usually consist of one-half written test and one-half SemNet-based test. This provides direct assessment of each student's SemNet and knowledge organization skills. The instructions for a SemNet-based test might take the form of "Provide as complete a description of a eukaryotic cell as you can from memory, including the structure and function of its various components" or "Summarize the process of cell division in a somatic cell as completely as you can, including both hierarchical and temporal relationships, with robust descriptions of each stage or event." This sort of question reveals quite dramatically the amount of knowledge the student has about a topic as well as the quality of organization of the student's ideas.

Sometimes it is useful to constrain the task by providing a set of relations and/or concepts to students in both a printed list (for easy reference) and in a SemNet (so they don't need to enter the information). Students are then asked to assemble the given ideas into a coherent network about a topic. This is especially useful when there isn't enough time for students to generate a net in its entirety. This approach has the advantage of allowing comparisons across all students on the exact same content.

You might think that this would be an easier task, since all concepts and relations are provided to students. In fact, it appears to be more challenging for students than working from memory. They must discipline themselves to use the ideas that are given rather than to freely follow their thought patterns. Many of my students are unable to do this consistently, so their constructions are inevitably a mix of their own ideas and the provided ideas.

Assessment of Prior Knowledge

Once students learn how to construct a network, it is easy to elicit their prior knowledge so long as there is a sense of trust. Prior knowledge is best assessed without forewarning. Students are asked to share their knowledge about a given topic to the best of their ability, are assured that the exercise will not be graded, and are also assured that the reader will respect their beliefs and ideas. No books, notes, or other references are permitted. SemNet-based assessment of prior knowledge is an especially useful research strategy.

STRATEGIES FOR EVALUATING STUDENT-GENERATED SEMANTIC NETWORKS

The same basic pattern for evaluating semantic networks is useful whether the goal is to assess or diagnose student difficulties, to monitor student progress through embedded assessment, or to evaluate students' summative or prior knowledge. The basic steps include (1) obtaining an overview of what each student or group has done, (2) assessing the quality of the relations that were employed, and (3) reviewing the quality of the concept descriptions. Sometimes it is also useful to examine special features such as (4) the hierarchies or temporal linkages that are used or (5) the key concepts that were included (and those that are missing). The ways in which SemNet can help with each of these evaluative aspects are illustrated below.

With larger networks, one can order students' nets according to size in the finder and predict the approximate outcome of the evaluation. There is a close but not perfect correlation between net size and net quality.

Overview—About Net

The most useful overview in SemNet is the About Net summary on the Display menu (Figure 2).

The top of the frame in Figure 2 shows the number of concepts, relations, and instances in the net. Associated with the 585 concepts are 25 synonyms, 10 texts, 65 pictures, and 610 names (585 concepts plus 25 synonyms). The 38 relations have one text and 69 names associated with them (there are usually almost twice as many relation names as there are relations because each asymmetric relation has two names, one in each direction). An asymmetric relation is one that requires different names for each relation ray, as in *has parent/has child*. A symmetric relation uses the same name in both directions, as in *is spouse of/is spouse of*.

A useful figure that is not displayed in About Net but is easily calculated from it is the ratio of instances to concepts, which gives a measure of the

About Net: Anatomy

Net Elements	# Elements	# Synonyms	# Texts	# Pictures	# Names
Concepts	585	25	10	65	610
Relations	38	—	1	0	69
Instances	878				

Counts of Concepts Having Various Numbers of Instances

# Instances	# Concepts	% of Total Concepts
0	0	0.0
1-2	357	61.0
3 or more	228	39.0
6 or more	85	14.5
10 or more	23	3.9
20 or more	3	0.5

Maximums

Most developed concept(s) with 21 instances: eye
Most embedded concept(s) with embeddedness of 123: cranial nerves
Most used relation(s) used in 406 instances: has a part/is a part of

FIGURE 2

About Net Display in a human anatomy net by Hugh Patterson, University of California Medical School, San Francisco.

interconnectivity of a network. The instance/concept ratio in Patterson's net is 1.5—reflecting a typically robust, highly interconnected expert network. I encourage my students to create at least 1.25 and preferably 1.3 or more times as many instances as concepts.

The center of the About Net Display shows the number and percentage of concepts having various numbers of connections to other concepts (0, 1–2, 3 or more, etc.). Three or more connections is the minimum or threshold level for providing an adequate description of a concept. In the anatomy net, 39% of the concepts have 3 or more connections. My students are urged to create nets in which at least 25% of the concepts have 3 or more connections, a robust net for students.

Sometimes an individual creating a net will create a concept and then decide not to use it. Such a concept will not be connected to the network and will appear in About Net having 0 connections. The anatomy net does not have any unconnected concepts. I encourage my students to polish their nets by deleting unconnected concepts and unused relations.

The lower part of the frame shows the most developed concept, which is the one having the greatest numbers of links or instances. It also shows the most embedded concept, which has the greatest number of unique paths to two nodes away. And finally, it identifies the most frequently used relation.

Quality of Relations

The second Display to examine in reviewing a net is Relations in Creation Order. Figure 3 shows the 31 relations in a student net describing mitochondrial function. Some of the relations were provided to the students by the instructor and they created others. The clock settings in Figure 3 refer to the location where each relation ray points on the screen. The Times Used column shows how many times each relation was used.

Since this network describes a process, it does not follow the usual pattern of having high numbers of *part*, *type*, and *characteristic* relations. However, it does illustrate some of the problems encountered in early student-generated nets. Here are the problems that I see in these relations:

- Most of the student-generated relations share the same locations— 6:00 and 12:00 o'clock—instead of being distributed around the screen; SemNet uses the metaphor of a clock to indicate where relation rays point on the screen; relations should be distributed fairly evenly around the clock for clear displays.
- In 10 cases the students did not name the reverse relation ray and it contains the default "inverse of" form generated by SemNet.
- Two seemingly identical relations, the first and the third, each called *has part/part of*, should be merged together; one of each of the seemingly identical relation rays must contain an extra space—they look identical to us but are not identical to the computer.

First Relation Ray	Second Relation Ray	Clock Settings	# Times Used
has part	part of	4:00/12:00	3
passes through	invert of passes through	8:00/12:00	2
has part	*part of*	*6:00/12:00*	7
has example	example of	4:00/12:00	4
diffuses	*inverse of diffuses*	*9:00/12:00*	1
expels	*inverse of expels*	*3:00/12:00*	1
carries	*inverse of carries*	*9:00/12:00*	2
has characteristics	characteristics of	3:00/12:00	20
form	*inverse of form*	*8:00/12:00*	1
has structure	structure of	9:00/12:00	3
passes	is passed from	5:00/12:00	4
has definition	definition of	3:00/2:00	5
contains	*inverse of contains*	*9:00/12:00*	4
excretes	*inverse of excretes*	*4:00/12:00*	1
releases glucose to	receives glucose from	8:00/2:00	11
passes CO2 to	receives CO2 from	3:00/9:00	11
forms	is formed by	6:00/12:00	3
releases	is released from	6:00/10:00	1
turns into	*is created by*	*6:00/12:00*	2
when added to	*inverse of when added to*	*6:00/12:00*	1
creates	*inverse of creates*	*6:00/12:00*	1
without	*inverse of without*	*6:00/12:00*	1
with	*inverse of with*	*6:00/12:00*	1
enters	*inverse of enters*	*6:00/12:00*	2
passes to	*receives ATP from*	*6:00/12:00*	4
passes ATP to	*inverse of passes ATP to*	*6:00/12:00*	3
site of	occurs at site	8:00/2:00	3
has type	type of	7:00/1:00	3
has output	output from	3:00/12:00	1
has input	input to	3:00/9:00	1
receives	pass to	9:00/3:00	1

FIGURE 3

Relations in Creation Order with the relation ray orientations and the number of times each relation has been used, from a net describing the mitochondrion by student group 5. This net contains 103 concepts, 31 relations, and 108 instances. Incorrect relation names are shown in boldface and italics and are described in the text.

- The relation, *turns into/is created by*, violates the rule of using the same main word in each half of a relation.
- The correct relation, *passes* ATP *to/receives* ATP *from*, is divided between two ill-formed relations (*passes to/receives* ATP *from, and passes* ATP *to/inverse of passes* ATP *to*).

In all, 15 of 31 relations in Figure 3 have a problem. If all relations were used with equal frequency, this would mean that almost 50% of the instances in this net are incorrect in one direction—an unacceptable situation.

Assessing Content

The main reason for using semantic network representations to support science learning is to help students improve their abilities to organize domain-specific knowledge and to construct robust networks of ideas. Thus it makes sense to evaluate the content of a semantic network as one would evaluate an essay. This includes recognition that there is more than one correct way to organize a given set of ideas, that some organizations are more effective than others, that elegance and style matter, and that the four C's are ultimately critical: coherence, completeness, correctness, and conciseness. Frequent detailed feedback (coaching) is valuable in helping learners increase their effectiveness as learners.

Quality of Concept Descriptions

The best way to assess content is to review concepts graphically either on screen or in print, typically printed six to a page. The display of each central concept with its related concepts is called a frame. Figure 4 illustrates a single frame having *Golgi apparatus* as its central concept; this is linked to eight related concepts with five relations rays. One concept, linked with the relation *has function*, is actually a phrase that is three lines long. Various means of selectivity can be used to determine which concepts to print (e.g., flagged

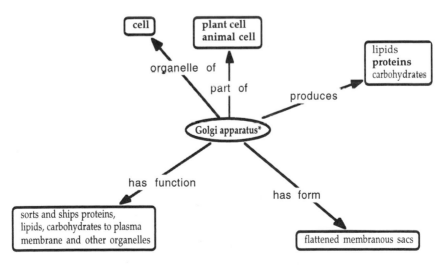

FIGURE 4

A concept, *Golgi apparatus*, displayed graphically with all of its direct links to related concepts. There is one such frame for every concept in the net, or 245 frames in all. From a net created by student group 2. This cell net contains 245 concepts, 39 relations, and 287 instances.

concepts only, all concepts). The default setting prints concepts with 3 or more connections, which is generally the most useful criterion. Printouts are especially helpful for formative assessment since it is possible to give students detailed feedback.

Sometimes it is particularly useful to review a semantic network on the computer. One approach is to Traverse the net (Move menu). Traverse is a SemNet command that provides automatic review of all concepts meeting the designated selection criteria.

Another approach is to Mask the central concept (Concept menu) and use the Random Jump command (Move menu). Masking the central concept engages the reviewer in specifically evaluating concept descriptions. It can sharpen the reviewer's ability to distinguish between adequate and inadequate concept descriptions. As long as the descriptions are adequate, the reviewer can identify the masked concepts. This is also a good way for students to assess the quality of their nets.

A third approach is to click through a network. This is especially useful when the reviewer is looking for particular temporal or hierarchical sequences. In nets about the circulatory system, for example, I ask students to trace the flow of blood around the body. Complex flows such as this are best reviewed either in this manner or using the hierarchy display (Figure 6).

We use the spatial arrangement as well as words to convey information. Thus, we find that frames are easier to read when the larger ideas are above the central concept, the smaller ideas are below, and temporal flows move from left to right. It takes some time for students to acquire the skills to make these subtle distinctions.

Identifying Main Ideas—Concepts by Embeddedness

It is often desirable to determine if students have included most or all of the main ideas about a topic in a network. The easiest way to do this is to review concepts in order of Embeddedness (Figure 5). The embeddedness calculation (number of unique paths to two nodes away from a concept) identifies the ideas that are most central to a given network. Important or central concepts appear in the top of the embeddedness list.

An interesting thing to note in Figure 5 is the degree of interconnectedness in a well-developed network. With a total of 2463 concepts, there are 534 different ways to access the most embedded concept, DNA, from just two nodes away! In fact, all the ideas in a well-developed network are close together in psychological and computer space, whereas in a linear list there would be 2461 nodes between the first and last concept. Another way to examine this interconnectivity is by assessing the shortest distance between any two concepts, which can be done easily in SemNet. The maximum "shortest path" we were able to find between any two concepts in this entire 2463-concept net was 11 nodes! This illustrates why the high interconnec-

Embed.	2463 Concepts by Embeddedness
534	DNA
492	nucleus
461	ATP
456	RNA
439	transcription
421	nucleic acid
384	translation
371	stroma
348	energy
320	mRNA

FIGURE 5

This shows the top of the list of molecular concepts by embeddedness in a semantic network created by the author that describes general biology and contains 2463 concepts.

tivity of expert knowledge facilitates retrieval and application of knowledge. It also shows the value of promoting integrated student learning.

Hierarchies and Temporal Flows

With the Display Hierarchy command, it is possible to extract any hierarchy or temporal flow from a semantic network. One can follow a single relation as in Figure 6 (*passes blood to*) or any combination of flagged relations. This provides a quick means for checking on students' hierarchical, temporal, or spatial organization, and facilitates the evaluation of tests designed specifically to assess students' organizational abilities.

Peer Review of Nets

Not only is it valuable for teachers to be able to "look into students' minds," but students benefit as well from seeing how their peers organize knowledge in the domain being studied. From some nets they obtain ideas for improving their own knowledge organizations. In others they see clear examples of what not to do. Overall, they have a much better appreciation of the possible variations in knowledge representations and of the distinct range of quality that is apparent.

Assessing Contributions of Members of a Group

When a group of students work together to construct a semantic network, the instructor evaluates the end product, the net itself, without much insight as to what was contributed by each member of the group. Under

	receives blood from right atrium	
	receives blood from right ventricle	
	receives blood from pulmonary (lung) arteries	
	receives blood from pulmonary (lung) capillaries	
receives blood from pulmonary (lung) veins		
left atrium		
passes blood to	left ventricle	
passes blood to	aorta	
passes blood to	carotid (neck) arteries	
passes blood to	cranial (head) capillaries	
passes blood to	jugular (neck) veins	
passes blood to	superior vena cava	

FIGURE 6

About one-fifth of the hierarchy showing the flow of blood to and from the left atrium of the heart, using the relation *passes blood to/receives blood from* in a small net that superficially describes the circulation of blood in the human body, as extracted with the Display Hierarchy command.

such circumstances it is valuable to ask group members to evaluate the contributions of each group member, including themselves. In my experience, the consensus among peer evaluations is very high, so much so that it is justifiable to raise or lower an individual student's score relative to the grade given to the overall project.

INCORPORATING SEMNET-BASED ASSESSMENT INTO PRINTED TESTS

It isn't always practical to give computer-based generative assessments, but teachers can still prompt integrated thinking by using the graphic displays from SemNet to create printed questions. SemNet frames can be incorporated into multiple-choice and short-answer tests. At first glance you might think that such SemNet-based tests would be no different from more traditional tests. However, students consistently report that they have to "think differently" with a SemNet-based test. Four types of printed, SemNet-based assessments are illustrated below, respectively assessing main ideas, details, relations, and discrimination.

Assessing Knowledge about Main Ideas

It is possible to mask the central concept in each SemNet frame (e.g., Figure 7). The student can then be asked to identify (fill in) the masked concept or to select the correct idea from a list of choices (such as, in this case, centromere, mRNA, gene, chromosome arm). A student has to evaluate all the information in the frame to choose the best response. Some students find

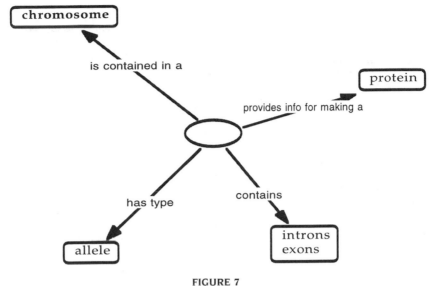

FIGURE 7
Identify the masked central concept.

this requirement challenging and will focus on just one or two choices of links to related concepts that have caught their attention. Students using this strategy miss the mark often. Other students scan all choices and focus on what appears to them to be key "clues." These students would be likely to decide that the masked concept in Figure 7 is a *gene*.

Assessing Knowledge about Details

It is also possible to mask the related concepts in each SemNet frame and to unmask them one by one, leaving one or more masked related concepts (e.g., Figure 8). A question of this type gives as well as asks for information and so can promote learning and integration of ideas even in the context of an examination.

Assessing Knowledge about Relations

Learning to use relations consistently and accurately is a key to successful biology learning. It is especially useful for biology students to be able to distinguish between members of a class, as signified by a relation such as *has type*, *has example*, or *is a set containing the member*, and physical parts of a whole, as signified by *has part*, *has component*, *composed of*, or *contained in*. There are many ways to examine this ability with SemNet (e.g., Figure 9).

The relation *is part of* would be correct pointing to *eukaryotic cell* in the first frame and *giraffe population* in the second frame.

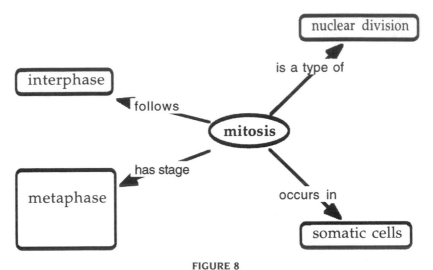

FIGURE 8
Identify the three masked related concepts in the order in which
they occur.

Assessing Ability to Make Fine Discriminations

Experts are better at making fine discriminations than novices. Questions such as that shown in Figure 10 can both assess and promote students' abilities to discriminate.

Aside from the Latin species names, which may not be useful to many students, the best distinguishing features between dogs and cats are their behaviors: barks or meows, wags tail or doesn't wag tail.

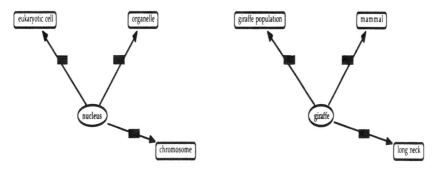

FIGURE 9
Check the one relation box in each of the two frames in which you would
insert the relation *is part of*.

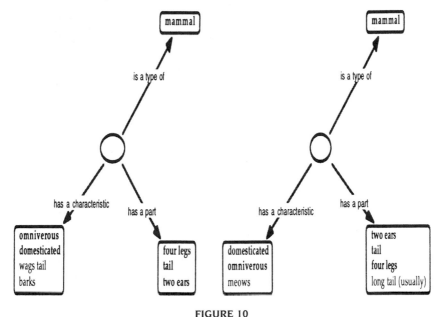

FIGURE 10
Identify the two masked concepts.

When generating SemNet-based questions of this type, it is important to monitor the frames for possible ambiguities. Also, it helps to keep it simple. A frame that contains too much information can be overwhelming and confusing.

SUMMARY: A VISION FOR THE FUTURE

The U.S. Department of Education and National Science Foundation have produced a *Statement on Principles of Assessment in Mathematics and Science Education* (1994). In their view, a basic principle of assessment is that "an assessment program at every level should be aligned with rigorous and challenging content standards of what students should know and be able to do" (p. 2). This proposed alignment represents a particularly challenging obstacle in the reform movement.

The move toward more meaningful learning, which involves teaching fewer concepts so as to achieve deeper understanding of each, is gaining wide acceptance around the world (except for pockets of resistance from the radical right in the United States). However, the predominant mode of testing in the United States remains the multiple-choice test (MC test), a wonderfully efficient, inexpensive, reliable, valid mode of testing. Unfortunately,

MC testing usually assesses fragments of knowledge based primarily on a low cognitive level of performance, recognition of correct responses. The most devastating outcome of MC testing is the way in which it induces and rewards rote learning, producing repeated cycles of memorization and forgetting under the guise of learning. The problem is succinctly described by Rothman (1995, p. 3):

> In the twenty-first century, they [educators] reasoned, all young people would have to be able to use their knowledge to solve problems, analyze information, and communicate clearly. But traditional tests not only failed to provide information on those abilities, they discouraged schools from tapping them by placing a premium on the quick recall of facts. Moreover, while the traditional system allowed some to excel, it also permitted many students simply to get by.

Because economics drives everything, it is not likely that MC testing will be replaced until another method is developed that is equally easy, efficient, valid, reliable, and automated. If a new method is developed that has all the benefits of MC testing, plus the added benefit of being aligned with the reform movement, it may gradually be adopted. The only challenge would be that of overcoming inertia, of replacing the familiar with the unfamiliar.

I believe that a computer-based semantic networking program has the potential to augment or replace multiple-choice testing in this manner. If knowledge nets could be scored automatically, the conflict inherent in the combination of reform teaching and MC testing could be overcome.

Semantic network-based testing would facilitate learning and integrative thinking consistent with the reform movement. Constructing semantic networks is generative. Students could be expected to describe an entire topical area, such as structure and function of a cell or a kidney. Their constructions would allow evaluation of higher order thinking (how their knowledge is organized) as well as evaluation of factual knowledge, as advocated by the Department of Education (1994). They also would allow diagnosis of specific student problems, thus empowering the instructor to give targeted corrective feedback to expedite the learning process. This specificity is akin to the "silver bullets" (monoclonal antibodies) being used to treat some cancers today.

The following questions remain to be answered: Can the evaluation of student-generated semantic networks be completely automated without reducing the task to one of memorizing and regurgitating the teacher's network? And if this is the case, would such testing be as valid, reliable, and efficient as multiple-choice testing is today? I believe that this is the promise for the future. It seems likely that with a combination of word recognition, structural analyses, and quantitative net descriptors, it will be possible to produce a testing system that gives reliable, valid, reproducible evaluations of knowledge along with specific, diagnostic feedback. A new cross-platform semantic networking program is currently under development. Much work remains to be done to develop the algorithms necessary for automatic scoring and for rigorously assessing the reliability and validity of the method. However, assessment based on automatic scoring of student-generated knowledge nets offers a tempting solution to the problem described by Cohen (1991):

> If the recent reforms are to succeed, students and teachers must not simply absorb a new body of knowledge. Rather, they must acquire a new way of thinking about knowledge and a new practice of acquiring it. They must cultivate new strategies of problem solving that seem to be quite unusual among adult Americans. They must learn to treat knowledge as something they construct, test and explore, rather than as something they accumulate.

With a semantic networking learning tool in the hands of every student, and assessment via generative knowledge construction, we could enjoy the benefits of a radical shift from rote to meaningful learning and solid alignment of assessment and instruction within the reform movement!

Note.   My reverse relation rays for the exercise presented earlier in the chapter:

- wheel *is part of* car
- glucose *is an input to* glycolysis
- prophase *is followed by* metaphase
- natural selection *has component* predation

Acknowledgment

This chapter builds upon collaboration with Ellen Gagne several years ago. I am grateful for her insights and suggestions.

References

Baars, B. J. (1988). A *Cognitive Theory of Consciousness*. Cambridge, UK: Cambridge University Press.

Campione, J. C., & Brown, A. L. (1990). Guided learning and transfer: Implications for approaches to assessment. In N. Frederiksen, R. Glaser, A. Lesgold, & M. G. Shafto (Eds.), *Diagnostic monitoring of skill and knowledge acquisition*. Hillsdale, NJ: Lawrence Erlbaum.

Chase, W. G., & Simon, H. A. (1973). The mind's eye in chess. In W. G. Chase, Ed., *Visual information processing*. NY: Academic Press.

Cohen, D. K. (1991, fall). Revolution in one classroom (or then again, was it?). *American Educator* 15(2).

Derry, S. D. (1990). Learning strategies for acquiring useful knowledge. In B. F. Jones & L. Idol (Eds.), *Dimensions of thinking and cognitive instruction*. Hillsdale: Lawrence Erlbaum.

Faletti, J., & Fisher, K. M. (1996). The information in relations in biology or, the unexamined relation is not worth having. In K. M. Fisher & M. Kibby (Ed.), *Knowledge acquisition, organization and use in biology* (pp. 182–205). Berlin: Springer Verlag.

Fisher, K. M. (1988a). SemNet: Software for student for faculty construction of large relational networks of concepts. Presented in the Symposium, From Concept Maps to Computer Representations of Large Bodies of Disciplinary Knowledge: Progress and Problems in Development and Utilization. Presented at the Annual Meeting of the American Educational Research Association, New Orleans, April 5–9.

Fisher, K. M. (1988b). Relations used in student-generated knowledge representations. Presented in the Symposium on Student Understanding in Science: Issues of Cognition and Curriculum, Annual Meeting of the American Educational Research Association, New Orleans, April 5–9.

Fisher, K. M. (1988c). Hidden meanings in biology: What's in a link? Presented to the Department of Natural Science & Center for Research in Mathematics & Science Education, San Diego State University, San Diego, CA, March 18.

Fisher, K. M. (1990). Semantic networking: The new kid on the block. *Journal of Research in Science Teaching*, 27(10), 1001–1018.

Fisher, K. M. (in press). Using the SemNet® Knowledge Mapping Tool. In K. M. Fisher, J. H. Wandersee, D. E. Moody, *Mapping biology knowledge*. Dordrecht, The Netherlands: Kluwer.

Fisher, K. M., & Thornton, R. M. (1987). Impact of teaching explicit formal relations between concepts in biology. Presented at the Annual Meeting of the American Educational Research Association, San Francisco, April.

Frederiksen, C. H., & Breuleux, A. (1990). Monitoring cognitive processing in semantically complex domains. In N. Frederiksen, R. Glaser, A. Lesgold, & M. G. Shafto (Eds.), *Diagnostic monitoring of skill and knowledge acquisition*. Hillsdale, NJ: Lawrence Erlbaum.

Frederiksen, J. R., & White, B. Y. (1990). Intelligent tutors as intelligent testers. In N. Frederiksen, R. Glaser, A. Lesgold, & M. G. Shafto, (Eds.), *Diagnostic monitoring of skill and knowledge acquisition*. Hillsdale, NJ: Lawrence Erlbaum.

Gentner, D. (1978). On relational meaning: The acquisition of verb meaning. *Child Development*, 49, 988–998.

Gordon, S. E., & Gill, R. T. (1989). The formation and use of knowledge structures in problem solving domains. Manuscript available from S. E. Gordon, Department of Psychology, University of Idaho, Moscow, ID 83843.

Gorodetsky, M., & Fisher, K. M. (1996). Generating connections and learning in biology. In K. M. Fisher & M. Kibby (Eds.), *Knowledge acquisition, organization and use in biology* (pp. 135–154). Berlin: Springer Verlag.

Hoffman, R. P. (1991). Use of relational descriptors by experienced users of a computer-based semantic network. Unpublished Master's Thesis, San Diego State University.

Johnson, D. W., Johnson, R., & Smith, K. (1991) *Active learning: cooperation in the college classroom*. Edina, MN: Interaction Book Company.

Keys, C. (1997). Understanding the concepts of freedom and privileging in inquiry teaching and learning. Presented in a symposium on Perspectives on Inquiry-Oriented Teaching Practice: Clarification and Conflict at the Annual Meeting of the National Association for Research in Science Teaching, Chicago, April 21–24.

Klausmeier, H. J. (1990). Conceptualizing. In B. F. Jones & L. Idol (Eds.), *Dimensions of thinking and cognitive instruction*. Hillsdale, NJ: Lawrence Erlbaum.

Langer, E. J. (1989). *Mindfulness*. Menlo Park, CA: Addison-Wesley.

Langer, E. J. (1997). *The power of mindful learning*. Menlo Park, CA: Addison–Wesley.

Lesgold, A., Lajoie, S., Logan, D., & Eggan, G. (1990). Applying cognitive task analysis and research methods to assessment. In N. Frederiksen, R. Glaser, A. Lesgold, & M. G. Shafto (Eds.), *Diagnostic monitoring of skill and knowledge acquisition*. Hillsdale, NJ: Lawrence Erlbaum.

Marshall, S. P. (1989). The assessment of schema knowledge for arithmetic story problems. Manuscript available from S. P. Marshall, CRMSE, San Diego State University, San Diego, CA 92182.

Perkins, D. N. (1981). *The mind's best work*. Cambridge, MA: Harvard University Press.

Quillian, M. R. (1967). Word concepts: A theory and simulation of some basic semantic capabilities. *Behavioral Science*, 12, 410–430.

Quillian, M. R. (1968). Semantic meaning. In M. Minsky (Ed.), *Semantic information processing*. Cambridge, MA: MIT Press.

Quillian, M. R. (1969). The teachable language comprehender. *Communications of the Association for Computing Machinery*, 12, 459–475.

Reif, F., & Larkin, J. (1991). Cognition in scientific and everyday domains: Comparisons and learning implications. *Journal of Research in Science Teaching*, 28 (9), 733–760.

Roberts, D. D. (1973). *The existential graphs of Charles S. Pierce*. The Hague: Mouton.

Rosenthal, J. W. (1996). *Teaching science to language minority students*. Bristol, PA: Multilingual Matters Ltd.

Roth, K. J. (1990). Developing meaningful conceptual understanding in science. In B. F. Jones, & L. Idol (Eds.), *Dimensions of thinking and cognitive instruction*. Hillsdale, NJ: Lawrence Erlbaum.

Sowa, J. F. (1984). *Conceptual structures: Information processing in minds and machine*. Menlo Park, CA: Addison Wesley.

Tweney, R. D., & Walker, B. J. (1990). Science education and the cognitive psychology of science. In B. F. Jones, & L. Idol (Eds.), *Dimensions of thinking and cognitive instruction*. Hillsdale, NJ: Lawrence Erlbaum.

U.S. Department of Education Office of Educational Research and Improvement and the National Science Foundation. (1994). *Statement of principles on assessment in mathematics and science education*. Washington DC: Department of Education PIP 94–1501.

Wandersee, J. H. (in press). Language, analogy and biology. In K. M. Fisher, J. H. Wandersee, & D. E. Moody. *Mapping Biology Knowledge*. Dordrecht, The Netherlands: Kluwer.

Woods, W. A. (1975). What's in a link: Foundations for semantic networks. In R. J. Brachman & H. J. Levesque (Eds.), *Readings in knowledge representation*. Los Altos, CA: Morgan Kaufmann.

Writing to Inquire: Written Products as Performance Measures

AUDREY B. CHAMPAGNE AND VICKY L. KOUBA

Center for English Learning and Achievement
University at Albany, State University of New York

This chapter examines the role of performance measures in the social construction of the understanding of inquiry and the development of the ability to inquire. Performance assessment is a powerful tool for science educators seeking to provide all students the opportunity to learn to inquire (Champagne, 1996). Writing, a particular form of performance measure, is a powerful tool for teachers seeking to provide all their students the opportunity to learn to inquire.

The topic is timely. Standards for science education set by national scientific organizations make inquiry a central goal for science education in this era of standards-based reform. The *Benchmarks for Science Literacy* (AAAS, 1993) call for all Americans to leave high school with an understanding of scientific inquiry. Standards for understanding the nature of scientific inquiry and the ability to inquire are set by the National Research Council of the National Academy of Science in the *National Science Education Standards* (NRC, 1996). These documents also acknowledge the importance of the ability to communicate scientific ideas.[1]

---

[1] Our project has conducted a detailed analysis communication and reasoning in the Benchmarks and Standard. The report of this work is contained in Kouba and Champagne (1998).

The importance of the ability to communicate scientific ideas is reflected in international, national, and state tests designed to measure students' progress toward meeting standards. The proportion of the test time students spend writing extended responses has increased, reducing the test time spent on short-answer items. For instance, on the grade 8 National Assessment of Educational Progress (NAEP) science test administered in 1996, 74 of the 194 questions were multiple choice, 100 were short constructed response, and 20 were extended constructed response[2] (Keiser, Nelson, Norris, & Szyszkiewicz, 1998). About 80% of the students' time taking the test was spent writing responses to constructed-response questions (Bourque, Champagne, & Crissman, 1997).

Inquiry takes on two distinct roles in K–12 science education as conceived by the developers of the NRC *Standards*. The framers of this document present inquiry as an activity in which students engage to develop understanding of the natural world *and* an ability that students are expected to acquire. As a consequence of the pronouncements in the AAAS *Benchmarks* and the NRC *Standards*, science teachers face the challenge of using inquiry, a highly complex activity, as an effective method of developing their students' understanding of the natural world, while simultaneously developing their students' understanding of the nature of scientific inquiry and ability to inquire.

Despite the importance of inquiry and the ability to inquire in the standards-based reform movement, research on students' construction of understanding has focused on the understanding of the knowledge products[3] of science rather than how students develop understanding of the way in which that knowledge is produced and becomes accepted by the community of scientists. Furthermore, little attention has been given to the role that writing has on the development of understanding of inquiry or on the ability to inquire.

Our chapter considers how writing might become an integral part of learning activities designed to develop the understanding and abilities of inquiry and the mechanisms by which writing enhances student learning. We begin with some definitions, assumptions, and perspectives.

DEFINITIONS, ASSUMPTIONS, AND PERSPECTIVES

The education literature is characterized by the use of terms that authors use in idiosyncratic ways. *Assessment, performance assessment, performance measures, understanding,* and *constructivism* are examples of these terms. Conse-

---

[2] Constructed-response items are of two types. Short constructed-response items require students to write a sentence or two, whereas extended constructed-response items require students to write a few sentences or a paragraph.

[3] By knowledge products we mean scientific principles, concepts, and theories that comprise scientific knowledge accepted by the scientific community.

quently, we begin our chapter on performance measures by laying out the ways in which we use some of these familiar terms as well as some of the assumptions and perspectives that underlie our chapter.

Assessment

Our definition of assessment and the principles of good assessment practices are taken from the *National Science Education Standards* (NRC, 1996). Assessment is a process. Assessment is data gathering with a purpose. Data are collected in many different ways, for many different purposes, and by many different organizations and individuals in the education system. Data are gathered by teachers, school districts, states, and the federal government to name a few. Data are collected for different purposes, for example, to grade students' work, to judge the quality of teachers' instruction, and to track progress in achieving standards.

Testing is but one form of assessment that occurs in the classroom. Tests are data-gathering devices whose purpose is to assign grades. However, testing is but one of the data gathering devices used in the classroom by teachers. Teachers gather data in their classrooms on an almost continuous basis. As they present a lesson, teachers observe student behavior, draw inferences about how the lesson is proceeding, and make necessary modifications in their lessons. Are the students engaged? Can students do the assigned activity? If not, is it because the directions are inadequate or because the students lack some prerequisite information? What implications are the students drawing from the experience? What have the students learned? On the basis of the inferences teachers draw from the data they have gathered, they either continue the lesson as planned or make on-the-spot adjustments to the lesson.

Gathering information about the progress of a lesson for the purpose of modifying the lesson as a means of assessment is quite different from the usual means of classroom-based assessment, which is testing for the purpose of grading. Our chapter focuses on other uses of assessment, namely on assessment as a method of gathering data for the purposes of (1) developing operational[4] definitions for educational standards; (2) planning K–12 science programs, courses, and lessons; and (3) using writing as a measure of students' understanding and abilities.

Performance Assessment

Alternative definitions for performance assessment abound. For Shavelson, Baxter, and Pine (1992) performance assessment is synonymous with alter-

---

[4] Our conception of operational definitions derives from Whitehead's position that concepts are defined by the way in which they are measured (Whitehead, 1925).

native assessment and characterized by performance of concrete, meaningful tasks that are scored on the basis of the reasonableness of the procedure, not just on getting the "right" answer (p.22). The tasks described in
Shavelson & Ruiz-Primo (Chapter 13) are of the "experimental" or problem-
solving type, requiring that the student plan and execute an approach to the
question or problem where the plan requires control of variables. Neill et al.
(undated) define performance assessment as any source of data or method
of data collection other than conventional testing (characterized by multiple-choice format, norm referencing) and cite as examples classroom observation, projects, portfolios, performance exams, and essays (p. 1). Our definition of performance assessment is consistent with those of Shavelson and
Neill. The data, student writing, is analyzed not only on scientific accuracy of
the writing but also on the quality of the reasoning. Thus, samples of writing comprise performance measures of students' understanding of inquiry
and their ability to inquire.

Opportunity to Learn

Opportunity to Learn (OTL) refers to the conditions under which experience
or theory suggests learning takes place. Our chapter is based on the
assumption that OTL is enhanced when (1) descriptions of the knowledge
and abilities students are expected to learn are stated in operational form
and (2) conditions in the classroom environment, physical as well as intellectual, match those that experience or theory suggests the targeted knowledge and abilities develop. If, for instance, the student is expected to learn
to inquire, the student's opportunity to learn to inquire will be enhanced if
(1) the teacher is clear about the knowledge and abilities required to conduct inquiry, and (2) the classroom has the equipment necessary to conduct
inquiries and the teacher creates an intellectual environment consistent
with inquiry.

Performance Expectations

Just as assessment often is equated with testing, so, too, performance
expectations often are equated with scoring rubrics. Performance expectations and scoring rubrics serve very different functions in standards-based
science education and are developed using different processes. Typically,
teachers use rubrics to score their own students' responses to test items
requiring brief or extended written responses. The scoring rubric is used to
assign points to individual responses; scores on individual responses are
totaled to compute a total score on a test. The total score, in turn, is used to
assign a grade.

Individual teachers develop scoring rubrics based on the objective the
item is designed to measure or, in other terms, the scoring rubric is based

on that which the teacher taught. Scoring rubrics as they are used in the classroom are based on individual teacher's expectations for student performance based on what the teacher has taught in his or her classroom.[5]

Performance expectations have a different function and are developed in a different way. Performance expectations are developed by groups of teachers in a district for the purpose of aligning the district's science program with state or national standards. Standards are by their very nature open to broad interpretation. Consequently, in the process of aligning its science program, the district must interpret the standards in the context of the district's student population and community. Performance expectations define the evidence that a district will accept that its students have met a national or state standard and the way in which that evidence will be collected. Thus, performance expectations are a measure of the district's success in achieving the standard, not a measure of an individual student's achievement of a standard.

Because performance expectations are developed by groups rather than by individual teachers, performance expectations define in broader terms the evidence that will be accepted that a district has met the standard than the evidence an individual teacher will accept that a student has met the objective he or she has set or some portion of that objective.

The broader definition of evidence in performance expectations is consistent also with the difference in specificity of standards and objectives.

We assume that engaging in the process of defining performance expectations in operational terms leads quite naturally to the identification of the characteristics of classroom environments in which students can meet expectations. Our experience with science teachers of students in grades K–14 supports our assumption.

Inquiry

The AAAS *Benchmarks* and the NRC *Standards* provide starting points for the definition of inquiry as it is practiced and learned in the K–12 classroom. However, these documents are not detailed enough to serve as the basis for the development of plans to provide all students with the opportunity to learn to inquire. This means that teachers and curriculum specialists must

---

[5] Scoring rubrics are also used in large-scale testing. The process for developing scoring rubrics in this context is different from the process used by teachers. In this case experts reach consensus on the knowledge and abilities an item is meant to measure. The item is field tested, that is, administered to a very large number of students of varying abilities and educational experiences. The scoring rubric for the item is based on the experts' analysis of the knowledge and abilities the item measures and how the students in the field test responded to the item. As in the case of teacher-developed rubrics for individual items, a student's score on a large-scale test will be computed from scores on individual items.

elaborate and refine the information about inquiry and teaching through inquiry contained in these documents. The documents pose another challenge. The authors of the documents recognize implicitly rather than explicitly that inquiry is practiced in different forms in the scientific community, in the lives of science-literate adults, and in the science classroom. What is never quite clear in these documents is whether the vision of scientific inquiry toward which teachers and students should aspire is the vision of the practice of inquiry in the scientific community or its practice by the ideal science-literate adult. Of even more immediate concern to K–12 science educators are the various forms of inquiry practiced in the science classroom. In the *Benchmarks and Standards*, the terms *scientific inquiry, inquiry, investigation*, and *experimentation* are used with little, if any, distinction made among them. We believe that the different terminology used reflects the authors' implicit recognition that what is called inquiry in the classroom takes on many different forms.

In another paper, we propose a typology for the various forms of science-related inquiry.[6] The typology distinguishes inquiry as it is practiced by natural scientists from inquiry practiced by science-literate adults, and inquiry as practiced by science literate adults from inquiry practiced by science students (Table 1). Our typology acknowledges that scientists, nonscientist adults, and students engage in inquiry for different purposes and that these differences in purpose are reflected in the ways in which inquiry is conducted. Scientists engage in inquiry to gain more complete understanding of the natural world—to formulate, test, and apply scientific principles. High school students may do experiments to test or verify scientific principles. Students perform investigations that involve hands-on laboratory work or that involve only the collection of information from print and on-line sources. Nonscientist adults do investigations that primarily involve the collection, evaluation, and analysis of information. In either the case of students or adults, the purpose of the investigations is often to get information on which to base personal or civic decisions. (Champagne, Kouba, & Hurley, 1999).

Whatever the form of inquiry, a tremendous amount of information and ability is required to perform the component parts of the inquiry, thus making the teaching and learning of inquiry a challenge to teacher and student alike. For each of several different forms of inquiry in our typology, we identified distinct phases in the process and began to characterize the knowledge, understanding, and abilities that must be learned in each of the phases. The phases common to all the forms of inquiry we have named the precursor, planning, implementation, and closure/extension phases (Champagne et al., 1999). While these individual phases may be taught separately, consistent

---

[6] The task of better definition of the forms of inquiry seen in science classrooms is further complicated by lack of distinction by science educators of scientific inquiry, the goal of which is to develop better understanding of the natural world, and engineering design, the goal of which is to create artifacts to meet human needs.

TABLE I
Types of Scientific Inquiry

Inquirers	Purpose
Natural scientists engaged in research	Develop, test, apply scientific theories
Science-literate adult	Collect, evaluate, and analyze information for the purpose of making personal, social and civic decisions
Science student	
Investigations	Collect, evaluate, and analyze information in the laboratory, the library, and on the Internet for the purpose of making personal, social, and civic decisions
Experiments	Collect, evaluate, and analyze information in the laboratory, the library, and on the Internet for the purpose of understanding or testing science principles

with the AAAS *Benchmarks* and the NRC *Standards*, all students should have the opportunity to engage in complete inquiry at least once a year.

Our chapter now turns to a description of the learning environment in which students will have the opportunity to learn to inquire. Our description of the learning environment is developed around a form of inquiry we call laboratory-based investigations. An example of a laboratory-based investigation is one that requires students to design an investigation testing claims by purveyors of breakfast cereal that their product meets all U.S. Department of Agriculture requirements for vitamin and minerals. The results of the investigation might be used to decide which product to purchase. An investigation of this type requires work in the laboratory and in the library or on the Internet. We distinguish this form of inquiry from experimentation because its purpose is not to learn more about the natural world—for instance, the vitamin A requirements of pregnant women—but to gain information about a commercial product on which to make a decisions about which product to purchase. While the knowledge, understanding, and many of the abilities required for successful performance of a laboratory-based investigation are the same as those required for performing a scientific experiment, the two forms of inquiry have different purposes, use different methodologies, and employ different language in reporting results (see Champagne et al., in press, for details about these differences).

THE LEARNING ENVIRONMENT

The learning environment has social, intellectual, and physical features. The teacher facilitates the development of the social and intellectual characteristics of learning environments. The environment that nurtures the ability to inquire has a social structure and an intellectual atmosphere that reflect certain aspects of the social structure and culture of the community of natural scientists. Civility and adherence to the norms of scientific discourse and rules of scientific evidence are characteristics of learning environments in which students can develop the ability to inquire. Students do not come to the science classroom knowing how to engage intellectually with their peers in a civil fashion or have knowledge of the norms of scientific evidence and discourse. These essential features of inquiry are learned and are as essential to being an inquirer as abilities such as observation and the use of scientific measuring instruments.

The discussion that follows describes the cultural and intellectual features of the learning environment in which the ability to inquire develops. The discussion is organized around the four phases of inquiry that we identified: the precursor, planning, implementation, and closure/extension phases of inquiry (Table 2). These phases are not distinct and are iterative. An inquirer may begin planning an approach to answering well-conceptualized questions only to learn that a reasonable plan cannot be developed to answer the question and, consequently, that the questions must be reformulated.

Posing and refining questions appropriate for scientific consideration are the activities of the *precursor phase* of laboratory-based investigation. These activities are highly interactive. Students pose questions motivated by their previous study of science, justify the scientific appropriateness of the questions, present their questions and justifications to their fellow students in written form, and refine their questions and justifications based on peer reviews. As members of the science learning community, students also have the responsibility for evaluating their fellow students' questions and justification. For these activities to be productive, all students must agree on the characteristics that make a question appropriate to scientific investigation as well as the characteristics of a well-structured justification for the appropriateness of the question. Our conception of the social and intellectual characteristics of the learning environment and the community of science learners is analogous to the characteristics of science and the communities of scientists that have norms for the discourse appropriate to the community, as well as defined attributes of questions appropriate for inquiry.[7]

Having posed a question appropriate to scientific inquiry, students enter the *planning phase* in which they develop a plan for the investigation of the questions they have posed along with written justification demonstrating that the plan is well matched with questions and that the plan is scientifically valid. The individual plans are evaluated by the classmates. Once again, for this activity to be productive, the community of science learners

---

[7] The level of sophistication of the characteristics of scientific questions will, of course, depend on the ages of the students.

TABLE 2
Phases of Inquiry

Phase	Activity
Precursor	Pose and refine questions
Planning	Develop a plan to answer questions
Implementation	Collect data
Closure/extension	Write report

must agree on how to judge the match of the questions to the plan and on the characteristics of a scientifically valid investigative plan.

The *implementation phase* of inquiry is the phase in which students engage in laboratory activities, manipulate equipment, collect and analyze data, and draw preliminary conclusions from their data. During this phase, students draw conclusions from their data and develop justifications for the validity of their conclusions. Conclusions and justifications are reviewed by classmates and modifications are made on the basis of the review. As before, the students under the guidance of the teacher must have agreed upon the scientifically acceptable forms of justification, that is, the form of arguments leading from the evidence (data) to the conclusions.

The *closure/extension* phase is the one in which students write reports of their work and consider the implications of the conclusions they have drawn to civic, social, or personal contexts. In this phase, as in the others, the community of inquirers, under the watchful guidance of the teachers, has developed criteria for scientifically acceptable reports.

In the learning environment we envision students spending as much time or more writing, planning, analyzing, and evaluating other students' work as in doing the hands-on portion of the investigation. Our experience is that many of the middle and secondary science teachers we work with are critical of this approach. They do not believe that so much time should be devoted to writing, or that students should be given responsibility for evaluating other students' work. Teachers also are highly critical of requiring students to demonstrate their understanding of science by writing.

Teachers' criticisms are understandable. Teachers are most familiar and comfortable with the processes of science, especially those associated with doing laboratory work.[8] Consequently, the focus in most classrooms has been on students' ability to engage productively in the processes associated with hands-on laboratory work rather than on their ability to choose appro-

---

[8] Process skills as defined in *Science: A Process Approach* (Walbesser, 1968) are observation, using space/time relations, classification, using numbers, measurement, inference, prediction, operational definitions, control of variables, experimenting, data interpretation, hypothesizing, and models.

priate processes and justify those choices. For instance, teachers are more comfortable making judgments about their students' ability to inquire on the basis of their skill in making accurate measurements than their ability to choose and justify a level of measurement accuracy that is required in a particular investigation.

Teachers' comfort aside, communication is a central component of national standards. Whether teachers are comfortable with writing in science or not, meeting the standards and scoring well on state and national tests will require that students become more proficient writers. However, as we will argue below, learning theory provides stronger justification for writing in the science curriculum than the threat of meeting standards and passing external tests. It is our contention that writing serves to keep students' minds on science as they engage in hands-on activities.

Teachers are not alone in their criticisms of writing in the curriculum. Certain university-based science educators are critical of the form of writing we advocate for school science. For instance, Hildebrand (1998, p. 345) is critical of "the hegemonic discourse on writing to learn science" that she claims is a consequence of the positivist view of science. (See Giere [1988] for a discussion of relationships among philosophies of science and language.) In her view, one method for disrupting hegemonic pedagogy is to incorporate hybrid imaginative genres in secondary school science. Our perspective is different. We argue that the form of writing developed in school science must be consistent with the forms of writing that characterize the discourse of the scientific community and the presentation of scientific information in the popular press, especially as presented by well-recognized science journalists. We justify our position by arguing that (1) if students are to learn about the nature of science they need to learn about science as it is practiced, and (2) most citizens get their information about science from the popular press and need to have the abilities to critically analyze this form of discourse.

DISCOURSE IN THE SCIENCE CLASSROOM

Discourse in the science classroom is consistent with the goals of science and science education and psychological theories about how science literacy develops. The National Research Council of the National Academy of Sciences recognizes communication as an essential to the construction of scientific knowledge and a fundamental responsibility of the scientific community (NRC, 1995). Science as a social process and the conventions of scientific discourse have been described in detail by sociologists and linguists (Connolly & Vilardi, 1989; Latour & Woolgar, 1986; Penrose & Katz, 1998). That students develop the ability to engage in scientific discourse at a level appropriate to their age is an essential goal of science education. That such engagement is essential to the development of science literacy and that the science classroom environment should reflect the social processes of science and the conventions of scientific discourse are fundamental assumptions underlying the science curriculum. Furthermore, the incorporation of these processes and conventions in the science curriculum is consistent with constructivist (Duit, 1995; Candace & Duckworth, 1996; Spivey, 1997; Sternberg, 1994) and social (Brown, Collins, & Duguid, 1989; Salomon, 1993: Vygotsky, 1986) theories of learning.

A fundamental assumption of constructivist and social learning theories is that engagement in discursive activities plays an essential role in the development of understanding of scientific principles and the ability to reason. These theories also provide insights into the mechanisms through which engaging in discursive processes results in learning and the characteristics of learning environments in which students develop understanding and the ability to reason. John Dewey (1933) said it most succinctly: We learn by doing. Thus, engaging in the construction, justification, and evaluation of scientific questions, plans for scientific inquiries, conclusions from such inquiries, and reports of scientific inquiries by writing and speaking is the way in which students develop the understanding and abilities of inquiry.[9] Because these abilities are learned in a social context, not only does each student develop individual abilities and personal understanding of the characteristics of appropriate forms of scientific discourse, but the community of learners engages in the process of constructing norms or conventions of appropriate forms of scientific discourse. Discourse not only is an essential mechanism for the development of science literacy but also provides evidence from which inferences about the extent to which students have learned can be made.

Evidence That Learning Has Occurred

Because neither the process of learning nor the results of that process are directly observable, teachers use student discourse, written work products, and speech to make inferences about what the students have learned. In the context of learning to inquire, teachers can make inferences about student learning from the students' reports of their own work and from their cri-

[9] These theories also suggest that engaging in discursive activities contributes to the development of understanding of scientific concepts, principles, and theories, that is, engaging in discursive activities develops understanding of the knowledge products of science as well as the nature of scientific inquiry. In the constructivist view, learning science is a process of making connections: connections among experiences with the natural world and mental representations of those experiences; and connections among concepts that result in the generation of principles new to the learner. These concepts and principles, in turn, are connected to events and experiences in the natural world. (See, for instance, Mintzes, Wandersee, & Novak, 1998.)

tiques of their peers' work. For instance, a student's written justification of the scientific validity of a question about which he or she plans to inquire is data from which the teacher can make inferences about the student's ability to pose a question amenable to scientific investigation, the student's understanding of the characteristics of such questions, and the student's ability to develop a well-constructed justification. Observations of individual students' interactions with their peers provide data teachers use to assess the extent to which the individual understands and applies the norms of interaction acceptable in the science classroom.

Observations of verbal interactions among students provide data teachers use to assess the progress of their classes' development into a science learning community. Physical behavior and the content of verbal interactions provide insights into the community's norms for proper collegial behavior. Inferring what an individual student has learned from observations of verbal interactions among students is complicated because the norms of the learning community influences individual behavior. Consequently, it is difficult in classroom situations to sort out an individual student's progress and the development of a learning community's norms.

WRITING TO INQUIRE

Writing is a process in which the private world of the mind is made overt. Inquirers sometimes engage in the process of writing simply to get ideas down on paper to clarify their own thinking. Often, however, the writer's purpose is to communicate ideas to others. In either case, writing involves much more than simply representing on paper the patterns of neuron activity in the brain. The effective writer engages in mental dialogue. When the purpose of writing is to clarify one's thinking, the effective writer asks: Does what I have written make sense to me, is it reasonable, is it logical, are the facts and principles correct? When the purpose of writing is to communicate to others, the writer engages in a mental dialogue with the individual or a representative member of the audience with which the writer wishes to communicate. The effective writer makes assumptions about the individual's knowledge and the kind of argument that will be compelling to that individual. As the writing progresses, the writer asks questions such as Will what I have written make sense to the person to whom I am writing? Does what I have written match the acceptable form of discourse for the audience to whom I am writing? Thus, writing to communicate precipitates a kind of mental dialogue different from that prompted by writing for personal clarification. The writer must ask if what has been written will make sense to the reader and if it will be convincing to the reader. To be successful, writers must put themselves in the minds of the audience to make inferences about what will be reasonable and convincing to the audience and craft the writing to the audience.

In the process of learning to inquire, engaging in writing serves both the introspective and communicative purposes.[10] *The introspective process of description evokes mental dialogue that produces understanding of the nature of scientific questions, plans, and reports, and the nature of well-structured justifications. The communicative process of justification evokes mental dialogues requiring that the writer make inferences about the audience's expectations, which leads to an understanding of community norms.*[11]

Communication serves many different purposes in inquiry. Among these are to convey information, to convince others of a position, or to reach consensus. For instance, a student provides her classmates with information about her plan for an inquiry and seeks to convince her classmates that the plan is a scientifically valid one. Based on the quality of the discourse and the plan's scientific validity, the student's classmates and teacher decide if the plan is scientifically valid and communicate their findings to the student along with their reason. When disagreements arise concerning the scientific quality of the plan, participants in the disagreement must work to convince each other of the scientific validity of their respective positions. During this process, community standards for scientific validity are established and refined.

In conventional classroom practice, students often direct their communication to teachers for the purpose of convincing their teachers of their understanding of science. In many classroom situations, students' internal dialogues in the development of communications to the teacher are *not* motivated by the questions of scientific validity or quality of argumentation. *Rather, the questions motivating the internal dialogues are: What did the teacher say about this? Does what I have written reflect accurately what the teacher said?*

Students have well-developed abilities to give back to their teachers that which the teacher has given them. We advocate the development of abilities that are analytical and based on the students' understanding of the criteria for scientific validity and quality of argumentation. Engaging students in writing and speaking that reflects the discourse of the scientific community will produce students who have the understanding of criteria for scientific validity and

---

[10] Writing serves another purpose in inquiry. Assuming that the writer has mental models of what constitutes reasonable and logical discourse and knows how to check the accuracy of information, the process of matching what has been written against those models is likely to result in the writer making new connections, that is, generating new knowledge. The relationship between writing and learning that stimulated writing across the curriculum is well established in the literature of English education. For instance, Britton (1970) and Britton et al. (1975) studied language as a means of discovery and distinguished between writing as personal expression and writing that engaged the writer in a larger community (McQuade, 1983).

[11] Students in external examinations face the formidable challenge of sizing up the audience. Students know what will convince their most important audience—the teacher, however, that which will convince the teacher may not convince the scorers of the external examination. A challenge science education faces is to define for the field of science education the criteria for scientific validity and quality of argumentation expected of students at various points in the K–12 continuum.

the ability to develop arguments that are required for an analytical approach. The constructivist approach we advocate here provides the student the opportunity to develop an understanding of the criteria for scientific validity.

This understanding is simultaneously learned, elaborated upon, and applied by the student in the course of conducting an inquiry. The student begins the process of inquiry by drafting the question he or she plans to investigate. Drafting the question and the justification contributes to the construction of personal knowledge about the nature of scientific questions. The student conducts an internal dialogue asking the question, Does my question meet the criteria for scientifically appropriate questions?

Refining the draft with the purpose of communicating the question and the justification to the members of the community requires students to imagine a dialogue with members of his or her learning community by asking the questions, Does my question meet the norms of the community? Does the way in which I have framed the justification make a convincing case? The process of refining the text contributes to broadening the student's understanding of the criteria for scientifically appropriate questions.

In addition, the process contributes to the development of skills of argumentation. For the argument to be convincing to the community, it must meet the community norms. This assumes that community norms are in place and that individuals in the community understand them, that is, can apply them in their evaluation of the individual student's work and can engage in thoughtful refinement of the norms.

What we have described here is the role writing and revision play in the construction of an individual's understanding of the nature of scientific questions and the forms of convincing argumentation. Furthermore, writing as we have described it here is a tool for developing reflective thinking, which we explore in greater depth in the theoretical section.

Writing to Develop Community Norms

One way to think about the community of inquirers is as an audience for scientific communication. As members of an audience in a science learning community, students cannot be passive receivers of scientific communication. They apply their knowledge and mental abilities to making critical judgments of the quality of communication and use their social skills to communicating judgments to their peers. As one student reads the work of another, the reader must engage in a mental dialogue matching what she is reading against her own standards for scientific validity and quality of argumentation. In justifying her evaluation of the work with her fellow students, she will learn more about her fellow students' standards as they learn more about hers. The process of debating individual standards serves to develop community norms. The process of reaching consensus on community norms is a continuous one. Consequently, at any point in time the community of learners is simultaneously constructing norms and using those norms to make judgments about the scientific quality of the communication.[12]

The Teacher

The teacher's knowledge of the attributes of scientifically valid inquiry, and the qualities of well-constructed justifications serve as the foundation for the design of learning environments for inquiry. The teachers' questions, plans for inquiries, methods of data analysis, strategies for relating conclusions to data, and justifications for each of these serve as models of excellent scientific practice. The characteristics of personal interactions in the learning environment are important as well. The teacher serves as the model for collegial interactions.

THEORETICAL PERSPECTIVE

The theoretical perspective underlying our work draws extensively on principles of social constructivism, the development of reflective thinking, and rhetoric.

Social Constructivism

Science is humanistic and inquiry is a social process. Our approach to inquiry situates science in humanism because it assumes a critical audience in the sense that Popper (1965) described:

> It is by this mutual criticism [that occurs when two individuals or groups argue a scientific theory or "myth"] that man, if only by degrees can break through the subjectivity ... of his own imaginative inventions, and the subjectivity of the historical accidents upon which these inventions may in part depend. For these standards of rational criticism and of objective truth [that emerge through the process of mutual criticism] make his knowledge structurally different from its evolutionary antecedents (even though it will always remain possible to subsume it under some biological or anthropological schema of action). It is the acceptance of these standards which creates the dignity of the individual man; which make him responsible, morally as well as intellectually; which enable him not only to act rationally, but also to contemplate and adjudicate, and to discriminate between, competing theories. These standards of objective truth and criticism may teach him to try again, and to think again; to challenge his own conclusions, and to use his imagination in trying to find whether and where his own conclusions are at fault. ... They may help him to grow in knowledge, and also to realize that he is growing. They may help him to become aware of the fact that he owes his growth to other people's criticisms, and

---

[12] To reach the literate adult level of critical judgment and communication implied in the standards, the process must begin in kindergarten and be sustained throughout all grade levels.

that reasonableness is readiness to listen to criticism. And in this way they may even help him to transcend his animal past, and with it that subjectivism and voluntarism in which romantic and irrationalist philosophies may try to hold him captive. This is the way in which our mind grows and transcends itself. If humanism is concerned with the growth of the human mind, what then is the tradition of humanism if not a tradition of criticism and reasonableness? (p. 384)

The process of mutual criticism and the emergence of standards of rationality are social phenomena that occur within communities of learners. Latour (1987) explains the social aspects as the need for scientists to be believed and to get others to read their work, where "reading" is an active, critical process. Knorr, Kron, and Whitley (1981) view the practice of science as a cultural activity with social processes that are open to study, for example, through the exploration of such questions as "How are problems formulated and selected; how are research opportunities recognized and exploited? How is scientific work presented, received and evaluated by other scientists? And so forth" (p. viii). Thus, for inquiry and the written performance assessments associated with inquiry, we are moving beyond Popper's critical rationality to a more contextualized or situated perspective where we treat knowledge as a social construction, rather in the sense and history that Gergen (1995) describes: "Surely the work of historians of science (e.g., Kuhn and Feyerabend) and sociologists of knowledge (Latour, Knorr-Cetina, and Barnes) have helped to underscore the importance of historical and social context in determining what becomes accepted as valid knowledge" (p. 20).

However, communities of learners are not totally free to work in isolation, ignorant of the larger community to which the context belongs. That is, classroom communities engaging in science must be true to the context of science in the larger communities. The standards used for criticism and for the structuring of scientific arguments cannot ignore the forms of rational criticism that make discussion viable in the larger community of science. Whereas the level of sophistication and complexity can vary, the socially constructed norms for scientific inquiry developed in individual classrooms still must follow genres established in the larger science community, or at least function in the same fashion.

Reflective Thinking

Our analysis of "reflective thinking" begins with Dewey's (1933) definition that reflective thinking is "the kind of thinking that consists in turning a subject over in the mind and giving it serious and consecutive consideration" (p. 3). Thus, reflective thinking is deliberate, conscious, and linked. Students engage in reflective thinking both when they generate a question, a plan of investigation, and a justification, and when they evaluate those products and processes. Both instances (generating and evaluating) involve an initial state of doubt or perplexity and an act of searching to find material that will bring resolution (Dewey, 1933). We agree with Dewey (1933) that the "nature of the problem fixes the end of thought, and the end controls the process of thinking" (p. 15).

In other words, if one is thinking reflectively about problems in science, then the context of science controls the process of the thinking. But how do students come to know the context of science or come to know the expectations or context within which to be, according to Dewey, sufficiently critical?

We turn to theories on culture and cognition. Thus, our definition of reflective thinking also involves the internalization of social speech as described by Vygotsky (Vygotsky, 1978) as the means for coming to know the context of norms for scientific discourse. Vygotsky wrote of words shaping future action in a dynamic interaction. We view the internal dialogue about the application of community norms for scientific discourse as one that shapes and interacts with the students' planning for writing and with the writing process itself. This places our work within the realm of activity theory, since

> "higher order mental functions" are complex functional systems that are formed during the course of an individual's development as the result of social experiences and activity. In other words, higher order abstract knowledge, ideas, and processing capacities develop in situations where these are functional in terms of the needs, expectations, and goals of the individual or cultural group. (Crawford, 1996, p. 133)

Rhetoric

Our perspectives on the place of writing in the classroom derive from the tradition of classical rhetoric, which has deliberative, epideictic (ceremonial oratory as, for instance, where an individual is praised), and forensic purposes. In all cases its purpose is to persuade and to induce to action, achieving these ends through the form of discourse as well as force of personality. While classical rhetoric is well matched to the requirements of government, law, and religion, modern writers in the field argue its more modern form has a place in the classroom. James Moffett, for instance, advocated dialogues between student writers and their audiences as the principle instructional method for teaching of writing. Moffett argued that writing should be "authentic," that is, delivered to the audience for which it is intended rather than to the teacher (McQuade, 1983). Moffett's views on teaching writing are quite consistent with our view of the role of writing in learning to inquire and in practicing inquiry. Our ideas about the form of well-structured justifications also draw extensively on the literature of rhetoric and English education.

PERFORMANCE EXPECTATIONS

Throughout this chapter we have referred to well-structured justifications and the characteristics of the elements of scientifically valid investigations. Volumes have been written about the characteristics of well-structured arguments (e.g., Cox & Willard, 1982; Halliday & Martin, 1993; Kuhn, 1991, 1992; Lakatos & Musgrave, 1970) and the nature of scientific inquiry (e.g., Bybee,

1997; Cohen & Nagel, 1934; Frank, 1957). However, there is relatively little in these volumes that speaks directly to the classroom practice of science education. Most of the literature on argumentation relates to argumentation in contexts other than science, while the literature on argumentation in science describes the attributes of argumentation in the scientific community. Similarly, the literature on the nature of science describes standards of practice in the scientific community. While the standards of practice in the scientific community should serve as the vision for science education, it is unreasonable to expect students after only 12 years of school science to attain that high level of performance. Without detailed performance standards to guide teachers and curriculum developers, we propose that developers and teachers use the basic ideas of performance expectations to guide the design of programs and lessons.

STRATEGIES FOR DEVELOPING PERFORMANCE EXPECTATIONS

Performance expectations describe curriculum designers' and teachers' visions for the performance of an ideal student upon completion of a program, course, or lesson. The strategy we propose for the development of performance expectations involves science educators working together to answer two questions: "What is convincing evidence that students have met a standard, for instance, have learned to inquire?" and "How would one go about collecting that evidence?" Answering these two questions is the first step in developing performance assessments. The answer to the second question describes the task the student will be asked to do or the conditions under which the student will be observed. The descriptions of the evidence are the performance expectations. These expectations guide the development of a program, course, or lesson. Students' performance on tasks given at the end the program, course, or lesson provides data to evaluate the effectiveness of the program, course, or lesson or to grade students' work.[13]

Developing performance expectations that will be convincing to other teachers, school board members, parents, and state officials requires that teachers engage in critical reflective thinking about evidence that demonstrates the attainment of some set of standards. The standards may be

---

[13] Performance expectations are used to guide the design and evaluation process. They describe the performance of an ideal student. Scoring rubrics also describe student performance. However, scoring rubrics define levels of performance, some of which are less than ideal. Different points are assigned to the levels of performance. Scoring rubrics are used to assign scores to actual students' performance. The scores, in turn, are used to give grades to students.

national, state, local, or some combination. The evidence and resulting performance expectations will need to be age appropriate across grade levels. The process of developing performance expectations is as social as that of setting community norms and requires teachers and other stakeholders within a school or district to reach consensus on the structure and sequence of the expectations across all grade levels. No subgroup can develop expectations for a single grade level in isolation from the grades that precede or follow, for to do so would be to ignore the consistency that students need to fully develop the ability to inquire and to think reflectively about science. In this respect the process teachers engage in to set performance expectations parallels the process students engage in to develop their understanding of the nature of scientific inquiry and the characteristics of high-quality argumentation.

AN EXAMPLE OF THE PROCESS OF DEVELOPING PERFORMANCE EXPECTATIONS

Performance expectations are more explicit than standards and, in essence, serve as a means by which standards may be interpreted appropriately within different contexts. Each school district is unique. The forces and issues at work in one district may not be the same as those at work in another district. Likewise, the needs and concerns of the teachers and students differ from district to district in ways that, at the least, subtly influence the nature and direction of the conversation within a community. Therefore, providing examples of performance expectations may be hazardous. Thus, we choose to provide an example of the process for developing performance expectations, with some articulations of the kinds of questions that might be considered in a discussion of performance expectations.

National Science Education Science as Inquiry Standard

Our example illustrates the thinking behind the development of a performance expectation based on the NRC Science as Inquiry Standard, in particular, the knowledge and abilities related to the ability of students to pose questions appropriate for scientific inquiry. The Science as Inquiry Standard is stated in broad terms (Table 3) and is elaborated in a "guide to the content standard," which contains "fundamental abilities and concepts that underlie [the] standard" (NRC, 1996, p. 122). These "abilities necessary and concepts to do scientific inquiry" are presented for each grade level, K–4, 5–8, and 9–12. The abilities and knowledge related to questioning appear in Table 4. Our example of a 9–12 performance expectation is based on the knowledge and questioning abilities for the K–4, and 5–8 standards, as well as the 9–12 Science as Inquiry Standard because to successfully meet the

TABLE 3
National Research Council's Science as Inquiry Standard

The Standard

National Research Council's Science as Inquiry Standard

As a result of activities in grades K–4, all students should develop
  Abilities necessary to do scientific inquiry
  Understanding about scientific inquiry
As a result of activities in grades 5–8, all students should develop
  Abilities necessary to do scientific inquiry
  Understanding about scientific inquiry
As a result of activities in grades 9–12, all students should develop
  Abilities necessary to do scientific inquiry
  Understanding about scientific inquiry

Abilities Necessary to Scientific Inquiry

K–4 Standard
Ask a question about objects, organisms, and events in the environment. This aspect of
the standard emphasizes students asking questions that they can answer with scientific
knowledge, combined with their own observations. Students should answer their questions by
seeking information from reliable sources of scientific information and from their own
observations and investigations (NRC, 1996, p. 122).

5–8 Standard
Identify questions that can be answered through scientific investigations. Students should
develop the ability to refine and refocus broad and ill-defined questions. An important aspect
of this ability consists of students' ability to clarify questions and inquires and direct them
toward objects and phenomena that can be describe, explained or predicated by scientific
investigations. Students should develop the ability to identify their questions with scientific
ideas, concepts, and qualitative relations that guide investigation (NRC, 1996, p.145).

9–12 Standard
Identify questions and concepts that guide scientific investigations. Students should
formulate a testable hypothesis and demonstrate the logical connections between the
scientific concepts guiding a hypothesis and the design of an experiment. They should
demonstrate appropriate procedures, a knowledge base, and conceptual understanding of
scientific investigation (NRC, 1996, p. 175).

9–12 standard, students must have the knowledge and abilities defined in
the K–4 and 5–8 standards.

Interpreting the Standard and Descriptions of the Abilities and Knowledge

The Science as Inquiry Standard and the knowledge and abilities necessary
to meet the standard are stated in such broad terms that they must be inter-

TABLE 4
Characteristics of Questions and Justifications from the National Science Education Standards

An Interpretation of the Standard	Related Statement from the National Science Education Science as Inquiry Standard
Abilities	
Students should have the ability to pose questions and hypotheses.	Students ask[ing] questions … (NRC, 1996, p. 122). Students should formulate a testable hypothesis (NRC, 1996, p. 175).
The questions and hypotheses are appropriate for scientific investi- gation, that is,	
The questions and hypotheses have foundations in scientific knowledge and observations of the natural environment.	Students ask[ing] questions that they can answer with scientific knowledge, combined with their own observations (NRC, 1996, p. 122).
	Students should develop the ability to identify their questions with scientific ideas, concepts, and qualitative relations … (NRC, 1996, p. 145). [questions are directed] toward objects and phenomena that can be describes, explained or predicated by scientific investigations (NRC, 1996, p. 145).
The questions are circumscribed.	Students [have the] ability to clarify questions and inquires (NRC, 1996, p. 145)
Question can be investigated using resources available to the student	
	Students ask questions that they can answer with scientific knowledge, combined with their own observations (NRC, 1996, p. 122).
Knowledge	Demonstrate the logical connections between the scientific concepts guiding a hypothesis (NRC, 1996, p. 175)
	Demonstrate appropriate procedures, a knowledge base, and conceptual understanding of scientific investigation (NRC, 1996, p. 175).

preted by local committees charged with the development of district perfor- mance expectations based on the standards.

One interpretation of the knowledge and abilities related to posing ques- tions is presented in Table 4. Contained in the NRC statements elaborating knowledge and questioning abilities are statements about knowledge related to scientific inquiry and other statements that go beyond question- ing to the design of investigations. For our example the interpretation is limited to abilities and knowledge related to questioning.

Elaboration of the Abilities and Knowledge

Because the information in the knowledge and abilities statements is not sufficiently detailed to inform classroom practices, further elaboration must be done at the local level.

For instance, the knowledge and abilities statements do not define in detail the characteristics of questions and hypotheses that are appropriate for scientific investigations. The statements leave open to interpretation the characteristics of questions that "can be answered with scientific knowledge, combined with their own observations" and the characteristics of a "testable hypothesis." Details must be developed at the local level.

The development proceeds by answering the question: What evidence will the district accept that students in grade 12 have met the standard and how will that evidence be collected? Assuming that the developers of the performance expectations have agreed that students at grade 12 would be required to pose hypotheses based on their knowledge of the natural sciences and develop written justifications for their hypothesis, the development group might proceed by collecting samples of hypotheses and justifications written by grade 12 students in their districts and deciding whether, on the basis of the work samples, the students have met the standard. This process is illustrated using the hypothesis and justification written by a grade 12 student that is contained in Table 5. In formulating a question related to the survival of a plant in an enclosed jar, has this student met the standard? The developers of a district's performance standards must match this student's work against the standards. Among the questions they might pose in making the comparison are:

Is the hypothesis testable using scientific methods?
Is the hypothesis sufficiently circumscribed?
Is the hypothesis based on scientific knowledge and observations?

TABLE 5
A Grade 12 Student's Hypothesis and Justification

A Student's Hypothesis and Justification

I propose to do an experiment testing the hypothesis that without a constant supply of carbon dioxide, green plants will not survive.

I have learned that to photosynthesize green plants must have carbon dioxide. I also have read somewhere that plants can live for long periods of time in containers like a sealed clear glass container that let light in but do not allow for the gases in the jar to mix with gases in the air. If the jar is really sealed, I think that the CO_2 in the jar will be used up. When the CO_2 is used up plants cannot photosynthesize and so the plants die. I am not sure how long it will take the plant to use up the CO_2 if the amount of time the plant is in the sun or if the volume of the container in relation to the size of the plant makes a difference, so I will have to think about these questions when I test my hypothesis.

Does the student's justification link the hypothesis to scientific knowledge?

Does the student's justification make the case that the hypothesis has
the characteristics required of a scientific hypothesis?

Does the student demonstrate the logical connections between the
hypothesis and the scientific ideas on which the hypothesis is based?

The answers to the first three questions will be based on inferences the
developers make about the student's understanding of the characteristics of
well-defined scientific hypothesis. If in the developer's judgment the
hypothesis is testable, then the developer infers that the student knows the
characteristics of a well-defined scientific hypothesis and can apply that
knowledge to pose a hypothesis. The answers to the last three questions
will be based on the information the student provides about the hypothesis
she has proposed and the quality of her justification. As the developers
answer the questions about this student's responses and the responses of
other students and provide reasons for their answers, individual developers'
expectations will be revealed and a district consensus for expectations will
evolve.

For instance, characteristics of the level of sophistication for a testable
hypothesis the district will require of its students will evolve from discussions of whether the hypothesis the student has stated meets local expectations. As stated, the hypothesis is subject to criticism because the student
cannot test all green plants or even a sample of certain species of green
plants. Does this mean that the hypothesis is ill defined and should be
restated in a more circumscribed manner, for instance, *without a constant supply of carbon dioxide, philodendron will not survive.*

Additionally, those working on a district consensus may discuss their
expectations regarding the students' understanding of the formal logical
reasoning involved in hypothesis testing. Does the district expect that students should recognize that conclusions from an experiment testing a
hypothesis cannot be generalized to all cases and involves the issue of support or nonsupport rather than an issue of proof? Does the district expect
that students understand the distinction between a hope for an expected
outcome and the need to use the null hypothesis in the actual testing and
drawing of conclusions? That is, in this particular case, does the district
expect the student to understand that starting from the hypothesis of *if a
plant does not have a constant supply of carbon dioxide, then it will not live* does not
allow for the same kinds of conclusions to be drawn as when one starts from
the null hypothesis of *the availability of a constant supply carbon dioxide will make no
difference in the survival of green plants?*

Discussions such as the kind suggested here allow districts to define
their own performance expectations. We hasten to note that the developers'
debates about the characteristics of testable hypotheses should be
informed by the writings of experts in the field.

In the development of performance expectations for the standard, all the questions in the list that appears above must be considered. The performance expectation development team considers the standards, student work, and information from experts in the development of performance expectations. The process is time-consuming and requires a level of analysis not often engaged by science educators. However, if students are to be provided adequate opportunity to develop the knowledge and abilities of scientific inquiry, the depth of knowledge we propose is essential. Classroom practices aligned with standards requires the detail that only deep analysis provides.

CONCLUSIONS

The AAAS *Benchmarks* and the NRC *Standards* encourage inquiry-based science and the development of scientific "habits of mind," or, in less formal terms, hands-on/minds-on science. In classroom practice the emphasis has been on strategies for hands-on science. This is consistent with most of the reform rhetoric that reflects less of a theory and philosophy of science as a liberal art (AAAS, 1990) than of science as technical skill. In this paper we argue that writing is a most effective strategy for keeping students' minds "on." Furthermore, writing to inquire models, to some degree, science as a liberal art and scientific habits of mind. Our perspective on writing as a performance measure provides an arena for the articulation of some middle-ground guidelines and criteria between the reform documents and the detailed local development of community norms for science literacy.

References

American Association for the Advancement of Science. (1990). *The liberal art of science: Agenda for action*. Washington, DC: American Association for the Advancement of Science.

American Association for the Advancement of Science. Project 2061. (1993). *Benchmarks for science literacy*. Washington, DC: American Association for the Advancement of Science.

Bourque, M. L., Champagne, A. B., & Crissman, S. (1997). *National Assessment of Educational Progress 1996 science performance standards: Achievement results for the nation and the states*. Washington DC: National Assessment Governing Board.

Britton, J. (1970). *Language and learning*. London: Allen Lane, The Penguin Press.

Britton, J., Burgess, T., Martin, N., McLeod, A., & Rosen, H. (1975). *The development of writing abilities* (pp. 11–18). London: Macmillan Education.

Brown, J. S., Collins, A., & Duguid, P. (1989). Situated cognition and the culture of learning. *Educational Researcher*, 18(1) 32–42.

Bybee, R. W. (1997). *Achieving scientific literacy: From purposes to practices*. Portsmouth, NH: Heinemann.

Candace, J., & Duckworth, E. (1996). A constructivist perspective on teaching and learning science. In C. T. Fosnot (Ed.), *Constructivism: Theory, perspectives, and practice*. (pp. 55–72). New York: Teacher College Press.

Champagne, A. B. (1996). Assessment and science curriculum design. In R. W. Bybee (Ed.), *National Standards and the Science Curriculum: Challenges, Opportunities, and Recommendations* (pp. 75–82). Colorado Springs, CO: BSCS.

Champagne, A. B., Kouba, V. L., & Hurley, M. (1999). Assessing inquiry. In J. Minstral & E. van der Zee (Eds.), *Examining Inquiry in science teaching and learning*. Washington, DC: American Association for the Advancement of Science.

Chi, M., Bassik, M., Lewis, M., & Glaser, R. (1989). Self-explanations: How students study and use examples in learning to solve problems. *Cognitive Science*, 13, 145–182.

Cohen, M. R., & Nagel, E. (1934). *An introduction to logic and scientific method*. New York: Harcourt, Brace.

Connoly, P., & Vilardi, T. (Eds.) (1989). *Writing to learn mathematics and science*. New York: Teachers College Press.

Cox, J. R., & Willard, C. A. (Eds.) (1982). *Advances in argumentation: Theory and research*. American Forensic Association. Carbondale, IL: Southern Illinois University Press.

Crawford, K. (1996). Cultural process and learning: Expectations, actions, and outcomes. In L. P. Steffe & P. Nesher (Eds.), *Theories of mathematical learning* (pp. 131–148). Mahwah, NJ: Lawrence Erlbaum.

Dewey, J. (1933). *How we think: A restatement of the relation of reflective thinking to the educative process*. Boston: D. C. Heath.

Duit, R. (1995). The constructivist view: A fashionable and fruitful paradigm for science education research and practice. In L. P. Steffe & J. Gale (Eds.), *Constructivism in education* (pp. 271–286). Hillsdale, NJ: Erlbaum.

Frank, Phillip. 1957. *Philosophy of Science: The Link Between Science, and Philosophy*. A Spectrum Book. Englewood Cliffs, NJ: Prentice-Hall; Belmont, CA: Wadsworth.

Gergen, K. J. (1995). Social construction and the educational process. In L. P. Steffe & J. Gale (Eds.), *Constructivism in education* (pp. 17–40). Hillsdale, NJ: Erlbaum.

Giere, R. N. (1988) *Explaining science: A cognitive approach*. Chicago, IL: The University of Chicago Press.

Halliday, M. A. K., & Martin, J. R. (1993). *Writing science: Literacy and discursive power*. Pittsburgh, PA: University of Pittsburgh Press.

Hildebrand, G. M. (1998). Disrupting hegemonic writing practices in school science: Contesting the right way to write. *Journal of Research in Science Teaching*, 35(4), 345–362.

Keiser, K. K., Nelson, J. E., Norris, N. A., & Szyszkiewicz, S. (1998). NAEP 1996 science: Cross-state data compendium for the grade 8 assessment. Washington, DC: U. S. Government Printing Office.

Knorr, K. D., Kron, R., & Whitley, R. (1981). *The social process of scientific investigation*. Boston: D. Reidel.

Kouba, V. L., & Champagne, A. B. (1998) *Literacy components in natural science and mathematics standards documents: Communication and reasoning*. Albany, NY: National Research Center on English Learning and Achievement.

Kuhn, D. (1991). *The skills of argument*. Cambridge, UK: Cambridge University Press.

Kuhn, D. (1992). Thinking as argument. *Harvard Educational Review*, 62(2), 155–178.

Kuhn, T. S. (1962). *The structure of scientific revolutions*. Chicago: The University of Chicago Press.

Lakatos, I., & Musgrave, A. (1970). *Criticism and the growth of knowledge*. Cambridge, UK: Cambridge University Press.

Latour, B. (1987). *Science in action: How to follow scientists and engineers through society*. Cambridge, MA: Harvard University Press.

Latour, B., & Woolgar, S. (1986). *Laboratory life: The construction of scientific facts*. Princeton, NJ: Princeton University Press.

McQuade, T. F. (1983). *Proposition analysis: A curriculum to teach high school students how to organize essays*. Doctoral Dissertation. Pittsburgh, PA: University of Pittsburgh.

Mintzes, J. J., Wandersee, J. H., & Novak, J. D. (Eds.). (1996). *Teaching science for understanding*. Orlando, FL: Academic Press.

Myers, G. (1990). *Writing biology: Texts in the social construction of scientific knowledge*. Madison, WI: University of Wisconsin Press.

National Research Council (1995). *On being a scientist: Responsible conduct in research* (2nd ed.). Washington, DC: National Academy Press.

National Research Council. (1996). *National science education standards.* Washington, DC: National Academy Press.

Neill, M., Bursh, P., Schaeffer, B., Thrall, C., Yohe, M., & Zappardino, P. (Undated). *Implementing performance assessments: A guide to classroom, school and system reform.* Fairtest: The National Center for Fair & Open Testing.

Penrose, A. M., & Katz, S. B. (1998). *Writing in the sciences: Exploring conventions of scientific discourse.* New York: St. Martin's Press.

Popper, K. R. (1965). *Conjectures and refutations.* New York: Harper & Row.

Salomon, G. (Ed.) (1993). *Distributed cognitions.* New York: Cambridge University Press.

Shavelson, R. J., Baxter, G. P., & Pine, J. (1992). Performance assessments; political rhetoric and measurement reality. *Educational Researcher,* 22–27.

Spivey, N. N. (1997). *The constructivist metaphor: Reading, writing, and the making of meaning.* San Diego, CA: Academic Press.

Sternberg, R. J. (Ed.) (1994). *Thinking and problem solving.* San Diego, CA: Academic Press.

Toulmin, S. E. (1972). *Human understanding.* Princeton, NJ: Princeton University Press.

Vygotsky, L. S. (1978). *Mind in society.* Cambridge, MA: Harvard University Press.

Vygotsky, L. S. (1986). *Thought and language,* Revised Edition. (A. Kozulin Ed.). Cambridge, MA: MIT Press.

Walbesser, H. (1968). *Science: a process approach: An evaluation model and its application.* Washington, DC: American Association for the Advancement of Science, Commission on Science Education.

Whitehead, A. N. (1925). *Science and the modern world.* New York: New American Library, The MacMillian Company.

CHAPTER 11

The Relevance of Multiple-Choice Tests in Assessing Science Understanding

PHILIP M. SADLER

Harvard Graduate School of Education and Harvard-Smithsonian Center for Astrophysics

Item 1. I believe that multiple-choice questions:

a. are an outdated assessment technique

b. measure only factual recall

c. should have no role in science education

d. all of the above

e. none of the above.

The primary goal of science education is to bring students closer to the scientist's way of understanding the world. As teachers of science, we encourage the development of skills, factual knowledge, conceptual understanding, attitudes, and curiosity that scientists have developed and exhibit. Yet as teachers, one cannot exactly recreate the identical experiences for students that we have undergone. One should refrain from any of the unproductive activities we have experienced in our science courses. Teachers must be sensitive to the fact that students are in many ways very different from them as learners. I have yet to meet a teacher who does not feel that he or she cannot shorten and make less arduous difficulties that they encountered in coming to understand science.

One of the most exacting elements of schooling is the "on-demand" production of proof that students have learned what is taught. Rarely do students feel that their performance on these tests fully captures and reflects their understanding. It seems as though it is always the test-makers who have the most confidence in the test's validity in measuring the knowledge in question, whether classroom teachers or psychometricians. Tests are usually administered subsequent to studying a particular topic, so they can measure only what is known at the end of study. One cannot tell how much students have gained. Administered afterward, such tests are not used for diagnostic purposes. Many tests are so replete with jargon that, used as a diagnostic, students could never answer questions correctly even if they understand the concepts.

In particular, standardized tests are easy to hate. There is usually much at risk for those who take them. There can be even more at stake for those who teach the test-takers. Standardized tests are shrouded in secrecy, crafted using complex statistical tools. They are administered in an environment that is often stressful. These tests purport to place everyone on a scale from the best to the worst. No one likes to think of themselves as below average; one always wishes for higher scores. With norm referencing, half the test-takers are bound to be disappointed.

Standardized tests are often characterized by their most common component, the multiple-choice question: a short stem followed by five answers. "How can all of knowledge be reduced to choosing between five short phrases?" many ask. How can it be that recognition of the "right" answer is all that is left of a year or a lifetime of study? How can such tests assess the practical performance skills that are learned in laboratory or in the science class (Welch, 1995)? Teachers know about multiple-choice items; they construct them and know how hard it is to create ones with which they are satisfied. How is it that such a simple tool is still in use, seemingly unchanged from a hundred years ago. Medical testing has evolved. Health clubs use the latest methods to assess physical performance. Shouldn't the testing for knowledge have evolved beyond such simple probes?

Other forms of testing have proliferated in an attempt to deal with the perceived weakness of standardized tests. They are often ingenious. Their supporters argue for their value in assessing, more genuinely, the skills and knowledge that predict student success. Many claim that such assessments give students an opportunity for additional learning while being assessed. Others argue that they are less susceptible to bias. The *National Science Education Standards* call for multiple methods of assessment (authentic if possible) that focus on ability to inquire and on the content that is most important for students to learn (Council, 1996)

In this chapter, I discuss the weaknesses of multiple-choice items for assessing conceptual understanding. I explore the opportunities for strengthening this much used, but underrated tool as a diagnostic instrument focused on uncovering students' conceptual frameworks, assessing learners' conceptual shifts, and aiding the design of curricula. Creating new such tests, grounded in cognitive research, will help teachers diagnose student difficulties and provide a shortcut to extensive interviewing on the part of teachers (Treagust, 1995). Such tests have the potential to bring order to the profusion of student ideas reported on in the research literature (Driver, Squires, Rushworth, & Robinson, 1994). Much as Darwin's discovery of evolution through natural selection brought order to the variety of nature's species, testing has the ability to help organize and codify the knowledge we wish to impart.

This effort fits well with my own interests in the clinical interviewing of students concerning their scientific ideas, made popular and brought to many teachers' attention though video interviews (Schneps & Sadler, 1988). A *Private Universe* and its follow-on series, *Minds of Our Own*, probe understanding by asking students to predict outcomes of experiments and exploring their reasons for the predictions that they make. Such qualitative techniques have been used extensively by those interested in understanding the cognitive underpinnings of student understanding (Duckworth, 1987, Osborne & Gilbert, 1980; Piaget & Inhelder, 1929). Moving from qualitative understanding to quantitative evidence requires that the models to be tested are well formulated. In this regard, the learning theories that underlie most of the assessment tools used today are suspect; they are based on old models that are still convenient, but do not reflect our current understanding of cognitive development.

I am also interested in creating tools for teachers that not only help them to measure student understanding after teaching is completed, but aid them in diagnosing the difficulties that students have in learning particular scientific topics. The building of a teacher's knowledge base of the strategies and models that students use is perhaps the most the most effective professional development activity of all (Rhine, 1998). Teachers deserve more than relying on their "gut feeling" for how well a curriculum works (Boone, 1990a). This is the primary focus in my work with those who are preparing to teach science and with experienced teachers who have returned to the university for deeper study. My work in curriculum development has been driven by finding ways to help students move from novice to expert understandings of science through the use of carefully developed curricula and computer simulations.

BACKGROUND ISSUES

History of Multiple-Choice Tests

Formal testing in the United States can be traced to the Boston Survey of 1845, in which printed tests were first used to assess student understanding in domains that included science (Doran, Lawrenz, & Helgeson, 1994). After several decades of such tests, researchers set to formalize a theory that related a student's ability with their performance on test. Foremost at the time was Charles Spearman's success at characterizing and understanding errors in testing, leading to recognition of the need for measurements of reliability. One could utilize such methods to design tests that gave reproducible results. Content could be embedded in such test items and the percentage of correct responses on the test could be viewed as indicative of an underlying ability (Mislevy, 1993b). With a nod to a desire for high reliability, responses to items required a high correlation with the total score on the test (Mislevy, 1993a). Those items that did not correlate well were modified or dropped. Shorter tests could be constructed by using only highly correlated items. This method of testing was dubbed *classical test theory* (CTT). Performance was simply measured by the total test score, with each item carrying equal weight. Test scores were assumed to be linearly related to the underlying trait to be measured (Weiss, 1983).

Item response theory (IRT) as developed by Frederick Lord and Georg Rasch was based on the idea that tests can be designed to measure a single ability and that this ability follows a Gaussian distribution in the population. IRT was developed to surmount the apparent limitations of classical test theory in which measurements are highly dependent on a test population (Hambleton, Swaminathan, & Rogers, 1991). More mathematically sophisticated than CTT, IRT depends on computer software to calculate item and test parameters. Originally, comprising a single-item parameter, the wide availability of computers saw a proliferation of alternatives with more degrees of freedom. IRT is found to offer several advantages over CTT in solving testing problems:

- Closely related tests can be built from a subset of items (Baker, 1985).
- Item parameters can be generalized to a population larger than those taking any particular test.
- Subjects of vastly different abilities can be placed on the same stable measurement scale (Sadler, 1998).
- Item bias can be measured for subpopulations of students (Hambleton et al., 1991).
- Individual responses to a test can be examined based on item characteristics, aiding in the discoveries of irregularities such as cheating (Trabin & Weiss, 1983).

Standardized Tests

So-called "standardized tests" are constrained in several ways. They are most often collections of multiple-choice items given, over time, to a large body of test-takers. Results from the tests are used to formulate norm-referenced scores, assuming that the traits measured fall into a normal distribution of results. Guidelines for test-taking conditions are specified. Most often students may not use any additional reference materials or aids. Time limits are strictly enforced. Group work is not allowed. Distractions are kept to a minimum. Test-takers are not allowed to remove materials, which helps to insure the secrecy of the test questions.

Test items are generally created by domain experts and judged adequate by calculating their psychometric profile. The key measure is "discrimination," that is, the degree to which student performance on a single item corresponds to how well students do on the entire test. Items are generally viewed as unacceptable if they are answered correctly by lower performing students, but wrong by higher performing students. The characteristics of individual items can be aggregated to create measures for any collection of items.

Perhaps one of the most interesting properties of such a psychometric analysis is that bias can be examined through analyzing the performance of items for different subsets of the population (Hambleton et al., 1991). In recent years certain items have been shown to be highly biased when groups of differing gender or race are compared. Such analysis can help test-makers eliminate such questions and make the test fairer for all (Trabin & Weiss, 1983).

Standardized tests have come under a withering assault and are criticized for "taking over" education, exercising great influence over what is taught and how it is taught (Neil, 1996). It appears to be a common view among many educators that students are "overtested and undereducated." Estimates by groups such as Boston College's Center for the Study of Testing, Evaluation, and Educational Policy have alarmed the public with estimates of 20 million student-days consumed in standardized testing. Yet these large numbers are misleading. What is not considered is that when divided by the 40 million students in school this huge number drops to a-half-day/student/year (Phelps, 1997). Even with test preparation time taken into account, Phelps found that standardized testing accounted for less than 1% of the time students spend in school. The view among average citizens is quite different than that among educators, with strong support for a national high school graduation exam testing (Phelps, 1997). Parents generally want an independent check on how effective their schools are, not trusting the educational establishment to police themselves and spend tax dollars wisely.

Moreover, the amount of standardized testing pales in comparison to the quantity of "homemade" tests that teachers create and give to students, probably consuming 10% of a student's time in school. Many complain that these tests measure only lower level skills and knowledge, that higher order thinking, characterized by Bloom as analysis, synthesis, and evaluation, cannot be measured in this fashion (Bloom, 1950).

Underlying Theories

The triumph of cognitive psychology in the last two decades has forced a rethinking of how we view learning. No longer does the "banking" method of instruction seem reasonable (Freire, 1993). Learning is now seen as chaotic, quantized, nonlinear, and idiosyncratic.

In the traditional model of learning the foundation of future knowledge can be acquired with little cognitive demand. Rote learning is sufficient to memorize vocabulary, algorithms, and facts. Novices are viewed as empty vessels, ready to be filled with knowledge. Concepts are considered to be more easily understood when isolated from their applications. All knowledge is viewed as cumulative, building gradually, banked away until called upon by future demands. Curricula are designed to provided a broad and shallow familiarity with a topic, allowing a great number of topics to be covered in little depth.

The cognitive model of learning finds that every level of learning is cognitively demanding, as schemas are continually restructured to include more relationships and examples. Novices hold preconceptions about most topics, which they must eventually discard or change to progress. Meaningful learning grows in fits and starts, recapitulating what we know of the development of science. A deep understanding of relatively few topics can be a great boon to learning. Rather than assuming that people possess inherently different abilities, current beliefs about learning have moved to an emphasis on finding ways to allow all students to succeed (Nichols, 1994).

The placement of learners on a single ability scale in IRT is a rather limited description of their knowledge, even if they are measured twice in a pre- and post-test. To be instructionally relevant, a test must describe a student's state of understanding fully so that a teacher can make decisions. Cognitive science has revealed that there are significant differences between novice and expert understandings. These differences are qualitative and include:

- Inconsistent beliefs that are held simultaneously
- Conceptions that depart from accepted scientific beliefs
- Inability to match problems with efficient strategies for solution
- Differences in the speed of solution of posed problems

Examination of incorrect responses can be indicative of student misconceptions and can add sophistication to a test rather than examining only right/wrong proficiency (Mislevy, 1993a). Assessment for novice levels of understanding are primarily tests for exposure, being able to recognize and produce information when the form is similar to that in which it was presented to the learner (Feltovich, Spiro, & Coulson, 1993). Whereas more expert understanding requires an ability to recognize applicable situations and apply knowledge productively. Students use inappropriate or inefficient models for scientific processes (Masters & Mislevy, 1993). Tests should be capable of identifying "unobserved states of understanding" through student responses (Masters & Mislevy, 1993).

The Origins of Testing for Preconceptions

The earliest attempts at investigating children's prior knowledge were those of Jean Piaget. Working at the start of his career on intelligence testing in France, Piaget's formal training in biology helped to direct his attention to the phenomena of adaptation of children's thoughts to the realities manifest by the world (Driver, 1973; Novak, 1977). The "pre-concepts" that children held were the early steps in a process of assimilation and accommodation, building more powerful cognitive structures (Anderson & Smith, 1986).

David Ausubel realized that Piaget's pre-concepts do not all evolve as a child develops. Many are amazingly tenacious and almost impossible to change through instruction (Ausubel, 1968). He viewed preconceptions not only as early stages in the formation of a cognitive framework, but as elements of an often very stable and comprehensive view of the world, and that formal instruction vies for, but often loses in the battle for, the student's beliefs. In his *Educational Psychology* (1968, p. 336), he states, "the unlearning of preconceptions might very well prove to be the most determinative single factor in the acquisition and retention of subject-matter knowledge." Ausubel clearly distinguishes learning that incorporates new concepts and facts through the restructuring of a student's knowledge from that of simple rote learning.

Many researchers utilized interviews to conduct extensive studies of students' ideas in the sciences. Early work in these domains include optics (Jung, 1987), the phases of the moon (Cohen & Kagan, 1979; Dai, 1990; Za'rour, 1976), seasons, (Furuness & Cohen, 1989; Newman & Morrison, 1993), mechanics (Caramazza, McCloskey, & Green, 1981; Champagne, Klopfer, & Anderson, 1980; Clement, 1982; McDermott, 1984), natural selection (Brumby, 1984), anatomy (Arnaudin & Mintzes, 1985), cosmography (Nussbaum & Novak, 1976; Sneider & Pulos, 1983; Vincentini-Missoni, 1981), chemical equilibrium (BouJaoude, 1992; Gorodetsky & Gussarsky, 1987), heat (Erickson & Tiberghien, 1985), magnetism (Finley, 1986), photosynthesis (Roth, 1985), and electricity (Shipstone, 1985).

Researchers recommend that teachers interview their students to identify students preconceptions (Driver, 1987; Langford, 1989; Novick & Nussbaum, 1978; Nussbaum & Novak, 1982). It is hoped that such activities clarify teachers' own ideas and lead to an appreciation of "children's science" (Osborne & Bell, 1983). While this is an admirable suggestion, I have seen that both preservice and practicing teachers have great difficulty developing expertise in clinical interviewing. They generally make two mistakes. First, an inability to mask approval of the "right answer" skews the conversation to one where the subject is looking to the interviewer for approval. Second, upon uncovering some degree of correctness (often simply the use of scientific jargon) the novice interviewer assumes that the subject has a sophisticated understanding and ends any probing. While it may be a goal for teachers to understand their students' knowledge state (Borko & Livingston, 1989), this can be very hard to accomplish through teacher interviews. Yet clinical interviews can be used as a step in understanding the knowledge structure of students by identifying the common "wrong answers" and testing their relationship to one another by posing them as foils to subjects (Bart & Krus, 1973; Haertel & Wiley, 1993; Sadler, 1995). Students will often comment on how others' views compare to theirs with "I used to think that, but I changed because..." or "that really couldn't be because..." Tracing the path of conceptions from one to another helps to build a pattern of growth that can lead to building of useful tests or supportive curricula.

Once students' ideas have been examined and categorized, written tests that offer a choice between a single correct answer and one of several alternative conceptions drawn from interviews can be constructed (Freyberg & Osborne, 1985). The weakness of this scheme is that alternatives are limited to responses to previously identified alternative conceptions, so effective items can be created only after exhaustive interviews or through open-ended tests (Haladyna, 1994).

Constructing a test in which students must judge which view is closest to their own requires that they be able to discriminate between and identify their own idea from several others. This is quite different from producing their own view. It is reasonable to question whether such test items could perform better than open-ended questions. Open-ended questions have the advantage of uncovering unexpected misconceptions, whereas multiple-choice tests produce standardized answers that are easily compared (Sadler, 1992).

Multiple-choice tests that utilize distractors based on student misconceptions look very similar to those that employ test-builder's original distractors. Unless one is familiar with the literature concerning these particular misconceptions, often the only way to identify the distractors that describe these alternative views is to inspect the frequency of student answers. The inclusion of such distractors often serves to raise the difficulty, of the item while lowering its discrimination (Narode, 1987; Schoon, 1988). This explains why it was not the creators of standardized tests (e.g. Education Testing Service) that discovered that student held alternative ideas. In their goal to attain high discrimination, items that did not fit this exacting profile were dropped by professional test-makers. Distractor-driven multiple-choice items must litter the cutting room floor of the major test creators.

TEST CONSTRUCTION

Item Construction

How does one construct a test item that embodies the ability to discern between learner's alternative conceptions? One must first know the relevant literature. Work attempting to elicit student ideas may take the form of interviews, open-ended written tests, or earlier attempts at multiple-choice questions. Often the nature of the interview question that reveals a particular conception holds within it the seeds for an excellent multiple-choice question. Such questions are often predictive in nature, asking students to describe the outcome of a possible observation or experiment. The variety of predictions can encompass the variety of alternative conceptions.

An example of such ideas gleaned from interviews can be found in elementary students' efforts to describe the reason for day and night (Vosniadou & Brewer, 1994). Students invoke a variety of changes involving the sun, including it being blocked by objects (clouds) or moving into a "shadow." Others found that students told of the sun moving to the other side (Klein, 1982) or under the Earth (Nussbaum, 1986). Older students appear to consolidate their views, using a single concept to explain a variety of phenomena. Heliocentrism is emphasized in our school to the point that students will fabricate evidence to support their beliefs: "All our pictures and telescopes and space flights tell us that there is one big star, the Sun, with several smaller planets (moving) around it" (Touger, 1985, T-8). Such were the reports on open-end written tests of undergraduate students taking an introductory astronomy course. Yet, pictures of the planets in motion around the sun do not exist.

An item released from the 1969 National Assessment of Educational Progress of 9-year-old (third-grade) students identifies three possible alternative views along with the correct answer: One reason that there is day and night on Earth is that the: Sun turns. (8%); Moon turns. (4%); Earth turns. (81%); Sun gets dark at night. (6%); I don't know. (1%) (Schoon, 1988).

The following item was constructed drawing on prior research:

What causes night and day?

A. The Earth spins on its axis.

B. The Earth moves around the sun.

C. Clouds block out the sun's light.

D. The Earth moves into and out of the sun's shadow.

E. The sun goes around the Earth.

The correct answer is the shortest, not the longest. There is a tendency among test writers to be exceedingly careful in constructing the right answer, extending it with caveats. We have avoided this by making the correct answer the best of the four, but by no means universally appealing to the scientific community. Note that the correct answer involves no jargon; "moves" and "goes around" are terms that are preferable to the textbook terminology of "rotates" and "revolves." By posing an answer using vocabulary with which a student is familiar, the question is less dependent on knowledge of specialized words and more suitable as being used as a pretest. Disputes about the quality of an item are not settled through opinion, but by the choices that scientists make when presented by the problem. If scientists choose the wrong answer, then the item is simply not valid and must be changed or removed from the test. While useful in determining the correct answers, subject matter experts are not always helpful in judging the quality of distractors. I have had many scientists chastise me for including in an item a distractor that "makes no sense." While it may make no sense to scientists, such answers are often quotes drawn from interviews or written answers of students. They clearly make sense to students and are chosen more often than other distractors.

One should guard against premature exclusion of distractors. Often one can identify conceptions that occur with some frequency in the literature or through one's own interview that seem silly or nonsensical. Answers that rise to a level of 10% of responses should always be tested as a possible distractor. Test items should be crafted to reveal known misconceptions (Feltovich et al., 1993). Conventional item forms, such as "The reason for ___ is:" are often not as useful as an item that offers a prediction, such as "What would happen if ___ :"

Examples of Constructivist Tests in Science

Diagnostic multiple-choice tests have been constructed, validated, and used in several different areas of science: light (Bouwens, 1986), mechanics (Halloun & Hestenes, 1985), cosmology (Lightman & Miller, 1989), electricity (Shipstone, Rhoneck, Jung, Karrqvist, Dupin, Joshua et al., 1987), chemistry (BouJaoude, 1992), and earth science (School, 1988). These multiple-choice tests produce standardized answer that are easily compared. Such tests are easily scored, even by those with no knowledge of alternative conceptions, and their results can be used immediately. They are useful not only for studies, but as diagnostic tools for teachers to easily ascertain alternative conceptions in their own classrooms.

To test basic ideas in mechanics, the Force Concept Inventory was developed (Hestenes, Wells, & Swackhammer, 1992). It uses a multiple-choice format. Drawn from the rich literature in teaching mechanics, the test is now widely used throughout the world.

The Project STAR Astronomy Questionnaire was developed to inform the developers (including the author) of the success of their new high school level astronomy course (Sadler, 1992). The test began as a two-tiered misconception test combining the elements of an open-ended test with a multiple-choice test (Treagust, 1986). Each two-part test item first asked students to *predict* the outcome of a situation. The second part requested that they provide a *reason* for their answer.[1] In interpreting these multiple-choice tests, responses that drew more than 10% of the answers were examined in depth (Gilbert 1977). These items were drawn from interviews reported in the literature that related to astronomy.

The reliability of these open-ended written questions were ascertained by interviewing 25 ninth-grade students. Interviews were similar to responses to the written instrument. As the curriculum project progressed, each year a new pre- and post-test was developed to match the year's evolving curriculum objectives. Items that teachers deemed to be unclear were rewritten. Items that were answered correctly more than 80% of the time were deemed "anchors" and were incorporated into the curriculum materials as ideas that students would probably know and on which they could build. These facts were removed from subsequent tests. Distractors—items that were chosen less than 5% of the time—were rewritten and replaced so that they would have greater appeal to the students. Often this meant combing the recent literature for more popular alternatives or inserting "scientific-sounding" jargon.[2] These changes tended to make the test more difficult each year as the distractors became more attractive (Sadler, 1992).

---

[1] An example from this test:

On August 7, 1654, J. Kepler went outside, looked up and saw a star explode, a supernova. When do you think the star really exploded?
  a. at least a few years before August 7, 1654.
  b. on August 7, 1654.
  c. at least a few years after August 7, 1654.
  d. at some other time.
Give your reason: _____

[2] In 1987 the question dealing with the cause of the seasons was:
   What causes the seasons?
      A. The Earth's distance from the Sun.
      B. The Earth's axis flipping back and forth as it travels around the Sun.
      C. The Sun's motion around the Earth.
      D. The Earth's axis always pointing in the same direction.
      E. The shifting seasons on the Earth.
   By 1990 the question had evolved into a different form:
      The main reason for it being hotter in the summer than the winter is:
         A. The Earth's distance from the Sun changes. (46%)
         B. The Sun is higher in the sky in the summer. (12%, the correct answer)
         C. The distance between the northern hemisphere and the Sun changes. (37%)
         D. Oceans carry warm water north. (3%)
         E. An increase in greenhouse gases. (3%)

PSYCHOMETRIC TOOLS

Item Response Theory

It is useful to think of IRT as a sophisticated system of curve fitting, where the logistic family of functions is relied on to model the probability of choosing an answer. The Item Response Model calculates curves for each test item as a function of a latent trait, usually described as *ability*. This trait is measured in units of standard deviation from the mean. IRT has evolved to the extent that three parameters are generally calculated for each item in a test: difficulty, discrimination, and a guessing parameter (Walsh & Betz, 1995).

Figure 1 shows a typical graph of a item analyzed using IRT. Ideally, the correct answer rises from an asymptotic guessing probability on the left to unity on the right. The difficulty of the item is derived from the value of the ability corresponding to the inflection point (or alternatively, $p = 0.50$) of the correct answer. Discrimination is a measure of the maximum slope of the correct answer trace line. Wrong answers are expected to drop from the guessing probability to zero as ability increases. In the traditional IRT model, all curves are monotonic.

Although the generally accepted profiles for these trace lines are monotonic (Haladyna, 1994), an extensive analysis of the Project STAR Astronomy Questionnaire finds that items that attempt to measure a concept for which student often have misconceptions are fitted better by nonmonotonic functions (Sadler, 1998). The IRT model we turn to for analysis is not constrained to be monotonic, but is of the form in Equation 1:

$$P(x_j = k;\ \theta,\ a,\ c,\ d) = \frac{e^{z_k} + d_n e^{z_0}}{\displaystyle\sum_{h=0}^{m_j} e^{z_k}}$$

where x_j is the response to the item and $k = 1, 2, \ldots, m_j$ for multiple-choice item j with m choices; θ is the ability; a, c, and d are the item parameters; $z_0 = a_0\theta + c_0$, a linear function of q for the "don't know" category; and $z_k = a_k\theta + c_k$, a linear function of q for each of the item responses.

This model has the additional benefit of estimating a "don't know" parameter, accounting for student guessing as a function of ability for each item without the need for including such a distractor on each item (Thissen, Steinberg, & Fitzpatrick, 1989). All items are fit simultaneously, with the ability parameter a measure of how well students do on the entire test.

Analysis of Two Items and the J-Curve

Let us examine sets of trace lines for two different items on the Project STAR Astronomy Questionnaire. The first item assess students' under-

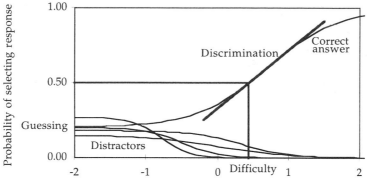

FIGURE 1

The item response model. Test data are fitted to a logistic equation for the probability of selecting an answer as a function of a common theta. Three parameters establish a guessing estimate for low ability students and the difficulty and discrimination for each item.

standing of the reason for day and night (Figure 2). The shape of the trace line for the correct answer shows a preference for the correct answer (the Earth spins on its axis) even at very low ability levels. This preference dips at moderate ability levels before it rises to unity at an ability level of 2.0. This dip accounts for an observed reduction in the number of students of moderate ability who chose the correct answer. The correct answer has a difficulty of −0.30 as measured by where it has a probability of 0.50 [P_c (−0.03) = 0.50]. Half the students are choosing the correct answer at this ability level.

This dip in the preference for the scientific view has been reported in the testing literature along with a corresponding increase in preference for misconceptions. It is described as U-shaped (Welch, 1995). Several researchers have examined the relative prevalence of students' conceptions at different ages, finding an increase and subsequent decline in preference for misconceptions as a function of age. Belief in the shadow of the Earth causing the moon's phases peaks at ages 13–14 then declines (Baxter, 1989). Students' explanations for the seasons being caused by the sun being farther away in the windter peaks at age 11–12 then declines (Baxter, 1989). Shipstone reports that the belief in a "current consumed model" of electricity peaks at age 14 then declines for students aged 12–17 (Shipstone, 1985). Roughly 70% of 230 5- to 8-year-olds classified a whale as an animal and nearly 100% of 50 17-year-olds did (Bell, 1981). One could reasonably assume that students between those ages would answer correctly in the 70–100% range. However, the preference for the correct response drops under 40% for the

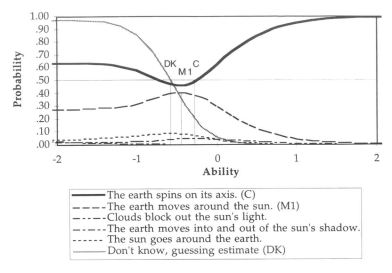

FIGURE 2

IRT model for "What causes day and night?" The probability of selecting the correct answer (C), that the Earth spins, is lower in students of moderate abilities than in those of low abilities or high abilities. This corresponds to an increase in preference for the incorrect notion of the Earth's orbit being responsible (M1). The estimate of guessing (DK) falls dramatically as ability increases in the population.

326 12- to 13-year-olds in the study. I prefer to characterize this response as J-shaped in that the left hand side is always lower than the right. Such a shape for a test item, independent of name, is enough for test-makers to exclude it from a conventional test.

The DK (don't know) trace line falls from near unity on the left smoothly to zero on the right. Students with higher ability guess more rarely than students with lower ability. In this case the trace line has a theta value of −0.55 when its probability is 0.50 [$P_{DK}(0.55) = 0.50$]. This is an estimate of the ability at which students guess 50% of the time.

The dip in this trace line for the correct answer is accompanied by an increase in the probability of choosing the M1 distractor (the Earth moves around the sun [in a day]). We have found that a J-shaped trace line is always accompanied by hump-shaped trace lines for one or more distractors. The value of theta where this maximum value of a distractor appears is the ability level for which this particular conception is the most attractive. In this case it is a value of theta of −0.43 [$P'_{M1}(0.43) = 0.00$, where $P_{M1}(0.43) = 0.41$]. This is a convenient measure to associate with a particular alternative conception.

The second example item deals with the cause of the moon's phases (Figure 3). It forces the selection of the best explanation for the moon's changes from the one's listed. The moon's phases are caused by the fact that our view of the lighted side of the moon changes as the moon orbits the Earth. The moon has no light of its own and is illuminated by the sun. Although the correct answer, E. None of the above, is difficult, astronomy teachers all get this problem correct.

The moon phase item is more difficult than the day/night problem. Half of the population chooses the correct answer when theta is 1.75. The trace line for the correct answer exhibits a substantial dip corresponding to two misconceptions. The peak for M1 occurs at a theta value of 0.96. The peak for M2 occurs at −0.55. The 50% level for DK is −0.45. This graph

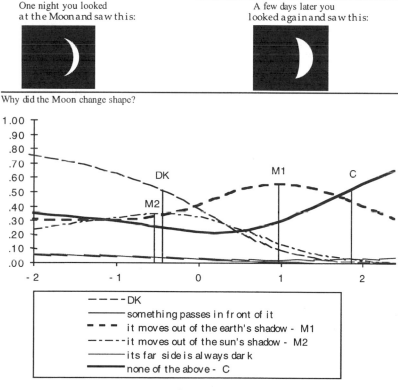

FIGURE 3
What causes the moon's phases? Three of the trace lines for this item exhibit nonmonotonic behavior. The correct answer is more popular among lower level students than among those at moderate levels of knowledge. Two misconceptions appear attractive to students.

shows that the belief that the phases are caused by the moon's movement out of the Earth's shadow is a fairly sophisticated belief. Comparing this graph to Figure 2, one can assume that students who hold this incorrect view have probably already learned the correct reason for day and night.

As students gain more knowledge, they move on the ability scale from left to right. One interpretation of the item characteristic curves (ICC's) is that students move from guessing (don't know) through one or more misconceptions until they reach the correct answer. Instead of being thought of as errors, misconceptions may be stepping stones to scientific understanding. Since IRT has the capability of assigning theta levels to each correct answer and misconception, hierarchies can be built that help reveal a structure internal to a particular scientific domain.

Test Characteristics

Each test item has its own set of item parameters and trace lines. Aggregating items to describe an entire test is simply a matter of averaging together all the items on the same common scale. The resulting Test Characteristic Curve (TCC) gives a general picture of the test, displaying the overall difficulty and discrimination. In Figure 4, one can see two forms of the TCC for the Project STAR Questionnaire.

The guessing parameter is estimated at 0.25 and dips for moderate-ability students before it rises for those with high ability. Figure 3 shows that differing sets of items have very similar response curves. In each case, the test has an overall difficulty of about 0.85 and a DK value of –0.80.

The "test information function" plays an important role in test development by estimating its precision at varying levels of ability:

$$I(\theta) = \sum_{i=1}^{n} \sum_{a=1}^{m} \frac{|P_i'(\theta)|^2}{P_i(\theta)[1-P_i(\theta)]}$$

where $I(\theta)$ is the information provided by the test, P is the probability of answering each answer as a function of θ, P' is the first derivative of the probability function, i is the test item where n is the total number of items, and a is the answer whem m is the total number of answers/item.

The information function is high for a range of abilities, signifying that the test can more precisely measure ability in that range (Hambleton et al., 1991). The information in the Project STAR Questionnaire is increased at lower ability levels by utilizing all the answers reported by students, rather than the correct answer alone. This argues for the inclusion of distractors in test analysis especially in cases where there are nonmonotonic trace lines. The information function is responsive to the slope of the trace lines. Items

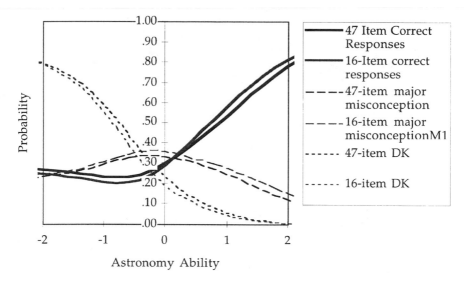

FIGURE 4
Comparison of test characteristic curves for a complete test and a 16-item subset. Note that both tests have similar trace lines for correct responses, the major misconception, and the "don't know" estimate.

(and test) where trace lines show more "bumps and dips" contain more information that can be used if accounted for (Figure 5).

MEASURING CONCEPTUAL CHANGE

Conceivably inspired by the quantum revolution in science, cognitive psychologists have come to generally agree that learning takes place in stages; there is nothing constant or seamless about it. Just as electrons are quantized in their energy states, cognition too moves in jumps as knowledge is reformulated by the individual. While this phenomenon can be viewed as chaotic, just as in science, one can make as a goal an understanding of the underlying processes. As scientists used the available tools used to study the Newtonian world (magnets, spectroscopes, cathode-ray tubes, and microscopes) and adapted them to study the subtle shifts in nature, so too psychometricans have begun to refine tools to explore the underlying structure of how we learn.

Placement along a Continuum

The most straightforward psychometric measurement of learning is the movement of a student's position along a continuum measured by a test. A

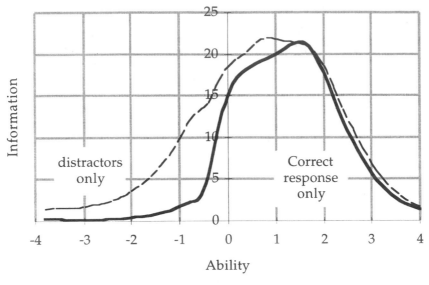

FIGURE 5

The test information function. Here two information functions are graphed, one using only the correct answers on the Project STAR Questionnaire, the other incorporating the four distractors. Utilizing distractors raises the information values substantially at lower ability levels, indicating that the test has useful information contained in the distractors. Using distractors in analysis extends the range of theta for which the test has high precision.

single measure before and a single measure afterward is enough to establish the size of (or lack of) gain. For example (Figure 6), the average high school student in a conventional year of astronomy or earth science study gained 0.16 standard deviations (from a starting point of 0.22) in a study of conceptual gain (Sadler, 1998). This can be compared to the gain predicted by teachers at this level of their students or 1.40 SD.

Comparing populations along this ability continuum reveals some intriguing issues. The performance of Harvard undergraduates on this test is not all that much different from that of the average high school student, but astronomy majors are clearly more advanced over the average undergraduate. Astronomy graduate students are closer to the knowledge levels of Harvard professors in their astronomical knowledge (when measured in units of standard deviation). High school teachers appear quite accurate when predicting the level at which their students begin their study. Teachers are inaccurate when attempting to predict their students' performance at the end of a year of instruction. Teachers predict that their high school students will know nearly as much about the basic conceptions in astronomy as Harvard

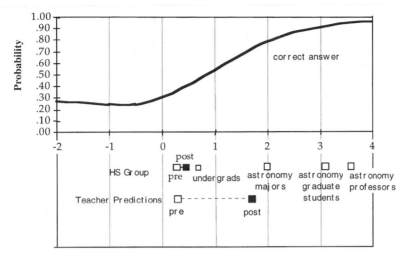

FIGURE 6
Test characteristic curve and plot of group means. The performance of
groups is represented by their horizontal position along the ability axis.
The trace line is the average for all 47 items on the Project
STAR Questionnaire.

astronomy majors. Measuring twice, using either predictions or actual performance, can allow comparisons between curricula or populations by using
a unidimensional ability scale in a domain.

Curriculum Maps

Key among the components of a curriculum is the characterization of order.
The notion of progression here is central, that there are better and worse
ways of arranging the experiences and topics that we place before students
(Millar, Gott, Lubben, & Duggan, 1993). Are there not some concepts that
should proceed others? How then can we identify such prerequisites? Measuring item difficulty is a help here. Teachers typically order concepts
sequentially from easy to hard.

Curriculum maps rank relevant test items by difficulty. They make visual
groupings of items and large gaps between item difficulties. Such rankings
"suggest a natural ordering of material in class" (p. 6) (Boone, 1990b) in
that a teacher may wish to proceed from the topic indicating the lowest
difficulty, in order, to the hardest. One can also plot individual students on
the same scale to compare the level of students with the difficulty of an
item. In Figure 7, student B has mastered the concepts below theta = 0.75,
involving the propagation of light and is ready to move on to the inverse

square law. Student A has probably mastered these simpler ideas and is ready to move on to the topics of filtering light and mixing colors of light. Yet, there are limitations to this kind of analysis. Mastery of some randomly chosen simple concept will probably have no influence on learning a difficult one. Moreover, the misconceptions that students hold are not utilized.

Cognitive Range

Representing the alternative conceptions or misconceptions of students along with the scientifically correct answers reveals more information about the structure of learning a particular set of topics. IRT models (as described above) are used to calculate the theta level for a 0.50 probability of the don't know answer and a 0.50 probability of the scientifically correct answer. This is the gray region in Figure 8. The data from an equivalent curriculum map are preserved in this chart as the right edge of the gray area. Added to this region are the theta values at which each misconception peaks. Misconceptions are always found at lower theta (and to the left) of the correct response. For many items there are several distractors that represent misconceptions.

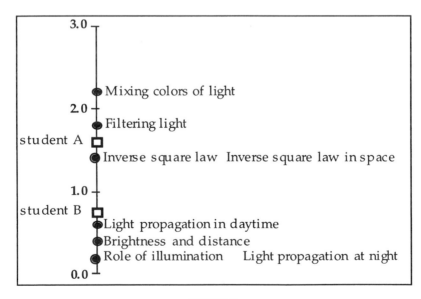

FIGURE 7

Curriculum map for a light and color subtest. Item difficulty is plotted along the vertical scale for eight items along with the ability level of two students.

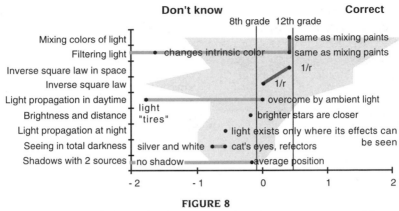

FIGURE 8

Cognitive range of light and color items. This chart is constructed from the item characteristic curves of each of nine items. The gray area represents the extent of difference between the guessing dominating and the correct answer dominating for each item. Items are arranged in order of increasing difficulty. The dots mark the ability levels corresponding to the peak of each wrong answer and are connected together horizontally by item. Vertical lines mark the ability means for eighth- and twelfth-grade students.

The range between the DK and correct thetas marks the domain between which half the students are guessing and half know the correct answer. When this range is small, students may learn a concept quickly. When it is large, coming to understand the scientific view may take years.

Most of what astronomers have learned about the universe results from analyzing light. We have touched and tested relatively few objects, and these only in our solar system. Light behaves in predictable ways that reveal much about the nature of its source. Through analysis of shadows, angle, flux, color and lack of it, and photon energy, astronomers determine chemical composition, size, temperature, pressure, density, and distance of objects too far away to be reached.

Groups of students of different ability levels can also be represented on these cognitive ranges. At the eighth-grade level, most students do not hold key scientific ideas about light that are used in understanding astronomy: that vision is a passive process (we see only when light enters our eyes), that shadows result from blocking light, that sources appear brighter when closer, and that light can exist even where its effects cannot be seen. By twelfth grade, the majority of students in our sample have come to understand these scientific ideas, but the inverse square nature of light propagation and the behavior of color still allude them.

Note that at levels below eighth grade, students believe that light "tires" as it fades out. They also believe that many objects are "naturally bright" and can be seen without illumination (Eaton, 1984; Jung, 1987). Substantial apparent progress in high school of many students shows that these are appropriate concepts to teach in astronomy courses, even though they are often glossed over by many books. While teachers optimistically predict that students will master virtually all of these concepts, color and $1/r^2$ notions may be too difficult for high school. Students hold a model of mixing light that is quite similar to the mixing of paint. The $1/r$ view of propagation is applied to Earth-bound systems (candles on tables) and later to astronomical objects. However, the $1/r^2$ notion, when it is understood, is applied correctly without regard to context.

Logical Networks

Psychometrics was originally designed to ascertain the position of subject on a continuous underlying variable in a population. Nichols (1994) views this as focusing on the "amount of content" acquired, not on the structures and strategies that students use to arrive at the answer that they do. While efficient for ranking students, the weak cognitive foundation of psychometrics (DiBello, Stout, & Roussos, 1993; Jiang, DiBello, & Stout, 1996) lacks "explicit psychological models of the structures and processes that underlie domain performance" (Nichols, 1994). Without some compelling reason to use the mathematical relationships on which it is based, psychometrics lacks a strong foundation.

Undergirding a new psychometrics utilizing the foundation of cognitive science has been proposed as the "Unified Model" (DiBello et al., 1993). Mislevy has proposed that a test structure should align with the structure of the domain. Tests should reveal and encompass the patterns of thought of novices and experts alike. Any "instructionally relevant patterns" should be embedded in the test itself (Mislevy, 1993a). Such a system would be similar to the shape of an airplane being determined by the underlying physics. The choices made in the overall structure are defensible down to the placement and number of rivets. Assessment tools, too, should not be a haphazard assembly of items, refined by tools with no cognitive foundation. Tests that are structured in justifiable ways is a goal.

Assessments tools utilizing cognitive models could have great value for teachers as a diagnostic test for students (Nichols, 1994), but they require that one be able to build hierarchical cognitive information from often non-ideal response patterns (Snow & Lohman, 1993). The sequence of states that students must pass through would be embedded in tests, along with the "end states" that have been the focus of tests to date (Haertel & Wiley, 1993). Psychometricians are attempting to develop the mathematics to make inferences about knowledge states where evidence is incomplete and certainty is low (Everson, 1995).

Within a population of students it is possible to determine which concepts appear to be prerequisite for others. The tool for establishing these relationships is the contingency table. Statistical measures can allow us to calculate the probability of the actual value being significantly different from the expected value with a chi-square test. Such a technique was developed and applied to logical and mathematical knowledge by Airasian and Bart in 1973 (Airasian & Bart, 1993). In the same fashion, we can compare expected with observed values for the answers to two different test items that examine students' conceptual understanding. A cell with a zero value would indicate that one concept may be a prerequisite for another. Of course, the multiple-choice format would change the minimum value of the key cell if the items are not similar in difficulty. Fisher's exact test is useful for calculating the probabilities in this case (Bart & Read, 1984). By comparing every question on the test with every other, one can establish which are the statistically significant prerequisite relationships in the population of students. This means that 47×47 contingency tables must be tested and evaluated, a job that is straightforward, although time-consuming even using a microcomputer.

An example is given in Table 1 for the contingency table relating the cause of night and day (item 1) and the knowledge of how long it takes the Earth to turn on its axis (item 21). One can use these numbers to settle the question of which comes first, knowing the reason for day and night, or knowing that the Earth spins in 24 hours. There are only 30 students in the population (1%) who know the Earth turns in 24 hours who do not know the cause of day and night. There are 406 who know the cause of day and night who do not know that the Earth turns in 24 hours. There are many who both know or do not know both. One can argue that knowing the cause of day and night is a prerequisite for knowing that the Earth spins in 24 hours. A value of 0% in the observed cell corresponding to an incorrect day and night and correct 24-hour rotation implies a prerequisite relationships. Fisher's exact test shows the statistical significance of the difference between the observed table and what one would expect under the null hypothesis of no prerequisite relationship (at the $p \leq .05$ level).

Even though all of the concepts covered on the Project STAR test reveal student misconceptions and can be placed on a continuum of difficulty, a smaller set are actually related to each other in a prerequisite fashion. Figure 9 shows an analysis of several items from the Project STAR Questionnaire. This diagram can be interpreted on the following basis. The difficulty of concepts increases vertically. Items that are pointed to by arrows have prerequisites in that there are very few students who hold this concept who do not already understand the prerequisite concept. Yet, students may have prerequisite knowledge and not have the more difficult concept.

Figure 9 shows that certain elementary knowledge appears prerequisite for more difficult concepts. The understanding of day and night and the Earth's yearly revolution about the sun appears to be key to mastery of the sun's motion in the sky, an understanding of seasons, and many other concepts. Many of the arrows lead to nodes (A, B, and C) that are not repre-

TABLE 1
Testing a Prerequisite Relationship between Two Test Items.

		24-Hour Rotation				24-Hour Rotation		
	Observed	Incorrect	Correct	Total	Expected	Incorrect	Correct	Total
Subjects	Incorrect	393	30	423	Incorrect	151	272	423
day and	Correct	406	1407	1813	Correct	648	1165	1813
night	Total	799	1437	2236	Total	799	1437	2236
Percent day	Incorrect	18%	1%	19%	Incorrect	7%	12%	19%
and night	Correct	18%	63%	81%	Correct	29%	52%	81%
	Total	36%	64%	100%	Total	36%	64%	100%

Note. Here the observed frequencies of response are displayed in a contingency table along with the expected frequencies using only the marginal (total) values. The low value of one of the cells in the observed table compared to the expected table implies that a prerequisite relationship is present.

sented by individual test items. Such an analysis may lead one to theorize about what concepts they represent. Items could then be generated to see if these items replace the nodes for which they were designed. In this way, prerequisite analysis could help to build more robust and complete tests. This form of analysis does not use information on student misconceptions, but a more complex model (now under investigation) may reveal links between students alternative ideas as well.

This chart shows the great difficulty students have in mastering advanced concepts without processing the prerequisite knowledge. This type of analysis suggests that understanding of science may be constructed much like astronomy's cosmic distance scale: Accurate measures of more and more distant objects are dependent on the ways in which we measure closer objects. It may be impossible for students to acquire powerful scientific ideas without great attention to the basics (Sadler, 1995).

IMPLICATIONS

Multiple-choice tests have suffered criticism in recent years for an inability to measure higher order thinking. They are utilized extensively in standardized tests, and many teachers find them useful and convenient. There is a tendency among test-makers and teacher alike to create multiple-choice items that avoid popular alternative conceptions, which lowers the cognitive level of a problem and makes it less valuable as a diagnostic instrument. For test-makers, inclusion of misconception distractors tends to lower the discriminating power of an item and the fit to a theoretically vaunted ideal. For teachers, inclusion of powerful distractors increases the difficulty of items

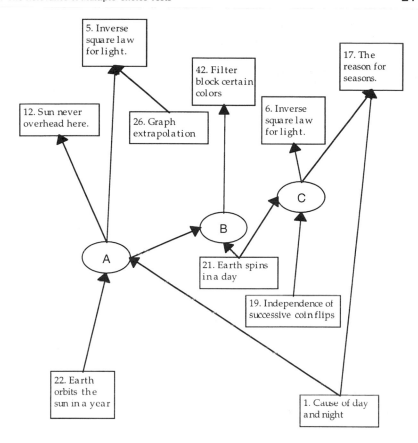

FIGURE 9

Prequisite relationships between astronomical concepts. The result of analyzing approximately 2000 contingency tables comparing test items is
shown in these 14 prerequisite relationships. The inclusion of three nodes
simplifies the diagram.

to the point that it is difficult to meet the 80% average that many desire.
Misconceptions are just too attractive to students.

The J-shaped response curve lends support to the observation that
instruction can sometimes appear to reinforce misconceptions. Students
can increase their preference for nonscientific views over scientific views
while they increase their knowledge overall. This appears to be virtually universal for all concepts measured using our tests, and other researchers have
noted this as well. This phenomenon diminishes with time studying a particular topic, adding support to the view that students should study few topics in great depth. The TIMSS Study has found that in countries in which

there is reduced coverage, students score higher on international tests (see chapter 12). In a study of nearly 2000 students, we have found evidence that those having taken high school courses covering fewer topics were more successful in college physics courses (Sadler & Tai, 1997).

We have also found that prerequisite relationships exist between concepts that affect the ease of learning a particular concept. For example, students who do not know the reason for day and night and the role of the Earth's rotation fare quite badly at learning more advanced concepts. We question the usefulness of moving on to new topic when students have not yet mastered what appears to be fundamental to their later understanding. Teachers might well reduce the scope of their science courses and concentrate on the key concepts that underpin others in the field.

Those who have an interest in the measurement of learning in science might be well served by reexamining the use of multiple-choice test items that distinguish between alternative conceptions and scientific views. Such items, when assembled into tests and analyzed using nonmonotonic IRT models reveal structures that match those found by cognitive scientists.

Acknowledgments

This research has been supported by grants from the National Science Foundation (MDR 85–50297 and MDR 88–50424), the Smithsonian Institution, and Apple Computer. I thank my Harvard and Smithsonian colleagues Hal Coyle, Bruce Gregory, Roy Gould, Judith Peritz, Susan Roudebush, Irwin Shapiro, Judy Singer, and Terrence Tivnan for their comments and support. Marcus Lieberman carried out the multiple IRT calculations with great patience and good humor. Project STAR teachers from across the United States have contributed immensely by agreeing to open their classrooms to our research. Portions of this paper are drawn from my earlier works, especialy my March 1998 article in the Journal of Research in Science Teaching.

References

Airasian, P. W., & Bart, W. M. (1993). Ordering theory: A new and useful model. *Educational Technology*, May, 56–60.

Anderson, C. W., & Smith, E. L. (1986). *Children's conceptions of light and color: understanding the role of unseen rays* No. ERIC ED 270 318). Institute for Research on Teaching, Michigan State University.

Arnaudin, M. W., & Mintzes, J. J. (1985). Students' alternative conceptions of the human circulatory system: A cross-age study. *Science Education*, 69(5), 721–733.

Ausubel, D. P. (1968). *Educational Psychology: A Cognitive View*. New York: Holt, Rinehart & Winston.

Baker, F. B. (1985). *The basics of item response theory*. Portsmouth, NH: Heineman.

Bant, W. M., & Krus, D. J. (1973) An ordering-theoretic method to determine hierarchies among items. *Educational and Psychological Measurement*, 33, 291–300.

Bart, W. M., & Read, S. A. (1984). A statistical test for prerequisite relations. *Educational and Psychological Measurement*, 44, 223–227.

Baxter, J. (1989). Children's understanding of familiar astronomical events. *International Journal of Science Education*, 11, 502–513.

Bell, B. (1981). When is an animal not an animal? *Journal of Biological Education*, 15(3), 213–218.

Bloom, B. (1950). *A taxonomy of Educational Objectives: Handbook 1, the cognitive domain*. New York: David McKay.

Boone, W. J. (1990a). How psychometric analysis can help teachers realize a curriculum. In AERA, ED342727. Boston: ERIC.

Boone, W. J. (1990b). *How psychometric analysis can help teachers realize a curriculum* (Paper No. ERIC ED342727). AERA.

Borko, H., & Livingston, C. (1989). Cognition and improvisation: Differences in mathematics instruction by expert and novice teachers. *American Educational Research Journal*, 26, 473–498.

BouJaoude, S. B. (1992). The relationship between students' learning strategies and the change in their misunderstandings during a high school chemistry course. *Journal of Research in Science Teaching*, 29(7), 687–699.

Bouwens, R.E.A. (1986). Misconceptions among pupils regarding geometrical optics. GIREP – *Cosmos – an educational challenge*. Copenhagen: European Space Agency, 369–370.

Brumby, M. N. (1984). Misconceptions about the concept of natural selection by medical biology students. *Science Education*, 68(4), 493–503.

Caramazza, A., McCloskey, M., & Green, B. (1981). Naive beliefs in sophisticated subjects: Misconceptions about trajectories of objects. *Cognition*, 9, 117.

Champagne, A. B., Klopfer, L. E., & Anderson, J. H. (1980). Factors influencing the learning of classical mechanics. *American Journal of Physics*, 48(12 Dec), 1074–1079.

Clement, J. (1982). Students preconceptions in introductory mechanics. *American Journal of Physics*, 50, 66.

Cohen, M. R., & Kagan, M. H. (1979). Where does the old Moon go? *The Science Teacher*, 46, 22–23.

Council, N. R. (1996). *National science education standards*. Washington; DC: National Academy Press.

Dai, M. F. (1990). Misconceptions about the Moon held by fifth and sixth graders in Taiwan. In National Science Teachers Association.

DiBello, L. V., Stout, W. F., & Roussos, L. A. (1993). Unified cognitive/psychometric diagnostic assessment likelihood-based classification techniques. In P. D. Nichols, S. F. Chipman, & R. L. Brennan (Eds.), *Cognitively diagnostic assessment* Hillsdale, NJ: Lawrence Erlbaum.

Doran, R. L., Lawrenz, F., & Helgeson, S. (1994). Research on Assessment in Science. In D. L. Gabel (Eds.), *Handbook of research on science teaching and learning* (pp. 388–441). New York: Simon & Schuster Macmillan.

Driver, R. (1973) *The representation of conceptual frameworks in young adolescent science students.* Ph D. dissertation, University of Illinois.

Driver, R. (1985). Pupil as scientist. Milton Keynes, England: Open University Press.

Driver, R., Squires, A., Rushworth, P., & Robinson, V. -W. (1994). *Making sense of secondary science: Research into children's ideas*. New York: Routledge.

Duckworth, E. (1987). *"The having of wonderful ideas"* & *other essays on teaching and learning*. New York: Teachers College Press.

Eaton, J. F. (1984). Student misconceptions interfere with science learning: case studies of fifth-grade students. *Elementary School Journal*, 84, 365–379.

Erickson, G., & Tiberghien, A. (1985). Heat and temperature. In R. Driver, E. Guesne, & A. Tiberhien (Eds.), *Children's ideas in science* (pp. 52–84). Philadelphia: Open University Press.

Everson, H. T. (1995). Modeling the student in intelligent tutoring systems: The promise of a new psychometrics. *Instructional Science*, 23, 433–452.

Feltovich, P. J., Spiro, R. J., & Coulson, R. L. (1993). Learning teaching and testing for complex conceptual understanding. In N. Frederikson, R. J. Mislevy, & I. Bejar (Eds.), *Test theory for a new generation of tests* (pp. 181–217). Hillsdale, NJ: Lawrence Erlbaum.

Finley, F. N. (1986). Evaluating instructing: the complementary use of clinical interviews. *Journal of Research in Science Teaching*, 23, 635–660.

Freire, P. (1993) The "banking" concept of education. In D. Bartholomae and A. Petrosky, *Ways of Reading*. 3rd Ed. (pp.207–221). Boston: Bedford.

Freyberg, P., & Osborne, R. (1985). Constructing a survey of alternative views. In R. J. Osborne & P. Freyberg (Eds.), *Learning in science, the implication of childrens' science* (pp. 166–167). Auckland, New Zealand: Heineman.

Furuness, L. B., & Cohen, M. (1989). Children's conception of the seasons: A comparison of three interview techniques, April 1, 1989.

Gilbert, J. K. (1977). The study of student misunderstandings in the physical sciences, Research in Science Education 165–171.

Gorodetsky, M., & Gussarsky, E. (1987). The role of students and teachers in misconceptualization of aspects of "chemical equilibrium". In *Second international seminar: Misconceptions and educational strategies in science and mathematics*, (pp. 187–193). Ithaca, NY: Cornell University (Dept. of Education).

Haertel, E. H., & Wiley, D. E. (1993). Representations of ability structures: Implications for testing. In N. Fredericksen, R. J. Mislevy, & I. I. Bejar (Eds.), *Test theory for a new generation of tests* (pp. 359–384). Hillsdale, NJ: Lawrence Erlbaum.

Haladyna, T. M. (1994). *Developing and validating multiple-choice test items*. Hillsdale, NJ: Lawrence Erlbaum.

Halloon, I. A., & Hestenes, D. (1985). The initial knowledge state of college physics students, *American Journal of Physics*, 53, 1043–1055.

Hambleton, R. K., Swaminathan, H., & Rogers, H. J. (1991). *Fundamentals of item response theory*. Newbury Park, CA: Sage.

Hestenes, D., Wells, M., & Swackhammer, G. (1992). Force concept inventory: *The Physics Teacher*, 30(3), 141–158.

Jiang, H., DiBello, L., & Stout, W. (1996). An estimation procedure for the structural parameters of the unified cognitive/IRT model. In NCME (pp. 1–20). New York: ERIC.

Jung, W. (1987). Understanding students' understandings: the case of elementary optics. In J. D. Novak (Ed.), *2nd international seminar on misconception and educational strategies in science and mathematics*, 3 (pp. 268–277). Ithaca, NY: Cornell University Press.

Klein, C. A. (1982). Children's concepts of the Earth and the Sun: A cross cultural study. *Science Education*, 65(1), 95–107.

Langford, P. (1989). *Children's thinking and learning in elementary school*. Lancaster; PA: Technomic.

Lightman, A. P., & Miller J. D. (1989). Contemporary cosmological beliefs. *Social Studies of Science*, 19, 127–136.

Masters, G. N., & Mislevy, R. J. (1993). New views of student learning: Implications for educational measurement. In N. Frederikson, R. J. Mislevy, & I. Bejar (Eds.), *Test theory for a new generation of tests* (pp. 219–242). Hillsdale, NJ: Lawrence Erlbaum.

McDermott, L. C. (1984). Research on conceptual learning in mechanics. *Physics Today*, July, 24–32.

Millar, R., Gott, R., Lubben, F., & Duggan, S. (1993). Children's performance of investigative tasks in science: A framework for considering progression. Liverpool: British Educational Research Association, ERIC ED364417.

Mislevy, R. J. (1993a). Foundations of a new test theory. In N. Frederikson, R. J. Mislevy, & I. Bejar (Eds.), *Test theory for a new generation of tests* (pp. 19–39). Hillsdale, NJ: Lawrence Erlbaum.

Mislevy, R. J. (1993b). Introduction. In N. Frederikson, R. J. Mislevy, & I. Bejar (Eds.), *Test theory for a new generation of tests* (pp. ix–xii). Hillsdale, NJ: Lawrence Erlbaum.

Narode, R. (1987). Standardized testing for misconceptions in basic mathematics. In J. D. Novak (Ed.), *2nd international seminar on misconception and educational strategies in science and mathematics*, 1 (pp. 222–333). Ithaca, NY: Cornell University Press.

Neil, M. (1996). How the "principles and indicators for student assessment systems" should affect practice. In AERA, ED399292. New York: ERIC.

Newman, D., & Morrison, D. (1993). The conflict between teaching and scientific sense-making: The case of a curriculum on seasonal change. *Interactive Learning Environments*, 3(1), 1–16.

Nichols, P. D. (1994). A framework for developing cognitively diagnostic assessments. *Review of Educational Literature*, 64(4), 575–603.

Novak, J. D. (1977). A *theory of education*. Ithaca, NY: Cornell University Press.

Novick, S., & Nussbaum, J. (1978). Using interviews to probe understanding. *The Science Teacher*, November, 29–30.

Nussbaum, J. (1986). Students perception of astronomical concepts. In J. Hunt (Ed.), GIREP – *cosmos – and educational challenge,* (pp. 87–97). Copenhagen: European Space Agency.

Nussbaum, J., & Novak, J. (1976). An assessment of childrens' concepts of the earth utilizing structured interviews. *Science Education,* 60(4), 535–550.

Nussbaum, J., & Novak, J. (1982). Alternative frameworks, conceptual conflict and accommodation: toward a principled teaching strategy. *Instructional Science,* 11, 183–200.

Osborne, R. J., & Bell, B. F. (1983). Science teaching and childrens' views of the world. *European Journal of Science Education,* 5(1), 1–14.

Osborne, R. J., & Gilbert, J. K. (1980). A technique for exploring students' views of the world. *Physics Education,* 15, 376–379.

Phelps, R. P. (1997). The extent and character of system-wide student testing in the United States. *Educational Measurement,* 4(2), 89–121.

Piaget, J., & Inhelder, B. (1929). *The child's conception of space* (F. J. Langdon J. L. Lunzer, Trans.). New York: W. W. Norton.

Rhine, S. (1998). The role of research and teachers' knowledge base in professional development. *Educational Researcher* (June–July), 27–31.

Roth, K. J. (1985) *The effect of science texts on students misconceptions about food for plants.* Ph.D. dissertation, Michigan State University.

Sadler, P. M. (1992) *The initial knowledge state of high school astronomy students.* Ed.D., Harvard Graduate School of Education.

Sadler, P. M. (1995). Astronomy's conceptual hierarchy. In J. Percy (Eds.), *Proceedings of the ASP astronomy education meeting.* San Francisco: Astronomical Society of the Pacific.

Sadler, P. M. (1998). Psychometric models of student conceptions in science. Reconciling qualitative studies and distractor-driven assessment and instruments. *Journal of Research in Science Teaching.* 35(3), 265–296.

Sadler, P. M., & Tai, R. (1997). High school physics: Its role in preparing students for college physics. *The Physics Teacher,* May.

Schneps, M. H., & Sadler, P. M. (1988). A private universe. In New York: Annenberg/CPB.

Schoon, K. J. (1988) *Misconceptions in Earth and space sciences, A cross-age study.* Ph.D. dissertation, Loyola University.

Shipstone, D. (1985). Electricity in simple circuits. In R. Driver, E. Guesne, & A. Tiberhien (Eds.), *Children's ideas in science* (pp. 33–51). Philadelphia: Open University Press.

Shipstone, D. M., Rboneck, C., Jung, W., Karrgvist, C., Dupin, J. J., Joshua, S., & Licht, P. (1987). A study of students understanding of electricity in five European countries. *European Journal of Science Education,* 10(3) 303–316.

Sneider, C., & Pulos, S. (1983). Childrens' cosmographies: understanding the Earth's shape and gravity. *Science Education,* 67(2), 205–222.

Snow, R., & Lohman, D. (1993). Implications of cognitive psychology for educational measurement. In R. L. Linn (Eds.), *Educational measurement.* New York: American Council on Education, Macmillan.

Thissen, D., Steinberg, L., & Fitzpatrick, A. R. (1989). Multiple-choice models: The distractors are also part of the item. *Journal of Educational Measurement,* 26(2), 161–176.

Touger, J. S. (1985). Students' conceptions about planetary motion, January 23, 1985.

Trabin, T. E., & Weiss, D. J. (1983). The person response curve: Fit of individuals to item response theory models. In D. J. Weiss (Eds.), *New horizons in testing: Latent trait theory and computerized adaptive testing* (pp. 83–108). New York: Academic Press.

Treagust, D. F. (1986). Evaluating students' misconceptions by means of diagnostic multiple choice items. *Research in Science Education,* 363–369.

Treagust, D. F. (1995). Diagnostic assessment of students' science knowledge. In S. M. Glynn & R. Duit (Eds.), *Learning science in the schools* (pp. 327–346). Mahwah, NJ: Lawrence Earlbaum.

Vincentini-Missoni, M. (1981). Earth and gravity: Comparison between adult's and children's knowledge. In W. Jung (Ed.), *Problems concerning students' representation of physics and chemistry knowledge.* Frankfort: University of Frankfort.

Vosniadou, S., & Brewer, W. 1994. Mental models of the day/night cycle. *Cognitive Science*, 18, 123–183.

Walsh, W. B., & Betz, N. E. (1995). *Tests and assessment* (3rd ed.). Englewood Cliffs, NJ: Prentice Hall.

Weiss, D. J. (1983). Introduction. In D. J. Weiss (Eds.), *New horizons in testing: Latent trait theory and computerized adaptive testing* (pp. 1–8). New York: Academic Press.

Welch, W. W. (1995). Student assessment and curriculum evaluation. In B. J. Fraser & H. J. Walberg (Eds.), *Improving science education* (pp. 90–116). Chicago: National Society for the Study of Education.

Za'rour, G. L. (1976). Interpretation of natural phenomena by Lebanese school children. *Science Education*, 60, 277–287.

National and International Assessment

PINCHAS TAMIR

The Hebrew University

Evaluation[1] has always been an important cornerstone of education. The main reason for this is the basic need of educators to know whether their educational intentions are realized, to what extent their educational activities achieve their goals, how these activities affect different students, and how best to plan for continuous and optimal instruction.

STUDENT ASSESSMENT

Student assessment may be defined as a systematic collection of information about student learning and other variables that are associated with particular learning experiences. Student assessment has traditionally relied on measures, instruments, and methodologies developed by measurement experts and based on measurement theories which yield quantitative data that served to rank-order individuals within given groups such as a classroom, a school, or a particular age cohort. The results of assessment have been typically used for selection and classification, for example, serving as criterion for admitting candidates to prestigious schools.

[1] Evaluation and assessment are synonymous. However, I prefer to use evaluation as the more general and comprehensive process, whereas assessment is reserved for student achievement.

Curriculum Reform and Student Assessment

For many decades, assessment has acted as a barrier to many innovations. There are at least two major reasons why testing would act as a barrier. First, teachers teach and students study toward success in the tests. *Innovations that compete with tests are bound to fail.* Second, tests that do not match the innovation fail to reveal the impact of the innovation. The commonly heard statement that the "new" curricula of the 1960s have failed to achieve their goals has been based on results of paper and pencil multiple-choice questions that favor rote learning and memorization and, consequently, cannot reveal gain in higher-order thinking. Finally, quite often the implementation of innovations has not been actualized even when the class was using the "new" text. In these cases the teachers continued to teach in their traditional manner with the new text. Consequently, the intended opportunities to learn have not taken place. Under these circumstances, no wonder that the intended has not been attained.

A Balanced Student Assessment

Ideally, an assessment program should reflect the goals and experiences of the curriculum to such an extent that when students study toward the tests they will do what they are intended to do in their school studies. For example, high school students who specialize in biology in Israel have been assessed at their graduation from school by a series of external examinations as well as by their teachers. The final grade is the average of the two grades: the teacher's and the average of all components of the external matriculation examination. A description of the comprehensive matriculation (Bagrut) examination in biology can be found elsewhere (e.g., Tamir, 1974, 1985; Doran, Laurenz, & Helgeson, 1994; Lazarowitz & Tamir, 1994).

Types of Assessment

Most of the literature on assessment in schools deals with student achievement and factors associated with meeting the goals assigned to it. Until recently, two modes of assessment dominated the educational system: school-based assessment, designated as *internal* assessment, and *external* assessment, often based on standardized tests produced by commercial organizations or by the governments of certain countries. The most common tests of the latter are end-of-high-school examinations, known as O and A levels in the United Kingdom, baccalaureate in France, Arbitur in Germany, and matriculation (Bagrut) in Israel. No such centralistic *external* examinations are used in some countries such as the United States and Sweden.

Assessment, like other topics and issues in education, may be assumed to be dependent on the subject matter. Hence, our comparisons will focus on science. Having made this decision, I note that the proposed study will yield results that will be relevant to other disciplines as well. The major sources of our data are three international studies: The Second International Science Study (SISS), the Third International Mathematics and Science Study (TIMSS), and a recently published study entitled *Examining the Examinations: An International Comparison of Science and Mathematics for College Bound Students* (designated ETE) (Britton & Raizen, 1996). SISS and TIMSS were designed, carried out, and analyzed by the International Association for the Study of Educational Achievement (IEA). ETE was conducted by the National Center for Improving Science Education (NCISE) in Washington, DC, but had strong connections to TIMSS (Britton, 1996, pp. 4–5). A common feature of the three studies is the use of international studies as a source of information on national educational systems (e.g., Beaton et al. 1996).

Recently, I have published two chapters in two handbooks (Tamir, 1996, 1997). These chapters provide a comprehensive review of the field of assessment in science. The topics of national and international assessment have not been included, yet interesting developments have taken place in these fields all over the world.

NATIONAL ASSESSMENT

Countries vary in their approach to student assessment. Within countries, different schools and different teachers use their own assessment program. Internal assessment includes, among other sources (e.g., teacher observation), the use of classroom tests. "Classroom tests are created or chosen by individual teachers or small groups of teachers for use in the classroom or sometimes the school level. Classroom tests usually matter much more to students and teachers" (Stiggins & Bridgeford, 1985, as cited in Haertal, 1990). Some differences in internal and external examinations are given in Table 1.

Some patterns of assessment are typically used by the majority of teachers in each country. For example, most teachers in the United States base their assessment on paper and pencil multiple-choice tests. In Britain, France, and Germany, on the other hand, multiple-choice items are hardly ever used in classroom tests. In some countries student grades are determined by classroom tests only. This is generally the case in the United States, as well as in the elementary and middle schools in Israel. However, in high schools, namely in grades 10, 11, and 12, all efforts of both students and teachers are directed to prepare for the end of school matriculation examinations. A strong impact of examinations is generally found regarding high-stake examinations.

Scoring

For many students and for many teachers the main function of assessment is assigning grades. However, there is no universal method of scoring and grad-

TABLE 1
Characteristics of External and Internal Assessment

Attribute	Internal	External
Proportion of use in the Unied States	Relatively low	Relatively high
Authors	Teacher or team of teachers	Government, examination boards
Quizzes	Common	Not relevant
Classroom test (unit and midterm tests)	Yes	No
Final examination	Yes	Sometimes
Student project	Yes	Sometimes
Domain content coverage	Narrow, small	Broad, large
Prior trial	Not done	Often done
Printed or typed	Partially	Always
Length of test	Short	Long
Matching with instruction	Usually good, adequate	Usually not sufficient
Feedback to teachers	High	Limited
Feedback to students	High	Does not exist
Reliability	Usually low ($r \sim 0.4$)	Usually high ($r \sim 0.8$)
Standard	Criterion referenced	Usually norm referenced
Number of examinees	Small	Great
Diagnostic potential	High	High, but less than internal
Match the curriculum	Very good, easy to get	There are many mismatches; difficult to get
Time allocated	As much as the teachers wish	Limited usually to one period
Scoring	Criteria and weights by teacher	Criteria and weights by outside agent
Makeup (e.g., sickness)	Possible, no real trouble	Usually impossible right away; repeat at other dates
Costs	Relatively low	Relatively high

ing. The variation has at least two explanations: First, in free-response items different teachers use different criteria; hence, the same answers will receive different scores from different teachers. Second, in different educational systems different scoring scales are used. For example, in Israel a perfect answer will get a grade of 100. The same answer will probably receive the grade of A+ in the United States, while in Russia, where a 5-point scale is used, the top grade is 1. Sweden also uses a 5-point scale, but in this case, 1 is the lowest and 5 the top score (Gisselberg, 1996). Table 2 presents the scoring system typically used in Israel and the meaning associated with the scores.

How can we explain the fact that this particular scale is used in Israel? We do not know for sure, but since this was decided on at the beginning of the century, it is reasonable to assume that its origin is in Europe, from which most of the residents of the country, Eretz Israel, then known as Palestine, have immigrated. Let us discuss the merits of a 0 to 100-point scale. Such a scale fits well the metric or decimal system, which is used by most countries

TABLE 2
Scores Used in Israel and Their Meaning

10-Point Scale	100-Point Scale	Meaning
0 to 4	0 to 44	Unsatisfactory/fail
5	54 to 54	Hardly satisfactory/partially fail
6	55 to 64	Pass
7	65 to 74	Fairly good
8	75 to 84	Good
9	85 to 94	Very good
10	95 to 100	Excellent

Source. Taken from Tamir (1987, p. 91).

to measure, to weigh, to classify, and to subdivide currency. In all those countries, people's quantitative thinking is performed in terms of the decimal system. Why should quantification of student performance be any different? One of the skills acquired by Israeli teachers as they accumulate experience is that of designing tests for which mean raw scores will fall within the range of 65 to 74. A weighting procedure is used to raise scores when the tests appear to be too difficult. Hence, while the scoring system is essentially criterion referenced, it may be and indeed frequently is augmented by adjustments which are not too different from a norm-referenced approach. The meaning of the scores is usually clear to everyone, much like the meaning of an A or B student in the United States or Britain.

The Meaning of Scores

It is often argued that raw scores carry little meaning and therefore should be substituted by verbal qualitative assessment. Undoubtedly, verbal assessments that identify strengths and weaknesses may be very useful, especially to students and parents. However, this kind of assessment is very hard to summarize for a whole class and it renders any comparison that one wishes to make (e.g., the differences in achievement between groups) very difficult to accomplish. Quantification has limitations but at the same time carries advantages such as brevity and ease of communication. Perhaps one solution to the dilemma is the use of profiles. Profiles can be provided by reporting item-by-item results or by creating subtests, each representing a particular cognitive level (e.g., knowledge, comprehension, application), a particular skill (e.g., observation, hypotheses formulation, making a graph), or a particular topic (e.g., photosynthesis, diffusion, cell structure). In recent years such profiles of the biology matriculation examination results have been regularly communicated to schools.

As far as the public is concerned, the strategies described above augment communication among schools, students, and parents as well as between schools, the Ministry of Education, and the public at large. Everyone in the country has a pretty good general idea what the scores mean. Teachers have used the scoring systems to convey a variety of messages. For example, often teachers design easy tests at the beginning of the school year, thereby letting students gain relatively high scores to enhance their self-confidence, hoping that this will encourage and motivate them to learn. This has been especially true with less able students. Another example is the impact of the matriculation examinations. Naturally these examinations strongly influence both students and teachers, who tend to distribute their efforts in light of the demands and emphasis of these examinations. Usually the results of these examinations are communicated as students' individual scores, as well as in the form of mean scores and standard deviations. In addition to the total test scores, subtest scores and item-by-item scores are also communicated. Both students and teachers can compare the scores earned in their class with those earned by students in other schools. This feedback is very important and may contribute significantly to the improvement of instruction. Moreover, not only do the matriculation examinations affect curriculum and instruction, but they have direct impact on the nature of teachers' tests (e.g., Tamir, 1977).

A novel kind of practical laboratory test which evaluates the skills associated with inquiry-oriented laboratory work has been developed and used successfully in Israel as a part of the biology matriculation examination for the last twenty years (Tamir, 1974; Doran et al., 1994). In this examination students are presented with novel problems (sometimes a novel situation that requires problem identification) and are required to formulate a relevant hypothesis, design a plan to test this hypothesis, actually perform the experiment, collect the data, communicate the findings in acceptable ways (e.g., graphs, tables, drawing), draw conclusions, suggest explanations, and apply the knowledge gained to new relevant questions. About 100,000 students have taken these examinations during the last twenty years. Normally one examiner monitors the tests of 10 to 15 examinees.

Scoring Key: An Example

Scoring is based on the written answers and is carried out in the regular matriculation examination scoring center. One way to raise the quality and usability of student assessment by this test is to build a performance profile. To do so it is necessary to develop assessment instruments consisting of categories of answers. Each of these categories should convey a clear meaning and at the same time allow for quantitative explanations and comparisons. One such instrument is the Practical Tests Assessment Inventory (PTAI; see Tamir, Nussinovitz, & Friedler [1982]). PTAI consists of the following 21 categories:

1. Formulating problems
2. Formulating hypotheses

   3. Identifying dependent variable
   4. Identifying independent variable
   5. Designing control
   6. The fitness of the experiment to the tested problem or hypothesis
   7. Completeness of experimental design
   8. Understanding the role of the control in experiment
   9. Making and reporting measurements
   10. Determining and preparing adequate dilutions
   11. Making observations with a microscope
   12. Describing observations
   13. Making graphs
   14. Making tables
   15. Interpreting observed data
   16. Drawing conclusions
   17. Explaining research findings
   18. Examining results critically
   19. Applying knowledge
   20. Understanding and interpreting data presented in a graph
   21. Suggesting ideas and ways to continue the investigation

For more details, see Tamir (1987).

INTERNATIONAL ASSESSMENT

A Brief Introduction to TIMSS

As the twenty-first century approaches, the demand for mathematical, scientific, and technological understanding and expertise will be greater than ever before. Students at the forefront of developments in the future will require very high levels of mathematical and scientific skills. These students will need to develop critical thinking, processing, and interpreting skills far beyond those required in the previous decade. Competence as well as skills in mathematics and science will be crucial as students leave school and enter higher education and the workplace. Welch, Walberg, and Fraser (1986) successfully predicted elementary science learning using national assessment data.

TIMSS is the largest and most ambitious international study of mathematics and science achievement at school level ever undertaken. It is the first time that mathematics and science studies have been combined as an integrated study. TIMSS is also the largest comparative study of its kind conducted under the auspices of the International Association for the Study of Educational Achievement (IEA), an independent international organization of national research institutions and governmental research agencies. Its primary purpose is to conduct large-scale comparative studies of educational achievement, with the aim of gaining an in-depth understanding of the effects of policies and practices within and across systems of education. The IEA has conducted more than 15 studies of achievement involving groups from different countries since its inception in 1959.

TIMSS was developed to assess the effects of the national curricula, schools, and social environment on the achievement in science and mathematics and on student attitudes toward science and mathematics in different kinds of participating countries and different evaluation systems of education around the world. TIMSS instruments were designed to measure mathematics and science achievement to help inform governments, policy makers, and educators about the mathematics and science proficiency of their students at key points in the educational process. The questionnaires were aimed at collecting information about factors related to students' learning of mathematics and science. Special attention was given to the state of scientific literacy (Orpwood & Garden, 1998).

Conceptual Framework for TIMSS

IEA studies traditionally have recognized the importance of the curriculum as a variable for explaining differences among national school systems and for explaining the students' results. These studies represent an effort to understand education systems and to make valid comparisons between them. The curricula and teaching practices have been investigated and compared with the students' results. These three factors have become the focus areas for TIMSS. It was believed that differences in achievement could be explained in terms of variations in curriculum, teaching practices, and other variables. It was also hoped that the study would help countries to evaluate national curricula and provide a research basis for future national curriculum reform.

The conceptual model for TIMSS was derived mainly from the models used in earlier IEA studies, especially for SIMS (Second International Mathematics Study) and SISS (Second International Science Study). In this model, three stages of curriculum are envisaged: the intended, the implemented, and the attained. The educational environment should be understood from the perspective of these three curriculum levels. It is believed that there are also factors outside of formal schooling that affect the students' achievement. Therefore, there is a unique set of contextual factors that influence the educational decisions for each stage of the curriculum (Martin & Kelly, 1996).

The model, adopted by TIMSS as its conceptual framework, provides a rationale and context for the key research questions in TIMSS. Five questions are central to the study:

- What are students expected to learn?
- Who provides the instruction?
- How is the instruction conducted?
- What have students learned?
- What are the factors associated with the various learning outcomes?

TIMSS Curriculum Framework

Since the curriculum is regarded as an important variable for explaining achievement differences, a framework to describe and classify the different aspects of the curriculum was designed (see Figure 1). In this framework, different aspects of the curriculum are classified under three broad headings: content or subject matter; performance expectations, what is the student expected to be able to do; and attitudes and views of the students that can influence learning. The detailed categories within the science and mathematics frameworks differ, but the structure and rationale of the two frameworks are the same. The major categories of these frameworks are presented in Figure 1.

The framework allows any test question or proposed teaching activity to be classified in detail. For example, a question on naming the different parts of an insect would be classified as a life science question with the performance expectation being "knowing." A question on solving a problem in geometry would be classified by content under geometry, with the performance expectation being "mathematical reasoning" and/or "problem solving." The content and expectation categories were used in curriculum analysis, whereas the perspectives aspect of the framework was used when analyzing documents such as textbooks or curriculum guides.

CONTENTS	PERFORMANCE EXPECTATIONS
Mathematics	1. Knowing
1. Numbers	2. Using routine procedures
2. Measurement	3. Investigating and problem solving
3. Geometry	4. Mathematical reasoning
4. Proportionality	5. Communicating
5. Functions, relations and equations	6. Theorizing, analyzing and solving problems
6. Data, probability and statistics	7. Using tools, routine procedures and scientific processes
7. Elementary analysis	
Science:	8. Investigating the natural world
1. Earth sciences	
2. Life sciences	**PERSPECTIVES**
3. Physical sciences	Attitudes
4. Science, technology and mathematics	Careers
5. History of science and technology	Participation
6. Environmental issues	Increasing interest
7. Nature of science	Safety
8. Science and other disciplines	Habits of mind

FIGURE 1

Major categories of the TIMSS curriculum framework for mathematics and science from Martin and Kelly (1996, pp. 1–6).

Who Was Tested

Population 1: Students in the pair of adjacent grades containing the most 9-year-olds.

Population 2: Students in the pair of adjacent grades containing the most 13-year-olds.

Population 3: Students in their final year of secondary school, regardless of age.

Data Collection

TIMSS brought a variety of different and complementary research methods to bear on the important education questions posed in the study. Five different instruments were used: examinations, questionnaires, curriculum content analyses, videotapes of classroom instruction, and case studies of policy topics. Table 3 presents details on the instruments used in the study.

Rigorous Quality Control

The entire assessment process was scrutinized by international technical review committees to ensure its adherence to established standards. An international curriculum analysis was carried out prior to the development of the assessments to ensure that the tests reflected the mathematics and

TABLE 3
The Instruments Used for TIMSS Population 2 Age Group Survey

Survey Instrument	Purpose of Instrument	Who Had to Fill in Each Instrument
Test booklet 1–8	To distribute 135 science questions and 151 mathematics questions to assess students' knowledge, ability and understanding	One-eighth of the students in each sampled class filled in each of the 8 test booklets
Student questionnaires	Students' perceptions about mathematics and science and about the conditions which influence learning in these subjects	All students in the sampled class who wrote a TIMSS test.
Mathematics teacher's questionnaire	Information about teaching conditions for mathematics in schools.	The mathematics teacher of the sampled class.
Science teacher's questionnaire	Information about teaching conditions for science in schools.	The science teacher of the sampled class.
Principal's questionnaire	Information about the general teaching conditions.	The principal of each sampled school.

science curricula of the variety of TIMSS countries and did not overemphasize what is taught in only a few. International monitors carefully checked the test translations and visited many classrooms while the tests were being administered in each of the 41 countries to make sure that the instructions were properly followed.

The Israeli matriculation examination has been described. Four more countries will be introduced: the United States, the United Kingdom, France, and Germany. Readers who are curious can find more interesting information in the book *Examining the Examinations* related to seven countries: the United States, the United Kingdom, Sweden, France, Germany, Japan, and Israel (Britton & Raizen 1996).

United States

Two major national assessment operations have been employed in the United States: (1) NAEP, the National Assessment of Educational Progress, and (2) tests distributed by commercial publishers as part of their K–12 assessment packages. In both tools the predominant question format has been multiple choice.

National Assessment of Educational Progress

The NAEP was established in 1969 to serve as a barometer of the nation's educational progress by periodic assessment. Currently NAEP assesses students in grades 4, 8, and 12, using representative samples on a 4-year cycle. NAEP assessment results are used primarily to monitor the status of educational progress in the country as a whole. Occasionally and increasingly they are used for other purposes, such as a source for developing new national level indicators of student achievement. Since 1990, 33 states have been provided with data of their own students' performance so that they can monitor better their own schools and assist in making policy decisions.

Recently, first steps have been taken toward using more free-response items as well as higher order thinking skills assessment techniques (Blumberg et al., 1986). This is a very desirable initiative that will significantly raise the benefits that may be derived from NAEP.

Commercially Developed Science Assessment in the United States

These tests are developed by measurement experts assisted by teachers. The most popular science tests are the Comprehensive Test of Basic Skills (CTBS), the Iowa Test of Basic Skills (ITBS), and the Iowa Test of Educational Development (ITED). These commercial tests have the advantages and disadvantages of using multiple-choice items.

Schools use nationally normed tests for a variety of purposes, the main ones being to assist teachers in monitoring student progress, determine student placements, monitor and evaluate instructional programs, and establish accountability. As a tool for assisting instruction these tests tend to be of little or no value (Hudson, 1990, p. 71).

Further details on science examinations in the United States may be found in Hawkins, Gandel, and Britton (1996). Some sources related to SISS and TIMSS are cited in the Bibliography.

United Kingdom

Britain is known as one of the most developed countries in educational assessment. Even in times and places wherein the headmaster of the school was free to make all pedagogical decisions, along with SB assessment an examination system has been developed, consisting of "boards of examinations" that were established to produce end-of-school tests in all school subjects. These independent examination boards have been responsible for the quality and adequacy of examinations such as the O level (ordinary) and A level (advanced).

The boards recruit the experts who determine the structure of the tests and actually write them. The Ministry of Education prescribes the curriculum, so the intended is national. Usually chief inspectors, subject matter specialists (e.g., scientists), and teachers are among the authors of the tests. A pass grade in three subjects at A level is required for admission to universities. In 1992, 25% of the age cohort passed at least one A level examination (Stevenson et al., 1994). The majority of students take examinations for the General Certificate of Secondary Education. Those intending to continue their academic studies are expected to earn a grade not lower than C. More details on external examinations in the United Kingdom may be found in Hawkins et al. (1996).

Assessment of Performance Unit (APU)

The United Kingdom has occupied a very special position regarding educational reforms. In the early 1960s the United Kingdom joined the United States in the massive reforms of science and mathematics education. Along with the Physical Science Study Committee (PSSC), Biological Science Curriculum Study (BSCS), and Chemistry Curriculum Study (CHEM) supported by the National Science Foundation (NSF) in the United States. The United Kingdom established similar projects supported by the Nuffield Foundation. In certain issues the United Kingdom has advanced more than other countries, including the United States. Two of these issues are known as STEP (Science Teacher Education Project) and APU (Assessment of Performance Units). Both projects were initiated to meet the needs of the progressive inquiry-oriented science curricula. One such need is the assessment of practical laboratory work outcomes. The APU was set up in 1975 within the Department of Education and Science (DES) "to promote the development of methods of assessing an monitoring the achievement of children in school and to identify the incidence of under-achievement."

The APU existed to provide objective information about national standards of children's' achievement at all levels of ability (Johnson, 1989, cover page). The major contribution of APU was developing and validating performance techniques and the implementation of practical tests on a national scale. The last large-scale APU science survey was in 1984, and follow-up studies were carried out in 1987 and 1989. With the introduction of the National Curriculum in Science in April 1984, the APU ceased to exist. More about the APU can be found in Black (1991) and in Doran et al. (1994, pp. 399–400).

France

The baccalaureate is awarded on the basis of performance on a set of examinations taken during the final year. This is a very high-stake examination— It is the ticket to higher education. There are two types of baccalaureate: technical and academic. About half of the age cohort receive this certificate in both types. There are two levels: brevet and lycee. Students must pass the brevet to proceed to the lycee. About 75% of the age cohort pass the brevet. Both types consist of free-response questions and no multiple choice. Since 1995 three tracks have been offered: literary (formerly called A), scientific (formerly C, D, D', and E), and economic and social science (formerly called B). Students take the baccalaureate at the end of the third year in the lycee. Most examinations are written, but some sections are oral. The examination and all that is included are the responsibility of the Ministry of National Education. Inspectors ensure that the Ministry retains final authority over the examination standards.

Each examination is developed by a committee of four teachers, assisted by the inspector, and subject specialists from universities. A student's final score is determined by taking a composite score of all the examinations. The examinations are scored regionally by teachers, under the guidance of the inspectors. Teachers may not score their own students. The scoring scale ranges from 0 to 20, with 20 being the top score. The certificate indicates how well the student did: 16 or above, very good; 14–15.9, good; 12–13.9, fairly good; 10–11.9, satisfactory (Hawkins et al., 1996).

Germany

In Germany, schooling is primarily the responsibility of each of the 16 states (Lander, in German). Compulsory education lasts 10 years. Possession of the Arbitur (matriculation) certificate is required for admission to higher education. About one-third of the age cohort earn the Arbitur. Secondary schools offer three tracks: Hauptschule—the most basic level lasting through the ninth year; the Realschule—a more advanced level lasting through the tenth year; and the gymnasium—the most rigorous academically, preparing for admission to the university. In 1992 student enrollments were Hauptschule, 32%; Realschule, 27%; Gymnasium, 28%; and comprehensive schools, 13% (Stevenson, 1994).

The majority of school teachers are responsible for developing the Arbitur examinations that will be given to their own students. The tests are sent to the Ministry of Education for approval. The Arbitur certificate is awarded based on a combination of students' grades over the last two years and their score on the examinations. Out of 840 possible points, 540 reflect course work and 300 reflect the examinations. A total score of 280 is considered passing.

Israel

Israel belongs to the large group of countries that employ a national curriculum. The matriculation (Bagrut) examination and the Israeli scoring system have already been discussed, with special emphasis on the structure of the biology Bagrut because of its uniqueness. Here some additional information on assessment in Israel is presented. In 1992 about one-half of the age cohort earned the Bagrut certificate. Students performing very well in their classes may elect to replace one external Bagrut examination with an individual in-depth research project, usually with the guidance of academic experts. After completion of the typed report, the national subject supervisor nominates an external examiner who examines the student orally, by conversation, on matters related to the project. The scores awarded by this examiner are based on the assessment of the written report and the answers in the oral. These scores are treated like other parts of the Bagrut. The Bagrut examination in each subject is developed by a Bagrut committee, appointed by the Ministry of Education and consisting of a measurement specialist, a researcher in science education, an expert in the subject matter, and a teacher elected by the national supervisor. The development of the inquiry practical laboratory test, which constitutes a component of the Bagrut in biology, requires a creative scientist who is able to devise novel tasks every year. We are fortunate to have on our staff such a biologist who devotes half of her time to the development. The biologist devotes half of her time to the development of the laboratory test and writing samples of possible answers, and a scoring key based on the Practical Test Assessment Inventory (Tamir et al., 1982). After being used in the Bagrut, all the materials that were developed are published and become curriculum resources. Close to 15 articles on SISS in Israel were published in the professional literature (see the Bibliography).

Science Education: International

The comparative nature of international studies helps to reveal and identify the meaning of differences that have emerged, for example, the distinction between nationally centralized and uncentralized educational systems. In TIMSS, the indicators of centralization were defined by those who made the decisions regarding (1) curriculum and syllabi; (2) textbooks; and (3) examinations. The data indicated that the United States is not centralized in all three populations in all three measures. Israel is centralized regarding the syllabi for all three populations, not centralized regarding textbooks in all three populations, but differs regarding examinations. In populations 1 and 2, assessment is not centralized, but in population 3 students take the matriculation examinations, which are centralized. More generally, in 31 countries the curriculum syllabi of the eighth grade are centralized, whereas in only 13 countries are the examinations not centralized.

Teachers' Autonomy

When the centrally prescribed curriculum and the Bagrut are considered together, it would appear as if teachers are heavily constrained and that very little room is left for autonomy. To some extent this is certainly true. However, both curriculum committees and the Ministry have taken a variety of steps that, in effect, provide teachers with a lot of freedom. We shall illustrate the nature of this "guided freedom"[2] using the Israeli high school biology program (IHBP) as an example.

High school biology teachers enjoy guided freedom of two kinds: (1) that built into the educational system in general, and (2) that offered particularly in biology.

Freedom Built into the System
(Not Specific to Biology)

1. There is a general Ministry guideline according to which local communities, including individual schools and their teachers, are free to follow their own chosen topics outside the prescribed syllabus for up to 25% of class time.
2. In general, schools and teachers are free to choose the textbooks and other learning materials, as long as they match the syllabus.
3. Although the requirements for the Bagrut examinations are highly specific, schools, teachers, and students still have some important opportunities for alternatives:

[2] I am indebted to Jerald Zaccharias for this term.

(a) Within the regular Bagrut requirements there are built-in choices, for example, a large list of writers and books to choose from for the Bagrut examination in literature.
(b) As already mentioned, students may substitute a Bagrut examination in one subject by an individual research project.
(c) Schools and teachers are free to design and propose "special programs." In all of these cases, the school teacher designs the examination, which is subsequently checked for quality and adequacy by a qualified inspector of the Ministry of Education.
(d) Every subject is offered in two levels, designated as High and Low. A Bagrut program can be completed by taking some subjects as High and others as Low. A High level weighs more than a Low level; the relative weight is usually 3:5 for Low and High, respectively.
(e) While in many countries, such as the United Kingdom, the final grade of a student is determined by his/her performance on the external final examinations, in Israel these examinations determine only *one half* of the final score. The other half is contributed by the teacher and reflects the student's work in grades 11 and 12 based on any criteria that individual teachers choose to employ. This kind of power contributes very significantly to teachers' autonomy.

Particular Features of the Biology Program

In addition to the general provisions for choices, described above, biology teachers and students enjoy some special opportunities that promote teachers' autonomy:

1. Curriculum patterns. Different portions of the curriculum fit different patterns.
   1.1 Prescribed topics with prescribed coverage. This part corresponds to the content of the Israeli version of *Biological Science: An Inquiry into Life* (based on the U.S. BSCS yellow version). It provides a survey of major concepts, principles, and phenomena at a rather elementary level. In addition students are expected to develop, through the study of biology, certain intellectual and manipulative inquiry skills.
   1.2 Teachers are expected to choose two out of six broad areas for in-depth study (energy transformations, reproduction, hormonal and nervous regulation, genetics, microbiology, ecology and evolution). No official texts are prescribed for these topics.
   1.3 Teachers are offered an extensive repertoire of inquiry-oriented laboratory investigations (based on practical Bagrut examinations of previous years) from which they may choose what they see fit.
   1.4 Analysis of research papers is required; however, the choice of particular papers is made by the teachers.

1.5 Identification of plants with the aid of a key is required; however, the particular plants, the particular time, the place, the instructional strategies, and even the administration of the pertinent matriculation test are determined entirely by the teachers.

1.6 Every student is required to carry out an individual ecology project that lasts over a period of several months. The choice of specific topics is usually made by the individual students. The organization, guidance, and assessment of the students' final reports is the teachers' responsibility.

2. Teachers are invited to participate in the design, administration, and assessment of the matriculation examination. Their role and involvement differs in different parts of this examination, which consists of paper and pencil as well as practical components.

2.1 Paper and pencil test. This accounts for 60% of the total matriculation score. Only a few teachers participate in the design of this test.

2.2 Plant identification test. This accounts for 5% of the total matriculation score; it is administered and assessed by the class teacher according to central prescribed guidelines.

2.3 Inquiry-oriented practical laboratory test (see Tamir, 1974). The test accounts for 20% of the total matriculation score; it is designed centrally and administered to all the examinees all over the country on the same day by the class teachers, who also assess their students' manipulative work. In addition, most teachers who teach twelfth-grade biology serve as external examiners of the Practical. The written answers are assessed like the answers of the paper and pencil tests, as described in 2.1.

2.4 The ecology project described under 1.6 also serves as a basis for an oral test that accounts for 15% of the total matriculation score. The teachers serve as external examiners in these oral tests, but they examine students from other schools, not their own. In this capacity the teachers play an important role in setting standards for this component of the curriculum. By examining students of other schools face to face, teachers learn much from each other.

Empowering Teachers

Based on the analysis of the IHBP in terms of modes of curriculum development and the roles that teachers actually play within the Israeli educational system in general, and the IHBP in particular, it may be concluded that for all practical purposes, teacher autonomy must not necessarily be associated with a noncentralistic system. If an effective dialogue is maintained between teachers, administrators, supervisors, inspectors, curriculum developers, and boards of examinations, the operational curriculum, that which is actually implemented in the classroom and experienced by the students, can greatly benefit. While teachers' autonomy may suffer a bit under circumstances similar to those that exist in the IHBP, on the average, their power and potential effectiveness increase considerably as they take advantage of the contributions of other agents in the system. Most often the kind of guided freedom described in this paper will work better than total freedom.

Differences between SISS and TIMSS

SISS took place in the mid 1980s, while TIMSS was conducted in the mid 1990s. The International Study Center of SISS was in Melbourne, Australia, whereas TIMSS' center was first in Vancouver, Canada, and later moved to Boston, Massachusetts.

Although SISS and TIMSS were similar in purpose and in certain other features (e.g., the emphasis on Opportunity to Learn [OPL], the attention given to the effects of the home on schooling and achievement), there were some differences as well. The differences are listed in Table 4. For some of the differences, references are cited. Where no reference is available, the information source is my own experience as National Research Coordinator (NRC) for both studies, as well as a member of the Subject Matter Advisory Committee.

TABLE 4
Comparing SISS and TIMSS

Feature	SISS	TIMSS
Staff and finance	Limited	Practically unlimited
Study center	Melbourne, Australia	David F. Robitaille
Study director	Malcolm Rosier	Albert Beaton
Final report	M. Rosier & J. Keeves	A. Beaton & D. Robitaille
Students' age	Population 1—10	Population 1—9
(most frequent)	Population 2—14	Population 2—13
	Population 3—17	Population 3—17
Grade level	Population 1—fifth	Population 1—fourth
(most frequent)	Population 2—ninth	Population 2—eighth
	Population 3—twelfth	Population 3—twelfth
Subject specialization	Earth science	No science, no math
in grade 12	Life science	Math, no physics
	Physical } Physics	Physics, no math
	Science } Chemistry	Both physics and math
Number of participating	21 (practical = 6)	41 (practical = 21)
countries		
Study organization	Steering	Steering
committees		Technical advisory
		Subject matter advisory
		Free response item coding
		Performance assessment
		Quality control

continued

TABLE 4 (continued)

Feature	SISS	TIMSS
Instruments used	Students, teachers, and school questionnaires	Students, teachers, and school questionnaires
Subjects and test levels	Populations 1 and 2—science test	Scientific literacy test
	Population 3—science, biology, chemistry, physics, earth science	Population 3—specialists math or physics, advanced tests
	Population 3—earth science, biology	Advanced tests
		Independent sample science literacy test
Video tapes	No classroom video tapes	Classroom video tapes prepared
Administration date	Spring 1985	Spring 1994–1995
Involvement of U.S. in study	Like other countries	Very broad and deep
Quality control by the center	No external control	Very rigorous external control
Publications	Relatively few	About 20 cited in IEA (1998)
Publicity	Weak	Strong
Impact	Limited	Substantial
Data analysis	Partially centralized	Totally centralized
Cost	SISS	TIMSS
Consulting experts	Relatively infrequent	Relatively frequent
Involvement of NSF	Some	A lot
Syllabus analysis	Not done	Done, very comprehensive
Textbook analysis	Not done	Done, very comprehensive
Special director for content analysis	None	Bill Schmidt, USA, Michigan State University
Publications	Relatively few	Relatively many
Meetings of national coordinators	One – twice a year in different countries	Twice a year in different countries
Presentations in professional conferences	Hardly seen, rarely discussed	Widely recognized, frequently discussed
Ph.D. dissertations based on the study	Eleven in the United States One in Israel	Not available yet A few in Norway

Looking at the table, one may observe that TIMSS was much larger, more formal, and, in some aspects, such as practical tests or free response items, more progressive. However, the most striking feature is the stronger emphasis on publicity and communication with educators all over the world, especially in the United States. In spite of the great number of publications by the TIMSS centers in Boston and Vancouver, the United States published about ten publications that show how the U.S. results compared with results of other countries. The United States also invested a very handsome sum of money to support a study of the curriculum. In this study, content analysis was carried out by a separate team under the guidance of the

United States at Michigan State University (Schmidt et al., 1998). Some publications of TIMSS are presented in the Bibliography.

When students are asked to respond to TIMSS tests and questionnaires, they often do not cooperate because the results do not count for determining their grades. On the other hand, high-stake external examinations, such as the A level in the United Kingdom and Arbiter in Germany, usually motivate the students to study and prepare themselves for the examination so that they pass and receive the invaluable certificate.

As already stated there are three international science studies that served as data sources for this chapter: SISS, TIMSS, and ETL. A good description of TIMSS may be found in more than 20 publications that were written by the TIMSS staff and some affiliated researchers. Close to ten publications were written in the United States, presenting information about TIMSS from the American perspective. Other countries may use these U.S. publications as a model for writing their own reports.

SISS is described in detail by Rosier and Keeves (1991). Some publications about SISS are Doran and Jacobson (1991), Doran and Tamir (1992), Jacobson et al. (1987), and Jacobson et al. (1988). A special issue of the *International Journal of Educational Research* (1991, 15:567–568) was devoted to SISS. Several countries contributed articles to that issue. Many countries published reports about SISS. Very few articles about SISS have been published in journals, with two exceptions: one in Israel and one in the United States (see the Bibliography). Furthermore, a whole issue of *Studies in Educational Evaluation* (SEE) was devoted to SISS practical tests (Doran & Tamir, 1997).

Selected findings

The findings of such a comprehensive study can be analyzed from a variety of perspectives, both in *national* and *international* contexts. As examples we shall present findings related to eighth grade, published by the U.S. Department of Education (1997, pp. 11–17).

U.S. *National Context*
- Eighth-grade students of different ability levels are typically divided into different classrooms in the United States (p. 14).
- Gender differences found in achievement of eighth graders are usually in favor of boys.

Practically all the findings reported in the U.S. Department of Education publications are presented in an international context. Following are some examples:

U.S. *International Context*
- In science our eighth-grade students score above the international average of 41 TIMSS countries (p. 11).

- The number of topics in the U.S. eighth-grade science curricula is similar to that of other countries (p. 12).
- U.S. teachers have more college education than their colleagues in all but a few TIMSS countries (p. 13).
- U.S. teachers do not receive as much support when they enter the teaching profession as their German and Japanese colleagues do (p. 13).
- U.S. eighth graders spend more hours per year in mathematics and science classes than German or Japanese students (p. 12).

What are the implications of these findings?

The division of students with different abilities to different classes may have negative effects. The United States should attempt to employ a process that has proved successful in teaching mixed ability classes in other countries, such as Japan and Israel. The superior achievement of eighth-grade U.S. students shows how it was possible to make significant progress in science achievements in the middle schools.

It is satisfying to find out that the U.S. teachers learn more than teachers in other developed countries such as Japan or Germany. However, just more may not be enough. The level and quality of teacher education will rely on what they learn and how they learn it, as well as in the support that they get in their first and second years of teaching. The finding that U.S. eighth graders spend more hours per year than their counterparts in other countries in the study of mathematics and science may be an indication that the "what and how" of U.S. teacher education should be checked.

CONCLUSIONS

One characteristic of our modern technology-based, computerized society is a tremendous mobility, which tends to make a small world. Yet, even though differences diminish and distances shrink, we can still learn much by preparing, sharing, and collaborating. Student assessment, like many other human enterprises, has a mix of similar as well as different attributes. There is always something building with classrooms—the building may be very big or very small, but in each classroom you will find a chalkboard, a teacher's desk, and student desks. The teacher and students quickly develop a routine for their activities and this routine is quite similar for many different classes. Yet, as we try to sum up the status of student assessment in the various countries, we find vast differences in certain aspects. The diversity is the justification for conducting national and international comparative studies so that we may learn from the experiences of other society and other countries.

Student assessment in each country reflects the habits and values of its citizens. Many problems are being handled in different ways. Often the solutions proposed in one school system will be different from those proposed in other countries. In this paper the important area of student assessment has been discussed. The opportunities to benefit from national and international assessments are many. This paper attempts to highlight these opportunities, thereby making some contributions to the improvement of science education.

References

Beaton, A. E., Martin, M. O., Mullis, I. V. S., Gonzales, C. J., Smith, T. A., & Kelly, D. L. (1996). *Science achievement in the middle school years*. IEA Third International Mathematics and Science Study, Chestnut Hill MA, Boston College, Boston.

Black, P. (1991). APU science: The past and the future. *School Science Review, 72*, 13–26.

Blumberg, F., Epstein, M., Macdonald, W. P., & Mullis, I. (1986). *A pilot study of higher order thinking skills assessment techniques in science and mathematics*. Princeton, NJ: National Assessment of Educational Progress.

Britton, E. (1996). Study background. In E. Britton & S. Raizen (Eds.), *Examining the examinations: An international comparison of science and mathematics examinations for college bound students*. Boston: Kluwer Academic Press.

Britton, E. D., & Raizen, S. (Eds.) (1996). *Examining the examinations: An international comparison of science and mathematics examinations for college bound students* (pp. 1–16). Boston: Kluwer Academic Press.

Britton, E. D., Dossey, J., Dwain, E. L., Gisselberg, K., Hawkins, S., Raizen, S., & Tamir, P. (1996). Comparing examinations across subjects and countries. In E. Britton & S. Raizen (Eds.), *Examining the examinations: An international comparison of science and mathematics examinations for college bound students*. Boston: Kluwer Academic Press.

Doran, R. L., Laurenz, F., & Helgeson, S. (1994). Research on assessment in science. In D. Gabel (Ed.), *Handbook of research in science learning and teaching* (pp. 388–442). New York: Macmillan.

Gisselberg, K. (1996). Physics examination. In E. Britton & S. Raizen (Eds.), *Examining the examinations: An international comparison of science and mathematics examinations for college bound students* (pp. 121–163). Boston: Kluwer Academic Press.

Haertal, E. H. (1990). Form and function in assessing science. In A. D. Champagne, B. L. Lovitz, & B. J. Calinger (Eds.), *Assessment in the service of instruction* (pp. 15–28). Washington, DC: The American Association for the Advancement of Science (AAAS).

Hawkins, S., Gandel, M., & Britton, E. (1996). Examination systems in seven countries. In E. Britton & S. Raizen (Eds.), *Examining the examinations: An international comparison of science and mathematics examinations for college bound students*. Boston: Kluwer Academic Press.

Hudson, L. (1990). National initiatives in assessing science education. In A. D. Champagne, B. L. Lovitz, & B. J. Calinger (Eds.), *Assessment in the service of instruction* (pp. 61–80). Washington, DC: The American Association for the Advancement of Science (AAAS).

Johnson, S. (1989). *National assessment: The APU science approach*. London: Department of Education and Science.

Lazarowitz, R., & Tamir, P. (1994). Research on using laboratory instruction. In D. Gabel (Ed.), *Handbook of research in science learning and teaching*. New York: Macmillan.

Martin, M. O., & Kelly, D. L. (Eds.) (1996). *Third international mathematics and science study: Technical report* (Vol. 1). Boston: Boston College.

Orpwood, G. O., & Garden R. L. (1998). *Assessing mathematics and science literacy*. Vancouver: Pacific Educational Press.

Rosier, M. J., & Keeves, J. P. (Eds.) (1991). *The IEA study of sciences; Science education and curricula in twenty-three countries*. Oxford, UK: Pergamon.

Stevenson, H., et al. (1994). *International comparisons of entrance and exit examinations: Japan, United Kingdom, France and Germany*. Draft. Washington, DC: U.S. Department of Education.

Tamir, P. (1974). An inquiry oriented laboratory examination. *Journal of Educational Measurement, 11*, 25–33.

Tamir, P. (1977). Questioning practices in the teaching of high school biology in Israel. *Journal of Curriculum Studies*, 9, 145–156.

Tamir, P. (1985). The Israeli Bagrut examination in biology revisited. *Journal of Research in Science Teaching*, 22, 31–40.

Tamir, P. (1996a). Biology examinations. In E. Britton & S. Raizen (Eds.), *Examining the examinations: An international comparison of science and mathematics examinations for college bound students.* Boston: Kluwer Academic Press.

Tamir, P. (1996b). Science assessment. In M. Birenbaum & J. R. C. Dochy (Eds.), *Alternatives in assessment of achievements, learning processes and prior knowledge* (pp. 93–130). Boston: Kluwer Academic Press.

Tamir, P. (1997). Assessment and evaluation in science education: Students, teachers and programs. In B. Fraser and K. Tobin (Eds.), *International handbook of science education* (pp. 751–991). Boston: Kluwer Academic Press.

Tamir, P., Nussinovitz, R., & Friedler, Y. (1982). The design and use of Practical Tests Assessment Inventory. *Journal of Biological Education*, 16, 42–50.

Welch, W. W., Walberg, H. D., & Fraser, B. (1986). Predicting elementary science learning using national assessment data. *Journal of Research in Science Teaching*, 23, 699–706.

Bibliography

United States Publications about TIMSS

Department of Education (1997). *Attaining excellence: Introduction to TIMSS, the third international mathematics and science study.*

Department of Education (1997). *Attaining excellence: Guidebook to examine school curricula.*

Department of Education (1998). *Pursuing excellence: A study of U.S. eighth grade mathematics and science teaching, learning, curriculum and achievement in an international context.*

Office of Educational Research and Improvement, U.S. Department of Education (1997). *Pursuing excellence: A study of U.S. fourth grade mathematics and science achievement.*

Schmidt, W. H., & Macnight, C. (1995) Surveying educational opportunities in mathematics and science: An international perspective. *Educational Evaluation and Policy Analysis*, 17, 337–353.

Schmidt, W. H., & 12 co-authors (1998). *Eighth grade tests. Facing the consequences: Using TIMSS for a closer look at mathematics and science education* Boston: Kluwer Academic Press.

SISS in Israel: Publications in Educational Journals

Doran, R., & Tamir, P. (1992). Results of practical skills testing. *Studies in Educational Evaluation*, 18, 302–318.

Doran, R., Tamir, P., & Bathory, Z. (1992). Conditions for teaching laboratory practical skills. *Studies in Educational Evaluation*, 18, 291–300.

Kay, C., Rosier, M., & Tamir, P. (1992). Instruments and supporting materials for practical skills testing in science. *Studies in Educational Evaluation*, 18, 319–354.

Tamir, P. (1987) Some factors which affect science achievement of high school seniors in Israel. *Research in Science and Technological Education*, 5, 69–92.

Tamir, P. (1991). Factors associated with acquisition of functional knowledge and understanding of science. *Research in Science and Technological Education*, 9, 17–38.

Tamir, P. (1991). Selected findings of the Second International Science Study in Israel. *International Journal of Educational Research*, 15, 351–361.

Tamir, P. (1992). Ethnic origin, socioeconomic status and science learning outcomes of high school students in Israel. *Curriculum and Teaching*, 7, 27–35.

Tamir, P. (1994). Israeli students' conceptions of science and views about the scientific enterprise. *Research in Science and Technological Education*, 12, 99–116.

Tamir, P., & Doran, R. (1992). Conclusions and discussion of findings related to practical skills testing in science. *Studies in Educational Evaluation*, 18, 393–408.

Tamir, P., & Doran, R. (1992). Scoring guidelines. *Studies in Educational Evaluation*, 18, 355–363.

Tamir, P., Doran, R., & Chye, O. Y. (1992). Practical skills testing in science. *Studies in Educational Evaluation*, 18, 263–275.

Tamir, P., Doran, R., Kojima, S., & Bathory, Z. (1992). Procedures used in practical skills testing in science. *Studies in Educational Evaluation*, 18, 277–290.

Vari, P., Tamir, P., Miyake, M., Jn-Jae, I., Chye, O. Y., Jacobson, W., Doran, R., & Miller, J. (1992). Profile of educational systems of countries participating in the practical skills testing. *Studies in Educational Evaluation*, 18, 301–318.

SISS Publications: United States

Doran, R. L., & Jacobson, W. J. (1991). Science achievement in the United States and sixteen other countries. In S. K. Magruder, I. M. Rosenfeld, P. A. Rubba, E. W. Miller, & R. F. Shmalz (Eds.). *Science education in the United States: Issues, crises and priorities*. Eastern Pennsylvania Academy of Sciences.

Doran, R. L., & Tamir, P. (1992). An international assessment of science process skills. *Studies in Educational Evaluation*, 18, 263–406.

Farko, A., Jacobson, W. J., & Doran, R. L. (1991). *Advanced science student performance*. Washington, DC: National Science Teachers Association.

Humrich, E. (1992). *Sex differences in science attributes and achievement*. Washington, DC: National Science Teachers Association.

IEA (1988). *Science achievement in seventeen countries: A preliminary report*. New York: Pergamon.

Jacobson, W. J., Doran, R. L., Chang, E., Humrich, E., & Keeves, J. P. (1987). *The second IEA science study*. New York: Teachers College, Columbia University.

Jacobson, W. J., & Doran, R. L. (1988). *Science achievement in the United States and sixteen countries*. Washington, DC: National Science Teachers Association.

Jacobson, W. J., Doran, R. L., Humrich, E., & Kanis, I. (1988). *International science report card*. New York: Teachers College, Columbia University.

Kanis, I., Doran, R. L., & Jacobson, W. J. (1990). *Assessing science process laboratory skills at the elementary and middle/junior high levels*. Washington, DC: National Science Teachers Association.

chapter 13

On the Psychometrics of Assessing Science Understanding

RICHARD J. SHAVELSON AND MARIA ARACELI RUIZ-PRIMO

Stanford University

Quite remarkably, the National Academy of Sciences' science education standards (National Research Council, 1996) address not only content and teaching, but also assessment. Equally remarkable, the standards include a wide range of assessments. Some of these assessments have a long history of psychometric research (e.g., pencil and paper "objective" tests), others are currently being researched intensively (e.g., performance assessment), and still others are more speculative (e.g., portfolios, interviews, observing programs, students, and teachers in classrooms). This chapter focuses on the psychometric qualities of "alternative" or "authentic" assessments of students' science understanding that fall within the currently-being-researched category.

Many of the "new" assessments include holistic tasks, in contrast to a set of stand-alone items found in multiple-choice tests. These new assessments pose a holistic problem or task, where students have to display their knowledge in a particular domain to solve the problem, by planning and carrying out the task. For example, the "Bugs" performance assessment (Shavelson, Baxter, & Pine, 1991) asks students to conduct an investigation using laboratory equipment to determine sow bugs' environmental choice behavior (e.g., choice of light or dark environment). Moreover, students are asked to provide extended responses to the task. They might, for example, be asked to write down the procedures that they used to conduct the investigation, what they found out in the investigation, and what they concluded from the findings. The students' performance is evaluated and scored by trained judges.[1] And students might perform the investigation with sow bugs and equipment, or on a computer with software that simulates the actual investigation (e.g., Baxter & Shavelson, 1994).

Needless to say, what counts as a science achievement test today varies far more than in the past when the almost sole emphasis was on pencil-and-paper, "objective" tests. The "technology" that had been developed for evaluating the quality of multiple-choice and short-answer tests—classical reliability and validity theory—is no longer up to the challenge of evaluating these more complex tests.

The purpose of this chapter is to present and exemplify methods for examining the reliability and validity of test scores that incorporate but go beyond what was standard practice in the past. The methods presented here are used to evaluate alternative assessments in large-scale (e. g., statewide) testing programs, where score interpretations and their potential consequences are at issue.[2] The methods can also be applied to classroom assessments, although more relaxed psychometric criteria are appropriate when teachers integrate test information with other information available to them.

We begin by presenting a sampling framework for evaluating the wide range of tests being employed in science education today. We then sketch a theory for modeling this sampling framework, *generalizability theory*, and show how it goes beyond classical reliability theory to model the complexity of alternative assessments. Next we sketch an expanded theory of validity, one that takes into account cognitive process interpretations of test scores as well as overt performance interpretations. We conclude the chapter with applications of these "psychometric" methods to concept-map and performance-assessment scores.

SAMPLING FRAMEWORK FOR EVALUATING ALTERNATIVE SCIENCE ACHIEVEMENT TESTS

The framework views tests as samples of student behavior. Inferences are made from this sample to a "universe" of behavior of interest. From this perspective, a score assigned to a student is but one possible sample from a

---

[1] To be sure, qualitative judgments need not be reduced to a single score or a set of scores. Such clinical judgments are perfectly appropriate for the teachers in everyday contact with their students. But these judgments should not be mistaken for formal measurement. Our focus in this chapter is on the latter, when the teacher (or other trained rater) observes and evaluates the performance of her or his students and resists the temptation to teach at that teachable moment in order to learn something perhaps not heretofore believed about her or his students.

[2] Equity, fairness, and bias issues are relevant but go beyond the scope of the chapter.

large domain of possible scores that student might have received if a different sample of assessment tasks were included, if a different set of judges evaluated her performance, and the like. A sampling framework is constructed by identifying the *facets* that characterize the measurement. Facets include the *task* presented, the *occasion* of measurement, the *raters* who judged performance, and so forth. This means that for a particular type of assessment, the relevant measurment facets may vary. For example, the rater facet is irrelevant for multiple-choice tests, but the task, occasion, and method facets are relevant. For other assessments, other facets should be included.

To exemplify the idea of a sampling framework, we present the framework for evaluating performance assessments. We begin with a definition of a performance assessment. A performance assessment is a set of goal-oriented science *tasks* with an associated format for responses and a scoring system. The task is performed by a student on a particular *occasion* and is scored by an expert *judge*. The *method* for mediating the task might be hands-on (e.g., students manipulating equipment), computer simulated, or pencil-and-paper. The "Bugs" performance assessment, for example, contains three concrete, goal-oriented tasks in which students conduct an investigation to see if sow bugs gravitate to (a) wet or dry environments, (b) dark or light environments, and (c) environments defined by a factorial combination of the first two tasks. The performance assessment is usually given on a particular occasion (e.g., second week in May) and scored by expert judges who take into account the procedures used to carry out the task as well as the final product. The *method* for assessing performance might be "hands on" with responses recorded by an observer or written in a notebook, with a computer simulation, or possibly with pencil-and-paper (short answer or multiple choice)

The *tasks* in an assessment are assumed to be a representative sample of the universe of possible tasks defined by the substantive and methodological content in a subject domain. This is easily said, and even possible to implement, at least approximately, when the domain is a concrete curriculum such as the National Science Resource Center's *Science and Technology for Children* (see Hein & Price [1994] for a description).[3] Task sampling becomes more difficult at the state level. A curriculum framework such as California's *Science Framework for California Public Schools, Kindergarten through Grade Twelve* serves as the domain specification and the curriculum itself varies from one school or classroom to another (but see Baxter, Shavelson, Herman, Brown, & Valadez, 1993). The task sampling problems magnify at the national level when a curriculum framework is created solely for the purpose of constructing a test, such as the National Assessment of Educational Progress, and not for a national curriculum.

---

[3] Similarly in military job performance measurement, domain sampling is possible, approximately, because job tasks are enumerated in doctrine (Wigdor & Green, 1991).

Occasions are assumed to be sampled from a universe of all possible occasions on which a decision-maker would be equally willing to accept a score on the test. Typically science tests are given on only one occasion so that the effect of occasion sampling is confounded with other sources of variation in test scores, especially task sampling (Shavelson, Ruiz-Primo, & Wiley, 1999).

Raters are assumed to be a representative sample of all possible individuals who could be trained to score the test reliably, if the test is not an "objective" test. Rater sampling is not difficult to implement, but it is costly due to training, scoring, recalibration time, and human resource needs.

Finally, *methods* are sampled from all permissible measurement methods that a decision-maker would be equally willing to interpret as bearing on a student's achievement. Many large-scale assessments focus on a very narrow range of methods—mostly multiple-choice items—in large part because of costs and the *belief* that, in the end, overall student achievement does not depend on the method used to measure performance.

A student's science test performance, then, can be viewed as a *sample* of behavior drawn from a complex universe defined by a combination of all possible tasks, occasions, raters and measurement methods. Student performance may vary across different samples of tasks, raters, occasions, or methods. Traditionally, variation due to task, occasion, and rater sampling have been thought of as sources of unreliability in a measurement (cf. Shavelson, Baxter, & Gao, 1993; Shavelson, Webb, & Rowley, 1989). In contrast, the incorporation of measurement method into the specification of the universe from which sampling occurs, moves beyond reliability theory into a sampling theory of validity (Kane, 1982; see also Baxter & Shavelson, 1994). When performance varies from one task sample to another, or from one occasion to another, or from one rater to another, we speak of measurement error due to sampling variability. When performance varies from one measurement method to another, we speak of the lack of convergent validity due to method–sampling variability.

PSYCHOMETRIC APPROACHES TO MODELING SCIENCE ACHIEVEMENT SCORES

From a sampling perspective, then, a test score, broadly defined, is but one of many possible samples of behavior that might be drawn from a large domain defined by a particular combination of facets—for example, a *task*, an *occasion*, a *rater*, and a measurement *method*. Note that for any particular type of achievement test, some subset of these facets may define the sample of behavior collected. Once a test score is conceived of as a sample of performance from a complex universe, both classical reliability theory and generalizability theory can be brought to bear on the score's technical quality.

Classical Reliability Theory

Reliability theory evaluates an achievement-test score one facet at a time. The variation in an individual's relative standing among his or her peers from one *task* or test item to another is evaluated by correlating scores among tasks. The average intertask or interitem correlation is adjusted with the Spearman–Brown prophecy formula to estimate the overall reliability of the test. This kind of reliability is called *internal-consistency reliability* or "Cronbach's alpha."

The variation in an individual's relative standing on a test among his or her peers from one occasion to the next is evaluated by correlating total test scores (summing/averaging over tasks or items). This correlation is called *test–retest reliability*.

When two samples of tasks from the same domain are given to students, variation in an individual's relative standing among peers across the samples, viz. "test-forms," is evaluated by correlating total scores from the two (or more) separate forms. This correlation is called *parallel-forms* or *equivalent-forms* reliability.

Finally, when two judges ("raters") evaluate students' performance, variation in an individual's relative standing across the sample of raters is indexed by correlating the first rater's scores with the second rater's scores (and so on for more than 2 raters). This correlation coefficient is called *inter-rater* reliability.

Generalizability Theory

In contrast to classical reliability theory, generalizability (G) theory evaluates the quality of a test score, taking all facets (e.g., task, occasion, rater) into consideration *simultaneously* (Cronbach, Gleser, Nanda, & Rajaratnam, 1972). Moreover, G theory incorporates method sampling variability into an expanded framework that includes some aspects of validity (Kane, 1982). G theory focuses on the magnitude of sampling variability due to tasks, raters, and so forth, and their combinations, and provides statistical estimates of the magnitude of each source of measurement error. The statistical estimates of sampling variability due to each facet of a test, and their combinations ("interactions") are called variance components. These variance components can be combined to estimate a standard error of measurement for relative decisions (rank-ordering students) and absolute decisions (e.g., describing levels of student performance). In addition, G theory provides a summary coefficient reflecting the "reliability" of generalizing from a sample score to the much larger universe of interest (e.g., the score achieved over all possible tasks, occasions, and raters) called a *generalizability coefficient*.

From a generalizability perspective, sampling variability due to raters, for example, speaks to a traditional concern about the viability of judging complex performance in an assessment—interrater reliability (cf. Fitzpatrick &

Morrison, 1971). Initially, with constructed response tests (any test where the answer is provided by the student, not selected from a set of alternatives), greatest concern was attached to rater sampling variability: Complex behavior was assumed to be too difficult to judge either in real time or from a written record. Recent research is quite clear on this issue: Raters can be trained to evaluate complex performance reliably (e.g., Shavelson, Baxter & Gao, 1993). Nevertheless, not all individuals can be trained to score performance consistently and raters must be continually checked and recalibrated.

Sampling variability due to tasks speaks to the complexity of the subject-matter domain. One goal of test developers has been to make "items" homogeneous to increase reliability. Within the sampling framework, task-sampling variability is dealt with not by homogenizing the tasks but by stratifying the tasks within a domain, increasing task sample size, or both (see Shavelson, Ruiz-Primo, & Wiley, 1999). The findings on task-sampling variability are remarkably consistent across diverse domains such as writing, mathematics, and science achievement (Baxter et al., 1993; Dunbar, Koretz, & Hoover, 1991; Shavelson, Baxter, & Gao, 1993): task-sampling variability is large. A large number of tasks (say 6 or more) is needed to get a reliable measure of student performance.

Sampling variability due to occasions corresponds to the classical notion of retest reliability. From a sampling perspective, the occasion facet reminds us that decision-makers are willing to generalize a student's performance on one particular occasion to many possible occasions. Occasion sampling variability is also large (Ruiz-Primo, Baxter, & Shavelson, 1993). Cronbach, Linn, Brennan, and Haertel (1997) pointed out that task and occasion sampling are often confounded, because a set of tasks (or items), typically, is given on only one occasion. One reason that task-sampling variability appears to be so large is that it also reflects the occasion confounding (Shavelson, Ruiz-Primo, & Wiley, 1999).

Finally, sampling variability due to measurement method bears on convergent validity. Large method-sampling variability indicates that measurement methods do not converge as has commonly been assumed in arguing for the cost efficiency of multiple-choice testing. We have found that method-sampling variability is sufficiently great to suggest that different methods may tap into different aspects of science achievement (Baxter & Shavelson, 1994). For example, paper-and-pencil tests appear to measure a different aspect of science achievement than do performance tests.

Item Response Theory

Item response theory (IRT) is a theory of scaling task or item scores, not a theory of measurement error (for an application in science education, see Sadler [1998] and chapter 11). IRT transforms observed scores, nonlinearly, to create scores on a latent trait that take into account not only the student's level of ability, but also the task's or item's difficulty. These transformed scores have a number of desirable properties, such as putting scores on a true interval scale and equating scores from parallel tests. Moreover, IRT can provide an estimate of the classical reliability coefficient. However, IRT cannot differentiate error in the way G theory does.[4] Consequently, since our focus is on improving the "quality" of test scores by reducing measurement error, not transforming them to a particular scale, we do not address IRT. Suffice it to say, IRT has been combined with G theory to obtain a score with well-known properties and the simultaneous estimation of the sources of measurement error (e.g., Candell & Ercikan, 1994).

A SKETCH OF GENERALIZABILITY THEORY

In our sketch of G theory, we focus on one type of test, performance assessment. Nevertheless, G theory can be and has been applied to all varieties of tests (e.g., Shavelson et al., 1989).

A science performance assessment is a set of standardized, hands-on investigations with equipment that reacts to the actions taken by the student in testing a hypothesis or solving a problem. Science performance assessment has been used in the Third International Mathematics and Science Study, in the National Assessment of Educational Progress, and in state assessment systems such as the California Learning Assessment System. In these large-scale testing programs, a student typically cycles through a series of investigations, like the "Bugs" investigation, by moving from one station to the next. Judges evaluate the student's performance on each investigation (or overall "task") and a total score for each task is assigned; each task score is usually the average of the judges' scores. A student's total performance score is the average of his or her task scores. The question raised by G theory is: *How well does the student's average score based on the sample of tasks generalize to the average score the student would have earned had the average score been based on all possible combinations of judges and tasks in the universe?*

More generally, the user of a performance score would like to know a person's average score over all combinations of conditions (all task and judge combinations in our example). This idealized datum is defined as the person's *universe score* (analogous to a person's "true score" in reliability theory). Unfortunately, this ideal datum cannot be known; it can only be estimated from a sample of tasks and a sample of judges. This is where error enters a measurement. The particular tasks and judges used in the science performance measurement are small samples from an indefinitely large universe.

---

[4] Item response theory incorporates one or another error facet (e.g., rater "main effect") in a limited way. These developments are beyond the scope of this chapter.

To identify the magnitudes of particular sources of measurement error, a study, called a *generalizability study*, is designed. The facets over which potential decision-makers might want to generalize (tasks and judges in our example) should be included. If, however, decision-makers want to generalize not just from one task or observer to another, but also from the score on one set of tasks to any other set of tasks, and differences in task might influence performance levels, multiple tasks should be incorporated into the G study. Likewise, if the decision-maker wishes to generalize from one judge's scoring to another's, and performance scores are expected to vary from judge to judge, multiple judges should be incorporated into the G study. More generally, a G study should be designed in anticipation of the multiple generalizations that different decision-makers might be interested in.

Consider an assessment system that contains three science performance assessments: (a) "Bugs"; (b) "Electric Mysteries"—using wires, batteries, and bulbs, hook up a circuit to a mystery box to discover its contents (e.g., bulb, two batteries); and (c) "Paper Towels"—using the equipment provided, determine which of three brands of paper towels soaks up the most water and which the least (Shavelson et al., 1991). In a G study of fifth and sixth graders' performance, a sample of over 300 students performed a sample of 3 tasks while being evaluated by a sample of 2 judges. The design of the G study was fully crossed with each person (student) being evaluated on all tasks by both judges (i.e., $p \times t \times j$). The students, tasks, and observers were considered representative of their corresponding populations.[5] In this case, the G study design is fully random (compare random-effects analysis of variance).

With data collected in a G study, an observed score is obtained on an individual under each combination of conditions. In our example, a student would receive a score on each task from each judge. An individual's score on any combination of a task and a judge can be decomposed into a component for the universe score, and one or more error components (facets). Then the magnitude of each source of error can be estimated.

More specifically, the performance score for a particular person on a particular task as evaluated by a particular judge can be decomposed into eight components as shown in Equation 1 of Table 1. The first component is the grand mean—a scaling device that depends on the metric used. The second component is the *object of measurement*, the student. (The object of measurement is not a source of error and therefore is not called a facet.) The remaining components, because they are samples of tasks and judges, introduce error into the measurement—error when generalizing

---

[5] Even if conditions of a facet have not been sampled randomly, the facet may be considered random if conditions not observed in the G study can be exchanged for conditions that were observed without changing the results (see Shavelson & Webb, 1981, for details).

TABLE 1

Equations for Observed and Component Scores, Measurement Error, and Summary Coefficients

No.	Equation	Description
(1)[a]	$\mathbf{X}_{ptj} = \mu$	Grand mean
	$+ \mu_p - \mu$	Person effect
	$+ \mu_t - \mu$	Task effect
	$+ \mu_j - \mu$	Judge effect
	$+ \mu_{pt} - \mu_p - \mu_t + \mu$	Person × task effect
	$+ \mu_{pj} - \mu_p - \mu_j + \mu$	Person × judge effect
	$+ \mu_{tj} - \mu_t - \mu_j + \mu$	Task × judge effect
	$+ \mathbf{X}_{ptj} - \mu_p - \mu_t - \mu_j + \mu_{pt} + \mu_{pj} + \mu_{tj} - \mu$	Residual
(2)[b]	$\sigma^2_X = \sigma^2_p + \sigma^2_t + \sigma^2_j + \sigma^2_{pt}\ \sigma^2_{pj} + \sigma^2_{tj} + \sigma^2_{residual}$	Overall score variation
(3)	$\sigma^2_{Rel} = \sigma^2_{pt}/n'_t + \sigma^2_{pj}/n'_j + \sigma^2_{res}/n'_t\ n'_j$	Relative measurement error
(4)	$\sigma^2_{Abs} = \sigma^2_t/n'_t + \sigma^2_j/n'_j + \sigma^2_{pt}/n'_t + \sigma^2_{pj}/n'_j$	Absolute measurement error
	$+ \sigma^2_{tj}/n'_t\ n'_j + \sigma^2_{res}/n'_t n'_j$	
(5)[c]	$\mathbf{E}_\rho = \sigma^2_p/\sigma^2_p + \sigma^2_{Rel}$	Generalizability coefficient
(6)	$\phi = \sigma^2_p/\sigma^2_p + \sigma^2_{Abs}$	Dependability coefficient

[a] Decomposition of observed scores where $\mathbf{X}_{ptj}$ denotes an observed score for person p on task t evaluated by judge j, and μ denotes a parameter, the mean.

[b] σ^2 denotes a parameter, the variance, and n' denotes "number of" where the number can be varied depending on alternative decision-study designs (see below). In a G study, $n' = 1$.

[c] $\mathbf{E}$ denotes the expectation operator.

from these samples to the broad universe defined by all possible tasks and judges. Hence tasks and judges are considered to be facets of measurement error.

Each component in Equation 1, other than the grand mean, may vary from one condition to another (e.g., from one task to another), and so each has a distribution. The variances associated with the components are called *variance components*. The variance of the collection of all persons, tasks, and observers included in the universe is the sum of the variance components (i.e., Equation 2 in Table 1). In other words, the variance of the observed scores can be partitioned into independent sources of variation because of the differences between persons, tasks, observers, and their interactions.

An estimate of each variance component can be obtained from the analysis of variance. The estimated variance component for person (see Equation 2) indexes universe-score variance and is analogous to reliability theory's "true-score variance." The remaining variance components represent independent sources of error variance. G theory focuses on these variance components. Their relative magnitudes provide information about sources of error influencing a science performance assessment.

TABLE 2
Estimated Variance Components for the p × t × o Design: Notebook Scores

Source of Variation	Estimate	Percentage of Total Variation
Persons	7.40	51.15
Tasks	0.25	1.74
Judge	0.00	0.00
PT	6.04	41.75
PJ	0.00	0.00
TJ	0.00	0.00
Residual (PTJ, e)	0.78	5.36

Source: Based on Sharelson, Gao, and Baxter (1996, Table 3).

The G study results for science assessment data (Shavelson, Gao, & Baxter, 1996) are presented in Table 2. The variance components were estimated with the analysis of variance (GENOVA, Brennan [1992]; the VARCOMP procedure in SAS and BMDP8V provide estimates of variance components). Because G theory focuses on the magnitude of variance components—not their statistical significance—Table 2 omits the usual F tests. Instead, standard errors for variance component estimates (though not provided in Table 2 for simplicity of exposition) give more important information than statistical tests about sampling variability of estimated variance components (e.g., Brennan, 1992; Brennan, Harris, & Hanson, 1987; Gao, Shavelson, & Baxter, 1994; Othman, 1995; Searle, Casella, & McCulloch, 1992).

The variance component for persons, the universe-score variance, represents systematic variation among students' performances and is relatively high compared to other components (7.4 or 51% of total score variation). Moreover, the variance components for the two sources of error variance—tasks and observers—differ markedly.

Task sampling introduced relatively large amounts of error into the performance measurement: 1.74% of total variation in scores was due to systematic differences in the difficulty of the tasks in the sample (the task effect, $\sigma^2_t = 0.25$), and inconsistencies in the levels of individuals' performances across the tasks accounted for 42% of the total score variation (p × t interaction, $\sigma^2_{pt} = 6.04$). The large task-sampling effect shows the importance of measuring science achievement on a variety of tasks—the more the better—to get a good fix on a student's performance.

In sharp contrast, the sampling of judges did not influence the performance measurement. All of the effects due to judges were negligible. Judges used the same part of the scale (judge effect, $\sigma^2_j = 0.0$) and rank ordered students' performance similarly (p × j interaction, $\sigma^2_{pj} = 0.0$). And the zero task × judge interaction component ($\sigma^2_{tj} = 0.00$) indicates that judges were consistent in their evaluation of the relative performance difficulty of the 3 tasks.

One implication of the small judge-sampling effect is that future studies might save money and time by using a single judge (rater). Another implication of the small effect is that different judges could evaluate the performance of different students without jeopardizing the findings, thereby reducing data collection time.

Finally, the residual that includes the person × task × judge interaction confounded with other sources of unexplained score variation such as occasion ($\sigma^2_{res} = \sigma^2_{ptj,e} = 0.78$) was small. This indicates that the G study design accounted for the major sources of measurement error.

Relative and Absolute Decisions

G theory recognizes that the decision-maker might want to make two distinct types of decisions based on a performance measurement. The first, called a *relative decision*, concerns the rank ordering of individuals. When correlations between assessment scores are estimated, the consistency of rank ordering individuals on each score is important. Or when the percentile rank of an individual is determined, accurately placing an individual at the 70th percentile in the population depends on the consistency of rank ordering people.

When a decision-maker wants to know the *level* of a student's performance, regardless of the performance of the student's peers, this type of decision is called an *absolute decision*. For example, knowing that the level of an individual's science achievement is at the 90th percentile is not enough; if everyone in the population has little knowledge in a subject domain, receiving a score at a high percentile would not indicate high achievement in an absolute sense. [The Third International Mathematics and Science Study (e.g., Beaton et al. 1996) showed that a student in one country achieved at the 90th percentile in that country but also scored below the mean of students in another country!] Other common examples of absolute decisions from everyday life involve written driving tests (number of correct responses). Passing the test depends on the level of performance, not on the rank order among a group of individuals. As might be expected, the consistency of scores may not be the same for relative and absolute decisions. For example, a person could score at the same rank, but also show different absolute levels of performance from one occasion to another.

Measurement Error

The definition of measurement error depends on the type of decision to be made. For relative decisions, the error consists of all variance components that affect the relative standing of individuals, except for universe-score variance. For the fully crossed performance-assessment study, error variance includes all interactions with person: $p \times t$, $p \times j$, and $p \times t \times j$, e or residual (see Equation 3 in Table 1). The variance components that do not enter error variance for relative decisions are those for the main effects of task and judge, and the interaction $t \times j$. In crossed designs, the effects of task, observer, and their interaction are the same (constant) for all persons and thus do not influence the rank ordering of students. For example, the task variance component in Table 2 suggests that the average performance level across persons is slightly higher for some tasks than others; that is, some tasks were easier than others. Because all persons respond to the same tasks in a crossed design, however, the difference in mean scores across tasks does not affect the rank ordering of people.

For absolute decisions, the error variance consists of all variance components except that for universe scores (see Equation 4 in Table 1). The error variance for absolute decisions reflects differences in mean scores across tasks and judges as well as disagreements about the ranking of persons. When a decision-maker is concerned with the absolute level of performance, the variance components associated with the effects of task, observer, and their interaction are included in the definition of error. The particular task sample (e.g., easy or hard) and the particular judge sample (e.g., lenient or stringent observers) will affect the *level* of a student's performance.

Estimation of Generalizability and Dependability Coefficients

Although G theory stresses the importance of variance components and measurement error, it provides a *generalizability coefficient* analogous to reliability theory's reliability coefficient—namely, true-score variance divided by observed-score variance: $\sigma^2_{True}/\sigma^2_{Observed}$. The G coefficient is defined as the universe-score variance divided by the expected observed-score variance (Equation 5 in Table 1). G theory also provides a *dependability coefficient* that is analogous to classical test theory's criterion-reference reliability coefficient. The dependability coefficient is defined in Equation 6 in Table 1. Both coefficients range from 0 to 1 and, like the reliability coefficient, their magnitude is influenced by variation among scores and the number of observations made. As the number of observations increases, error variance decreases, and the coefficients increase.

To estimate a G coefficient, the decision-maker specifies a set of facets over which she or he is willing to generalize (see below). Suppose a legislator were willing to use 3 tasks and 2 judges as in the example G study to examine students' performance. In this case, the G coefficient would be 0.78 (see Table 3). This indicates that 78% of the expected observed score variance is accounted for by systematic, consistent differences in students' performances.

TABLE 3
Generalizability Study and Some Alternative Decision Studies for Performance Assessments

Source of Variation	$\hat{\sigma}^2$	G Study $n'_t = 1$ $n'_j = 1$	D Studies $n'_t = 2$ $n'_j = 1$	$n'_t = 1$ $n'_j = 2$	$n'_t = 3$ $n'_j = 2$
Person	$\hat{\sigma}^2_p$	7.40	7.40	7.40	7.40
Task	$\hat{\sigma}^2_t$	0.25	0.13	0.25	0.08
Judge	$\hat{\sigma}^2_j$	0.00	0.00	0.00	0.00
PT	$\hat{\sigma}^2_{pt}$	6.04	3.02	6.04	2.01
PJ	$\hat{\sigma}^2_{pj}$	0.00	0.00	0.00	0.00
TJ	$\hat{\sigma}^2_{tj}$	0.00	0.00	0.00	0.00
Residual	$\hat{\sigma}^2_{ptj,e}$	0.78	0.39	0.39	0.13
Relative error	$\hat{\sigma}^2_{rel}$	14.22	10.81	13.83	9.54
	$\hat{\sigma}^2_{abs}$	14.47	10.94	14.08	9.62
Coefficients					
Generalizability	$\hat{\rho}^2$	.52	.68	.54	.78
Dependability	$\hat{\phi}$	.51	.68	.53	.77

Generalizability and Decision Studies

G theory enables the decision-maker to pinpoint sources of measurement error (e.g., due to tasks, judges, or both) and to improve the measurement by increasing (or decreasing) the appropriate number of observations accordingly, so that error "averages out." The science assessment, then, might be carried out with a large sample of students, and the number of tasks and judges needed to produce consistent estimates of the level of students' performance—the design of this decision study—would be determined from the G study. That is, the variance components from the G study would be used to determine the major sources of measurement error and the number of tasks and judges needed in the decision study to obtain generalizable measures of performance. Hence, the results of the G study are used to determine the best possible design for the D study.

Table 3, based on the science assessment study (Shavelson et al., 1996), presents variance components and generalizability and dependability coefficients for different number of tasks and judges—that is, different possible D studies. As expected, increasing the number of judges from 1 to 2 has almost no influence on the variance components or coefficients associated with judges. Simply put, variation among judges does not contribute error to the measurement. Increasing the number of tasks, however, has a large impact. With 3 tasks, a G coefficient of 0.78 is achieved. Since the task and rater main effects were negligible, the dependability coefficient is about as high: .78.

In some cases, the decision-maker does not want to generalize beyond the conditions of a facet sampled in the G study. This facet, then, is called a *fixed facet*. For example, an achievement test might consist of 2 physics tasks,

2 chemistry tasks, and 2 biology tasks. While tasks may be randomly sampled (at least in an exchangeability sense, see footnote 4), the subject-matter domain might reasonably be considered to be fixed. Hence, subject matter is a fixed facet. Depending on the results of the G study, further analyses could average over the conditions of the fixed facet or treat the conditions (physics, chemistry, and biology in the example) separately (for details, see Shavelson and Webb, 1981).

Validity of Proposed Interpretations of Assessment Scores

Validity refers, in large part, to the empirical and logical grounds for claiming that a proposed interpretation of a test score is warranted against alternative interpretations and their consequences. Validation of a proposed test-score interpretation is driven by a conceptual framework that underlies the test score—that is, test scores don't just happen, they arise from some conception or construct, explicit or implicit. For example, performance assessments are posited to tap into both propositional (declarative) knowledge (knowing that something is true) and procedural knowledge (knowing how to do something like conducting a comparative experiment) (Shavelson & Ruiz-Primo, 1999). Proposed interpretations, not tests, are validated. A discussion of validity theory is beyond the scope of this chapter (see especially Cronbach, 1971, 1984; Messick, 1989, 1994, 1995). In our research on alternative assessments, we have used four different techniques for examining proposed test-score interpretations: convergent validity, expert–novice comparisons, cognitive analyses, and task quality analyses.

Convergence of Measurement Methods

In G theory, we include a *method* facet in the design of a G study in order to study convergence. When we speak of sampling variability due to method, we refer to the convergence of different methods on similar scores for each student. Of particular interest, then, is the *person × method* variance component. If a student's relative performance is roughly constant across different measurement methods, the variance component will be negligible and we have evidence of convergence. It doesn't matter which method the student receives in a test, his or her performance relative to peers will be about the same. If, however, the p × m component is large, measurement method does matter. The particular method used on the test could advantage or disadvantage the student, depending on which method is sampled.

Expert–Novice Comparison

Expert–novice or instructed/uninstructed comparisons address the question of whether the proposed interpretation of a test score can be supported empirically. Assuming that the assessment taps an important aspect of propositional and/or procedural knowledge, experts in the domain should perform better than novices. The expectation is that if the assessment is measuring what it is intended to measure, experts should differ from novices in expected ways. For example, one characteristic of expertise is well-structured knowledge. Consequently, we should expect experts to demonstrate more highly structured, accurate knowledge on an assessment of knowledge structure than novices.

Cognitive Analyses

Most interpretations of test scores on alternative assessments include claims about the cognitive processes and declarative and/or procedural knowledge involved in performing a task. That is, an assumption of science assessment reform is that new forms of tests require more complex cognitive processes—reasoning, understanding, and problem-solving strategies—than traditional assessments (e.g., multiple-choice tests). Think aloud protocols, interviews, and observational procedures are tools used to provide evidence about the type of reasoning and understanding required by the assessment. For example, science performance assessment scores are often interpreted as providing evidence of "higher order thinking" involving both content and procedural knowledge, but research has found that this is not always the case (Baxter & Glaser, 1998; Hamilton, Nussbaum, & Snow, 1997).

Task Quality Analyses

Task quality addresses the opportunities the assessment task provides to the examinee/student to show what she or he understands and can do. This technique analyzes the level of complexity of the assessment task by examining its properties and objectives. For example, a highly structured performance assessment is less likely to require from students a deep understanding of the content and/or procedural knowledge that is being measured. Analytic frameworks have been developed to guide this kind of analysis (e.g., Glaser & Baxter, 1997).

EVALUATION OF ALTERNATIVE ASSESSMENTS: EXAMPLES AND SUMMARY OF FINDINGS

In this section we exemplify the psychometric evaluation of two different types of tests that have been used to evaluate students' understanding in science: concept maps and performance assessments. At the outset, we wish to highlight two points. The first point is that the sampling framework is fitted to the nature of the assessment. Consequently, the concept map framework will, inevitably, address concept sampling, while the performance assessment framework for will address task sampling. Nevertheless, other facets will remain the same; notice that the judge, occasion, and method facets might very well be included in the sampling framework for both concept maps and performance assessments. The second point is that a single G study is unlikely to be comprehensive. Since inclusion of all possible facets often is not practical, more than one study is usually needed before drawing conclusions about the appropriate use and quality of an assessment technique.

For both concept maps and performance assessments, we (1) define the assessment and how its key characteristics are reflected in the sampling framework; (2) describe one of our studies that exemplifies the application of the sampling framework, the use of G theory, and the interpretation of results; (3) present findings from different studies; and (4) generalize conclusions across studies.

CONCEPT MAPS

Research on expertise in science (Chi, Feltovich, & Glaser, 1981; Chi, Glaser, & Far, 1988; Glaser, 1991) has shown that richly structured, declarative knowledge is characteristic of experts, not novices. That is, understanding in science involves a rich set of relations among important concepts in that domain (e.g., Novak, 1990; Wallace & Mintzes, 1990; Wandersee, 1990). To access students' connected understanding—that is, relations between concepts—two approaches have been used. Indirect approaches probe a student's knowledge structure by asking the student to rate the similarity between concepts (e.g., Goldsmith, Johnson, & Acton, 1991), to associate words (e.g., Shavelson, 1972, 1974), or to sort concepts into groups based on their similarity (e.g., Shavelson & Stanton, 1975). A more direct approach is to ask a student to construct a "map" or labeled graph that makes explicit how the student relates concept pairs. Concept-map assessment scores are interpreted as representing, at least partially, the structure of an individual's declarative knowledge in a content domain (Novak & Gowin, 1984). We evaluate here the use of a direct, "construct-a-concept-map" approach to the structural representation of declarative knowledge (Ruiz-Primo & Shavelson, 1996a).

Definition

We (Ruiz-Primo & Shavelson, 1996a) have defined a concept map as a graph in which the nodes represent concepts, the lines between nodes represent relations, and the labels on the lines represent the nature of the relation between two concepts (Figure 1). A pair of nodes and the labeled line connecting them is defined as a *proposition*, the basic unit of meaning in a concept map (Novak, Chapter 1, this volume). We conceive of a concept-map-

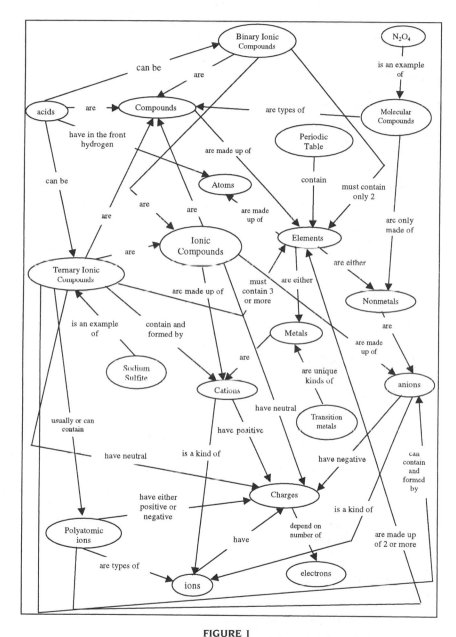

FIGURE 1

A student's concept map on the topic ions, molecules, and compounds.

based assessment to be composed of a (1) *task* that invites students to provide evidence bearing on their knowledge structure in a content domain; (2) format for the student's *response*, and (3) *scoring system* by which the student's concept map can be evaluated accurately and consistently.

Types of Maps

We (Ruiz-Primo & Shavelson, 1996a) have identified different ways in which concept-map tasks, response formats, and scoring systems vary in practice (Table 4). Concept-map tasks vary as to (1) *task demands*—the instructions given to students in generating their concept maps (e.g., fill-in a skeleton map, construct a map from scratch, or talk about the relation between concepts to an interviewer); (2) *task constraints*—the boundaries of the task (e.g., students may or may not be asked to construct a hierarchical map, or to use more than one link between concepts, or to provide the concepts for the map), and (3) *task content structure*—the intersection of the task demands and constraints with the structure of the subject-domain to be mapped (e.g., there is no need to impose a hierarchical structure if the content structure is not hierarchical).

Three types of response variations have been identified in concept mapping: (1) *response mode*—whether the student's response is paper-and-pencil, oral, or on a computer (e.g., students may be asked to draw the concept map on a piece of paper or to enter the concepts and relations on a computer); (2) *response format*—the characteristics of the response requested usually fitting the specifics of the task (e.g., if the task asks students to fill in a skeleton map, a skeleton map and concepts are provided); and (3) *the mapper*—who draws the map (e.g., student, teacher, interviewer).

Three scoring strategies have been used in practice (1) *score map components* (e.g., the number of nodes, links, cross-links); (2) *compare a student's map with a criterion map* (e.g., an expert's concept map); and (3) *a combination of both strategies* (e.g., an expert's concept map is used to validate a student's links and concepts).

From the characterization presented above, it is clear that concept-mapping techniques can vary widely in the way they elicit a student's knowledge structure, which in turn can produce different representations and scores.

Evaluating Reliability and Validity

We have asked the following questions about concept-map-based assessments. With respect to generalizability, we have asked: Can judges consistently score concept maps? Are map scores sensitive to the sampling of concepts (or linking lines) used? Do different types of scores reflect student's connected understanding similarly? With respect of validity, we have asked:

TABLE 4
Variations among Concept Map Components

Map Assessment Components	Variations	Instances
Task	Task demands	Students can be asked to Fill in a map Construct a map from scratch Organize cards Rate relatedness of concept pairs Write an essay Respond to an interview
	Task constraints	Students may or may not be: Asked to construct a hierarchical map Provided with the concepts used in the task Provided with the concepts links used in the task Allowed to use more than one link between nodes Allowed to physically move the concepts around until a satisfactory structure is arrived at Asked to define the terms used in the map Required to justify their responses Required to construct the map collectively
	Content structure	The intersection of the task demands and constraints with the structure of the subject domain to be mapped.
Response	Response mode	Whether the student response is Paper and pencil Oral On a computer
	Format Characteristics	Format should fit the specifics of the task
	Mapper	Whether the map is drawn by a Student Teacher or researcher
Scoring system	Score components of the map	Focus is on three components or variations of them: Propositions Hierarchy levels Examples
	Use of a criterion map	Compare a student's map with an expert's map. Criterion maps can be obtained from One or more experts in the field One or more teachers One or more top students
	Combination of map components and a criterion map	The two previous strategies are combined to score the student's maps.

Source. After Ruiz-Primo and Shavelson (1996b).

Do different concept mapping techniques produce scores that can be interpreted in the same way, as representing the same aspect of student's connected understanding? Do different mapping techniques pose different cognitive demands on students? Are mapping techniques able to differentiate between more and less competent students?

One main focus of our studies has been to evaluate the equivalence of different mapping techniques. The critical question here is whether different mapping techniques (e.g., construct-a-map with concepts provided or fill-in-a-skeleton-map) provide a similar "picture" of students' connected understanding. The characteristics of the observed structural representation portray important aspects of students' underlying knowledge structures (e.g., a highly connected, integrated, organized structure characterizes experts and competent students; and isolated, less integrated structures are typical of students who are novices, less competent). However, the observed characteristics of a representation of a student's knowledge structure may depend to a large extent on how the representation is elicited, not a minor issue.

Another issue examined across studies is the scoring system used to evaluate students' concept maps. We have examined three types of scores in our research: (1) *proposition-accuracy score*—the sum of the accuracy ratings assigned to each proposition in a student's map (assessed on a 5-point scale from 0 for inaccurate/incorrect to 4 for excellent/outstanding in that the student provided a complete proposition that shows deep understanding of the relation between two concepts); (2) *convergence score*—the proportion of accurate propositions in the student's map out of the total possible valid propositions in a criterion map; and (3) *salience score*—the proportion of accurate propositions out of all the propositions in the student's map.

Our sampling framework defines and integrates the following facets: mapping techniques, raters (i.e., judges), and terms (i.e., concepts).[6] G theory has been used to evaluate the generalizability of a student's average map score over mapping techniques, raters, and concepts. Other procedures, along with G theory, have been carried out for supporting score interpretations. Different facets have been included in different studies. In what follows we describe in detail a study that illustrates the evaluation of concept map scores. We then describe very briefly other studies, findings, and our general conclusions on concept-map assessments.

Sources of Map-Score Sampling Variability

Is anything lost in representing a student's knowledge structure when the assessor provides the concepts instead of student generating the concepts for building a map? (Ruiz-Primo, Schultz, & Shavelson, 1996). To answer this

---

[6] Other facets can be included in the framework (e.g., occasions, method) that we have not yet studied.

question, we varied the source of the concept sample used to construct a map: student-generated sample (Mapping Technique 1) or assessor-generated sample (Mapping Technique 2). Technique 1 asked 43 high school chemistry students to provide the concepts with which to construct the map; Technique 2 provided the concepts for mapping (Figure 2).

To study the sensitivity of concept map scores to the sampling variability of assessor-generated concepts, we also randomly sampled concepts from the subject domain (Sample A and Sample B). Each of the students was tested on three occasions: (1) on the first occasion, students were asked to construct a map with terms they provided; (2) on the second occasion, students were asked to construct a map with the first list of assessor-provided concepts; and (3) on the third occasion, students were asked to construct a map with the second list of assessor-provided concepts. Half of the students

Instructions When No Concepts Are Provided to the Students	Instructions When Concepts Are Provided to the Students
You recently studied the chapter on Chemical Names and Formulas.	Examine the concepts listed below. They were selected from the chapter on Chemical Names and Formulas that you recently studied. The terms selected focus on the topic Ions, Molecules, and Compounds.
Construct a concept map that reflects what you know about Ions, Molecules, and Compounds.	
The concept map should have 10 concepts in it. We are providing you with 3 concepts: ions, molecules, and compounds.	Construct a concept map using the terms provided below.
Select another 7 concepts to construct your map. The 7 concepts should be the ones that you think are the most important in explaining ions, molecules, and compounds.	Organize the terms in relation to one another in any way you want. Draw an arrow between the terms you think are related. Label the arrow using phrases or only one or two linking words.
Organize the terms in relation to one another in any way you want. Draw an arrow between the terms you think are related. Label the arrow using phrases or only one or two linking words.	You can construct your map on the blank pages attached. When you finish your map check that: (1) all the arrows have labels; (2) your concept map has 10 concepts, and (3) your map shows what you know about ions, molecules, and compounds.
You can construct your map on the blank pages attached. When you finish your map check that: (1) all the arrows have labels; (2) your concept map has 10 concepts, and (3) your map shows what you know about ions, molecules, and compounds.	After checking your map redraw it so someone else can read it. Staple your final map to this page.
After checking your map redraw it so someone else can read it. Staple your final map to this page.	**LIST OF CONCEPTS:** acids anions cations compounds electrons ions metals molecules molecular compounds polyatomic ions

FIGURE 2

Instructions to construct concept maps using techniques that differ in the demands imposed on the students.

constructed their maps using Sample A first (sequence 1) and the other half using Sample B (sequence 2). A multiple-choice test was administered to all students prior to concept mapping.

To evaluate the equivalence of mapping techniques (i.e., student- and assessor-generated concept list), we examined whether the means and variances across techniques were similar. We also compared the similarity of the reliability and validity indices of the techniques. To test mean differences between techniques, a repeated measures ANOVA over the three conditions (No Concepts, Sample A, and Sample B) was carried out for proposition accuracy and salience scores.[7] To examine the generalizability of proposition accuracy and salience scores across raters and mapping techniques, we carried out two person × rater × assessment condition G studies, one per score.

No significant differences were found among means (proposition accuracy: Hotelling's $T^2 = .05$; $p > .05$; salience: Hotelling's $T^2 = .06$; $p > .05$) or variances (Mauchly's test of sphericity for proposition accuracy: .94, $p > .05$; for salience = .90, $p > .05$) for either type of score across techniques. G study results (see Table 5) indicated that patterns of variability across types of scores were the same. The largest variance component was for systematic differences among persons followed by the error component, person by condition interaction. Raters did not introduce error variability into the scores (percentage of variability is negligible). The magnitude of the person × condition variance component indicated that students' relative standing varied from one condition (or sample of concepts) to the next (some students did better with Sample A, others with Sample B, and still others when they selected the concepts). The generalizability and dependability coefficients varied across type of score. For proposition accuracy, both relative and absolute coefficients were high, suggesting that concept maps scores can consistently rank students relative to one another ($\hat{\rho}^2 = .90$) as well as provide a good estimate of a student's level of performance, in addition to how well their classmates performed ($\hat{\phi} = .90$). However, coefficients for the salience scores were lower ($\hat{\rho}^2 = .79$, $\hat{\phi} = .79$). Furthermore, the percentage of variability among persons is higher for the proposition accuracy score than for the salience score. This indicates that the former score better reflects the differences in students' structure of knowledge.

To examine convergence, we correlated scores across the three mapping techniques and examined the patterns of correlations, as well as compared the correlations to reliability estimates (Table 6).[8] To begin, *interrater reliability coefficients (in parenthesis on the diagonal of Table 6) across types of scores were high,*

---

[7] Convergence scores were not available for the "No Concepts" technique because no criterion could be established to determine the expected number of propositions

[8] Although the three types of scores are presented in Table 6, information related to convergence scores applies only to the two assessor-generated concept samples, A and B (Technique 2).

TABLE 5
Estimated Variance Components and Generalizability Coefficients for a Person × Rater × Condition G Study Design for No-Concept, Sample A, and Sample B Conditions Using the Propositions Accuracy and Salience Scores

Source of Variation	Estimated Variance Components	Percentage of Total Variability
Proposition accuracy score (NC, A, B)		
Person (P)	46.991	73.47
Rater (R)	0.074	0.12
Condition (C)	0.000*	0.00
PR	0.000*	0.00
PC	13.526	21.15
RC	0.000*	0.00
PRC, e	3.365	5.26
$\hat{\rho}^2$ ($n_r = 2$; $n_c = 3$)	.90	
$\hat{\phi}$	.90	
Salience score (NC, A, B)		
Person (P)	0.03682	52.48
Rater (R)	0.00018	0.26
Condition (C)	0.00007	0.10
PR	0.00000*	0.00
PC	0.02469	35.19
RC	0.00000*	0.00
PRC, e	0.00840	11.97
$\hat{\rho}^2$ ($n_r = 2$; $n_c = 3$)	.79	
$\hat{\phi}$	.79	

* Negative variance components set to zero; in no case was the variance component more than −0.08910 for proposition accuracy and 0.0036 for salience score.

TABLE 6
Multiscore–Multitechnique Matrix

| | Student-Generated | | Assessor Provided | | | | | | |
| | No-Concept | | Sample A | | | Sample B | | | |
	PA	S	PA	C	S	PA	C	A	Multiple-Choice Test
No-concept									
Proposition Accuracy (PA)	(.91)								.57
Salience (S)	.81	(.79)							.43
Sample A									
Proposition Accuracy (PA)	.73	.47	(.98)						.63
Convergence (C)	.68	.48	.96	(.97)					.64
Salience (S)	62	.47	89	94	(96)				.61
Sample B									
Proposition Accuracy (PA)	.73	.53	.83	.83	.72	(.96)			.64
Convergence (C)	.62	.47	.70	.74	.61	.95	(.93)		.56
Salience (S)	.63	.50	.72	.76	.71	.90	.91	(.90)	.50

Note. Interrater reliability on the diagonal.

confirming the results obtained from the G *studies.* Raters can consistently score concept maps. The lowest coefficients were found with Technique 1— concepts given by student.

To examine the convergent validity of the two techniques, we focused on the first two columns of the matrix. Coefficients are higher for the proposition accuracy score (r_{avg} = .73) than for salience score (r_{avg} = .48). This suggests that the salience score may rank students differently depending on the technique used. This result is confirmed by comparing the correlations between different types of scores using different techniques (correlations in italics). Finally, if concept maps measure somewhat different aspects of declarative knowledge than multiple-choice scores, the correlation between these two measures should be positive and moderate (last column of Table 6). *We interpreted the correlations to mean that concept maps and multiple-choice tests measure overlapping, yet somewhat different aspects of declarative knowledge.*

To evaluate whether different concept samples, Sample A and Sample B, influenced students' map scores we compared means and variances across samples and types of scores (Table 7). Results from the analyses across techniques (see Table 5) indicated no significant difference between means for proposition accuracy and salience scores. For the convergence score, available only for Sample A and Sample B, no significant difference was found between means (Hotelling's T^2 = .16; p = >.05) or variances (F_{Max} = .80; p = >.05).

The generalizability of scores across raters and concept samples was examined in three, person × judge × concept sample, G studies, one for each type of score. The pattern observed was the same across techniques. The largest variance component was for persons, followed by the interaction of person by concept–sample; variability between raters was negligible. The proposition accuracy scores had the highest relative and absolute coefficients (.89 for both coefficients). Convergence and salience scores had similar coefficients. However, the convergence score had a higher percentage of variability among persons, meaning that it better reflected the differences in students' knowledge than the salience scores.

Findings from this study led to the following tentative conclusions: (1) *The two mapping techniques produced equivalent scores reflecting similar aspects of students' knowledge structures.* However, with the student-generated concept technique students were probably given too much credit for propositions that did not provide evidence of their knowledge of the topic assessed. We are currently exploring this issue further before reaching a final conclusion about the equivalence of these mapping techniques. (2) Sampling variability from one random sample of concepts to another is negligible; *the two random samples of concepts provide equivalent map scores (when the concept domain is carefully specified).* (3) *Concept maps can be reliably scored, even when complex judgments such as proposition quality are required.* (4) *The relationship between multiple-choice scores and concept-map scores suggests that they measure overlapping and yet somewhat*

TABLE 7
Estimated Variance Components and Generalizability Coefficients for a Person × Rater × Concept-Sample G Study Design for Sample A, and Sample B Across the Three Types of Scores

Source of Variation	Estimated Variance Components	Percentage of Total Variability
Proposition accuracy score (A, B)		
Person (P)	52.85513	79.82
Rater (R)	0.00000*	0.00
Sample (S)	0.05353	0.08
PR	0.64103	0.97
PS	11.37147	17.17
RS	0.05897	0.09
PRS, e	1.24103	1.87
$\hat{\rho}^2$ ($n_r = 2$; $n_s = 2$)	.89	
$\hat{\phi}$	.89	
Convergence score (A, B)		
Person (P)	0.00668	70.02
Rater (R)	0.00001	0.10
Sample (S)	0.00000*	0.00
PR	0.00003	0.31
PS	0.00244	25.58
RS	0.00001	0.10
PRS, e	0.00037	3.88
$\hat{\rho}^2$ ($n_r = 2$; $n_c = 2$)	.83	
$\hat{\phi}$	.83	
Salience score (A, B)		
Person (P)	0.04660	67.08
Rater (R)	0.00014	0.20
Sample (S)	0.00077	1.11
PR	0.00000*	0.00
PS	0.01727	24.86
RS	0.00011	0.16
PRS, e	0.00458	6.59
$\hat{\rho}^2$ ($n_r = 2$; $n_c = 2$)	.83	
$\hat{\phi}$	.82	

* Negative variance components set to zero; in no case was the variance component more than −0.01603.

different aspects of declarative knowledge. And (5) the convergence score—the proportion of valid propositions in the student's map to the number of all possible propositions in the criterion map—is the most time-and-effort-efficient measure of the three score types.

Other Studies

We also evaluated the differences between mapping techniques that imposed a hierarchical or nonhierarchical structure on students' knowledge representations in two types of content domains—one that is naturally hierarchical and the other that it is not (Ruiz-Primo, Shavelson, & Schultz, 1997). Regardless of the type of organization, we expected that as subject-matter knowledge increased, the structure of the map should increasingly reflect the structure, hierarchical or not, in the domain as held by experts. Therefore, topics for this study were selected as having different structures according to experts' concept maps. On average, student's scores did not depend on whether the instruction to produce a hierarchical map matched a like content domain (i.e., no topic by mapping technique interaction was found in any type of score). We are still working on indicators to evaluate the hierarchical structure of the students' maps.

In a third study, we compared two other mapping techniques (Ruiz-Primo, Schultz, Li, & Shavelson, 1998): (1) The high-directed *fill-in-a-skeleton-map* technique required students to fill-in the blank nodes or blank linking lines of a skeleton concept map. (2) The low-directed *construct-a-map-from-scratch* technique asked students to construct a map with assessor provided concepts. Students were tested on three occasions: On the first occasion, students were asked to construct a map from scratch using all 20 concepts provided by the assessor. On the second occasion, students were asked to fill in a blank-*node* skeleton map. On the third occasion students filled in a blank-*linking-line* skeleton map. High-directed and low-directed map techniques led to different interpretations of students' connected understanding. Whereas scores obtained under the high-directed technique indicated that students' performance was close to the maximum possible score, the scores obtained with the low-directed technique revealed that students' knowledge was incomplete compared to a criterion map. Furthermore, the low-directed technique provided a symmetric distribution of scores, whereas the high-directed technique scores were negatively skewed due to a ceiling effect. We concluded that the construct-a-map technique better reflected differences among students' knowledge structures.

To study the sensitivity of fill-in-the-map scores to the variability of sampling blank nodes or blank linking lines, we randomly sampled the nodes and the linking lines that needed to be filled in by the students from the criterion map (Ruiz-Primo et al., 1998). As in the previous study, students filled in two types of skeleton maps: node skeleton map and linking-line skeleton map. Each student was tested on two occasions. On the first occasion, students were asked to fill in a blank-node skeleton map; half the students filled the Sample A node skeleton map and half of the students filled in the Sample B node skeleton map. On the second occasion students filled in a blank-linking-line skeleton map; half the students filled in the Sample A linking-line skeleton map and half of the students filled in the Sample B linking-line skeleton map. The sequence in which students took the skeleton maps was controlled by randomly assigning students to one of the four sequences. No sequence effects were found. Results indicated that fill-in-the-map scores were not sensitive to the sample of concepts or linking lines to be filled in. Nevertheless, the fill-in-the-node and fill-in-the-linking line techniques were not equivalent forms of fill-in-the-map.

To address the cognitive validity of cognitive structure interpretations of concept-map scores, we have sought evidence about the correspondence between intended map-task demands and the cognitive activities evoked, as well as the correspondence between quality of cognitive activity and students' performance scores. We asked two questions: Is there a difference in cognitive processes observed across different mapping techniques? Does the cognitive activity vary qualitatively between more and less proficient students? Twelve high school chemistry students (three top, three average, and three low), two chemistry teachers, and one chemist were asked to think aloud (concurrent verbalization) as they were engaged in three concept-mapping techniques: construct a map from scratch, fill in the nodes, and fill in the linking lines. After they finished each assessment, they were asked to describe, retrospectively, the strategies used. To evaluate the nature and quality of cognitive activity, we developed a system that includes a set of coding categories (e.g., explanation, monitoring, conceptual errors) for classifying the content of the respondents' protocols, and higher-level categories for describing the planning and the strategies they used to address the assessment tasks. Two raters are currently coding students' protocols independently.

Preliminary results from the analysis of one high- and one low-scoring student under the construct-a-map-from-scratch condition show a difference in cognitive activity. For example, although both students provided a plan, the planning of the high-scoring student showed a clear procedure. Before starting the drawing of the concept map, the student provided a definition of almost all the concepts in the list and made groups of concepts:

> The charge has negative, electrons are negative charges, anions have negative charge, so cations are positive charge, so they are related" [student goes on and defines and groups the concepts] ... so periodic table is the most general one, so the periodic table is in the middle.

The low-scoring student read all the concepts, selected one, with no justification for doing so, and started drawing the map:

> I am just going to go over the list of concepts ... [reads each one of concepts aloud] ... I am going to use the periodic table as my starter.

The high-scoring student's plan was composed of actions (defined the concepts and grouped them) that helped him anticipate the map to be drawn—a sort of trial run through the solution strategy. The low-scoring student lacked a plan. Also, higher percentages of accurate, coherent, and complete explanations and monitoring statements were provided by the high-scoring student (40.54 and 37.84, respectively) than by the low-scoring student (4 and 16, respectively). We believe that our coding system can capture differences across students and, we hope, differences across assessment techniques.

General Conclusions

Results across all the studies are clear about the effect of human judges ("raters"): *judges can reliably score students' maps.* Judges, in general, did not introduce error variability into the scores (Ruiz-Primo et al., 1996, 1997,

1998). Moreover, results from the first two studies showed that the largest variance component was due to systematic differences among students' map scores—the purpose of measurement. The major source of measurement error was the interaction of persons by mapping technique: Some students performed better with the student-generated concept sample, whereas others performed better using the assessor-generated concept sample. The magnitude of both relative and absolute reliability ("generalizability") coefficients has been high (>.79) and both coefficients have been of similar magnitude. *This suggests that map scores can consistently rank students relative to one another as well as provide a good estimate of a student's level performance, regardless of how well his or her classmates performed.*

Results also suggest that the type of score selected for scoring concept maps might be an issue. Results from the G studies showed that the percentage of variability among persons ("universe score" variability) is highest for the proposition-accuracy score, followed by the convergence score, and finally the salience score. Relative and absolute generalizability coefficients were higher for the proposition accuracy score (~.90) than for the other two scores (~.79). Proposition-accuracy scores, then, better reflect systematic differences in students' knowledge structures than convergence or salience scores. However, based on the amount of work and time involved in developing a proposition-accuracy scoring system, we recommend the use of convergence scores for large-scale assessment. Finally, *correlations between multiple-choice test scores and concept map scores across the different studies are all positive and moderately high (r ~.50). We interpret these findings to mean that concept maps and multiple-choice tests measure overlapping, yet different aspects of declarative knowledge.*

Performance Assessment

Science performance assessments invite students to conduct a hands-on investigation to test a hypothesis or solve a problem. Students plan and carry out an investigation, and report and interpret their findings. Performance assessments provide evidence bearing on procedural and strategic knowledge (e.g., Baxter, Elder, & Glaser, 1996).

Definition

A science performance assessment is composed of a (1) *task* that poses a meaningful problem and whose solution requires the use of concrete materials that react to the actions taken by the student, (2) *response format* that focuses the student's report of the investigation (e.g., record procedures, draw a graph, construct a table, write a conclusion), and (3) *scoring system* that involves professionals judging both the reasonableness—scientific defensibility—of the procedures used to carry out the task and the accuracy of findings (Ruiz-Primo & Shavelson, 1996b). The "Bugs" performance assessment described before exemplifies this definition (Shavelson et al., 1991).

Types of Performance Assessments

There are as many performance tasks as there are investigations in science. We have attempted to reduce the range by classifying them according to regularities in their characteristics (Figure 3; see Ruiz-Primo & Shavelson, 1996b; Shavelson, Solano-Flores, & Ruiz-Primo, 1998). While our categories (as would any other category system) oversimplify the complexity and uniqueness of each assessment, they focus on commonalities that have proven useful in developing other assessments within the same category. The *other* category in our classification scheme acknowledges our ignorance and the possibility of discovering other types of tasks. Table 8 provides examples of each type of assessment and the focus of its corresponding response format and scoring system. Here we briefly define each category and describe each example.

Technical Quality

The sampling framework used to evaluate performance assessments has already been described. We are interested in how generalizable a student's average performance score is across tasks, occasions, judges, and measurement methods. As with concept maps, we have carried out a series of stud-

Types of Scoring Systems		Types of Tasks				
		Comparative Investigation	Component Identification	Classification	Observation	Others
Analytic	Procedure Based	• Paper Towels • Bugs • Incline Planes • Saturation				
	Evidence-Based		• Electric Mysteries • Mystery Powders			
	Dimension-Based			• Rocks & Charts • Sink & Float		
	Data Accuracy-Based				• Day-Time Astronomy	
	Others					?
Holistic	Rubric			• Leaves (CAP Assessment)		
	Others					?

FIGURE 3

Types of tasks and scoring systems in performance assessments.

Richard J. Shavelson and Maria Araceli Ruiz-Primo

TABLE 8
Examples of Different Types of Assessments

Type of Assessment	Task	Response Format	Scoring System
Comparative investigation: Saturated Solutions	Given three powders, students determine which one saturates water most readily and which least readily.	Asks students to write in detail how they conducted the investigation as well as their finding.	Procedure-based: Focuses on the scientific defensibility of the procedure used and the accuracy of the findings.
Component Identification: Mystery Powders	Given bags of powder mixtures, students determine which powders are in each bag.	Asks students to report the tests they used to confirm and/ or disconfirm the presence of a substance as well as their observations.	Evidence-based: Focuses on the evidence provided to confirm or disconfirm the presence of a particular powder and the accuracy of the finding.
Classification: Sink and Float	Given 12 plastic bottles of different colors, sizes, and weights, students create a classification scheme, based on the relevant attributes for flotation, and use it to predict whether other bottles would sink or float.	Asks students to show the classification scheme they constructed, explain why bottles sink or float, use the classification for predicting other bottles behavior.	Dimension-based: Focuses on the relevance of the attributes selected to construct the scheme and the accuracy of the use of the classification scheme.
Observation: Daytime Astronomy	Given an earth globe, students model the path of the Sun from sunrise to sunset and use direction, length, and angle of shadows to solve location problems. ·	Asks students to provide results of their observations and to explain how they collected the information.	Data accuracy-based: Focuses on the adequacy of the model used to collect the data and the accuracy of the data collected.

ies to evaluate different types of performance assessments. Research on the "sink and float" assessment illustrates our work in developing and evaluating this type of assessment (Solano-Flores et al., 1997).

A Classification Assessment: Sink and Float

Classification is a fundamental science activity and, unfortunately, is often conceived as just the ordering or grouping of cases based on their similarity on critical attributes. However, classification is much more than organizing objects or events. It usually involves a purpose, either conceptual or practi-

Problem 2:
Sort your bottles.

In the space below make a chart or a drawing to sort your bottles by size and weight. Refer to the bottles with their letters. Show which bottles are floaters by circling their letters.

Problem 3:
Explain how size and weight make bottles float or sink.

In the chart below your bottles are sorted by size and weight.

White boxes show | floaters | Shaded boxes show | sinkers |

	small	medium	large
1 ounce	J		
2 ounces	N and G	T	V and P
3 ounces	D and K	B	R and C
4 ounces			H

FIGURE 4

Two problems from the "sink and float" assessment.

cal (see Sokal & Sneath, 1963). Besides the process of classifying, classification is also the end result of that process, or the use of that end result. A classification task, then, encompasses a *process* (e.g., identify categories to which objects belong, identify which dimensions are needed to construct a goal-oriented classification scheme), an *end result* (e.g., a classification scheme based on critical dimensions, a description of how those dimensions are related), and an *application* (e.g., use a classification scheme to make inferences or predictions about certain objects).

To develop the classification assessment we selected flotation, a physics topic covered by many hands-on science curricula (e.g., Full Option Science System, Science for Early Educational Development, and National Science Resource Center). Using this content domain, we devised *sink and float*, a classification assessment for fifth and sixth graders intended to assess knowledge of flotation (Figure 4). The core concept of flotation is *density (d)*: the relation between weight (*w*) and volume (*v*).[9] Therefore, the problems

---

[9] Strictly speaking, we should use the word "mass." However, we found that most students are not familiar with it, so we decided to use "weight." For the same reason, in the assessment we used the word "size" instead of "volume."

included in a classification assessment on flotation should involve identifying weight and volume as critical dimensions to floating and sinking, creating and using a classification scheme based on those dimensions, and defining how those dimensions are related.

The general characteristics of the task, the response format, and the scoring system are provided in Table 8 (for details see Solano-Flores et al. [1997]). The assessment includes four *tasks*: (1) *Find out what makes bottles float or sink*—identify the bottles as floaters or sinkers and determine the dimensions that are critical to floating-sinking; (2) *Sort your bottles*—classify the bottles according to size, weight, and whether they are floaters or sinkers; (3) *Explain how size and weight make bottles float or sink*—when provided with an accurate classification scheme, determine how the dimensions of weight and volume are related to identify an object as a floater or a sinker; and (4) *Tell floaters from sinkers without using water*—based on the information about weight and size for a new set of bottles, but without actually having the bottles, classify bottles as floaters or sinkers. The *response format* consists of a notebook that poses the problems and provides directions for using the equipment. The notebook is also intended to capture the students' responses—both their solutions to the problems and the reasoning and strategies they used to arrive at those solutions.[10] In all the problems, the students are allowed to provide answers with words, drawings, or both. The scientific defensibility of a classification system depends on how well some formal criteria (e.g., exhaustiveness and mutual exclusiveness) are met, as well as how relevant the dimensions used in the classification system are to the conceptual or practical purposes intended. Therefore, the *scoring system* for classification tasks is *dimension-based*—it focuses on the relevance and accuracy of the dimensions used by a student to construct or use classification schemes with specific conceptual or practical purposes.

The evaluation of the assessments focused on interrater reliability and two aspects of validity: (1) knowledge domain specification—the ability of the four *sink and float* problems to distinguish different kinds of knowledge; and (2) sensitivity to differences due to instruction. We administered the assessment to two classes of fifth-grade students. In one of the classes (class 1), students studied the sink and float unit and the curriculum emphasized hands-on science. The other class did not study the unit (class 2). Both classes were tested at the same time on two occasions, before and after class 1 studied the unit.

---

[10] Since problem 3 provides an accurate classification scheme, whereas problem 2 asks students to construct a classification scheme, the notebook is divided in two parts. When students complete Part 1 (problems 1 and 2), they return their notebooks and get Part 2 (problems 3 and 4). This reduces the possibility of carrying forward mistakes made in solving problem 2 to problems 3 and 4; it also prevents students from seeing an accurate classification scheme (problem 3) when solving problems 1 and 2. Figure 1 shows problems 2 and 3.

Two student × rater × problem G studies were carried out, one per class (Table 9). Averaging across classes and occasions, the problem variance component accounted for 46.59% of the score variability, indicating substantial differences in difficulty across problems. The large score variability due to the student × problem interaction (which, averaged across classes and occasions accounts for 30.56 of the total score variability) indicates that a given problem was not equally difficult for all students. Thus, the four problems seem to distinguish different kinds of knowledge. Variability due to raters was negligible. Indeed, interrater reliability coefficients for pretest and post-test total scores were reasonably high (on average .87 and .83, respectively). Generalizability coefficients were higher ($\hat{\rho}^2 = .40$ averaging across groups and occasions) in magnitude than domain-referenced coefficients ($\hat{\phi} = .23$ averaging across groups and occasions), reflecting especially the difference in problem difficulty. *The most striking result is that mean scores are, in general, lower on occasion 2 in both classes, even for the class that had instruction*(!). A series of split-plot ANOVAs performed for both problem scores and total

TABLE 9
Estimated Variance Components and Generalizability Coefficients for a Student × Rater × Problem Design in the Sink and Float Assessment

Source of Variation	Pretest		Post-Test	
	Estimated Variance Component	Percentage of Total Variability	Estimated Variance Component	Percentage of Total Variability
Class 1—Instruction				
Student (S)	0.00306	4.31	0.00958	9.66
Rater (R)	0.00004	0.05	0.00002	0.02
Problem (P)	0.03593	50.65	0.05108	51.53
SR	0.00000*	0.00	0.00123	1.24
SP	0.02185	30.80	0.02739	27.63
RP	0.00013	0.18	0.00000*	0.00
SRP, e	0.01006	14.18	0.00983	9.92
$\hat{\rho}^2$ ($n_r = 2; n_p = 4$)	.31		.52	
$\hat{\phi}$	.16		.31	
Class 2—No Instruction				
Student (S)	0.00945	16.58	0.00134	1.42
Rater (R)	0.00020	0.46	0.00074	0.79
Problem (P)	0.03970	37.90	0.04362	46.30
SR	0.00000*	0.00	0.00000*	0.00
SP	0.01785	24.48	0.03754	39.85
RP	0.00000*	0.00	0.00016	0.17
SRP, e	0.00572	7.84	0.01097	11.64
$\hat{\rho}^2$ ($n_r = 2; n_p = 4$)	.65		.11	
$\hat{\phi}$	.38		.05	

* Negative variance components set to zero; in no case was the variance component more than −0.00124.

scores revealed no significant differences ($p > .05$) between classes (C), across occasions (O), or their interaction (C×O) for problems 1, 2, and 3 and Total Score (problem 1: $F_C = .21$, $F_O = .98$, $F_{C×O} = .11$; problem 2: $F_C = .15$, $F_O = .01$, $F_{C×O} = .06$; problem 3: $F_C = 1.39$, $F_O = .35$, $F_{C×O} = .78$; Total Score: $F_C = 2.57$, $F_O = .001$, $F_{C×O} = .19$). In problem 4 we found a significant difference between classes ($F_C = 9.78$, $p < .05$), but not between occasions or for their interaction ($F_O = .06$, $F_{C×O} = 1.47$; $p > .05$).

Possible interpretations for these findings, taken together, are (1) *students either had some naive knowledge of what makes things sink or float (receiving, on average, 17 out of 24 possible points) or could attain this score through trail and error; and (2) whatever the conceptual difficulties that led to less than perfect performance, these difficulties were not ameliorated by instruction.* Hence, essentially no gain from pre- to post-test and no between classroom mean differences were observed. In the end, the assessment may not sufficiently overlap the instruction students received to show changes. Indeed, the teacher found the instructional unit difficult to teach and spread across many important ideas.

Other Studies

We have carried out numerous studies to evaluate performance assessments (e.g., Jovanovic, Solano-Flores, & Shavelson, 1994; Klein et al., 1997a; b; Shavelson et al., 1991, 1993, 1996; Solano-Flores, Jovanovic, Shavelson, & Bachman, 1999; Solano-Flores & Shavelson, 1997; Stecher et al., 1998). We just describe very briefly one study that evaluates the cognitive validity and task quality of performance assessments.

Performance assessments are intended to capture, in large part, students' procedural knowledge as they conduct investigations. Whether the assessment captures this knowledge depends on the quality of the assessment. By observing students conduct investigations, interviewing them about their investigations, examining their written work, and analyzing assessment characteristics, Baxter and Glaser (1998) concluded that the characteristics of the task, response format, and scoring system, together, significantly influenced the assessment's ability to tap procedural knowledge. Baxter and Glaser proposed a framework for examining assessment characteristics. For example, they argued that knowledge rich tasks require in-depth understanding of both subject matter and procedures for their completion compared to tasks in which a successful solution is not dependent on prior knowledge but rather on the information given in the assessment situation. In sum, *assessment tasks that provide step-by-step instructions for conducting an investigation may prohibit students from demonstrating how they can apply their knowledge to solve the problem. Indeed, this type of task may only show that a student is able to follow directions.* Finally, Baxter and Glaser (1998) showed that scoring systems inconsistent with the task do not tap students' meaningful use of knowledge and problem solving procedures.

General Conclusions

Initially, greatest concern about performance assessment was attached to rater sampling variability: Complex behavior was assumed to be too difficult to judge either in real time or from a written record. Research is quite clear on this issue: *Raters can be trained to evaluate complex performance reliably (e.g., Shavelson et al., 1993). Nevertheless, not all individuals can be trained to score performance consistently and raters must be continually checked and recalibrated* (Wigdor & Green, 1991).

The findings on task-sampling variability are remarkably consistent across diverse domains, such as writing, mathematics, and science achievement (Baxter et al., 1993; Dunbar et al., 1991; Shavelson et al., 1993) and performance of military personnel (Wigdor & Green, 1991): task sampling variability is large. *A large number of tasks is needed to get a generalizable measure of student performance, creating substantial costs* (Stetcher & Klein, 1997).

One study, and perhaps the only study, of occasion sampling variability with science performance assessments indicates that this source of variability may also be large (Ruiz-Primo et al., 1993; Shavelson et al., 1993). Indeed, occasion sampling variability is often confounded with task sampling variability because assessments are given only at one point in time (Cronbach et al., 1997). *We have found that both task- and occasion-sampling variability combined give raise to the major source of measurement error in performance assessment.*

Finally, method-sampling variability is sufficiently great to suggest that different measurement methods may tap into different aspects of science achievement (Baxter & Shavelson, 1994). A student's score depends on the particular task sampled and the particular method used to assess performance (see Baxter & Shavelson, 1994). Research suggests that paper-and-pencil methods (e.g., multiple-choice and short-answer tests) are less exchangeable with direct observation ($r < .30$) than other methods (e.g., computer simulations). Direct observation, notebooks, and computers simulations—all methods that react to the actions taken by students in conducting an investigation—seem to be more exchangeable ($r \sim .50$; Shavelson, Ruiz-Primo, & Wiley, 1999). *The important lesson to learn from this research is that performance assessment scores are sensitive to the method used to assess performance.*

CONCLUDING COMMENTS

Alternative types of tests are being used to assess understanding in a science domain. These new types of tests are welcome in that they expand our knowledge of what it means to achieve in science.

Nevertheless, these new assessments also pose challenges for psychometric theory. Their structure, for example, is more complex than that of multiple-choice and open-ended tests. Generalizability theory provides a flexible framework for evaluating the quality of these alternative assessments, especially the sources of error affecting these measurements.

Combined with fairly traditional approaches to validity and recent developments in cognitive analysis, we are in a good position to provide evidence
about the technical quality of these tests.

Research on concept maps and performance assessments has shed light
on the technical quality of these assessments, for both large-scale and
classroom assessment. In the large-scale context the following are the key
lessons: (1) Increasing the number of judges (i.e., raters or scorers) has little effect on measurement error or "reliability." Perhaps the most credible
explanation for this conclusion is that the scoring systems used were generally well designed and defined, and judges have been well trained. (2)
Increasing the number of tasks in performance assessments substantially
decreases error variance and increases reliability. Because performance
assessments typically are given on only one occasion, task and occasion
sampling are confounded. Consequently, stratifying tasks into homogeneous subsets will not appreciably affect task-sampling variability. The only
solution appears to be to increase the number of tasks, which is costly. And
(3) the construct-a-concept-map technique seems to be the most robust
assessment, when the concepts are carefully selected.

The lessons learned from large-scale assessments have implications for
classroom use, as well. (1) Teachers should use more than one source of
information for drawing conclusions about what their students understand
and can do in science. Different assessments, as well as their own observations and knowledge about students, provide different kinds of information
about students' achievement in science (e.g., concept maps focus on connected understanding, whereas performance assessment focuses on procedural and strategic knowledge). (2) Teachers need to recognize the importance of the quality of the assessments they use in class. Although
psychometric criteria can be relaxed for classroom assessment, teachers
should constantly question the quality of the assessment task they are
using (e.g., degree of structured, nature of the response format and quality
of the scoring form). Low-quality assessments may provide misleading
information about what students understand and can do. And (3) teachers
should not draw conclusions about a student's performance based on a single task (i.e., a single investigation) because of significant task-sampling
variability. Multiple tasks, and a lot of wisdom, are needed.

A great deal of progress has been made in research and development on
science assessment. But much remains to be done. What is needed is time to
develop concept-map, performance-assessment, and other technologies that
reduce the time and cost for their development, administration, and scoring
while providing an expanded picture of science achievement.

References

Baxter, G. P., & Glaser, R. (1998). Investigating the cognitive complexity of science assessment.
    Educational Measurement: Issues and Practice, 17 (3), 37–45.

Baxter, G. P., & Shavelson, R. J. (1994). Science performance assessments: Benchmarks and surrogates. *International Journal of Educational Research*, 21(3), 279–298.

Baxter, G. P., Shavelson, R. J., Herman, S. J., Brown, K., & Valadez, J. R. (1993). Mathematics performance assessment: Technical quality and diverse student impact. *Journal of Research in Mathematics Education*, 24, 41–53.

Baxter, G. P., Elder, A. D., & Glaser, R. (1996). Knowledge-based cognition and performance assessment in the science classroom. *Educational Psychologist*, 31, 133–140.

Beaton, A. E., Mullis, I. V. S., Martin, M. O., Gonzalez, E. J., Kelly, D. L., & Smith, T. A. (1996). *Mathematics achievement in the middle school years: IEA's third international mathematics and science study.* Chesnut Hill, MA: Center for the Study of Testing, Evaluation, and Educational Policy, Boston College.

Brennan, R. L. (1992). *Elements of generalizability theory* (2nd ed.). Iowa City. IA: ACT.

Brennan, R. L., Harris, D. J., & Hanson, B. A. (1987). *The bootstrap and other procedures for examining variability of estimated variance components in testing contexts.* Paper presented at the Annual Meeting of the National Council on Measurement in Education, Washington, D. C.

Candell, G. L., & Ercikan, K. (1994). On the generalizability of school level performance assessment scores. *International Journal of Educational Research*, 21(3), 267–278.

Chi, M. T. H., Feltovich, P. J., & Glaser, R. (1981). Categorization and representation of physics problems by experts and novices. *Cognitive Science*, 5(2), 121–152.

Chi, M. T. H., Glaser, R., & Farr, M. J., (1988). *The nature of expertise.* Hillsdale, NJ: Lawrence Erlbaum.

Cronbach, L. J. (1971). Test Validation. In R. L. Thorndike (Ed.), *Educational measurement* (2nd ed) (pp. 443–507). Washington, DC: American Council on Education.

Cronbach, L. J. (1984). *Essentials of psychological testing* (4th ed.). New York: Harper & Row.

Cronbach, L. J., Gleser, G. C., Nanda, H., & Rajaratnam, N. (1972). *The dependability of behavioral measurements.* New York: Wiley.

Cronbach, L. J., Linn, R. L., Brennan, R. L., & Haertel, E. H. (1997). Generalizability analysis for performance assessments of student achievement or school effectiveness. *Educational and Psychological Measurement*, 57, 373–399.

Dunbar, S. B., Koretz, D. M., & Hoover, H. D. (1991). Quality control in the development and use of performance assessment. *Applied Measurement in Education*, 4, 289–303.

Fitzpatrick, R., & Morrison, E. J. (1971). Performance and product evaluation. In R. L. Thorndike (Ed.), *Educational Measurement* (pp. 237–270). Washington, DC: American Council Education.

Gao, X., Shavelson, R. J., & Baxter, G. P. (1994). Generalizability of large-scale performance assessments in science: Promises and problems. *Applied Measurement in Education*, 7, 323–342.

Glaser, R. (1991). Expertise and assessment. In M. C. Wittrock & E. L. Baker (Eds.), *Testing and cognition* (pp. 17–30). Englewood Cliffs, NJ: Prentice Hall.

Glaser, R., & Baxter, G. P. (1997, February). *Improving the theory and practice of achievement testing.* Paper presented at the conference, Science Education Standards: The Assessment of Science Meets the Science of Assessment. Washington, DC: National Academy of Sciences/National Research Council.

Goldsmith, T. E., Johnson, P. J., & Acton, W. H. (1991). Assessing structural knowledge. *Journal of Educational Psychology*, 83, 88–96.

Hamilton, L. S., Nussbaum, M., & Snow, R. E. (1997). Interview procedures for validating science assessments. *Applied Measurement in Education*, 10(2), 181–200.

Hein, G. E., & Price, S. (1994). *Active assessment for active science: A guide for elementary school teachers.* Portsmouth, NH: Heinemann.

Jovanovic, J., Solano-Flores, G., & Shavelson, R. J. (1994). Science performance assessments. Will gender make a difference? *Education and Urban Society*, 26(4), 352–366.

Kane, M. T. (1982). A sampling model of validity. *Applied Psychological Measurement*, 6, 126–160.

Klein, S. P., Jovanovic, J., Stecher, B. M., McCaffrey, D., Shavelson, R. J., Haertel, E., Solano-Flores, G., & Comfort, K. (1997a). Gender and racial/ethnic differences on gender and racial/ethnic differences on performance assessments in science. *Educational Evaluation and Policy Analysis*, 19(2), 83–97.

Klein, S. P., Shavelson, R. J., Stecher, B. M., McCaffrey, D., Haertel, E., Baxter, G. P., Comfort, K., & Solano-Flores, G. (1997b). *Sources of task sampling variability.* Manuscript submitted for publication.

Messick, S. (1989). Validity. In R. L. Linn (Ed.), *Educational measurement* (3rd ed., pp. 13–104). New York: Macmillan.

Messick, S. (1994). The interplay of evidence and consequences in the validation of performance assessments. *Educational Researcher, 23*(2), 13–23.

Messick, S. (1995). Validity of psychological assessment: Validation of inferences from person's responses and performances as scientific inquiry into score meaning. *American Psychologist, 50*(9), 741–749.

National Research Council. (1996). *National science education standards.* Washington, DC: National Academy Press.

Novak, J. D. (1990). Concept mapping: A useful tool for science education. *Journal of Research in Science Teaching, 27*(10), 937–949.

Novak, J. D., & Gowin, D. B. (1984). *Learning how to learn.* New York: Cambridge University Press.

Othman, A. R. (1995, January). *Examining task sampling variability in science performance assessments.* Unpublished doctoral dissertation, University of California, Santa Barbara.

Ruiz-Primo, M. A., & Shavelson, R. J. (1996a). Problems and issues in the use of concept maps in science assessment. *Journal of Research in Science Teaching, 33,* 569–600.

Ruiz-Primo, M. A., & Shavelson, R. J. (1996b). Rhetoric and reality in science performance assessments: An update. *Journal of Research in Science Teaching, 33,* 1045–1063.

Ruiz-Primo, M. A., Baxter, G. P., & Shavelson, R. J. (1993). On the stability of performance assessments. *Journal of Educational Measurement, 30,* 41–53.

Ruiz-Primo, M. A., Schultz, S. E., & Shavelson, R. J. (1996, April). *Concept map-based assessment in science: An exploratory study.* Paper presented at the annual meeting of the American Educational Research Association, New York.

Ruiz-Primo, M. A., Shavelson, R. J., & Schultz, S. E. (1997, March). *On the validity of concept-map-based assessment interpretations: An experiment testing the assumption of hierarchical concept maps in science.* Paper presented at the annual meeting of the American Educational Research Association. Chicago, IL.

Ruiz-Primo, M. A., Schultz, S. E., Li, M., & Shavelson, R. J. (1998, April). *Comparison of the reliability and validity of scores from two mapping techniques.* Paper presented at the annual meeting of the American Educational Research Association, San Diego, CA.

Sadler, P. M. (1998). Psychometric models of student conceptions in science: Reconciling qualitative studies and distractor-driven assessment instruments. *Journal of Research in Science Teaching, 35*(3), 265–296.

Searle, S. R., Casella, G., & McCulloch, C. E. (1992). *Variance components.* New York: Wiley.

Shavelson, R. J. (1972). Some aspects of the correspondence between content structure and cognitive structure in physics instruction. *Journal of Educational Psychology, 63,* 225–234.

Shavelson, R. J. (1974). Methods for examining representations of a subject-matter structure in a student's memory. *Journal of Research in Science Teaching, 11,* 231–249.

Shavelson, R. J., & Ruiz-Primo, M. A. (1999). Leistungsbewertung im naturwissenschaftlichen Unterricht. *Unterrichtswissenschaft. Zeitschrift für Lernforschung, 27*(2), 102–127.

Shavelson, R. J., & Stanton, G. C. (1975). Construct validation: Methodology and application to three measures of cognitive structure. *Journal of Educational Measurement, 12,* 67–85.

Shavelson, R. J., & Webb, N. M. (1981). Generalizability theory: 1973–1980. *British Journal of Mathematical and Statistical Psychology, 34,* 133–166.

Shavelson, R. J., & Webb, N. M. (1991). *Generalizability theory: A primer.* Newbury Park, CA: Sage.

Shavelson, R. J., Webb, N. M., & Rowley, G. (1989). Generalizability theory. *American Psychologist, 44*(6), 922–932.

Shavelson, R. J., Baxter, G. P., & Pine, J. (1991). Performance assessments in science. *Applied Measurement in Education, 4*(4), 347–362.

Shavelson, R. J., Baxter, G. P., & Gao, X. (1993). Sampling variability of performance assessments. *Journal of Educational Measurement, 30*, 215–232.

Shavelson, R. J., Gao, X., & Baxter, G. P. (1996). On the content validity of performance assessments: Centrality of domain specification. In M. Birembaum & F. J. R. C. Dochy (Eds.). *Alternatives in assessment of achievements, learning processes and prior knowledge.* Boston, MA: Kluwer Academic.

Shavelson, R. J., Solano-Flores, G., & Ruiz-Primo, M. A. (1998). Toward a science performance assessment technology. *Evaluation and Program Planning, 21*(2), 171–184.

Shavelson, R. J., Ruiz-Primo, M. A., & Wiley, E. (1999). Note on sources of sampling variability in science performance assessments. *Journal of Educational Measurement, 36*(1), 61–71.

Sokal, R. R., & Sneath, P. H. A. (1963). *Principles of numerical taxonomy.* San Francisco: W. H. Freeman.

Solano-Flores, G., & Shavelson, R. J. (1997). Development of performance assessments in science: Conceptual, practical, and logistical issues. *Educational Measurement: Issues and Practice, 16*(3), 16–25.

Solano-Flores, G., Shavelson, R. J., Ruiz-Primo, M. A., Schultz, S. E., Wiley, E., & Brown, J. (1997). *On the development and scoring of classification and observation science performance assessments.* Paper presented at the annual meeting of the American Educational Research Association, Chicago, IL.

Solano-Flores, G., Jovanovic, J., & Shavelson, R. J. (1999). On the development and evaluation of a shell for generating science performance assessments. *International Journal of Science Education, 21*(3), 293–315.

Stecher, B. M., & Klein, S. P. (1997). The cost of science performance assessments in large-scale testing programs. *Educational Evaluation and Policy Analysis, 19*, 1–14.

Stecher, B. M., Klein, S. P., Solano-Flores, G., McCaffrey, D., Robyn, A., Shavelson, R. J., & Haertel, E. (In press). *The effects of content, format, and inquiry level on performance on science performance assessment scores.* Educational Evaluation and Policy Analysis.

Wallace, J. D., & Mintzes, J. J. (1990). The concept map as a research tool: Exploring conceptual change in biology. *Journal of Research in Science Teaching, 27*(10), 1033–1052.

Wandersee, J. H. (1990). Concept mapping and the cartography of cognition. *Journal of Research in Science Teaching, 27*(10), 923–936.

Wigdor, A. K., & Green, B. F. (Eds.) (1991). *Performance assessments in the work place* (Vol. 1). Washington, DC: National Academy Press.

CHAPTER 14

Cautionary Notes on Assessment of Understanding Science Concepts and Nature of Science

RONALD G. GOOD
Louisiana State University

A central question raised in this chapter is, What does it mean to say someone *understands* a science concept? Any theory of assessment in science education must explain what it means to understand science before progress in assessment can be achieved.

In Chapter 3 Mintzes and Novak talk about shared meanings (intersubjectivity), resolving inconsistencies (coherence), seeking simplicity (parsimony), and unpacking knowledge (transparency) as criteria for understanding. Identifying the natural scientist (e.g., biologist, chemist, geologist, physicist) as one who understands science, Mintzes and Novak say scientists master many ideas and techniques that are not explicitly taught, but are acquired informally as part of the socialization process within a community of scientists. According to this view understanding science, for the scientist, includes not only the formal coursework and other explicitly taught ideas and skills that are common to undergraduate and graduate studies in the natural sciences, but also the informal "socialization" process that occurs in a given scientific community. The shared meanings and understandings of a science are tied closely to the sense of community that exists among scientists trying to develop better knowledge of nature's operations.

I would add to Mintzes and Novak's *resolving inconsistencies* criterion, the process of *recognizing inconsistencies*. Realizing that an inconsistency exists between two ideas or explanations about how nature works precedes the process of trying to resolve the inconsistency. One of science's most important examples of recognizing inconsistency is Albert Einstein's "curious question" that led him to his theory of relativity:

> Why is there in Maxwell's theory one equation for finding the electromotive force generated in a moving conductor when it goes past a stationary magnet, and another equation when the conductor is stationary and the magnet is moving? (Holton, 1988, p. 212)

To resolve this inconsistency or anomaly, Einstein dismissed traditional conceptions of space and time (including simultaneous events) and worked out a more consistent, harmonious view of reality—relativity theory. This new understanding of nature led to a revolution in the way physicists, and others who understand relativity theory, construct reality.

This chapter identifies some ideas, including cautionary notes, on assessment that should be considered by those interested in translating school science standards into measures that can be used by classroom teachers and others to assess student understanding of science concepts and the nature of science itself. The first section, Defining Understanding, elaborates on what has just been said about what it means to say someone understands a science concept such as *acceleration, density, natural selection, conservation of energy,* or *electromagnetism.* Here and in the second section, Assessing Understanding of Science Concepts, I refer to some of the many prescientific conceptions that have been identified in science education research as widespread among nonscientists, including many who teach school science.

In a third section, Assessing Beliefs about Science and Scientists, I focus on the *nature of science* and the difficulties involved in reaching agreement on this rather fuzzy construct. And finally in the last section, Reasonable Expectations for Science Teachers, I caution against placing unreasonable burdens on teachers for detailed assessment of student achievement.

DEFINING UNDERSTANDING: EXPERT–NOVICE STUDIES

The expert–novice studies in science education, inspired by Newell and Simon's *Human Problem Solving* (1972), identify expertise in problem solving as a critical component of understanding. Research in which I have participated (Smith & Good, 1984; Camacho & Good, 1989) and many other studies attribute successful problem solving in school science to recognition of the correct conceptual structure of a problem, access to needed technical information, and command of the procedures that can be used to achieve a solution. Novices are less successful because they lack facility in one or more of these areas. *According to the Newell and Simon definition of understanding, problem solving success is the ultimate test.* In science when highly interesting problems are solved, Nobel Prizes and other forms of recognition go to scientists who finish first as judged by those in the scientific community.

In university graduate studies problem solving becomes more of a focus, with thesis and dissertation research dominating a student's program of studies. Unlike undergraduate studies, where formal coursework is the main focus, graduate-level study is centered on identifying and researching a question that can add to the knowledge base of the natural sciences. If an interesting problem can be identified and solved by the graduate student (and successfully defended to a supervising committee) it is assumed that understanding has been achieved.

In school science one of the difficulties of equating understanding to problem solving is knowing when a problem is really a problem, rather than a recall-of-algorithm exercise for a given student. Conceptual understanding in science involves more than algorithmic expertise. A more complete definition of understanding science concepts requires that *qualitative* means as well as *quantitative* means be used to assess understanding. The concept of *acceleration*, for example, can be defined in terms of quantitative problem solving ($a = F/m$, $a = V_2 - V_1/T_2 - T_1$, $a = 2d/T$, etc.) and in relation to predictions of what will happen to objects if they are dropped from an airplane or shot from a cannon. *Prediction* is a powerful tool both in science and in education. A scientific theory's power of prediction (especially in the physical sciences) is a mark of its validity and its value in creating new research areas. In science education student prediction of phenomena as a tool in the teacher's toolbox can be a powerful way to determine the extent to which a student understands a science concept.

Most of the research on students' misconceptions in science (see Wandersee, Mintzes, & Novak [1994] for a summary of this knowledge base), and especially the physical sciences, is based on prediction and related explanations. A student is shown a system of some sort (or a representation of the system) and asked to predict what will happen if such and such is done to the system, and then asked to explain the prediction or compare it with other predictions. Other work on prediction (Lavoie & Good, 1988) as a powerful pedagogical tool supports the many studies on students' misconceptions in identifying it as one of the keys to defining understanding in school science.

Explaining science concepts in terms of other concepts, predicting the outcomes of changes in systems, and solving problems that involve more than simple, algorithmic recall are three central ways to define understanding. Each of these ways of defining understanding has its own theory and research base. *Concept mapping* (see Novak & Wandersee, 1990) explains concepts in terms of their relationships to other concepts; *predicting outcomes* when a change is made in a system is a major strategy used in misconceptions research (especially in the physical sciences); and *problem solving* using the expert–novice model for research has a large data base as well. Each of these three pedagogical tools, in its own way, defines understanding in school science. The fact that three fairly distinct knowledge bases have developed out of these ways of defining understanding and that each knowledge base continues to be seen as a valid and fruitful research path, is reason enough to use all three approaches in our attempt to define understanding in school science.

In the next section on *assessing* understanding I use each approach to explore various ways of reaching agreement on the meaning and the means of assessment in school science.

ASSESSING UNDERSTANDING OF SCIENCE CONCEPTS

Defining understanding in terms of problem solving, prediction, and concept mapping takes advantage of the familiarity of most science educators with three large knowledge bases: (1) expert–novice research (problem solving), (2) misconceptions research (prediction), and (3) cognitive structure research (concept mapping). Each approach to studying student's understanding of science concepts is elaborated on in this section, with a view toward assessment by teachers of science.

Assessment as Problem Solving

As mentioned previously, in the many expert–novice studies (in chess, medicine, science, education, etc.) where specialized knowledge and skills are required to become an expert, problem solving is used as the test of understanding. In a recorded interview setting a problem is presented to the novice or expert and the subject is asked to *think aloud* as he or she tries to solve the problem (see Ericsson and Simon [1991] for protocol details). A brief example of a think-aloud interview is provided here to illustrate the procedure (from Smith & Good, 1984) The interviewer (I) has provided the student (NO3) with a Mendelian genetics problem; the student has drawn an incorrect Punnett square and appears confused:

NO3: I'm trying to think ... the chromatids and the separating and everything ... if they ... I think it was Mendelson's (sic) assortment, you know half and half, not a ... un ... See, Mendelson was corrected on the independent assortment of genes ... well not corrected, but there's a new...

I: Uh huh.

NO3: ...theory behind that, I believe, if I remember. And, ah, with this. (Points to Punnett drawn.) It would be like Mendelson, but...

I: OK.

NO3: ...not, ah ... What I'm trying to think is ... uh ... (laughs). I just see all these chromatids going wherever they want ... random assort ... that's what I'm thinking.

The resulting data show how the subject solves or tries to solve the problem. Novices can be compared to experts in terms of problem representation, number and type of solution paths, checks on internal consistency, time required for solution, and so on. For cognitive scientists interested in using computers to model human problem solving, these data can be used to develop programs that simulate expert or novice human problem solving. For educators interested in assessing students' understanding of science concepts these studies point out important differences between experts and novices, and they define understanding in terms of problem solving. It is clear that a major difference is the amount of specialized knowledge available to the expert that is not available to the novice. Also, the way this knowledge is structured in the expert seems to be quite different than the way knowledge is structured in the novice.

To focus on the nature of knowledge structure rather than on problem-solving methods, science education researchers and others use a tool called *concept mapping*, the topic of the next section and the focus of Chapter 2.

Assessment as Concept Mapping

The main assumption behind concept mapping is that expertise or understanding can be assessed by asking a person to construct a *map* by relating concepts in a hierarchical structure using propositional statements such as *is regulated by* and *results in* as the links or connections (see Chapter 2 for more details). The resulting map reflects the person's mental structure related to the concept(s) in question. The hierarchical nature of knowledge is reflected in concept maps and although little research has been done to relate problem-solving expertise to concept mapping, the expert–novice studies tend to support the assumption of hierarchically related concepts. Some research (Demastes-Southerland, Good, & Peebles, 1996) does indicate that cognitive structure, as reflected by concept maps, is influenced by factors other than expertise or understanding of concepts. Also, Ruiz-Primo and Shavelson (1996) have noted that better reliability and validity information on the effect of different mapping techniques is needed. They also recommend more research on students' facility in using concept maps. It is fair to say, however, that concept mapping is recognized by most science educators as a valid way to assess understanding and as a useful instructional tool. Much of the credit for popularizing the use of this tool in science education goes to Joe Novak, Professor Emeritus at Cornell University and for over 40 years an active science education researcher. He has been influential as well in the science misconceptions research, the topic of the next section.

Assessment as Prediction

Problem solving and concept mapping represent important kinds of tests or assessment tools for judging how well someone understands science concepts. Each tool seems to tap an important feature of what it means to understand, although it is clear that problem solving is seen by most scientists and members of Nobel Prize committees as the ultimate test. The third assessment tool or strategy to be considered here shares some of the qualities of problem solving and concept mapping, but I think it also taps a unique part of understanding. *Prediction* is a central part of many misconception studies (Wandersee et al. [1994] estimated about 2000) that probe science concept understanding. A student is presented with a system, or a representation of a system, and then is asked how the system might behave if something is done to it. The system can consist of any objects commonly found in school science laboratories that are used to demonstrate certain phenomena related to the science concept(s) in question. For the physical sciences Stepans (1996) has summarized the results of many misconceptions studies and has translated them into a useful guide for the teacher of science who wants to target students' science (mis)conceptions. Prediction is a central strategy in most of these studies and Franklin (1992) found that paper-and-pencil versions of the studies can be used in a valid and less time-consuming way by classroom teachers. Experienced classroom teachers often use a "talking" version of a prediction strategy to encourage students to think more carefully about science concepts and models being studied. The *thought experiment*, made famous by Galileo, Einstein, and other scientists also involves prediction as a strategy. *What would happen if...?* questions are the central feature of this strategy.

The science misconceptions data base is very convincing, showing that many students maintain prescientific conceptions of big ideas in science even after completing science courses in high school and college. Carefully structured questions, using prediction as a common strategy, can reveal the nature of the student's (mis)conception, and in the process help both student and teacher see the source(s) of the learning problem. The conceptual change model (see Posner, Strike, Hewson, & Gertzog, 1982) in science education assumes that a student must see the shortcomings/weaknesses of a prescientific conception in order to want to try to learn a more scientifically accurate conception. To the extent that this is true, targeting students' science (mis)conceptions should be an important part of science teaching, and using prediction, especially in the physical sciences, is a central feature of this strategy.

Up to this point in the chapter little has been said specifically about "cautionary notes"; however, in the remainder of this chapter I offer some cautionary notes, first on assessing beliefs about the nature of science and then on reasonable assessment expectations for science teachers.

ASSESSING BELIEFS ABOUT SCIENCE
AND SCIENTISTS

The first chapter (The Nature of Science) of *Science for All Americans* (AAAS, 1990) contains many statements that describe a scientific world view, scientific inquiry, and the scientific enterprise. A few of these statements are listed here to help explain more concretely what is meant by the phrase *nature of science* (NOS):

1. Science assumes that the universe is, as its name implies, a vast single system in which the basic rules are everywhere the same (p. 3).
2. Although scientists reject the notion of attaining absolute truth and accept some uncertainty as part of nature, most scientific knowledge is durable (p. 4).
3. Sooner or later, the validity of scientific claims is settled by referring to observations of phenomena (p. 5).
4. A hypothesis that cannot in principle be put to the test of evidence may be interesting, but it is not useful (p. 7).
5. On issues outside of their expertise, the opinions of scientists should enjoy no special credibility (p. 13).

NOS research typically consists of questionnaires composed of questions or statements such as these, where the subject responds by choosing strongly agree, agree, no opinion, disagree, or strongly disagree. Occasionally subjects will be asked to explain their choice, but more often the response will go unexplained. Lederman (1992) has provided us with a nice summary of NOS research and one can conclude that the findings from the studies are inconclusive. There seems to be little agreement on the nature of science among the researchers themselves. Some of the problems involved in assessing beliefs in this area are now discussed in more detail.

NOS Assessment: Problems and Prospects

Problems

In the natural sciences it is nature that has the final say. Science concepts such as acceleration, work, and conservation of energy are well defined and agreed upon by scientists and this agreement is achieved because, ultimately, ideas must be consistent with nature's rules. Roger Newton (1997) identifies *coherence* as a central feature of scientific truths:

> Even though parts of the edifice may be found to be rotten, the coherence of a body of scientific truths accounts for its stability over long periods of time. "Scientific knowledge," John Ziman [Ziman, 1978, p. 83] rightly observes, "eventually becomes a *web* or *network* of laws, models, theoretical principles, formulae, hypotheses, interpretations, etc., which are so closely woven together that the whole assembly is much stronger than any single element." In contrast to many other kinds of truth, the truth of science does not rest on permanent acceptance of any one of its parts." (p. 209)

Unlike knowledge in the natural sciences, social science knowledge is much less stable and coherent, and knowledge about the nature of science and scientists is social science knowledge. Ideological factors, ultimately controlled by nature in the natural sciences, often play an important role in the social sciences. Also, the fuzziness or lack of precision of natural language contributes to the instability and lack of coherence of knowledge in the social sciences. Evolutionary biologist Edward Wilson (1998) suggests that little progress will be made in the social sciences until they are firmly grounded in the natural sciences.

Adding to the difficulties of achieving consensus on the nature of science is the complexity of the subject of study. The single word *science* refers to the process of doing science as well as to the knowledge produced by the process. Science is both a process and a product. However, when NOS research is done, especially via the questionnaire, it is often not clear if the word *science* refers to a process or a product (i.e., scientific knowledge). And to further complicate things the process of doing science is quite different in the early stage of developing new ideas compared to the later stage of testing the ideas. Holton (1988) refers to these two stages of doing science as *private* and *public* science. Private science is the early, imaginative, creative part of inventing or discovering new ideas to better explain nature, whereas public science is the later testing stage to see if the new ideas conform to nature and to related science knowledge (coherence). In an earlier paper (Good, 1996) I represented the complexity of the construct, NOS, by writing $NOS = (NOST_E + NOST_L) + NOSK$, where $NOST_E$ is nature of science thinking (early), $NOST_L$ is nature of science thinking (later), and NOSK is nature of science knowledge (product).

Science teachers, researchers, and others interested in assessing NOS beliefs should pose questions carefully so the student or research subject understands how the word *science* is being used.

Prospects.

So what are the prospects of actually making progress in assessment of students' ideas about the nature of science? I think we must begin by agreeing that the two major U.S. science education reform documents, *Benchmarks for Science Literacy* (AAAS, 1993) and *National Science Education Standards* (1996), should serve as the guideposts for NOS assessment questions. Both *Benchmarks* and *Standards* were developed by a large number of scientists, educators, and others who represent the science education community in the United States, so these documents are probably as close as we can get to a consensus about the nature of science.

A faculty colleague of mine, Catherine Cummins, and a current doctoral student, Gary Lyon, and I have begun to develop and field test a NOS questionnaire based on *Benchmarks* and *Standards*. Example questions are listed here:

1. Scientists assume that the universe is a vast single system in which the basic rules are the same everywhere. (AAAS, 1990, p. 2)
2. The modification of ideas, rather than their outright rejection, is the norm in the natural sciences. (AAAS, 1990, p. 3)
3. Many matters cannot usefully be examined in a scientific way. (AAAS, 1990, p. 4)
4. There is no fixed set of steps that scientists follow that leads them to scientific knowledge. (AAAS, 1990, p. 5)
5. Sooner or later, the validity of scientific claims is settled by referring to observations of phenomena. (AAAS, 1990, p. 12)

In an early report (Good, Cummins, & Lyon, 1999) on this effort we recommend that others interested in NOS research develop assessment instruments and other data-collection techniques based on *Benchmarks* and *Standards* so that research results can be compared with some assurance that we are comparing apples with apples. The results of many of the NOS studies summarized by Lederman (1992) and earlier by Munby (1983) are at best inconclusive primarily because there is little agreement among researchers regarding the nature of science. However, even the use of a single "consensus" questionnaire must be regarded as inadequate because of the nature of questionnaire data in general. NOS questionnaire data should be supplemented with individual interview data. Although time-consuming, individual interviews allow the researcher to clarify what the interviewee means by answering strongly agree or disagree or whatever on a questionnaire. The individual interview can serve as a check on the questionnaire, providing feedback for refining the questionnaire for future use.

It is unlikely that professional philosophers, historians, sociologists, scientists, and others who study and write about the nature of of science will ever agree on its many aspects. Studying the nature of science is not like studying nature. However, we have an opportunity to begin to make some progress in NOS research by taking seriously the reform documents *Benchmarks* and *Standards*. It will be interesting to see what happens.

REASONABLE ASSESSMENT EXPECTATIONS FOR SCIENCE TEACHERS

The main cautionary note in this chapter is saved for last. For a decade or so there has been a lot of talk about *authentic* assessment (apparently previous forms of assessment were not authentic), *alternative* assessment, *performance* assessment, *portfolios*, and so on. Champagne and Newell (1992) noted that much of the current enthusiasm for alternative methods of assessing scientific literacy has roots in political as well as intellectual concerns. Low test scores for U.S. students on international tests of science literacy cause some educators to blame shortcomings on multiple-choice tests and similar traditional measures of achievement. Other critics of education with a social constructivist bent disapprove of traditional tests because they do not allow students to "negotiate" their own knowledge (see Matthews [1994] and Nola [1998] for a critique of various forms of constructivism).

Whatever the reason(s) for rejecting traditional assessment in science, it is clear that many educators believe that traditional assessment procedures must be changed. As yet, however, there has been little evidence offered to show that traditional assessment procedures must be changed to ensure higher levels of science literacy.

One alternative assessment procedure is known as *performance* assessment (see Chapters 10 and 13 in this book for details). In performance assessment the teacher is expected to provide students with laboratory equipment, pose a problem, and determine whether the student can perform satisfactorily. Obviously, this requires much more teacher time and effort than a machine-scored, multiple-choice test or a short-answer, problem-solving exam and there is no guarantee that higher level thinking is being assessed. As the catchy phrase goes, "hands-on is not necessarily minds-on." For the classroom science teacher who teaches 150 students in six classes each day the large amount of extra time required for performance assessment had better show dramatic effects; and even if dramatic effects could be assured, where would the time be found? Most teachers are already using all their time doing the many things expected of them these days. The 1990s have not been an easy time to be a teacher and there is no reason to believe the job will be any less demanding in the next decade, so anything that places even more demands on teachers will be met with caution and skepticism.

Another of the "new" assessment techniques is known as *portfolio* assessment (see Chapter 8 for more details). Here students are asked to compile and maintain a record of the work they do related to their science class and teachers periodically check the portfolio and make written comments to the student. It is not at all clear how effective portfolios can be in determining a student's progress in understanding scientific ideas, the traditional goal of science education and presumably the focus of national or international standardized tests. And like performance assessment, portfolios demand more time from an already busy teacher. It is difficult to imagine how a secondary school science teacher could keep up with 150 portfolios on any kind of a regular basis, giving meaningful feedback to all the students, and continue to perform all of the other duties of a teacher.

Improving assessment of student achievement in science is a central goal of current science education reform efforts but it is not clear that so-called "authentic" assessment will contribute in a significant way to improved science literacy in the United States. The central goals of science literacy are improved understanding by students of (1) science concepts, (2) the nature of science itself, and (3) how science interacts with other components of society. The first goal (and traditionally the most important), improved understanding of science concepts, can be assessed in a number of ways, including the use of traditional problem solving, prediction, and concept mapping as described earlier in this chapter.

For assessment techniques that require excessive teacher time the computer offers a possible solution (see Chapter 8 for more details). Given adequate numbers of computers with appropriate software, teachers can expect many assessment chores to be transferred to these tireless, powerful educational tools. A wide variety of instructional and assessment methods can be carried out by well-designed computer programs, including simulations of natural events that allow students to conduct experiments, solve problems, and answer questions. The computer as intelligent tutor has the potential to blend instruction with assessment in a seamless way, a goal proposed by many assessment experts and prominently presented in the *National Science Education Standards* (e.g., "In the vision of science education described in the *Standards*, teaching often cannot be distinguished from assessment", p. 80).

Standards and *Benchmarks* have identified, in a fairly general way, what science content and related knowledge should be considered fundamental for defining a scientifically literate citizen. It has not been easy to reach a consensus on these standards within the science education community and it will be even more difficult to reach a consensus on standards for assessment. Especially for the science content standards identified in *Benchmarks* and *Standards*, it seems inevitable that statewide and perhaps nationwide tests based on reform documents will be developed to determine how students "measure up." In fact, according to a thoughtful account of assessment in school science found in *Blueprints for Reform* (AAAS, 1998), most states have aligned or are presently aligning state curriculum frameworks and related assessment systems with *Benchmarks* and *Standards*. We should be very careful not to overburden classroom teachers with paperwork, as some forms of assessment seem to do. Guarding against this problem as new forms of assessment are developed and field-tested is perhaps the biggest challenge facing the field of assessment reform.

References

AAAS (1990). *Science for all Americans*. New York: Oxford University Press.

AAAS (1993). *Benchmarks for science literacy*. New York: Oxford University Press.

AAAS (1998). *Blueprints for reform*. New York: Oxford University Press.

Camacho, M., & Good, R. (1989). Problem solving and chemical equilibrium: Successful versus unsuccessful performance. *Journal of Research in Science Teaching*, 26, 251–272.

Champagne, A., & Newell, S. (1992). Directions for research and development: Alternative methods of assessing scientific literacy. *Journal of Research in Science Teaching*, 29, 841–860.

Demastes-Southerland S., Good, R., & Peebles, P. (1996). Patterns of conceptual change in evolution. *Journal of Research in Science Teaching*, 33, 407–431.

Franklin, B. (1992). The development, validation, and application of a two-tier diagnostic instrument to detect misconceptions in the areas of force, heat, light, and electricity. Unpublished doctoral dissertation, Louisiana State University, Baton Rouge.

Good, R. (1996). Trying to reach consensus on the nature of science: Words get in the way. Paper presented at the annual meeting of the National Association for Research in Science Teaching, St. Louis, MO, March 31–April 3.

Good, R., Cummins, C., & Lyon, G. (1999). Nature of science assessment based on *Benchmarks* and *Standards*. Paper presented at the annual meeting of the Association for the Education of Teachers of Science, Austin, TX, January 14–17.

Holton, G. (1988). *Thematic origins of scientific thought: Kepler to Einstein*. Cambridge, MA: Harvard University Press.

Lavoie, D., & Good, R. (1988). Nature and use of prediction skills in a biological computer simulation. *Journal of Research in Science Teaching*, 25, 335–360.

Lederman, N. (1992). Students' and teachers' conceptions of the nature of science: A review of the research. *Journal of Research in Science Teaching*, 29, 331–359.

Matthews, M. (1994). *Science teaching: The role of history and philosophy of science*. New York: Routledge.

Munby, H. (1983). *An investigation into the measurement of attitudes in science education*. Columbus, OH: The ERIC Science, Mathematics and Environmental Education Clearinghouse, The Ohio State University.

Newell, A., & Simon, H. (1972). *Human problem solving*. Englewood Cliffs, NJ: Prentice-Hall.

Newton, R. (1997). *The truth of science: Physical theories and reality*. Cambridge, MA: Harvard University Press.

Nola, R. (1998). Constructivism in science and in science education: A philosophical critique. In M. Matthews (Ed.), *Constructivism in science education: A philosophical examination* (pp. 31–59), Boston, MA: Kluwer.

Novak, J., & Wandersee, J. (1990). Perspectives on concept mapping. Special issue of the *Journal of Research in Science Teaching*, 27, 921–1075.

Posner, G., Strike, K., Hewson, P., & Gertzog, W. (1982). Accommodation of a scientific conception: Toward a theory of conceptual change. *Science Education*, 66, 211–227.

Ruiz-Primo, M., & Shavelson, R. (1996). Problems and issues in the use of concept maps in science assessment. *Journal of Research in Science Teaching*, 33, 569–600.

Smith, M., & Good, R. (1984). Problem solving and classical genetics: Successful vs unsuccessful performance. *Journal of Research in Science Teaching*, 21, 894–912.

Stepans, J. (1996). *Targeting students' science misconceptions: Physical science concepts using the conceptual change model*. Riverview, FL: Idea Factory.

Wandersee, J., Mintzes, J., & Novak, J. (1994). Research on alternative conceptions in science. In D. Gabel (Ed.), *Handbook of research in science teaching and learning* (pp. 177–210). New York: Macmillan.

Wilson, E. (1998). *Consilience: The unity of knowledge*. New York: Knopf.

CHAPTER

15

Epilogue: On Ways of Assessing Science Understanding

JOSEPH D. NOVAK
Cornell University

JOEL J. MINTZES
North Carolina State University

JAMES H. WANDERSEE
Louisiana State University

ASSESSING SCIENCE UNDERSTANDING: A SUMMARY OF TOOLS, TECHNIQUES, AND IDEAS

We have sought in this volume to discuss some of the important issues and methodologies relevant to the improvement of assessment in the natural sciences. While many of these would apply to assessment in any domain of learning, our examples and discussions have emphasized application for science instruction. The problems in the sciences are especially acute, partly because there has been such enormous growth in knowledge in this field and because common instructional practices tend to emphasize memorization of science "facts" with little emphasis on the great unifying ideas or concepts of the sciences. While we agree with critics such as Hirsch (1996) who argue that the "Education Establishment" has placed too much emphasis on students' "self-realization" and acquisition of generic "higher order thinking skills," and too little emphasis on the acquisition of subject matter knowledge, there are methods of teaching and assessment that can help to achieve all of these goals. It is easy to go off in the wrong direction when teaching strategies and assessment approaches emphasize rote learning of science facts, problem-solving algorithms or "inquiry" activities, with little or no regard for the quality of understanding of powerful scientific concepts and methods of knowledge creation.

In the first chapter we presented key ideas from a theory of education that recognizes that every educational event involves five "commonplaces": (1) the learner, (2) the teacher, (3) the knowledge framework, (4) the context or social milieu, and (5) the assessment strategy. All five of the commonplaces operate in some way in every educational event and all interact with one another. The result can be high levels of meaningful learning for all students and concomitant acquisition of positive values and important skills, or instruction that results in little differentiation and improvement in student's knowledge structures and negative feelings and attitudes toward the sciences.

Chapter 2 presented the relatively new and powerful tool of concept maps, which can serve both as a facilitator for helping students to learn, create, and use knowledge, and also an assessment tool that can reveal to both students and teachers the quality and level of development of conceptual understanding for any domain of science, at any grade level (Novak, 1998). However, this tool cannot be used most effectively for evaluation if it is not also used as a tool to facilitate learning. Since teachers tend to teach the way they have been taught, and since concept maps are not yet used widely in college science or teaching methods courses, we face the challenge of breaking the cycle and encouraging teachers at all levels to use this tool. How does one get started if he or she has never been taught to use this tool? The only way is to begin using it! We believe the readers of this volume are the kind of innovative teachers who will benefit from the suggestions in Chapter 2 and apply this tool in both their teaching and in their assessment of student understanding.

Chapter 3 presented another tool, the vee heuristic, that can also be used to facilitate learning in sciences, especially learning from science laboratory work or inquiry studies, and can also be used for assessment of the quality of learning of science. Concept maps and vee heuristics are tools rooted in a theory of learning and knowledge-making that recognizes that all knowledge is constructed by individuals who are engaged in high levels of meaningful learning. Moreover, these activities are driven by high levels of positive feelings and value toward science knowledge and the process of knowledge creation. This symbiotic relationship between thinking, feeling, and acting that builds on high levels of meaningful learning underlies human constructivism.

Piaget (1926) pioneered the use of "clinical interviews" as a method for ascertaining patterns in children's thinking. Building on his work, many teachers and researchers have found value in using "structured interviews" to assess the degree of understanding, or misunderstanding, of their students. In Chapter 4, Southerland, Smith, and Cummins presented ideas on effective ways to design, conduct, and evaluate structured interviews. While it is true that a classroom teacher cannot routinely assess all of his/her students using this technique, it is nevertheless a powerful tool to be used occasionally, say once or twice a week with a sample of two or three students, to assess both the entry level of concepts or misconceptions held by students and their level of understanding after instruction. The rich, detailed picture of students' understanding revealed by interviews contributes importantly to the teacher's improvement of instructional design, and to students' awareness and understanding of their own cognitive development. This tool should be used by every teacher at least occasionally.

The chapter by Hogan and Fisherkeller described a type of interview format that is especially effective for understanding students' thinking and reasoning patterns. In Chapter 5 they present samples from such interviews to illustrate how this assessment approach is done and how it reveals a deeper understanding of student's developing understandings.

All science textbooks contain numerous pictures, diagrams, tables, charts, and other visual representations of knowledge. Research has shown that most students do not use or benefit from these illustrations. In Chapter 6, Wandersee presented strategies for encouraging better use of illustrations, and also methods for assessment of the quality of learning resulting from student's use of illustrations. His suggestions could be incorporated into any assessment program and would aid teachers, textbook authors, and students in gaining insights into the ideas represented in visual tools.

Careful observation is a key to acquiring knowledge in the sciences. In Chapter 7, Trowbridge and Wandersee provided a rationale for the careful use of observation strategies in assessment. They provide a variety of criteria that can be used to judge the quality of observations and students' reports on their observations. They provide criteria to compare the observations made by experts and novices. While it is true that our observations are constrained by the power of the "conceptual goggles" we wear, improving observation strategies can aid in the development of student understanding, together with the development of their "conceptual goggles."

Vitale and Romance (Chapter 8) provided examples and guidelines for using portfolios as an alternative assessment form. Their chapter does more than suggest things that can be included in portfolios; they go on to explain how certain items can contribute to assessment of student's cognitive development and they provide illustration of assessment strategies for portfolios. Too often portfolios are little more than miscellaneous collections of students' papers and drawings, with little explicit effort to show how they contribute to students' understanding of key concepts of a field. Vitale and Romance summarize some of the important work done to illustrate the potential value of portfolios as assessment tools.

SemNet is another useful knowledge-representation tool, developed by Kathleen Fisher and her colleagues at San Diego State University. Chapter 9 described the use of this tool and summarized research showing the positive impact of SemNet on student achievement of understanding. Fisher also provides numerous illustrations of SemNets done by students and shows how these evidence greater or lesser comprehension of science concepts. SemNet can be used together with concept maps and vee diagrams, since these tools provide somewhat different, yet complementary evidence of students' understandings.

For the foreseeable future, preparation of written text will continue to be an important form of communicating knowledge. In Chapter 10, Champagne and Kouba described relevant research and strategies for improving the science writing performance of students. As all readers have no doubt experienced, writing about something you have observed or studied can force a high degree of reflection on the knowledge you seek to present. While writing also entails skills in grammar, diction, and writing style, there are important elements that can be considered in the assessment of student's writing that can lead not only to improved writing skills, but also to better understanding of science. The authors suggest various scoring rubrics that can be employed to evaluate student writing and to assist them in writing better. Good writing can also build skills in reflective thinking and critical observation. Concept maps, vee diagrams, and SemNet can be used as adjunct tools to facilitate writing, but these tools are not a substitute for well-executed written exposition. With the guidelines provided by Champaign and Kouba, writing for assessment of science understanding can be much improved.

Multiple-choice testing will be with us for the indefinite future. In Chapter 11, Sadler presented ideas on how to improve the use of such tests by application of item response theory and the results of studies on student misconceptions that have been done in the past three decades. One interesting observation Sadler reports is that when alternative answer choices are based on common student misconceptions, some groups will score below chance levels on these items. Another observation is that such test items often show a decline in scores as students gain information on a topic, and then a subsequent rise. These effects lead to J-shaped score distributions and signal the difficult problems learners have in reconstructing their conceptual frameworks, integrating new information, and reconciling conceptual conflicts.

The Ausubelian (1968) psychological processes of progressive differentiation and integrative reconciliation of concept and propositional frameworks are illustrated in Sadler's work. He also shows ways that multiple-choice test items can be improved to measure much more than rote recall of information. Recently, Sadler was recognized by conferral of the JRST Award (1999) of the National Association for Research in Science Teaching (NARST) for this research effort.

With the globalization of world economies, every developed country finds itself increasingly in economic competition with every other country. Since the development of wealth is also becoming increasingly dependent on the quantity and quality of knowledge produced, in recent years there has been a growing interest in state, national, and international comparisons of student achievement in science and mathematics. Most of the early state, national, and international testing has relied primarily on multiple-choice, machine-scored tests. While these tests do provide a crude measure of the knowledge students possess, they are not highly valid indicators of how students can use their knowledge in new contexts. Tamir described in Chapter 12 the recent history and emerging patterns in national and international science and mathematics assessment programs. He also described the differences in enrollment patterns and curricula that make cross-comparisons between schools and nations difficult at best. There are also differences in the prevailing attitudes and values in different countries, and these need to be considered in developing tests and evaluating the results. All these problems notwithstanding, national and international assessment is probably here to stay, Tamir offers suggestions for the improvement of such evaluations.

All assessment requires that we consider the validity and reliability of the assessment measures we use. In Chapter 13, Shavelson and Ruiz-Primo carefully reviewed the various issues involved in establishing reliability and validity of assessment measures. Unless the latter are present, we cannot generalize from an assessment measure to expected performance on related tasks. With many alternative assessment strategies, such as concept mapping, numerous problems arise in scoring and interpreting student performance, thus posing threats to reliability and validity. The authors deal carefully with these issues and give numerous examples of how established assessment principles can be applied to alternative assessment approaches. While much research remains to be done, the authors express their confidence in the promise that new assessment strategies hold for improving science education.

Finally, in Chapter 14, Good presented some cautionary notes on assessment of science understanding. He reviewed some of the issues that need continuous attention and provided examples to illustrate possible pitfalls in assessment. Good noted some of the efforts to assess students' understanding of the nature of science and showed how some difficulties are rooted in the complex nature of scientific inquiry and the evolutionary character of scientific knowledge. Promising as some alternative assessment strategies are, Good cautioned that we cannot overload classroom teachers with time-consuming assessment strategies whose application in ordinary classrooms is unrealistic. We trust that these cautionary notes have been given adequate consideration in this volume.

LEARNING, TEACHING, AND ASSESSMENT: A HUMAN CONSTRUCTIVIST VIEW

Plato dreamed of a rational world ruled by philosopher-kings. Terman revived this dangerous vision but led his corp of mental testers in an act of usurpation. If all people could be tested, and then sorted into roles appropriate for their intelligence, then a just, and, above all, efficient society might be constructed for the first time in history. (Gould, 1981)

One of the repeating themes of this book has been the view that success in creating, learning, and using knowledge is not well captured by commonly used assessment practices that rely heavily on single, quantitative measures of subject matter attainment (Novak, 1998). Tests of this type, which purport to measure classroom achievement (and "intellectual ability"), have been a significant part of the educational landscape for nearly 100 years, but their use began to grow exponentially in the era following World War II, along with the explosive growth in the school-age population.

The "testing and measurement" movement had its origins in the practicalist era in American education (Mintzes, Wandersee, Novak, 1998) and was heavily influenced by the pioneers of educational psychology, most notably Spearman (1904), Binet and Simon (1911), Terman (1917), Thurstone (1924), and the inventor of the "Army Alpha Test," Robert Yerkes (1921). Although the current generation of teachers and university faculty has grown up with techniques such as multiple-choice, completion, and true/false tests, these and similar "objective" approaches were used quite sparingly in the years leading up to World War II, and became a prominent fixture of the assessment repertoire only after the "baby boom" generation entered the schools in the 1950s and 1960s (Bloom, Hastings, & Madaus, 1971). Interestingly, the widespread use of these testing devices has been, until very recently, a uniquely American phenomenon; unfortunately, however other countries have begun copying these methods.

Along with the ubiquitous *Stanford–Binet Test*, the *Peabody Picture Vocabulary Test*, and other standardized measures of intellectual ability and academic achievement (e.g., SAT, GRE, LSAT, MCAT), these assessment practices grew rapidly in the postwar years (together with "psychometric science") and soon became the sine qua non of evaluation, despite their lack of a sound theoretical foundation based on an understanding of human learning. In their zeal to become "scientific educators" many experts in test and measurement theory sought to create a "wissenschaft of evaluation"; to others, these efforts produced a kind of "tyranny of testing." These problems were compounded when classroom teachers began adopting assessments methods intended to identify "outliers" in large populations.

What pupils shall be tested? The answer is, all. If only selected children are tested, many cases most in need of adjustment will be overlooked... Universal testing is fully warranted. (Terman, 1923; quoted in Gould, 1981)

We must ... strive increasingly for the improvement of our methods of mental measurement, for there is no longer ground for doubt concerning the practical as well as the theoretical importance of studies of human behavior. We must learn to measure skillfully every form and aspect of behavior which has psychological and sociological significance. (Yerkes, 1923; quoted in Gould, 1981)

Among other claims, authors of these "scientific" measures of student learning proposed to offer efficient and inexpensive ways of selecting and sorting students; an increasingly important characteristic in an age of burgeoning applications and strongly competitive admissions policies at the nation's best colleges and universities. In heavily enrolled college science courses, the multiple-choice, machine-scored test offered a low-cost way of processing students; and the financial benefits accruing to academic science departments enabled colleges to offer a greater selection of upper division courses and expanded graduate programs (Pearsall, Skipper, & Mintzes, 1997). Mimicking their university professors, many secondary school science teachers soon adopted these time-saving techniques.

In contrast to these approaches, authors of this book have suggested a wide range of potentially valuable alternative assessment techniques that attempt to distinguish between *rote* and *meaningful* science learning. Among the implicit assumptions we make are two that are central to a human constructivist view of assessment: (1) that *understanding is not meaningfully revealed through "normalized" comparisons among students*, and (2) that *conceptual change is not adequately represented by a single, "standardized" alphanumeric score*. The former requires evidence of *intersubjectivity, coherence, parsimony, and transparency*; and the latter requires *multiple, longitudinal comparisons* of the same learner over extended periods of time. To illustrate how assessment practices might be improved, we cite one longitudinal study that followed science learners from the early elementary school years through grade 12 (Novak & Musonda, 1991), and others (Martin, 1998; Pearsall, 1995; Skipper, 1995) that examined knowledge restructuring in several semester-long, college level biology courses.

In a now-classic study, Novak and Musonda (1991) analyzed concept maps depicting students' understanding of the "particulate nature of matter" drawn from structured, clinical interviews over the course of 12 years. In grade 2, Paul recognizes that some substances (such as sugar) are made of "tiny chunks" (Figure 1). He also understands that these chunks may break up and become invisible when dissolved in water. Furthermore, he is clearly able to claim that water and ice are made of "the same stuff" and that water freezes, while ice melts. Additionally however, it appears that Paul has yet to understand that all physical substances (e.g., air, water, ice and cement) are also made of "chunks"; and he seems to believe that "smell" is a kind of substance that is composed of "oxygen or something."

By grade 12 Paul can assign a wide range of important, scientifically acceptable concept labels to these phenomena (Figure 2). The "chunks" have been replaced by "molecules" and his appropriate use of concepts such as solid, liquid, gas, sublime, vaporize, dissolve, energy, space, and nothing suggest that he has a fairly well-differentiated and highly integrated understanding of the molecular–kinetic theory of matter. Interestingly, it appears that his basic misconception about "smell" has been retained, but now it is

A- PAUL GRADE 2

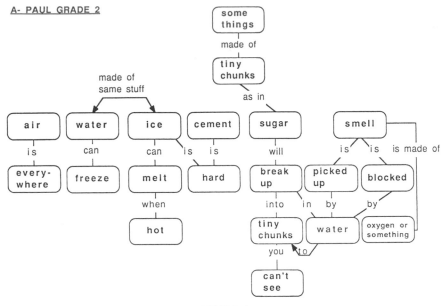

FIGURE 1

Paul's "tiny chunks" (grade 2).

embedded (and possibly undergirded) in an extremely complex framework of interrelated concepts. The finding that students' scientific misconceptions are "tenacious and resistant to change" has been recognized for over 30 years (Ausubel, 1968), and more recently has become a centerpiece in thinking about knowledge restructuring and conceptual change (Mintzes et al., 1998).

The notion that students' ideas undergo substantial change in structural complexity and propositional validity as a result of formal and informal learning, and that misconceptions are often retained despite the best efforts of good teachers, is further underscored by longitudinal studies of college and university science students (Pearsall et al., 1997; Martin, 1998). Several recent studies have explored the way learners restructure their knowledge in biology over the course of a semester by constructing concept maps at 4-week intervals throughout the term. The results of these studies suggest that a substantial amount of knowledge restructuring occurs, and that much of it can be described as a "weak" (Carey, 1986) type of reorganization, resulting in an incremental, cumulative, and limited form of conceptual change. It is probable that much of this weak restructuring is a product of subsumption learning (Ausubel, Novak, & Hanesian, 1978).

It is also clear, however, that the first few weeks in a learning sequence is typically characterized by a "strong" or radical form of reorganization that accompanies the introduction of a new set of "higher-order," superordinate

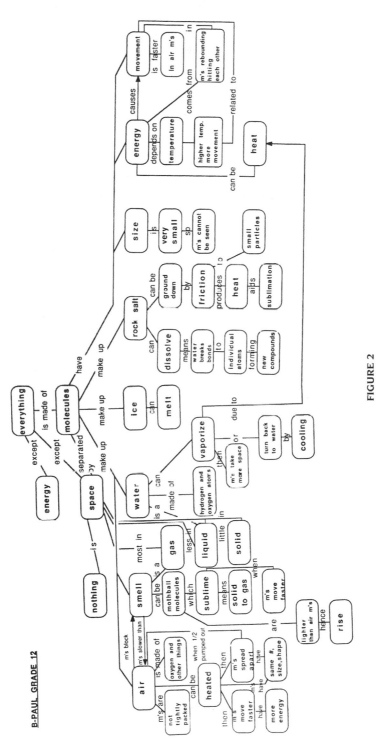

FIGURE 2

Paul's "molecules" (grade 12).

concepts. When these concepts become fully integrated into the learner's knowledge structure, a wholesale, abrupt, and extensive change in conceptual understanding may be expected. It is significant that the latent period required for substantive integration of superordinate concepts varies substantially among learners and knowledge domains.

To illustrate some of these issues, Lori enrolled in a one-semester, introductory biology course for nonscience majors and constructed her first concept map during the second week of the term (Figure 3). Her understanding of "living things" is structured around their requirements for oxygen, food, and water. She recognizes that plants get their food from photosynthesis, which requires carbon dioxide and water, and that animals require an exogenous source of food. Although her knowledge framework is relatively sparse, the only explicit misconception she depicts is the proposition that "oxygen helps plants eat." The notion that plants don't respire is a common one; it is seen among students of all age groups and ability levels (Songer & Mintzes, 1994; Wandersee, 1983).

In subsequent concept maps (Figure 4), her knowledge structure becomes progressively differentiated and significantly more complex. Among the important changes is the appearance of several new organizing nodes such as "cells," "DNA," "cellular respiration," and "biomes." Each of these nodes produces multiple branches, cross-links, and examples. Additionally, the newly emergent knowledge structure takes on many levels of hierarchy and a qualitative sophistication not found in her original concept map.

Lori's depiction of plant and animal nutrition has become substantially more complex; for example, she seems to understand that "animals are

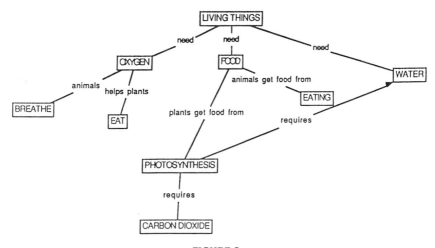

FIGURE 3
Lori's "living things" (1st year college: nonmajors).

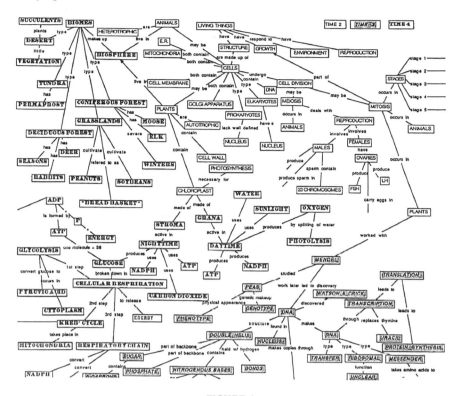

FIGURE 4
Lori's subsequent concept maps.

heterotrophic" and that "plants are autotrophic." Furthermore, she recognizes the chloroplast as the site of photosynthesis and apparently has a rudimentary grasp of cellular respiration. She even sees that glucose, the product of photosynthesis, is broken down in cellular respiration where energy is extracted. One misconception that Lori has apparently picked up in the course of her learning is that the "dark phase" of photosynthesis occurs only during the nighttime. This, too, is a common misunderstanding, seen in all age groups despite ability and previous instruction (Wandersee et al., 1994).

The concept maps of students enrolled in Lori's class (N = 93) were scored using a modified version (Markham, Mintzes, & Jones, 1994) of Novak and Gowin's (1984) rubric. A quantitative analysis of the scores (Figure 5) revealed a stepwise, incremental, and cumulative change in students' frameworks of "living things" over the course of the semester. A similar pattern of incremental change has been found among science majors in courses taken during the first (Pearsall, 1995) and third (Martin, 1998) years of the undergraduate program in the biological sciences.

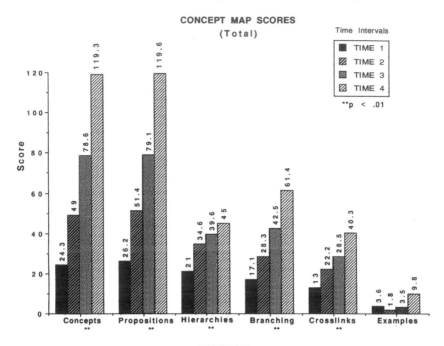

FIGURE 5
Summary of concept map scores (Weeks 2, 5, 9, 13).

Although we have championed the role of concept maps and V diagrams in assessing science understanding and conceptual change, we recognize that other techniques (including those described in the preceding chapters) make additional and complementary contributions to this overall effort. We clearly need a wide range of high-quality assessment tools that can be deployed in a variety of combinations and permutations as circumstances dictate. What remains to be examined is how best and in what circumstances to deploy these alternative strategies, and what role, weight, or value should be assigned to each of them.

ASSESSING ASSESSMENT AND VALUING STUDENT WORK

Assessing Assessment

What is needed for helping educators guide the organic growth of children's thinking toward formal knowledge of a discipline is a technique for knowledge representation

that faithfully portrays students' conceptions while simultaneously comparing them
to experts'. (Hogan & Fisherkeller, 1996)

We have suggested that the quality of an assessment system is ultimately a measure of how well it reveals *understanding* and *conceptual change*. Further, we have argued that *understanding* is a dynamic epistemological status conferred on individuals by a consensually recognized referent group (i.e., "experts") within a community of scholars. In the context of the science classroom, the teacher serves as the de facto local representative (or delegate) of this referent group. Additionally, we have suggested that intersubjectivity, coherence, parsimony, and transparency comprise the principal criteria used by the scientific community to confer this epistemological status.

In recognizing *understanding* as a dynamic epistemological status, we explicitly identify *conceptual change* as any significant modification or transformation in a conceptual or explanatory framework over time. In this context, the function of classroom assessment is essentially threefold: (1) to ascertain the epistemological status of an individual at a given moment in time, (2) to document changes in that status, and (3) to assign value to the status and its changes. With this in mind, it is clear that no single assessment strategy, by itself, can fulfill all of these functions and that some variable combination of techniques will be needed as circumstances dictate.

Hogan and Fisherkeller (1996) recently suggested that the fundamental challenge of assessment is to find ways of representing two aspects of students' knowledge, which they refer to as "compatibility with expert propositions" and "elaboration of ideas." Using a series of clinical interviews and a bidimensional coding system, they attempted to assess students' ideas about nutrient cycling in ecosystems. We agree that a good assessment mechanism must differentiate between two epistemologically related dimensions, which we prefer to label *understanding* and *conceptual change*.

To provide a way of thinking about the relative strengths and weaknesses of several assessment strategies, we offer a two-dimensional graphic (Figure 6), plotting these strategies in terms of their proposed usefulness in documenting *understanding* and *conceptual change*. As a meaningful intellectual exercise, we challenge readers to think about other assessment strategies and where each might fit within this schema.

We begin with the ubiquitous true/false test, which apparently retains its currency in some academic circles despite its many limitations. In our view, this form of assessment is of remarkably little value, as a measure of either understanding or conceptual change. We compare this form of testing with two other commonly used techniques: (1) attitude inventories or opinion polls, and (2) application tasks or problem sets.

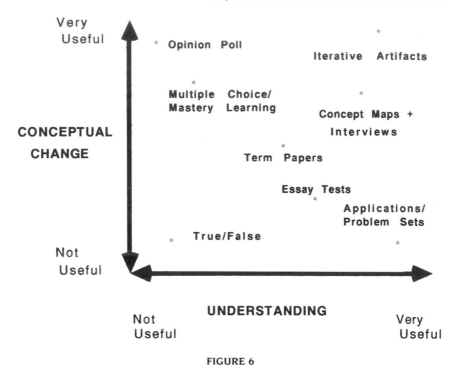

FIGURE 6
Strengths and weaknesses of several assessment strategies based on criteria of understanding and conceptual change.

The attitude inventory or opinion poll (as it is employed in the classroom and in other contexts) may be thought of as an exquisitely sensitive and often remarkably volatile measure of conceptual change. When used in the science classroom (before, during, and after instruction), it offers the teacher some insight into the way students' global views vary over the course of a semester or an academic year. "What do you think about Dar-win's views on natural selection?" "Do nuclear reactors offer a safe, efficient, and economically viable way of delivering electrical energy to large popula-tions?" "Is abortion a safe means of terminating an unwanted pregnancy?" "Should earthquake-prone areas remain off-limits for human habitation?" Responses to questions such as these may provide valuable feedback, a kind of formative evaluation, for teachers who want to know whether their efforts are "getting through" to students. In general, however, they *do not* offer much evidence of conceptual understanding (unless students are required to provide a thoroughly well-thought-out rationale for their responses).

In contrast, application tasks and problem sets, as they are often used in science classes, may be among the most effective ways of assessing understanding. As suggested by Toulmin (Chapter 3), "in showing that he recognizes how and when to *apply* these [explanatory] procedures a man gives all the proof needed for professional purposes that he has acquired a "conceptual grasp" of the discipline"; "we come to understand the scientific significance of those [scientific] words and equations, only when we learn their *application*" [emphasis our own].

The value of application tasks and problem sets has been recognized by generations of teachers, especially in knowledge domains such as physics, chemistry, and genetics. Novel problems that require a rationale or justification are clearly among the most valuable of these methods. Unfortunately, in the hands of less experienced science teachers, problems and applications often become an exercise in memorizing a solution path or a simple algorithm. In either case, however, application tasks and problem sets, as they are commonly used in science classrooms, are typically viewed as "one-shot" assessments; consequently, they do not offer a convenient way of exploring or documenting *conceptual change*.

By way of comparison, an assessment strategy that depends on the longitudinal construction of concept maps along with structured, clinical interviews (such as that described in the preceding section) seems to offer a readily accessible way of tapping into both *understanding* and *conceptual change*. Another approach that offers similar advantages is the iterative construction of classroom artifacts. One excellent example of this is the construction of hypermedia representations that reveal emerging student understanding of science concepts (Spitulnik, Zembal-Saul, & Krajcik, 1998). Spitulnik et al. use hypermedia authoring systems such as Hyper-Card and HyperStudio in high school chemistry classes and university-level science methods courses to enable students to depict their understandings at three times during the course of a semester. A comparison of these hypermedia artifacts reveals much about student understandings and the way they change over time.

Valuing Student Work

This volume has described many potentially useful ways of assessing science understanding. Yet, very little has been said about *assigning value* to student work, and the criteria instructors might consider as they do so.

Traditionally, evaluation (assigning value) has served two principal purposes: (1) providing feedback to instructors and students to improve teaching and learning, and (2) judging how well teachers and students have succeeded in performing their respective roles. The former is generally referred to as *formative evaluation* and the latter as *summative evaluation*.

Within a *human constructivist* perspective, we have suggested that the purpose of assessment is to document *understanding* and *conceptual change*. To help guide teachers as they begin to think about assigning value to these issues, we offer an initial series of analytical questions (Figure 7). In some ways, these questions may be thought of as a kind of *scoring rubric*, but we have purposefully omitted point values in order to encourage teachers to think about how much weight or emphasis should be placed on each. We also wish to encourage teachers, curriculum developers, school administrators, and others to add to and modify these questions as local conditions dictate.

WINDOWS ON THE MIND: CONCLUDING REMARKS

In this volume we have attempted to present a view of assessment in science education that departs significantly from the traditional "selecting and sorting" model that has become standard fare in our schools. We have asserted that *good assessment practice must be built on a strong and intellectually defensible theory of human learning and knowledge construction* (Figure 8). We have also suggested that *no single assessment technique, by itself, adequately reflects the entire multidimensional nature of understanding and conceptual change* (although some techniques are better than others). Finally, we have joined with others in recognizing that *longitudinal assessment efforts that focus on knowledge restructuring are preferable to one-time measures of subject matter attainment.*

The theoretical framework that guides our thinking about assessment and other aspects of science teaching and learning has been summarized in depth elsewhere (Mintzes et al., 1998). Its principal axioms (highlighted in Figure 8) are that (1) human beings are meaning makers; (2) the goal of education is the construction of shared meanings; and (3) shared meanings may be facilitated by the active intervention of well-prepared teachers.

Recent work by Griffard and Wandersee (1999) and by Jones, Carter, and Rua (1999) supports our view that the most promising approaches to probing cognitive structure and exposing gaps in conceptual understanding rely on multiple assessment measures over extended periods of time. The study by Griffard and Wandersee employs "traditional" two-tiered tests paired with think-aloud interviews, coconstruction of concept maps, and computer simulations. In a similar vein, Jones, Carter, and Rua rely on concept maps, card sortings, clinical interviews, and student drawings. We think that these studies might become a model for those who wish to explore the multidimensional, longitudinal nature of good assessment practice.

We close this book with a plea that teachers, school administrators, curriculum experts, and researchers begin to see assessment as an opportunity to view *knowledge in the making*, and our best practices as *windows on the mind*. When this plea is finally taken seriously and acted upon, then and only then

Understanding

Intersubjectivity   Based on the available assessment data, is there convincing evidence that the student has:

A. Constructed a viewpoint about a natural phenomenon and described that viewpoint in verbal, graphic or pictorial form?
B. Engaged in self-reflective or metacognitive activities?
C. Shared his/her viewpoints with other students?
D. Attended to and considered viewpoints other than his/her own?
E. Examined primary or secondary sources that describe the prevailing scientific explanation?
F. Explored the empirical evidence for differing viewpoints and weighed the relative merits of each?
G. Sought ways to reconcile his/her views with those of others and/or the empirical evidence?

Coherence   Based on the available assessment data, is there convincing evidence that the student has:

H. Considered how the individual parts of his/her viewpoint fit into the larger picture?
I. Sought to explicitly relate one part of his/her viewpoint with another in verbal, graphic or pictorial form?
J. Attempted to reconcile inconsistencies among the parts?
K. Successfully engaged in one or more forms of analytical, analogical, inferential or integrative reasoning? (see Chapter 5).

Parsimony   Based on the available assessment data, is there convincing evidence that the student has:

L. Constructed a viewpoint that is 'complete' but concise and devoid of extraneous variables or unnecessary complexity?
M. Attempted to explain natural objects or events with the assistance of models, outlines, graphic representations or pictorial formats?

Transparency   Based on the available assessment data, is there convincing evidence that the student has:

N. Identified a focus question (or knowledge domain) that is amenable to scientific investigation?
O. Considered the objects and events that must be investigated in order to develop a tentative answer or hypothesis?
P. Described the concepts, principles, theories, and philosophical views that are necessary to answer the focus question?
Q. Suggested ways of recording information about an observation?
R. Attempted to transform, manipulate or rearrangement records?
S. Offered one or more knowledge claims that are consistent with the conceptual framework and logically inferred from the records and transformations?
T. Offered one or more value claims that are consistent with the knowledge claims?

Conceptual Change

Based on the available assessment data, is there convincing evidence that the student has:
U. Assimilated new concepts into his/her cognitive structure over the course of days, weeks or months?
V. Restructured connections among existing concepts?
W. Undergone a significant alteration in the structural complexity and propositional validity of his/her knowledge framework (concepts, relationships, hierarchy, branching, cross-links, examples)

FIGURE 7
Assigning value to student work: analytical questions.

Axiom 1: Human Beings Are Meaning Makers

- Meaning making is a fundamental adaptation of the human species and the driving force underlying all forms of conceptual change. It is characteristic of young children and mature adults, and the product of millions of years of evolution. The ability to make meaning is the principal selective advantage we enjoy.
- Human beings are fundamentally adapted to "making sense" out of conflicting sensory data. The conceptual understandings we construct are products of the interaction of our meaning making capacities and the objects, events, and other people we encounter.
- Science is best understood as a formalized and highly adaptive way of harnessing the meaning making capacities of the human mind. It is a way of codifying, socializing and channeling a natural capacity of all human beings.
- Understanding is a dynamic epistemological status conferred on individuals by a consensually recognized referent group. In science, that group consists of disciplinary experts; in the classroom, the science teacher serves as the de facto local representative (i.e., delegate; proxy) of that group.
- Within the scientific community, the principal criteria of understanding are: intersubjectivity (sharing meanings); coherence (resolving inconsistencies); parsimony (seeking simplicity); and transparency (unpacking/decrypting knowledge).

Axiom 2: The Goal of Education Is the Construction of Shared Meanings

- Genetic variation produces differences in the meaning making capacities of individuals (independently of gender and ethnicity).
- Social, political, economic, historical and other environmental factors strongly influence our opportunities to interact with objects, events and other people.
- As a result of genetic variation and environmental factors, no two people construct precisely the same meanings about natural phenomena. Consequently, the outcomes of science instruction are not entirely predictable.
- The teacher's role is to facilitate and negotiate meanings among diverse groups of learners with the aim of establishing "shared meanings." Her job is to challenge students' understandings by encouraging them to interact with a diverse array of objects, events and other people.
- The teacher's ultimate goal is to encourage learners to construct progressively more powerful explanations; to wrestle with and resolve inconsistencies and unnecessary complexities in their thinking; and to evaluate and challenge the knowledge and value claims of others.

Axiom 3: Shared Meanings May Be Facilitated by the Active Intervention of Well-Prepared Teachers

- Changing the way people think requires that personal meanings be clarified and "externalized." Concept maps and other representational techniques offer vehicles for making meanings public, and thereby subjecting them to the critical evaluation of others.
- The conceptual change process depends on the active restructuring of knowledge which involves both incremental, cumulative and limited alterations, as well as wholesale, abrupt and extensive modifications of cognitive structure.
- Teachers are catalysts who succeed when they reduce the "activation energy" required to restructure knowledge.
- Restructuring knowledge requires time and resources. These constraints limit the effectiveness of teachers and schools.

FIGURE 8

Three axioms of human constructivism.

will we be able to conclude that our schools do indeed have an authentic commitment to *assessing science understanding.*

References

Ausubel, D. P. (1968). *Educational psychology: A cognitive view.* New York: Holt, Rinehart & Winston.

Ausubel, D. P., Novak, J. D., & Hanesian, H. (1978). *Educational psychology: A cognitive view* (2nd ed.). New York: Holt, Rinehart & Winston.

Binet, A., & Simon, T. (1911). *A method of measuring the development of the intelligence of young children.* Lincoln, IL: Courier.

Bloom, B., Hastings, J., & Madaus, G. (1971). *Handbook of formative and summative evaluation.* New York: McGraw-Hill.

Carey, S. (1986). *Conceptual development in childhood.* Cambridge, MA: MIT Press.

Gould, S. (1981). *The mismeasure of man.* New York: W. W. Norton.

Griffard, P., & Wandersee, J. (1999). Exposing gaps in college biochemistry understanding using new cognitive probes. *Paper presented at the annual meeting of the National Association for Research in Science Teaching,* March 1999, Boston, MA.

Hirsch (1996). The schools we need: and why we don't have them. New York: Double day.

Hogan, K., & Fisherkeller, J. (1996). Representing students' thinking about nutrient cycling in ecosystems: Bidimensional coding of a complex topic. *Journal of research in science teaching,* 33, 941–970.

Jones, M. G., Carter, G., & Rua, M. (1999). Concept mapping, interviews, diagrams, observations, and card sorting: Which window into the mind? *Paper presented at the annual meeting of the National Association for Research in Science Teaching,* March 1999, Boston, MA.

Markham, K., Mintzes, J., & Jones, M. G. (1994). The concept map as a research and evaluation tool: Further evidence of validity. *Journal of Research in Science Teaching,* 31, 91–101.

Martin, B. (1998). *Knowledge restructuring in marine biology: Cognitive processes and metacognitive reflections.* M.S. thesis, University of North Carolina at Wilmington.

Mintzes, J., Wandersee, J., & Novak, J. (Eds.) (1998). *Teaching science for understanding: A human constructivist view.* San Diego: Academic Press.

Novak, J. (1998). *Learning, creating and using knowledge: Concept maps™ as facilitative tools in schools and corporations.* Mahwah, NJ: Larence Erlbaum Associates.

Novak, J., & Musonda, D. (1991). A twelve year longitudinal study of science concept learning. *American Educational Research Journal,* 28, 117–153.

Novak, J. D., & Gowin, D. B. (1984). *Learning How to Learn.* New York: Cambridge University Press.

Pearsall, N. R. (1995). *A longitudinal study of conceptual change in an introductory college biology course for majors.* M.S. thesis. University of North Carolina at Wilmington.

Pearsall, N. R., Skipper, J. E. J., & Mintzes, J. (1997). Knowledge restructuring in the life sciences: A longitudinal study of conceptual change in biology. *Science Education,* 81, 193–215.

Piaget, J. (1926). *The child's conception of the world.* New York: Harcourt Brace.

Skipper, J. E. J. (1995). *A longitudinal study of conceptual change in an introductory college biology course for non-majors.* M.S. thesis. University of North Carolina at Wilmington.

Songer, C., & Mintzes, J. (1994). Understanding cellular respiration: An analysis of conceptual change in college biology. *Journal of Research in Science Teaching,* 31, 621–637.

Spearman, C. (1904). General intelligence objectively determined and measured. *American Journal of Psychology,* 15, 201–293.

Spitulnik, M., Zembal-Saul, C., & Krajcik, J. (1998). Using hypermedia to represent emerging student understanding: Science learners and preservice teachers. In J. Mintzes, J. Wandersee, & J. Novak (Eds.), *Teaching science for understanding: A human constructivist view.* San Diego: Academic Press.

Terman, L. et al. (1923). *Intelligence tests and school reorganization.* Yonkers-on-Hudson, NY: World Book.

Terman, L. L. et al. (1917). *The Stanford revision extension of the Binet-Simon scale for measuring intelligence.* Baltimore: Warwick & York.

Thurstone, L. L. (1924). *The nature of intelligence*. London: Kegan, Paul, Trench, Trubner.

Wandersee, J. (1983). Students' misconceptions about photosynthesis: A cross-age study. *Proceedings of the international seminar on misconceptions in science and mathematics*. Ithaca, NY: Department of Education, Cornell University.

Yerkes, R. (Ed.) (1921). Psychological examining in the United States Army. *Memoirs of the National Academy of Sciences*, 15.

Index